CHANGING THE RULES

Changing the Rules enters into the debate between theoretical analyses of constitutional amendment provisions (considered the most important part of a constitution) and empirical research (which argues that amendment provisions have little or no significance). George Tsebelis demonstrates how strict provisions are a necessary condition for amendments to have low frequency and significance and provides empirical evidence from case studies and over 100 democracies to corroborate this claim. Examining various cultural theories that dispute these findings, Tsebelis explains why their conclusions have weak foundations. He argues that constitutional rigidity is also a necessary condition for judicial independence and provides theoretical argument and empirical evidence. Tsebelis also establishes a negative correlation between the length of a constitution and problematic indicators such as time inconsistency, low GDP/capita, high corruption, inequality, and lack of innovation. This title is also available as Open Access on Cambridge Core.

GEORGE TSEBELIS is the Anatol Rapoport Collegiate Professor of Political Science at the University of Michigan, where he works on political institutions. He is a member of the American Academy of Arts and Sciences and has received honorary degrees from the Universities of Athens, Crete and Milan. He is the author of (among other books) *Nested Games: Rational Choice in Comparative Politics* and *Veto Players: How Political Institutions Work*.

CHANGING THE RULES

Constitutional Amendments in Democracies

GEORGE TSEBELIS
University of Michigan

Shaftesbury Road, Cambridge CB2 8EA, United Kingdom

One Liberty Plaza, 20th Floor, New York, NY 10006, USA

477 Williamstown Road, Port Melbourne, VIC 3207, Australia

314–321, 3rd Floor, Plot 3, Splendor Forum, Jasola District Centre, New Delhi – 110025, India

103 Penang Road, #05-06/07, Visioncrest Commercial, Singapore 238467

Cambridge University Press is part of Cambridge University Press & Assessment, a department of the University of Cambridge.

We share the University's mission to contribute to society through the pursuit of education, learning and research at the highest international levels of excellence.

www.cambridge.org
Information on this title: www.cambridge.org/9781009597265

DOI: 10.1017/9781009597234

© George Tsebelis 2025

This publication is in copyright. Subject to statutory exception and to the provisions of relevant collective licensing agreements, with the exception of the Creative Commons version the link for which is provided below, no reproduction of any part may take place without the written permission of Cambridge University Press & Assessment.

An online version of this work is published at doi.org/10.1017/9781009597234 under a Creative Commons Open Access license CC-BY-NC 4.0 which permits re-use, distribution and reproduction in any medium for non-commercial purposes providing appropriate credit to the original work is given and any changes made are indicated. To view a copy of this license visit https://creativecommons.org/licenses/by-nc/4.0

When citing this work, please include a reference to the DOI 10.1017/9781009597234

First published 2025

A catalogue record for this publication is available from the British Library

A Cataloging-in-Publication data record for this book is available from the Library of Congress

ISBN 978-1-009-59726-5 Hardback
ISBN 978-1-009-59725-8 Paperback

Cambridge University Press & Assessment has no responsibility for the persistence or accuracy of URLs for external or third-party internet websites referred to in this publication and does not guarantee that any content on such websites is, or will remain, accurate or appropriate.

Dedicated to:
Barb Koremenos, my wife and my partner, for the persistence of her love and support through the years;
Selene Koremenos-Tsebelis, my daughter, for continuously bringing me pride and keeping me young.

CONTENTS

List of Figures		viii
List of Tables		x
Preface		xiii
Note on the Cover		xvi
	Introduction	1
1	The Landscape of Constitutional Amendments	23
2	An Institutional Approach to Constitutional Rigidity	54
3	Cultural Theories of Constitutional Amendments	76
4	Cases of Failed Amendments: Italy and Chile	99
5	A Case of Successful Amendments: Mexico	126
6	Constitutional Rigidity and Amendment Rate	147
7	Time Inconsistency and Other Correlates of Constitutional Length	170
8	Constitutional Rigidity and Judicial Independence	190
9	Conclusions	221
	Appendices	226
	Bibliography	277
	Index	300

FIGURES

2.1 Five-sevenths and six-sevenths cores in one dimension   56
2.2 Change of core in one dimension under five-sevenths and six-sevenths majority   57
2.3 Core of a unicameral legislature under qualified majorities and lack of core under simple majority   59
2.4 Constitutional core of a bicameral legislature   61
2.5 Constitutional core with two-thirds majority in both chambers and a majority of states (Mexico)   62
2.6 Core with alternative constitutional provisions   63
2.7 Large core produces smaller win-set, no matter where the status quo (SQ) is   64
2.8 Outcomes of a referendum   67
2.9 Referendum outcomes as a function of agenda setter   68
3.1 New constitutions do not come with new levels of constitutional rigidity   86
3.2 Summary of the number of countries that changed their constitution and the difference in rigidity scores   87
3.3 Correlations between amendment frequencies and the World Values Survey (WVS) and V-Dem Variables (variables used by Blake et al. [2023] in bold)   95
4.1 Constitutional core of Italy under Article 138   101
4.2 Constitutional core of Chile, three-fifths, and president   104
4.3 Constitutional core of Chile and two-thirds without president   105
4.4 Constitutional core of Chile with all alternatives   106
5.1 House and Senate support for constitutional amendments in Mexico from 2000 to 2013 by topic, coalition, and number of articles affected   143
5.2 Congressional support for constitutional amendments in Mexico from 2000 to 2013   145
6.1 Constitutional rigidity and amendment size and/or rate   155
6.2 The effect of constitutional rigidity on the rate of all amendments (amendments of constitutions in effect in 2013 in all democratic countries)   156

LIST OF FIGURES

6.A.1.1	The effect of constitutional rigidity on the rate of fundamental amendments (amendments of constitutions in effect in 2013 in all democratic countries)	163
6.A.1.2	The effect of constitutional rigidity on the rate of significant and fundamental amendments (amendments of constitutions in effect in 2013 in all democratic countries)	163
7.1	Writing and revising the constitution game	173
7.2	Amendment frequency and log length	177
7.3	Time inconsistency and log length	178
7.4	Scope and details in 187 countries	181
7.5	Log GDP and log length	184
7.6	Corruption and log length	185
8.1	Legislative core: the court can make any statutory interpretation inside it	202
8.2	Constitutional core larger than legislative core: any constitutional interpretation within the constitutional core stands	203
8.3	Low constitutional rigidity is a necessary condition for low judicial independence	208
8.4	The win-set of the status quo subject to constraints on judicial decision-making	208
8.5	The win-set of the status quo subject to constraints on judicial decision-making, with uncertainty	210
8.6	The effect of constitutional rigidity on court strikes	215

TABLES

I.1	Two-person game (Player A with three and Player B with two strategies)	4
I.2	Three levels of rulemaking	9
3.1	Difference between actual and formal rigidity: As n increases, the error term (difference) approaches zero	80
3.2	Effect of formal rigidity on another variable (constitutional amendments): As n increases, the coefficient approximates the true value	81
3.3	Estimation of coefficient of "culture" as a lagged dependent variable: When institutional data are serially correlated, including a lagged dependent variable will inflate its estimated effect and lead to misestimation of other variables including the wrong sign	88
3.4	Association of indicators of culture from Tarabar and Young (2021) with economic outcomes (based on IMF data) are not as expected	91
4.1	Reasons for "NO" vote of Chilean referendum in September 2022	119
4.2	Reasons for "NO" vote of Chilean referendum in December 2023	120
4.3	What are all the reasons why you voted "NO" at the referendum on the European Constitution?	122
5.1	Congressional seats of main parties in Mexico (1997–2015)	136
6.1	Correlation of veto player constitutional rigidity index with other indexes	154
6.2	Comparison of three models of effects of constitutional rigidity (null, mean only, and heteroskedastic) on amendment rate for POLITY2 ≥ 5 threshold 103 countries; likelihood ratio tests	159
6.A.1.1	Results of the heteroskedastic regression for fundamental amendments (POLITY2 ≥ 5)	161
6.A.1.2	Results of the heteroskedastic regression for the combination of fundamental and major amendments (POLITY2 ≥ 5)	162
6.A.1.3	Results of the heteroskedastic regression on all amendments (POLITY2 ≥ 5)	162
6.A.2.1	Comparison of three models of effects of constitutional rigidity (null, mean only, and heteroskedastic) on amendment rate for POLITY2 ≥ 6 threshold (ninety-five countries; likelihood ratio tests)	164

LIST OF TABLES   xi

6.A.2.2	Comparison of three models of effects of constitutional rigidity (null, mean only, and heteroskedastic) on amendment rate for POLITY2 ≥ 7 threshold (eighty-three countries; likelihood ratio tests)	165
6.A.2.3	Comparison of three models of effects of constitutional rigidity (null, mean only, and heteroskedastic) on amendment rate for POLITY2 ≥ 8 threshold (seventy-two countries; likelihood ratio tests)	165
6.A.2.4	Comparison of three models of effects of constitutional rigidity (null, mean only, and heteroskedastic) on amendment rate for POLITY2 ≥ 9 threshold (fifty-four countries; likelihood ratio tests)	166
6.A.2.5	Comparison of three models of effects of constitutional rigidity (null, mean only, and heteroskedastic) on amendment rate for POLITY2 ≥ 10 threshold (thirty-five countries; likelihood ratio tests)	166
6.A.3.1	OLS regressions of different amendment rates (POLITY2 ≥ 5 cutoff) on constitutional rigidity and social capital (n = 57)	167
6.A.3.2	OLS regressions of different amendment rates (POLITY2 ≥ 5 cutoff) on constitutional rigidity and each indicator of social capital separately (n = 57)	168
7.1	Time inconsistency as a function of constitution length	179
7.2	Constitutional length as a function of country characteristics	182
7.3	GDP per capita as a function of constitutional length and economic variables	182
7.4	GDP per capita as a function of length, economic variables, education, and corruption	183
8.1	Measures of de facto judicial independence	196
8.2	Measures of de jure judicial independence	197
8.3	Components of de jure judicial independence	198
8.4	Countries with constitutional courts	205
8.5	Effect of constitutional rigidity on percentage of strikes (sample: POLITY2 ≥ 5)	216
8.6	Comparison of three models of effects of constitutional rigidity (base, mean only, and heteroskedastic) on judicial strikes for POLITY2 ≥ 5 threshold (likelihood ratio tests, n = 30)	216
8.A.1	Data used in the analysis (constitutional and unconstitutional judgments) from the Comparative Law Database	219

PREFACE

I started writing this book many years ago. All these years I have been thinking about the distinct area (an intersection of political science and constitutional law) that is composed of the amendment rules (the articles of the constitution) and their consequences (the constitutional amendments). What makes them distinct is that in the overwhelming majority of countries there is a difference between the amendment rules and the rules of any other legislation.

The first article of the project,[1] coauthored with Dominic Nardi, focused on OECD countries under the assumptions that the relations uncovered in this set would be more stable and the data would be more readily available. Both assumptions were true, and the only dataset that included our independent variable (constitutional rigidity) was aggregating a series of indexes including the amendment frequency.

I realized that I had to expand the dataset to include democracies and change my independent variable (constitutional rigidity) so it would be derived only from the amendment provisions of the corresponding constitution. I got the idea from my book *Veto Players* to use two different approximations: the number of veto players and the qualified majority required for decisions. An article materialized,[2] and the previous results were corroborated for the whole set of democracies with both constitutional rigidity indicators. This is the basis for Chapter 7 of this book after reworking the variables according to later research results. I knew that I needed to combine these two independent variables, but I left that for the next article along with better measurements of amendments.

The next attempt took several years,[3] wherein I evaluated the significance of amendments in the more than 100 democratic countries, created

---

[1] Tsebelis and Nardi (2016). Reprinted with permission.
[2] Tsebelis (2017b). Reprinted with permission from John Wiley and Sons.
[3] Tsebelis (2022). Published by Cambridge University Press under Creative Commons Licence CC BY 4.0.

the composite measure of constitutional rigidity (presented now in Chapter 2), and used the appropriate statistical method for analysis of the data, which is based not only on the estimation of the effect of the independent variable but also on its variance. This is now presented in Chapter 6. During this long period of gestation of the argument, the idea of this book was beginning to emerge, reinforced by side events revolving around specific countries.

First, the senate of Italy in 2016 invited me to talk about the consequences of the upcoming constitutional revision which would reduce its powers; indeed, the amendment would abolish the famous "symmetric bicameralism" where the two chambers have identical powers to the extent that the constitution does not differentiate between the two, using the expressions "either chamber" or "both chambers." My talk was later published in a professional article,[4] and now parts of it are included in Chapter 4.

Second, I was invited by the Inter-American Development Bank and the government of Chile to a conference on constitutional reform in Chile (Santiago 2016), and my talk became an article in a professional journal,[5] which generated a discussion with two Chilean constitutional experts.[6] Parts of these articles and debates are also included in Chapter 4.

In the meantime, the results of my empirical analysis of the frequency of constitutional amendments had materialized, and the exceptional position of Mexico on the plot of countries demanded an explanation. How was it possible for a country with high constitutional rigidity (according to my indicators) to have so many amendments? The answer is provided in the article coauthored with Edwin Atilano-Robles.[7] I thank him for permitting me to include it in this book as Chapter 5.

There are some additional chapters in the book which were created in order to complete the picture. Chapter 1 shows the diversification of amendment institutions throughout the world. Chapter 3 puts together the different cultural approaches that are presented either as competitive or complementary to the institutional perspective presented in this book. Finally, Chapter 8 expands the work I had started some twenty years ago about the courts and the role of judges, but now with a focus on constitutional and supreme courts making decisions on constitutional issues. I was arguing then that the discretion of courts increases with the size of

---

[4] Tsebelis (2017a). Reprinted with permission.
[5] Tsebelis (2018c).
[6] Tsebelis (2018a).
[7] Tsebelis and Atilano-Robles (2024).

the legislative core because of how difficult it is for the political system to make decisions overruling them. The same argument is presented in this book about the decisions of constitutional or supreme courts, but the yardstick of difficulty this time is the amendment of the constitution. The results corroborate the expectations, but, as I argue, they are weak because the dataset is very small.

During this long journey I had many supporters and co-travelers for at least part of the way. A big part of the work was done while I was a visiting fellow at the Kellogg Institute. I would like to thank the Kellogg Institute and the University of Michigan for financial support. I would also like to thank the following colleagues that provided amendment significance ratings: Şener Aktürk, Eduardo Alemán, Rod Alence, Abel Djassi Amado, Ana Catalina Arango Restrepo, Jorge Baquerizo, Kamila Bezubik, Agnieszka Bień-Kacała, Eszter Bodnár, Catarina Santos Botelho, Mario Cajas, Cláudio Gonçalves Couto, Jesse Crosson, Javier Duque Daza, Boniface Dulani, Arolda Elbasani, Alan Fenna, Martina Flick, Claudio Fuentes, Venelin I. Ganev, Aris Georgopoulos, Marco Giuliani, Magnus Hagevi, Gábor Halmai, Allen Hicken, Giuseppe Ieraci, Christian Jensen, Aida Just, Yannis Karagiannis, Dean Knight, Thomas Koelble, Viktoriia Kolesnyk, Amie Kreppel, Ming-Sung Kuo, Nikolas Kyriakou, Tomáš Ľalík, Mahendra Lawoti, Sokol Lleshi, Małgorzata Lorencka, Emmett Macfarlane, Lára Magnúsardóttir, Robert Mattes, Mikko Mattila, Milan J. N. Meetarbhan, Wojtek Mojski, Woojin Moon, Juan Andres Moraes, Erika Moreno, Wolfgang Claudius Müller, Malkhaz Nakashidze, Noah Nathan, Gabriel Negretto, Joakim Nergelius, Bertil Emrah Oder, Eoin O'Malley, Reijer Passchier, Darko Pavlovski, Bjørn Erik Rasch, Julio Ríos-Figueroa, Tatiana Rizova, Juan Carlos Rodríguez-Cordero, Matt Ryan, Anna Rytel-Warzocha, Camilo Emiliano Saavedra Herrera, Sebastian Saiegh, Pascal Sciarini, Aqil Shah, Ulrich Sieberer, Güneş Murat Tezcür, Brian Turner, Wilson Tay Tze Vern, Arta Vorpsi, Jarle Weigård, Oya Yeğen, and Francesco Zucchini. I would also like to thank Nikos Alivizatos, Yannis Anastassakos, Rogerio Arantes, Paolo Carozza, Eric Chang, Michael Coppedge, Barbara Koremenos, Scott Mainwaring, Iain McLean, Kevin Quinn, Bjorn-Eric Rasch, Julio Ríos-Figueroa, Kaare Strom, and Vassilis Tzevelekos for critical comments; Tom Ginsburg for providing me with the data on amendments; and Richard Albert for providing me with the means to collect data on the significance of amendments through the blog site ICONnect. I am also indebted to Mitch Bosley, Jesse Crosson, Pedro Luz de Castro, Anna Halstenbach, Joe Klaver, Julia Maynard, Li-Hong Weng, and Hyeon Young Ro for excellent research assistance.

NOTE ON THE COVER

The images on the cover of this book are of the US Constitution (March 1787), the French Constitution (Declaration des Droit's de l'Homme et du Citoyen [August 1789]), and the Greek Constitution (Γ' Εθνοσυνέλευση Τροιζήνας [May 1827]).

Introduction

The subject of this book is understanding constitutional amendments, which are very significant, as well as unusual, national events. These events alter the way politics is run in the country. From the demand side, they must be modifications that cannot be addressed by ordinary legislation; from the supply side, they must clear obstacles specified by the constitution itself – namely, the amendment rules of constitutions. While some from both law and political science perspectives consider these rules fundamental (and consequential), others consider them of very little use. To the average reader, it may seem surprising that experts dispute the significance of amendment rules. If institutions are important, the institutions that regulate the change of rules should be the most important of all institutions. So, let me start by establishing this contradiction in the literature.

I.1 Are Constitutional Amendment Rules Important?

Arguing for the importance of amendment rules more than a century ago, John Burgess, a lawyer and one of the founders of American political science, dedicated four chapters of his most important book to the "amending clause" because it "describes and regulates … amending power. *This is the most important part of the constitution*" (Burgess 1890: 137; emphasis mine). This understanding is echoed by Herman Finer (1949), who argues that "we might define a constitution as its process of amendment" (127), as well as Richard Albert (2019), who states, "No part of a constitution is more important than the rules we use to change it" (2).[1] A similar position is taken by Dixon and Holden

---

[1] A series of researchers (Lutz 1994, Lorenz 2005, Rasch and Congleton 2006, Lijphart 2012, Anckar and Karvonen 2015) have built on these arguments and found a stronger or weaker negative correlation between constitutional rigidity and frequency of constitutional amendments.

(2012), for whom "constitutional amendments play a number of important functions in a constitutional democracy."

On the other side of the coin, Ginsburg and Melton (2015), in an article entitled, "Does the constitutional amendment rule matter at all? Amendment cultures and the challenges of measuring amendment difficulty," analyze 790 current and previous constitutions and conclude that "the institutional variables are never statistically significant and, often, they do not even have the sign one would expect" (711). In his book on constitutional amendments, Albert (2019) summarizes his findings this way: "I show also that rankings of comparative amendment difficulty have a fatal flaw: they either ignore or fail to account for nontextual sources of amendment ease or difficulty ... I ultimately arrive at two conclusions: first, that studies of amendment difficulty are doomed to failure; and second, that in any case they may not be worth the effort" (32). Marshfield (2018) writes, "A better measure of constitutional flexibility is a constitution's actual amendment rate because this presumably captures both the formal barriers to amendment contained in the amendment rules as well as cultural attitudes regarding formal amendment" (80). Versteeg and Zackin (2016) agree, saying, "The measure [of constitutional entrenchment] does not rely on formal amendment rules because these rules are mediated so dramatically by political norms" (661).

I will discuss these arguments later in the book, but I want to inform the reader right from the beginning that I side with the first approach on institutions, believing that institutions in general, constitutions in particular, and amendment rules even more so certainly matter. I will explain how we can use the texts to measure constitutional rigidity. I will also show that constitutional rigidity affects the frequency of amendments, as the first side of the literature suggests (although I will slightly modify the expectations and explain why).

However, I do not stop with the argument and evidence that constitutional rigidity affects the frequency of amendments. I go one step further and consider the difference between the expected (on the basis of rigidity) and actual frequency of amendments, calling this time inconsistency. Time inconsistency is the discrepancy between the intentions of the founders and the real development of the constitution (thinking from the collective point of view of the country, it is like a change of mind over time). I then study time inconsistency further as an independent variable. So, instead of arguing that constitutional rigidity does not matter at all and replacing it with amendment frequency as some of the literature does, I use it to determine time inconsistency and explain the reasons behind why some constitutions get revised more frequently than they were designed to (that is, have higher time inconsistency than others). Finally, I argue that higher constitutional rigidity leads to higher judicial independence of constitutional courts and possibly higher independence of constitutional interpretations of supreme courts, I explain the reasons for this, and I provide empirical evidence. Therefore, the argument in the book is not only that constitutional rigidity matters but also how and why it matters.

I will start my discussion by explaining why I study institutions and why I focus on amendment rules. None of these choices are uncontroversial, and I will address different points of view in this introduction. Throughout the book, I will present a theory of constitutional rigidity based on game-theoretic principles and then corroborate it with empirical evidence from the constitutions of all democratic countries. I will present case studies as well as aggregate results so that the reader will understand that the mechanisms described in the theory are in play and that the overall expectations of the theory are corroborated.

I.2 Importance of Institutions

This book presents an institutional approach to constitutions and their amendments. It is neither the first time such an approach has been taken nor the only way that one can study constitutions. However, my particular argument regarding the significance of institutions is both novel and theoretically rigorous given its game-theoretic foundations.

Any human interaction can be studied as a game. Von Neumann and Morgenstern (1944) argue that games can be presented equivalently either in extensive or in normal form and that the normal form lends itself to more theoretical developments while the extensive form helps with the identification of the equilibria of particular games. I will use the normal form, which is composed of three elements: (1) the players participating, (2) the strategies of each player, and (3) their payoffs (when each one of them selects one strategy). Table I.1 presents a very simple game with two players (A and B), three strategies for Player A, and two strategies for Player B. At the intersection of the different strategies, the table presents the payoffs of the players (named P for Player A and Q for Player B). So, for example, P_{11} and Q_{11} are the payoffs of A and B when they use strategies A_1 and B_1 respectively.

This game becomes more realistic when each player has more strategies, enlarging from 3×2 to $m \times n$ strategies, but it would still have two

Table I.1 *Two-person game (Player A with three and Player B with two strategies)*

	B_1	B_2
A_1	P_{11}, Q_{11}	P_{12}, Q_{12}
A_2	P_{21}, Q_{21}	P_{22}, Q_{22}
A_3	P_{31}, Q_{31}	P_{32}, Q_{32}

players. Note that making more strategies available to one player requires additional responses for the other and, of course, more corresponding payoffs in their intersection. In addition, one can consider adding a third player, which would require one additional dimension in our table. It would now be a three-dimensional object, and it would require more strategies for each of the previous two players and, of course, many more payoffs. Although it would be conceptually the same as a two-person game, it would be difficult to represent on a book page. One can continue complicating the interaction by adding more players, each one with their strategies, requiring more responses (strategies) from the other players and more payoffs for the possible outcomes. I have managed to present an intellectually simple but realistically very complicated situation as a game (a triplet of players, strategies, and payoffs). Yet, from this description, the word "institutions" is absent. How would the introduction of institutions modify this account?

First, institutions modify the strategies of the players. It is institutions that tell us when different players move; for example, unless there is a proposal on the floor of a parliament, there can be no vote, or unless there is a restriction of circulation for some reason, a citizen cannot be fined for being out late. Permissions and prohibitions are some simple examples, but institutions may also specify more complicated patterns. For instance, participation in an auction requires that the participants do not know the bids of their competitors (in game-theoretic terms, they move simultaneously, which is specified by the rules of the auction). This situation would be very different if some of the players knew the bids of others (that is, if they moved *after* the others had submitted their bids). Again, there are institutional structures that specify the sequence of moves among different players and, as a result, the strategies of the corresponding players. In cases in which we have an institutional structure that determines how exactly a procedure is going to work, the strategy space of the players is going to be seriously affected. In this book, we will analyze the amendment procedures of all democratic countries, and we will see that some of these countries describe several alternatives and endow certain actors to engage in one of the alternatives. Each one of these procedures generates a whole strategy space for the corresponding players, and the existence of multiple alternatives expands the strategy spaces even more. Chapter 2 will examine exactly how we can calculate the constitutional rigidity that procedures like these engender.

Second, institutions determine the payoffs of the actors. For example, prohibited moves are associated with negative payoffs (i.e., the penalties incurred when one violates the prohibiting rule). Similarly, there are "incentives" for desirable actions, helping players make the corresponding choices. If the payoffs are well-known among all the players, they can be used as hints about the effort they will undertake in order to achieve the desired outcome. If the first prize in a competition is accompanied by a ten-million-dollar check, the competition will become more fierce. One can anticipate how hard a politician will try to reach a particular goal if the achievement is a major requirement for his reelection strategy, and so on.

Third, institutions can specify the players of the game. It is not the case that every individual is entitled to participate in every game. State regulations decide whether only voters registered in the corresponding party can participate in the Republican and Democratic primaries. Laws that specify that every elementary school instructor must report bodily injuries on a child affect the participants in the injury protection game with the goal of impacting the final outcome of the game (reducing injuries). A similar strategy was used by the state of Texas for the prevention of abortion by enabling any person that observes any facilitation of abortion to report it. Again, an expansion of players will have dramatic effects on the equilibrium outcome of the game.

Clearly, institutions affect each of the items that determine the triplet of a game: players, strategies, and payoffs. Given that every interaction that involves this triplet is a game, I have demonstrated that institutions affect every human interaction in multiple ways.

Of course, I did not demonstrate that institutions are the *only* factor that affects human interactions. Other candidates could be preferences, ideologies, interests, cultures, and so on. I will consider the effect of the most general of these concepts: preferences. I consider it more general than the other concepts because it is more systematic and less idiosyncratic. People have tried to provide theories about *collective organizers* of preferences like interests, ideologies, and even cultures. The analyses cover how these concepts form and what their effects are; for example, workers can be argued to have more progressive ideologies, and they may prefer left-wing politicians. However, none of these arguments is expected to work all the time and determine the preferences of any particular individual.

In Chapter 3, I will address some cultural arguments that have been proposed to explain constitutional amendments and explain their insufficiencies. In Chapters 4 and 5, I will analyze specific cases of failed amendments (Italy and Chile) and successful amendments (Mexico) as my alternative approach to grafting politics to the institutional framework of the book.

I.3 Structure of Institutions

Although individuals may be located in different institutional environments at different times or places (they may, for example, operate under different rules in their family vs. at school or when they are at work vs. during the weekend), they are subject to the laws of their country at all times and, in addition, they can conform to the requirements and enjoy the benefits enumerated in their constitution. The laws of the country are expected to be in agreement with the constitution, and if they are not, they are invalidated by court decisions. Every constitution specifies the criteria that any legislation has to satisfy in terms of the procedure that engenders it and in terms of the general content that it should (or should not) have.

The fact that the constitution describes the conditions under which different laws or other types of decisions are valid means that it generates a constitutional equilibrium. The term equilibrium is game theoretic and implies that all the actors involved are selecting among their strategies the ones that are best responses to each other – a concept introduced by J. Nash (1951). As a result, no actor would modify their action if they had the opportunity.

As an example, the French Constitution (Article 34) specifies the areas that the Parliament can legislate. Any area not included in this article does not belong to the jurisdiction of the Parliament but to the government. This provision is unusual from a comparative perspective where parliaments have the authority to legislate on any issue of their choice. But, as a result, the French constitutional equilibrium is different from that of other countries in this respect. Similarly, different constitutions specify under what conditions war is declared (is it the jurisdiction of a president? Of government? Of parliament?) a referendum is proclaimed (who asks the question? Who triggers it?), and so on. It is obvious that different constitutions generate different constitutional equilibria.

From the point of view of this book, it is interesting to identify the formal conditions that every piece of legislation has to fulfill according to the constitution. For example, the constitution may define a whole hierarchy of laws.[2] If this is the case, there are different constitutional equilibria depending on the required majorities for different levels of laws. In addition, the constitution may generate different tiers of constitutional articles: It may prohibit the alteration of certain articles,[3] and it may make some articles more difficult to modify than the rest of them.[4] In each one of these cases, a different type of constitutional equilibrium is generated because of the difference in the regulating institutions.

Having established what a constitution is and how it generates a constitutional equilibrium, I now turn to the question of constitutional change. In order to simplify things, I will divide the issues into three levels.

At the first level, there are modifications *inside* the constitutional equilibrium. The constitution specifies rules for how each particular game is to be played. How is a law to be voted for? What happens if a particular law is defied? Who decides if there was a violation of the legal order? How does the nation go to war? How does it stop the war engagement? For some of these questions, the constitution may not

---

[2] Some countries like France, Spain, Chile, Ecuador, Panama, Peru, and Venezuela name them "organic," others like Portugal, Guatemala, and Nicaragua name them "constitutional," others like Brazil name them "supplemental," and in Columbia the name is "statutory," to list a few examples. These laws rank below the constitution but above ordinary laws and require higher parliamentary majorities to be enacted.

[3] In many Latin and Central American countries, for example, presidential term limits are enshrined in the constitution, and there are formal clauses that bar the revision of these clauses under any circumstances. Efforts by presidents to get around these barriers to reelection (cf. Landau et al. 2019b) and a theoretical treatment of Unconstitutional Constitutional Amendment Doctrine (UCA) are discussed later in this section.

[4] Canada, for example, has seven different amendment rules depending on the expansiveness of the proposed constitutional amendment. In all cases, majorities in the House of Commons and the Senate must agree to the amendment, but the number of provincial assemblies required varies by the expansiveness of the proposed reforms. When a proposed amendment only concerns a single province, that single province's legislature must assent, while proposed amendments that would materially affect all the provinces require ratification by at least two-thirds of Canada's ten provincial legislatures (and potentially all of them, depending on the severity of the proposed reform). For an in-depth discussion of the Canadian case, see Albert (2015d).

provide specific answers, but it may delegate the decision to particular agents. For example, it may include the phrase "according to the law," inviting the legislature to make more specific decisions, or the phrase "according to an executive order," giving jurisdiction on the subject to the executive. The two most important delegations that the constitution makes "in equilibrium" are for *legislation* (for the legislative procedure to be engaged) and for *judicial interpretation* (for the judiciary to apply the laws [statutory interpretation] or the constitution [constitutional interpretation] in particular). It goes without saying that every constitution specifies the exact scope and rules for these procedures.

At the second level, there are modifications *outside* the constitutional equilibrium (amendments). The constitution uses the provision of amendment rules in order to specify how specific provisions may be replaced. Amendment rules may divide the articles of the constitution into different categories, or it may not. This is a significant distinction for what follows. The constitution may specify that certain articles cannot be amended or can be amended by a more stringent procedure than the rest of the constitution. If there is only one amendment procedure, then this procedure has to be followed any time the constitution is considered inappropriate or insufficient. If there are multiple amendment procedures, then it has to be certified that the appropriate amendment procedure is used. Usually, it will be the judiciary that is enabled explicitly by the constitution or by convention to decide whether the procedure used is the appropriate one. This will be a procedural decision: The court will decide that the specific modification cannot occur because the article is unamendable or belongs to a more stringent amendment category than the one classified by the political system; therefore, the amendment procedure in use is not appropriate.

At the third level, there is the possibility of the replacement of the whole constitution. This may occur under a diversity of conditions, such as through a general agreement (e.g., recently in Chile), under a popular revolution (e.g., the French Revolution of 1789), or because of a military coup (e.g., the Greek colonels in 1967). The most interesting part of this category is that we do not know the payoffs of the different actors; therefore, we cannot describe it as a game until long after it is over. For example, the military coup in Greece failed after seven years, and democracy was restored in 1974. The leaders of the coup went from running the government to being in jail for life. Were the seven years in power worth life imprisonment? To determine this, we will argue whether the seven years of interruption of the democratic regime was a

Table I.2 *Three levels of rulemaking*

Level of rulemaking	Types of actions
1. Inside the constitutional equilibrium	Legislation Statutory and constitutional interpretation by courts
2. Outside the constitutional equilibrium (but within the constitution)	Constitutional amendments (respecting amendment rules if these rules are uniform and there is no distinction among articles) Unconstitutional constitutional amendments (if there are layers of amendment and the rules of amendment are not respected)
3. Outside the constitution	New constitution

long or a short period, and, according to the answer, we will make a different assessment of the payoffs and analyze the outcomes.

Table I.2 summarizes the argument. I want to emphasize here that the distinctions I am making are procedural and not substantive. It may be that a new constitution is a replica of an older one, but the procedures followed were not specified by the previous constitution. For example, Chile recently underwent two failed attempts to replace (as opposed to amend) the Pinochet Constitution through constitutional conventions (a procedure not included in the constitution).[5] The same logic applies to amendments, the significance of which varies from extremely important (e.g., slavery in the US) to completely insignificant (e.g., most constitutional amendments in Mexico). We will divide the amendments according to significance in Chapter 2, but here we will focus solely on their rules of adoption (they all followed the amendment rules of the corresponding constitution – that is, they belong to Level 2 of Table I.2).

Cases inside the constitutional equilibrium also vary in significance. Just like judicial interpretation, legislation may be significant or it may not be. For example, the constitutional interpretations of abortion (*Roe v. Wade*) or desegregation (*Brown v. Board of Education*) are more significant than most laws the political system of the US has produced. However, they are still constitutional interpretations – that is, they move

---

[5] I discuss the case of Chile in detail in Chapter 4.

inside the constitutional equilibrium. Similarly, Obamacare and Trump's tax cut law are much more significant than other laws produced by the US political system, but they are still laws – that is, they are decisions within the constitutional equilibrium.

Finally, an example that moves from outside of the constitutional equilibrium to inside of it is the issue of women's rights. Some fifty years after the original introduction of the Equal Rights Amendment (ERA) in 1923, both houses passed it with the required two-thirds majority in 1971 and 1972. However, the amendment never cleared the hurdle of approval by three-fourths of the states as required by Article V of the US Constitution. Because of this, there has been no ERA amendment in the US Constitution. On the topic of equal rights, Lilly Ledbetter was hired by Goodyear as a supervisor and was receiving, without knowing, a significantly lower salary than her male counterparts. When she found out, she sued the company for sex discrimination, but she lost her case in the Supreme Court because the legal limit to present the case was 180 days from the date of the discriminatory case (the day she received her first paycheck). The statutory interpretation of the Supreme Court was correct and demonstrated a movement within the constitutional equilibrium. In response, the first legislative act of the Obama administration was the Lilly Ledbetter Fair Pay Act, which enabled an actionable complaint within 180 days of any discriminatory act (therefore, the last paycheck received) and, consequently, enabled the plaintiff to win. This piece of legislation contradicted the Supreme Court decision and also represented a move within the constitutional equilibrium. We will see in subsequent chapters that the court can overrule the political system by issuing constitutional interpretations, which are also movements within the constitutional equilibrium. The latest such constitutional interpretation was the decision about presidential immunity. Despite the fact that, in the opinion of the court minority, many constitutional scholars, and the author of this book, this interpretation significantly modifies the equality under the law principle (that is, the common understanding of the constitution), it cannot be modified by legislation.[6]

In all discussions, what qualifies as law, statutory/constitutional interpretation, or amendment is defined alone by the procedures followed rather than by the significance of the outcome. In other words,

---

[6] An idea consistent with the rest of this book is that constitutional interpretations should require some form of qualified majority inside the court, just as constitutional amendments require qualified majorities of legislators (see also Table I.2).

I follow the procedure – the decision-making rule – with the same respect, dedication, and tenacity that a prosecutor or an economist follows the money in order to understand the motives of different actions. Throughout this book, I focus on Level 2 of Table I.2 – that is, constitutional amendments. I consider the totality of amendments without confusing them with judicial interpretations or legislation, no matter how significant these latter decisions are. In addition, I independently assess the significance of different amendments and study the adoption of insignificant, significant, and fundamental amendments as a function of the amendment rules. This is a defining characteristic of this book since the procedures determine the institutions that are involved in the analysis as well as the decisions that are taken. I will refer to this approach as "follow the decisions." No matter how significant a law is (e.g., the Franklin D. Roosevelt legislation or the Ledbetter Fair Pay Act), it is not a constitutional amendment, and no matter how insignificant a constitutional amendment, the reason that its content was adopted through the (more difficult) constitutional amendment procedure is that legislation to that effect would have been considered unconstitutional. Each one of these decisions follows a different procedure, and that is why they have a different name. I will follow the decisions.

I.4 Constitutional Moments and Unconstitutional Constitutional Amendments

The importance of following the decisions (that is, of defining terms on the basis of procedures rather than substantive significance) is not universally recognized. There are two different procedures that constitutional lawyers consider as being fundamental extensions of constitutional law: the first is the theory of "Constitutional Moments" presented by B. A. Ackerman (1991), and the second is the theory of "Unconstitutional Constitutional Amendments" whose birth is currently in progress (Dixon and Landau 2015, Yap 2015, Roznai 2017, Dixon and Uhlmann 2018, Torres-Artunduaga and García-Jaramillo 2020). Here is how Albert puts it:

> Briefly stated for now, Bruce Ackerman's theory of constitutional moments uncovers the dualist foundations of the U.S. Constitution to show how leaders have transformed constitutional meaning without a corresponding alteration to the constitutional text, while the basic structure doctrine, first articulated by the Indian Supreme Court, enforces implicit limitations on the power to amend the codified constitution. Each idea has disrupted how we understand the forms and functions of

constitutional amendment, each has caused us to rethink the very meaning of constitutionalism and how it translates democracy, legitimacy, and sovereignty into law, and each continues to generate important scholarship critiquing, applying, and extending it both inside and out of the domestic context from which it emerged.

(Albert 2019: 19)

I.4.1 *Constitutional Moments*

According to Ackerman, besides the "classical" system of amendment determined by the constitution (which is institutional and formal), there is also a "modern" system (which is revolutionary and informal). He states, "Here the decisive constitutional signal is issued by a President claiming a mandate from the People. If Congress supports this claim by enacting transformative statutes that challenge the fundamentals of the preexisting regime, these statutes are treated as the functional equivalent of a proposal for constitutional amendment" (Ackerman 1991: 268; see also Amar 1994). This "modern" system bypasses Article V of the US Constitution. According to Ackerman, this informal procedure has been used in adopting the constitution, the Fourteenth Amendment, and the New Deal legislation.[7] I do not know what inferences can be made from unique historical events like the first two, but the adoption of the New Deal legislation is a matter of constitutional interpretation by the Supreme Court, which was evaluated first as unconstitutional and subsequently as consistent with the US Constitution.[8]

The court is permitted to make a constitutional interpretation no matter what its position may be while staying within the constitutional equilibrium (Table I.2). The fact that it moved towards progressive positions also does not mean it will do that all the time or even ever

---

[7] For a thorough legal criticism of Ackerman's positions, see Tribe (1995). Other scholars, such as Dixon and Baldwin (2019), suggest that there are additional preconditions for the applicability of Ackerman's theory, such as "meaningful political competition among parties" (172).

[8] Ackerman (1991) refers to Justice Owen Roberts' "switch in time" from anti- to pro–New Deal legislation in 1937 (43). The historical context for this episode was that prior to 1936, President Roosevelt's New Deal legislation had been repeatedly struck down by the Supreme Court as unconstitutional. In 1936, Roosevelt won a sweeping electoral victory and used that momentum to propose court-packing legislation. Although the court-packing legislation ultimately failed, it exerted enough pressure that the court did not invalidate a subsequent New Deal labor rights legislation on constitutional grounds as they had before due to the "switch" of Justice Owen Roberts in 1937 from anti- to pro–New Deal. See also Goldman (2012) for an in depth review of this case.

again. The Dobbs decision on abortion in 2022 showed that the court moved against the political system (since all three legislative actors were democrats) as well as the will of the voters. Consequently, what happened during the New Deal was not a constitutional amendment but a change in the opinion of the Supreme Court with respect to the constitutionality of the New Deal legislation. The reverse occurred with respect to abortion rights when the court changed its interpretation in a conservative direction. Whenever such a change occurs (regardless of the reasons), we have a different constitutional interpretation, which is a move within the constitutional equilibrium. Therefore, it is *not* a constitutional amendment.

This is not the only blow that the extraconstitutional procedure of constitutional moments suffers from. The fact that the ERA failed to pass because of not satisfying the requirements of Article V indicates that the proposal presented by Professor Ackerman cannot be the basis of a constitutional amendment: if there are several procedures and one of them is easier than the others (because of the omission of the approval of three-quarters of the states), then no political actors would ever use the difficult procedure again in order to change the constitution.[9] Consequently, if there were alternative procedures (as Ackerman claims), ERA proponents would have never used Article V and thereby failed.

An alternative interpretation of Article V would be that it is an insurmountable obstacle as opposed to one that can be bypassed. Stohler et al. (2022) argue that Article V has become an instrument of constitutional position-taking, presenting the almost 12,000 unsuccessful amendment proposals that have been made in the history of the US as evidence. This position respects the rigidity of the US Constitution, exploiting historical analysis.

1.4.2 *Unconstitutional Constitutional Amendments (UCA)*

The term unconstitutional constitutional amendments indicates that a constitution constrains the people's constituent power. Some of the amendments undertaken may be against the constitution. There may be two different reasons for this: the first is procedural (it may be that some of the specified conditions were not fulfilled – for example, a required referendum may have been fraudulent), and the second may

---

[9] We will revisit this point more theoretically in Chapter 2 as there are many constitutions that provide alternative procedures for amendments (the US Constitution is not one of them).

have been a matter of content (for example, there may have been violations of eternity clauses in the constitution). Under these conditions, the court can judge that a particular amendment violates the eternity provision of an article (for example, if the regime type is protected by an eternity clause, then significantly modifying the powers of an institution may be a violation of this clause). If an amendment is prohibited preemptively on the grounds of unconstitutionality, the move is within the constitutional equilibrium; if it passes and is invalidated later by the court, then we are in the area outside the constitutional equilibrium. Germany, South Africa, and India are countries which are contemplating the case of unconstitutional constitutional amendments and are enabling the courts to make a judgment (Albert 2009).

However, arguments have been made about courts making unconstitutional constitutional amendment decisions even if the constitution does not include appropriate provisions. For example, in Colombia, Alvaro Uribe, who was elected as president in 2002, tried to change the constitution that limited presidents to serve only one term in office. Because Uribe maintained a very high approval rate until the end of his presidency term, he sought and received approval of a constitutional amendment that allows presidents to serve two consecutive terms. While the amendment was challenged both on procedural grounds and as an unconstitutional "substitution of the constitution," the Constitutional Court upheld the amendment (Dixon and Landau 2015). However, when Uribe sought another extension for the presidential term limit – to serve for three consecutive terms – the court blocked the attempted constitutional change. In this *second* re-election case, "the majority of the court struck down the proposed referendum, both on the grounds that the procedures for approval had been unconstitutional and on the grounds that the amendment constituted a substitution of the Constitution" (Dixon and Landau 2015).

Legal theorists consider unconstitutional constitutional amendments to be a way of preventing anti-democratic or "abusive" constitutional rules (Dixon and Landau 2015). Dixon and Landau identify conditions under which such a decision, which invalidates the decisions of elected representatives by non-elected courts, is permissible or, indeed, necessary (such as in the case of Colombia).[10]

---

[10] Specifically, they argue that "the key question a judge should ask is the following: based on the actual impact of this amendment and what has come before it or is occurring in parallel in a particular country, does this particular amendment clearly pose a substantial threat to democracy or to democratic constitutionalism? In the mold of Thayerian review

constitution or the success of the amendment (or its significance). As a result, the text of the constitution rules.

I will come back to this point in Chapter 2 to develop a theory that will translate the constitutional text of different countries into an index of constitutional rigidity and in Chapter 6 to defend this method against arguments that claim "in any case they may not be worth the effort" (Albert 2019: 32). Here, though, I want to defend the written legal text as an achievement of humanity, going back to all monumental forms of civilization, from Hammurabi, to Moses, to Lycurgus in Sparta, and to Solon in Athens. Constitutions are the fundamental form of law in all contemporary societies. Even the people who consider them flawed and who disagree with important parts of the text agree that the only way to change them is through constitutional amendments (that is, working outside the constitution, but applying the rules of amendment themselves). For example, it may be disappointing that the US Constitution does not respect the fundamental democratic principle of "one person, one vote" for presidential elections. However, nobody would claim that we could respect this principle without changing the constitution. A reference to Dean Ely comes to mind here: "A neutral and durable principle may be a thing of beauty and a joy forever. But if it lacks connection with any value the Constitution marks as special, it is not a constitutional principle and the Court has no business imposing it. I hope that will seem obvious to the point of banality" (Ely 1973: 949).[13]

I.5.2 Focus on Democratic Countries

The reason that so many constitutional scholars go beyond constitutions and consider their own theories and principles legitimate is that they care about democracy and they see democratic values being disputed or even trespassed. In other words, in many countries, the constitution itself is not respected, and what is quite clearly written and generally understood (like the impossibility of standing for a presidential election twice in some countries) is violated by the relevant actors. This is the reason for searching for other principles as well as other authorities (such as foreign organizations or powers). I respect the intentions of these researchers as well as their efforts to create consistent theories. Still, I will adopt a different method in this book. Throughout, I will restrict the countries

---

[13] Dean Ely announced this principle criticizing *Roe v. Wade* despite the fact that he was in favor of choice.

I study to democracies because in these countries the rule of law prevails and, as a result, the constitution is respected. Consequently, the written text is relevant and applicable.

An example of the democratic intentions of scholars focusing on nondemocratic countries is the work of Sadurski who, in studying countries of Central and Eastern Europe, comes to the conclusion of "relative insignificance of formal constitutional design" in one article (Sadurski 2020a: 324) and that "formal institutions must be underwritten by norms which are by-and-large shared, and by common understandings about what counts as a norm violation, even if formal legal rules are silent about it" in another (Sadurski 2020b: 59). Such conclusions/suggestions are not included or discussed in this book because of the focus on democracies.

As a factual example of disrespecting a constitution, consider the case of the military coup against Honduras in 2009 when President Manuel Zelaya was arrested and subsequently exiled by the Honduran military. Zelaya had been attempting to change the constitution to allow him to run for a second term as president by appealing to the people in a consultative referendum on whether to hold a constitutional convention. In the Honduran Constitution, this was not a formal avenue for constitutional change, and the Honduran Supreme Court issued an injunction to make him halt his attempts. Zelaya continued his efforts despite the injunction, and a group of Honduran elites, including the Supreme Court and the military, conspired to arrest him and deport him to Costa Rica. In this situation, neither side respected the constitution. Zelaya wanted to change the constitution illegally, and the Supreme Court, despite its claims that it did what it did to *protect* the constitution, did not respect the constitution when it conspired with the military to have him removed (Sosa 2015).

From a comparative constitutional point of view, if nondemocratic countries are included in the study, there is substantial noise that contaminates the results, so their reliability declines. One of the first experiments in statistics was conducted by Student, who, when asked whether milk was beneficial for infants, compared a small number of twins, one of which was offered milk and the other not, and claimed that his results were more reliable than other researchers who were comparing thousands of infants without being able to control for intervening factors (Student 1931). Whenever we can, we should also try to find "twins." Obviously, in this book we are not performing an experiment like Student, but we are selecting countries that respect their constitutions – that is, democracies – when we study constitutional amendments in as much of an approximation as possible.[14] Therefore, this book will focus on the amendment texts of democratic countries and a series of consequences that these texts have for the political life of the countries.

The distinction of different changes occurring inside and outside the constitutional equilibrium that I follow in this book highlights the logic the existence of a constitution imposes on these changes. Instead of calling what most people call constitutional interpretation an "amendment," or instead of calling an extraconstitutional interpretation constitutional, I use the existing terms and identify the reason for their use. This way, when I use existing datasets of constitutional amendments, I do not need to reevaluate them country by country (an enterprise appropriate for historical accounts) on the basis of new interpretations.

The restriction to democracies also affects the comparative part of the book, which uses statistical analyses. In the descriptive part of the book, when I present specific institutional structures or historical accounts, I am going to extend the universe of cases and speak of events that took place regardless of whether they happened in democratic countries or not or even whether they occurred in countries, states, or supranational organizations like the European Union. Finally, I will also not be restricted by time limits. In all cases, I will provide all the necessary information. These selection rules are to permit the necessary cases to be included if they are interesting and relevant to the issue under discussion.

I.6 Outline of the Book

This book is organized into eight chapters, beginning with a descriptive (Chapter 1) and theoretical (Chapters 2 and 3) account. Then, it moves to an individual country approach (Chapters 4 and 5) that focuses on the amendment provisions of several countries in detail in order to understand the institutional mechanisms proposed in the book. Finally, it moves to a comparative analysis in Chapters 6–8 where I provide evidence that constitutional amendment mechanisms define constitutional rigidity, which, in turn, decreases the frequency of constitutional amendments (Chapter 6), that these mechanisms affect time inconsistency of constitutions – that is, how often they are amended

---

[14] It can be argued the not even democracies respect their constitutions all the time as every country has a problem of interpretation of its constitution and laws. This objection is correct, and I will address it by considering different levels of democratic commitment (based on the POLITY2 index) in Chapter 6.

despite locking provisions (Chapter 7), and that constitutional rigidity is a necessary condition for the significance of the judiciary of a country (Chapter 8). I will now describe the contents of these chapters in more detail.

Chapter 1 provides descriptions of different amendment provisions, which range from simple ones, such as that a constitutional amendment can be decided by a simple majority in the parliament of a country, to more complicated provisions, such as when an amendment requires approval in both chambers of the parliament of a country by qualified majorities. Some other provisions discussed in this chapter include even more composite ones, such as parliamentary approval and referendum approval, or alternative paths, such as either qualified majority in parliament or simple majority and referendum. In addition, there may be time limits implemented to wait for certain procedures or to not exceed in others, double passages with or without an intermediate election, quorum requirements, and other provisions. All these procedures are so complicated that different actors may have disagreements as to which is appropriate, and they may be fighting for their opinions, or, even more frequently, they may be modifying the institutions in order to ensure their opinion prevails. All these descriptions are meant to persuade the reader that amendment procedures are not only very diversified across countries but are also very influential since the people involved disagree about them.

Chapter 2 presents the theory of the book and explains how this variety of institutions affects the constitutional rigidity of a country. I use two theoretical concepts: the win-set of the status quo (the set of outcomes that can defeat the status quo) and the core of the constitution (the features of the constitution that cannot be changed given the amendment rules and the preferences of the actors). These two concepts help us classify the different amendment provisions in terms of their difficulty since the constitutions that are easier to amend will have a smaller (or empty) core and a larger win-set of the status quo. Special attention is given to the institution of referendums for both theoretical and empirical reasons that will become obvious later on. This classification enables us to construct an index of constitutional rigidity that will be used in the empirical part of the book. The expectation is that higher constitutional rigidity will not only produce a lower rate of amendments but also a lower variance of this rate. Indeed, when a country has high institutional rigidity, amendments are very difficult, and there will be very few of them, but if it has low rigidity and amendments are possible, it does not mean that they will happen frequently.

Chapter 3 addresses different cultural theories that are presented as alternatives or complementary to my institutional approach. I argue that there are three different approaches that deal with constitutional amendments: one uses cultural analyses as idiosyncratic forces, one as a systematic omission, and one as an independent variable. I provide different reasons for why each approach needs further elaboration before they can be used in a comparative perspective.

Chapters 4 and 5 provide a concrete institutional answer to the cultural theories presented in Chapter 3. They demonstrate that political analysis complements the broad brush of comparative constitutional analysis provided in Chapter 2.

Chapter 4 analyzes the institutions of two different countries (Italy and Chile) that recently had either constitutional amendments or rejections of the whole constitution. First, I analyze their institutions and explain why they have high rigidity before focusing on the final step of the modification (whether amendment or whole constitution rejection) process, which involved a referendum. I then analyze the public opinion that led to a NO vote and present an institutional improvement to constitutional referendums, which are likely to become more frequent.

Chapter 5 examines the opposite situation (from Chapter 4), focusing on a case where constitutional amendments are very frequent: Mexico. I analyze the institutions in more detail and explain why Mexico in particular has less-rigid institutions than expected when applying broad comparative rules. I then show that the political conditions of the country have created oversized coalitions that clear all constitutional obstacles for amendment.

Chapter 6 applies the constitutional rigidity index presented in Chapter 2 to all 103 democratic countries. I argue that higher institutional rigidity produces not only lower amendment frequency but also lower variance, as anticipated in Chapter 2. I divide the over 900 amendments into three different categories, examine them according to their significance, and show that the higher their significance, the more important the institutional rules are for their adoption. Chapter 6 is the empirical demonstration that constitutional rigidity is significant in determining the frequency of amendments and that its significance increases with the importance of the amendment, unlike the minor importance or irrelevance that other analysts have claimed.

Chapter 7 uses constitutional rigidity as the basis for developing a measure of time inconsistency. Instead of adopting the idea proposed in the literature that amendment frequency depends on culture and is unrelated to constitutional rigidity, I use the difference between the actual frequency of amendments and the one expected on the basis of constitutional rigidity, calling this time inconsistency. I demonstrate that this difference depends on the size of the constitution and that longer constitutions are more time-inconsistent (locked and amended more frequently) than shorter ones. As a result, I expect longer constitutions to be more restrictive and have more negative economic outcomes than shorter ones – expectations that are then empirically confirmed.

Chapter 8 analyzes the role of the judiciary. I argue that the judiciary will have low independence when constitutional rigidity is low because it will not be able to interpret the constitution without fear of being overruled. However, high rigidity *may* generate high independence because, in this case, the judiciary will not be concerned about being overruled. Therefore, in case it disagrees with the executive, it will strike down existing legislation (exactly like how constitutional rigidity affected the frequency of amendments in Chapter 6). I expand on this idea because frequently in the social sciences relationships are presented as necessary conditions alone, and, therefore, the statistical tests should be different than the standard ones.

1

The Landscape of Constitutional Amendments

The constitutions of the world are incredibly diverse, and the rules governing what is needed for an amendment vary greatly across countries. In this chapter, I describe a series of constitutional amendment stories with the goal of impressing upon the reader this diversity. I will be describing the institutions and providing information about particular events that bring them into relief. Sometimes these events will refer to constitutionally permitted initiatives, while other times they will be stretching the existing constitutional rules (therefore pushing the countries further away from a democratic status). Also, some amendment rules in US states are quite original and, as such, deserve to be included in a chapter on the diversity of amendment rules even though we will not deal with US states in other chapters. I will divide the chapter into three sections.

In Section 1.1, I present the *elements and combinations* of amendment rules (simple procedures, multiple bodies, qualified majorities, referendums, time, or other constraints) – or, in other words, the *additive or alternative combinations* that create more complicated pathways for amendments.

In Section 1.2, I argue that these procedures are so convoluted, or that interests are so confrontational, that they can generate *institutional conflicts* among different constitutional players regarding what the appropriate process is.

In Section 1.3, I will show that sometimes these procedures may create *constitutional revisions* with the immediate goal of amending the amendment rules themselves so that ordinary amendments will become either feasible or impossible.

This division is not to be understood as creating mutually exclusive and collectively exhaustive categories because each one of the stories I will tell could be classified in different positions. For example, when we have alternative institutional paths for amendment (a case belonging in Section 1.1), it is possible that the actors involved will disagree on which route should be selected (turning it into a case for Section 1.2), and it is also possible that down the road the institutions are changed so that these conflicts will be eliminated (becoming a case for Section 1.3). Depending on what I want to focus on, I will classify the case in one of the three categories, and the reader should know that none of my stories has an exclusive belonging.

These complications, once identified and enumerated, will be compared in Chapter 2 where we will study the constitutional amendment rules of all democratic countries and assess constitutional rigidity.

1.1 Elements and Combinations of Amendment Rules

1.1.1 Simple Procedures

In Israel, the absence of a formal, written constitution contributes to the relative simplicity of their procedure for amendments. Israel operates under a set of laws, legal precedents, and parliamentary norms known collectively as the "Basic Laws." The Knesset, the Israeli Parliament, sets identical procedures for the enactment of regular laws and Basic Laws. Thus, a Basic Law can be passed by a simple majority; however, some Basic Laws include entrenchment provisions that require a higher threshold to change them. Specifically, two sections of the Basic Law "The Knesset" (1958) are entrenched, so a two-thirds qualified majority (80 out of 120) is required to extend the Knesset's term (Section 9A[a]) and amend emergency provisions (Section 44). Other provisions (such as the modification of the status of Jerusalem) require an absolute majority (61 out of 120). Clause 6 of the Basic Law "Jerusalem, Capital of Israel" (1980), which prohibits the transfer of authority to a foreign body, was entrenched in 2000, requiring an absolute majority of sixty-one members of the Knesset to amend it (Amendment 1). It was further entrenched in 2018 and now requires a super majority of 80 out of 120 (Amendment 2). Likewise, the entrenchment section itself was entrenched: Any further amendment now requires a majority of sixty-one Knesset members.[1]

The status of Jerusalem has been a multimillennial aspiration of Jewish people, so it is difficult to imagine that it will be disputed. Nevertheless, Article 7 creates a roadmap for institutional conflict: it creates different

---

[1] "The provisions of article 6 are not to be changed, save by a Basic law adopted by a majority of eighty Members of the Knesset. The provisions of this article are not to be changed save by means of a basic law adopted by a majority of the Knesset Members" (Basic Law Jerusalem The Capital of Israel, Article 7).

conditions for direct vs. indirect disputes of Article 6. For direct disputes, a majority of two-thirds is required, but for indirect disputes, a simple majority of the Knesset can modify Article 7 itself and can thereby also modify the non-protected Article 6. This analysis indicates that even the simplest amendment provisions become complicated and conflictual very fast.

This short institutional and political account of what was intended to be the simplest worldwide set of amendment rules indicates how these rules are most endowed with significance and can be changed to promote different actors' goals, which is the fundamental point being made throughout this book.

1.1.2 Multiple Bodies

In the Czech Republic, a constitutional amendment must be passed by a three-fifths majority in both houses of the Czech Parliament. In response to the terrorist attacks in Paris and Brussels in 2015 and 2016, the EU issued a directive in 2016 restricting the sale of semi-automatic firearms to reduce the risk of future attacks (Bank 2016). In the Czech Republic, which was slated to hold its national elections soon, the interior minister of President Miloš Zeman's cabinet proposed a constitutional reform that would provide Czech citizens the right to use firearms to protect the state against terrorism (Adamičková and Königová 2016). The proposed amendment passed the Chamber of Deputies, where Zeman enjoyed considerable support, with an overwhelming margin of victory. However, the vote in the Senate, where the center-left Social Democratic party still held a plurality of seats, missed the three-fifths threshold by seven votes, thus causing the proposed reform to fail (Williams 2018).

In response to another EU directive aimed at restricting gun ownership, another attempt was made in 2021 to enshrine the right to gun ownership in the constitution after a petition was signed by over 100,000 Czechs. Senate elections in 2018 and 2020 had weakened the Social Democrats, who now accounted for three of the eighty-one seats in the Senate rather than the twenty-five they held in 2016. As a result of a less hostile Senate, the second attempt to enshrine gun rights in the Czech constitution passed the supermajority threshold in both houses (Plevák 2021).

In the United States, where constitutional amendments must be approved by a two-thirds majority in both the House of Representatives and the Senate as well as three-quarters of the states, a proposed amendment to criminalize the burning of the US flag failed by one vote in the Senate after being ratified by the House (Morisey 2007).

This was the latest in a string of unsuccessful attempts to modify the constitution to prohibit flag burning. In 1989, the US Supreme Court ruled that flag burning was a constitutionally protected expression of free speech. In response, the US Congress attempted to amend the Constitution to criminalize the defacement of an American flag but was unable to achieve a supermajority of votes in the US Senate. While they did pass the Flag Protection Act, which allowed for the punishment of flag defacers, this act was struck down in the same year by the Supreme Court. Further attempts were made in 1998, 2000, 2001, 2003, and 2005, but they were unable to reach enough support from Democrats in the Senate to reach the supermajority threshold. While three-quarters of the US states would need to ratify the amendment even if it did pass the US Congress, every US state has signaled that they would ratify an anti-flag burning amendment (American Civil Liberties Union n.d.).

1.1.3 Qualified Majority

In Poland, a three-quarters majority of legislators in the lower house and a simple majority in the upper house must agree in order to amend the constitution. Since 2015, the Polish government has packed the Constitutional Court by mandating a retirement age, forcing the retirement of several judges and appointing its own partisans to the empty spots. In this way, by 2020 thirteen of the fifteen seats on the Constitutional Court had been appointed by Andrzej Duda, the far-right president of Poland (Bunikowski 2018). However, Duda's supporters in parliament have still struggled to pass constitutional amendments. For example, in 2020, members of Duda's nationalist party proposed two constitutional amendments: to extend the term of the president by two years because of the coronavirus crisis (Reuters 2020b) and to ban the adoption of children by LGBTQ couples (Reuters 2020a). While a majority of voters in the lower house voted in favor of both amendments, neither passed because they were unable to meet the required two-thirds threshold.

In South Korea, President Moon Jae-In proposed a constitutional amendment in 2018 that would replace a single five-year presidential term without reelection with two four-year terms with the possibility of reelection. The amendment would also have lowered the legal voting age from nineteen to eighteen and devolved power to local governments.

To pass, the amendment needed a two-thirds majority, but only 114 of 288 legislators took part in the vote (Kim 2021), causing the amendment to fail.

1.1.4 Multiple Votes in Successive Parliaments

Several countries require an extended time period for a successful amendment, where two *successive* parliaments agree on a constitutional revision.[2] In these cases, the first parliament identifies the proposed revisions, then there is an election of a new parliament which votes for the adoption of the final text. The required majorities of the two parliaments are specified in the amendment rules. Obviously, this procedure may fail in any one of the two votes and is significantly more difficult than the simple vote required by most constitutions.

In Benin, a constitutional amendment must pass a double vote of three-quarters (consideration stage) and then four-fifths of members of parliament (MPs) in the National Assembly (the formal substantive deliberation stage, or, alternatively, a referendum). A 2017 amendment failed when it did not even reach the second stage because it missed the three-quarter requirement by three votes (Adjolohoun 2017). Because the proposed amendments would have changed about one-third of the constitution's text, Adjolohoun believes that "the 22 MPs who voted against the proposal and the one who abstained blocked the entire process for fear of opening a Pandora's Box which they believed they may lack the political ability to control." The proposal sought to extend the current five-year presidential term by one year and to reduce the number of terms from two to one, which, in Adjolohoun's words, followed from the "desire to superimpose a personal pledge [that President Talon had made during his election campaign] onto the people's will." The presidential term limit was central to the controversy since it had been a "key pillar of the national consensus edifice" (Adjolohoun 2017).

In Greece, the required majorities are significantly lower, needing only a simple majority in one parliament and a three-fifths majority in the other. However, the Greek Constitution does not specify which parliament should have each majority. This generates two possibilities: either

---

[2] I am *not* discussing here repeated votes which are very often prescribed in the same parliament since we are discussing identical majorities, which, even if they are not completely achieved, will be approximated.

the first parliament will decide by simple majority in which case the second (after the election) will be required to decide by qualified majority, or the first parliament will decide by qualified majority enabling a simple majority of the second parliament to make a constitutional amendment at its will. This particular constitutional flexibility generates different strategic possibilities as a function of the anticipated electoral outcomes. If the same party is anticipated to win the election, then it will select the easier procedure. If a different party is anticipated to win, the most likely procedure will require the qualified majority to be used in the second parliament (which will make many attempted amendments fail). This is what happened (for the first time) during the 2019 election. The constitutional revision was initiated by the left-wing coalition government of the country and was completed by the right-wing majority.

This procedure resulted in the failure of many proposed amendments. For example, the proposal by the Left included a referendum by popular initiative (after the collection of 500,000 signatures) which was not included in the constitution.[3] Similarly, the separation of church and state was not included. Two significant modifications that survived the process were the separation of the election of the president of the republic from the dissolution of parliament and the reduction of qualified majorities for the selection of independent authorities. Article 32 required the dissolution of parliament, and the new election of a three-fifths qualified majority could not select a president of the republic. This provision led to the rise of the left-wing government in 2015 when the Right could not find the number of votes necessary for the election of a president of the republic. The left-wing government voted to modify Article 32 in the first parliament, thus enabling the upcoming right-wing government to modify it at will. As for the independent authorities, the four-fifths qualified majority of parliamentary support for their election was reduced to three-fifths (the significance of the numbers being that in the first case support by the main party of opposition is necessary while

---

[3] The coalition of SYRIZA–ANEL introduced a referendum in 2015 that indicated their opposition to the needs of economic restrictions and was advocated for by the EU due to the conditions for financial loans to the Greek government (see Tsebelis 2018b). This referendum passed but was then almost immediately abdicated as the coalition wanted to introduce the measure in the constitution. This proposal has often been made by other actors like the Greek Orthodox Church in order to support proposals such as the rejection of marriage between people of the same sex. I discuss the ambivalent role of referendums as constitutional devices later in this chapter.

in the second the support of some minor party of the opposition may be sufficient).

These two countries' examples indicate how difficult it is to overcome the multiple-votes procedures. However, failure is not the only option. I will describe here two more alternatives in order to indicate that political elites may find ways to deviate from restrictive rules (unconstitutional though they may be).

In Belgium, constitutional amendments must be passed in two votes separated by an election. The first vote requires an absolute majority and declares that there are reasons to revise such constitutional provisions as it determines. The substance of the amendment does not have to be specified until the second vote, which requires a two-thirds majority with a quorum of two-thirds (Article 195 of the Belgian Constitution). In 1962, the Catholic-Socialist governing coalition proposed a series of constitutional reforms with the goal of helping to reduce tensions between French and Dutch Belgians, which eventually started the transformation from a decentralized unitary state to a federation. The so-called first state reform in 1970 established guarantees against minorization by implementing (1) a procedure for preventing a parliamentary majority composed mainly of members of the majority ethnic group from passing a law that was harmful to the interests of the linguistic minority; (2) a guarantee of equal representation in the government, or, rather, in the cabinet (Council of Ministers); and (3) the guarantee that certain specified future laws that affected the basic relations between the linguistic communities would have to be passed by a special concurrent majority. These guarantees were enshrined in the constitution in exchange for cultural communities (mainly concerned with person-related matters) that the Flemish demanded to promote cultural and linguistic autonomy. Also, three regions (mainly concerned with economic and place-related matters) were created (the Flemish, Walloon, and Brussels-Capital regions) as "an answer to the call for more economic autonomy of the French-speaking population" (Goossens and Hendriks 2021: 24), although their competences were less clearly defined than those of the communities.

These proposals passed the first vote in 1965, after which the parliament dissolved and elections were called in accordance with the rules of amendment. However, as a result of the election, the Catholic-Socialist coalition lost its supermajority, and the Socialists were replaced by the Liberals in the governing coalition. Because the Liberals were opposed to the constitutional reforms, the second vote did not occur. However, in the aftermath of the Leuven Affair of 1968, an outbreak of the language war between Flemings and Walloons prompted legislative elections. The French section of the Catholic University of Leuven, a Francophone enclave on Flemish soil, announced plans for a major expansion of its facilities in the city, resulting in a split of the university with the French departments moving across the language frontier to Louvain-la-Neuve. The parliament concurred on the sustenance of the declaration of constitutional revision, which permitted the freshly established Catholic-Socialist coalition, led by Prime Minister Eyskens, to again prioritize the revision. Since the coalition lacked the necessary two-thirds majority, Eyskens' government started negotiating with the Liberals and occasionally with the linguistic parties, which had gained voter support in the 1968 election. After a period spanning over two years which were marked by substantial parliamentary debate and rigorous consultations with various special ad hoc commissions, Prime Minister Eyskens managed to gain enough backing to institute the major reform of the Belgian state in December 1970 (Dunn 1974: 152).

Decades later, the Belgian political elites sought to circumvent these complicated procedures and reduce the potential for failure of amendments. This only happened once in Belgian history and was applicable to the legislature elected on June 13, 2010.[4] This time, a new *transitional* provision in Article 195 omitted the need to dissolve the parliament (the second stage of the original amendment procedure) for reforms regarding the autonomy of regions, child allowance rights, federal elections, bicameral system reform, the powers of the Brussels Region's capital, the use of languages in legal matters, public prosecutions, tax matters' conflict of interest regulation, and European parliament elections over the remaining course of the legislature (Venice Commission 2012). In the remaining stage, two-thirds of the members and votes in each house were still needed for what constituted the so-called sixth state

---

[4] "The Houses, as they were constituted following their full renewal on 13 June 2010, may however, in common consent with the King, pronounce on the revision of the following provisions, articles and groups of articles, but only to the effect as indicated hereafter: [follows a list of revisions of fifteen parts of the constitution] ... The Houses can only debate on the items mentioned in the first paragraph provided that at least two thirds of the members who make up each House are present and no change is adopted unless it is supported by at least two thirds of the votes cast. This transitional provision is not to be considered as a declaration in the sense of Article 195, second paragraph" (Venice Commission 2012: 3ff.).

reform. According to Goossens and Cannoot (2015), "In light of the historical evolution of Belgian federalism, the sixth state reform is undoubtedly a major reform. The whole package of power transfers is extensive (ca. 20 billion euros), especially in comparison with previous state reforms. In addition, for the first time powers regarding social security were transferred to the federated entities, as the power concerning family allowances is decentralized from the federal level to the communities" (44). They conclude that "the power transfers of the sixth state reform have resulted in a paradigm shift, since the lion's share of powers – excluding social security – is now situated at the level of the federated states. The sixth state reform also thoroughly revised the Special Finance Act, which considerably increased the fiscal autonomy of the regions" (50).

In Luxembourg, a constitutional amendment also had to be passed by two successive votes (although the legislature consists of only one chamber) separated by an election. In addition, the grand duke had to sign the declarations of amendments and sanction (enact) the modifications that the Chamber of Deputies had decided. The Luxembourg political elites found another way to get around this restriction: Before the regularly scheduled dissolution of every parliament for an election, they simply stated their intention to revise the constitution, even if they did not plan on revising the constitution in the subsequent election (Gerkrath 2013). Sometimes, these declarations mentioned many articles at once. Gerkrath (2013) concludes that "virtually any new elected Chamber was also entitled to proceed to constitutional amendments" (451). Since 2003, however, the intervening elections have been removed, and constitutional reforms must now undergo two parliamentary votes, spaced at least three months apart, in order to enable a more efficient and comprehensive reform process of the constitution that had become less and less coherent, consistent, and transparent over regular and increasingly frequent amendments since 1868 and, strikingly, lacked the enumeration of a number of fundamental rights and liberties (Sauer 2021). Furthermore, in an effort to enhance direct public involvement, the 2003 revision of the constitutional amendment process introduced the option of a referendum to replace the second parliamentary vote either if at least one-quarter of the MPs (numbering sixteen) or if 25,000 voters eligible to vote in parliamentary elections, which is slightly less than one-tenth of the eligible voters, makes such a request (Sauer 2021). In addition, "the ultimate change in the revision procedure results indirectly from the reform of Article 34 by the revision act of 12 March 2009. By ending the power of the Grand Duke to 'sanction' acts of Parliament, this revision also removed the last prerogative of the Grand Duke in the field of constitutional revision. Now constitutional revision acts, like ordinary legislation, will simply be enacted 'within three months of the vote in the Chamber'" (Gerkrath 2013: 453).

1.1.5 Tiered Amendment Difficulty

Many countries include "eternal provisions" in their constitutions, such as Germany's Article 79.3 which specifies that "amendments to this Basic Law affecting the division of the Federation into Länder, their participation on principle in the legislative process, or the principles laid down in Articles 1 and 20 shall be inadmissible." Similarly, the Greek Constitution specifies (in Article 110.1) that "the provisions of the Constitution shall be subject to revision with the exception of those which determine the form of government as a Parliamentary Republic and those of articles 2 paragraph 1, 4 paragraphs 1, 4 and 7, 5 paragraphs 1 and 3, 13 paragraph 1, and 26."

Additionally, a constitution frequently specifies different tiers of permissibility of amendments. For example, the Chilean Constitution (Article 127) divides the articles into two different categories requiring different majorities for each one: "The proposed amendment will need to be approved in each House by the vote of three-fifths of the representatives and senators in office. If the amendment concerns chapters I, III, VIII, XI, XII, or XV, it will need, in each House, the approval of two-thirds of the representatives and senators in exercise." Similarly, the constitution of Malta (Article 66) specifies a series of subjects requiring two-thirds of the members of the house of representatives, while others require additional approval by a referendum.

1.1.6 Time Limits

The time limit in the amendment procedure of the Costa Rican Constitution is twofold and proceeds as follows. (1) The proposal to reform one or various articles must be presented to the legislative assembly in ordinary sessions, signed by at least ten deputies or by 5 percent at a minimum of the citizens registered on the electoral roll. (2) This proposal will be read three times at intervals of six days, to decide if it is admitted or not for discussion. (3) "In the affirmative case it will pass to a commission appointed by [an] absolute majority of the Assembly, for it to decide [dictamine] in a term of up to twenty working days" (Constitution of Costa Rica, Article 195). Obviously, having an amendment survive a vote three times instead of once makes survival more difficult, but it is not significantly more difficult since the same parliament is involved. Nevertheless, there is some challenge involved as shown in the next case, which indicates that this rule was relaxed.

In Nigeria, this process is followed:

> The end of Assembly of every legislative house breaks the cycle of the amendment process. Therefore, the Constitution amendment process cannot go beyond the fixed period stipulated for any given Assembly nor deliberations on the amendments continue at the convening of a new Assembly.
>
> Note however, that recent Rules of the House of Representatives [Order XIII, Rule 1 (11)] now allow for constitution amendment bills not concluded in a previous Assembly to be taken up by a new Assembly. This was seen in the 7th and 8th Assemblies where the latter continued and concluded work on some constitution alteration bills began by the former but vetoed by the President. This provision however goes more to the issues and does not dispense with certain procedural requirements. For instance, the bill will still have to be reintroduced and made to go through the legislative stages or readings. The benefit of the rule is that the same issues can be brought back on table. Those considered settled can be prioritized and accelerated while certain procedures like a public hearing may be dispensed with except there are new issues or provisions introduced in the bill that require further consultations.
>
> (PLAC 2014: 11)

In Guyana, where a constitutional amendment must pass within six months of originally being proposed, an amendment to the constitution that would have forbidden discrimination based on sexual orientation failed when, despite having unanimous support from Congress, the president refused to ratify the amendment after being targeted with a pressure campaign by Christian groups. Because of the president's refusal, the six-month threshold was reached without the amendment being passed, and the amendment failed (Bulkan 2004).

1.1.7 Alternative Pathways

In Colombia, a constitutional amendment can be passed either by a simple majority vote of both houses of the Colombian legislature or by a majority vote of citizens in a referendum, with the caveats that Congress must approve of the referendum and the turnout must reach

25 percent.[5] In 2003, Colombian president Álvaro Uribe submitted a list of fifteen reforms to a popular referendum. The reforms that were initially proposed included a ban on public office for those convicted of corruption, mandatory participation of regional legislatures in the creation of the national budget, the dissolution of the existing two houses of parliament followed by the establishment of a new unicameral parliament, and the limiting of the wages of politicians to no more than twenty-five times the country's minimum wage.

Before the vote, Uribe faced two setbacks. First, in order to secure Congress' support of the referendum, he was forced to abandon the proposed unicameral reconstitution of Congress, instead settling on a 20 percent reduction in the number of legislators in each body. Second, Uribe wanted all fifteen proposals to be bundled into a single question, but the Colombian Supreme Court ruled that, according to the constitution, each proposed reform needed to be considered separately. Consequently, every voter had to read each of the fifteen proposals and vote for or against the reform.

On October 25, 2013, Colombians went to the polls to vote on the proposed changes. While all fifteen proposals received support in excess of 80 percent among those who voted, only a single proposal – a ban on holding public office for those convicted of corruption – passed the 25 percent quorum requirement laid out in the Colombian Constitution. Following this failure, Uribe submitted his amendments for approval in the Colombian Congress where he was forced to substantially water down the most controversial proposals (Breuer 2008).

In France, where a constitutional amendment may pass either in Congress or by referendum, the French people voted in a referendum in 2000 to decide whether to reduce presidential term limits from seven to five years. The referendum was a success: 73.2 percent of voters supported the proposed constitutional amendment, though only 30.2 percent of eligible voters turned out (Rogoff 2008). In 2008, France considered another constitutional amendment that would impose term limits on

---

[5] Specifically, the Colombian constitution states that "the constitutional reforms must be submitted to a referendum approved by Congress when referring to the rights recognized in Chapter I of Title II and to their guaranties, to the procedures of popular participation, or to Congress, if so requested, within the six months following the promulgation of the legislative act, by one third of the citizens who make up the electoral rolls. The reform shall be understood to be defeated by a negative vote of the majority of the voters as long as at least one-fourth of those on the electoral rolls participate in the balloting" (Colombian Constitution Article 376).

French presidents and broadly restructured the relationship between the executive and legislative branches. Rather than pursue another referendum, a joint session of Congress was called, where the amendment passed the two-thirds supermajority threshold by a single vote (Rogoff 2008).

1.1.8 Referendums

Citizen Initiatives

In Switzerland, citizens can challenge any legal provision via referendum and may also initiate a process of constitutional amendment by gaining 100,000 signatures in support of a proposal. Recently, constitutional amendments that restrict migrants or the building of minarets, for instance, have been proposed and passed in this fashion (Dixon and Uhlmann 2018). In the case of the minaret ban, legal challenges against the initiative were made, but the Swiss federal court did not consider the challenges on the grounds that they did not have the right to overturn a citizen initiative.

In Spain, where citizen initiatives can also be a source of lawmaking, there are limits to the types of issues that can be decided via referendum. Spanish citizens cannot reform the constitution, tax law, or international treaties. Moreover, they may not submit an initiative that concerns matters that are regulated by constitutional law, such as fundamental rights and liberties (Cuesta-Lòpez 2012). Similarly, **in Italy**, "issues of taxation, budgets, criminal amnesty or pardons, and the ratification of international treaties cannot be put to popular vote" (Uleri 2012: 74), and **in Greece** a referendum on a legislative bill "regulating important social matters" that has been passed by Parliament can be declared if three-fifths of the Greek Parliament assent, so long as it does not concern fiscal policy (Constitution of Greece Article 44).[6]

Majority Requirements

In 1999, a set of over fifty constitutional reforms was (after much debate and many rounds of concessions) passed by the **Guatemalan** Congress and was submitted to a vote by the Guatemalan people in a referendum. The referendum failed, however, and all the hard-fought amendments

---

[6] The same article of the constitution states that "the President of the Republic shall by decree proclaim a referendum on crucial national matters following a resolution voted by an absolute majority of the total number of Members of Parliament, taken upon proposal of the Cabinet."

were abandoned (Lehoucq 2002). Since the Guatemalan constitution does not impose a quorum requirement on referendums, it is worth noting that even though less than 19 percent of Guatemalan voters actually cast a vote during the referendum, if the result had gone the other way it still would have been binding and the amendments would have passed.

Quorum Requirements

This was decidedly not the case **in Moldova** in 2009, where a referendum to reduce the number of votes needed by the Moldavian Congress to elect a president from sixty-one to fifty-one failed despite receiving 88 percent support from those voting. Much like the Colombian case where most of Uribe's proposed reforms did not achieve the 25 percent quorum threshold, only 30.3 percent of Moldavian voters participated in the 2009 Moldavian referendum, falling just short of the required 33 percent (Fruhstorfer 2016). In contrast, a 2001 constitutional amendment to impose restrictions on the appointment of judges in Botswana (where referendums are required for major constitutional amendments) was ratified in a referendum with only 5 percent of the population actually participating.

In Denmark, constitutional amendment also requires assent from both the Danish Parliament and from the people in a referendum. The Danish Constitution requires that 40 percent of all voters must participate in a constitutional referendum and that a simple majority of those voters must assent to a proposed constitutional change. This 40 percent requirement is actually reduced from the 45 percent requirement that prevailed prior to 1953. In 1939, a major set of constitutional reforms in Denmark that had included reducing the voting age to twenty-one narrowly failed, with 44.5 percent of the Danish voting population participating in the referendum (Elklit 2010).

In Australia, "a double majority referendum" is required for a successful constitutional amendment. This is defined by the Australian Electoral Commission (2024): "A national majority of all formal votes cast a majority of formal votes cast in a majority of the states (i.e. at least four out of six states)." This unusual procedure is a replication of the Swiss system of amending the constitution.

Five amendment proposals were rejected at the state stage despite having a majority of the popular vote. One salient example is the Simultaneous Election Bill of 1977, which aimed to change the duration of senator terms from a fixed term to two terms of the house. The bill had broad popular support, winning 62.22 percent of votes in the referendum, but it was narrowly rejected, gaining a majority in only three states instead of the required four. The actual discrepancy between the majority of the population and the blocking minority can be much higher because of the pronounced population differences among states. I calculated that, as of 2023, a 9.95 percent of the population is sufficient to form the majority in the three smallest states (Western Australia, South Australia, and Tasmania, who together comprise 19.90 percent of the population) and, consequently, block an amendment even if the remainder (over 90 percent of the population) is in favor (Centre for Population 2024).

In the state of Nevada, referendums are of great importance in both pathways that the state constitution may be amended. If the legislature (senate or assembly) proposes an amendment, the pathway is threefold (as stated in Nev. Const. art. 16, § 1).[7] First, the amendments must pass in the senate and the assembly by an absolute majority. Second, they must pass it again in the next consecutive biennial session – or, in other words, after the next general election when they are possibly composed differently. Third, a majority of the electors qualified to vote for members of the legislature must approve and ratify the amendment in a referendum.[8]

If the citizens initiate the amendment, the pathway is twofold and leaves out the legislature entirely. Before that pathway starts, any such initiative must obtain the signatures of registered voters that equal at least

---

[7] Nev. Const. art. 16, §1: "Any amendment or amendments to this Constitution may be proposed in the Senate or Assembly; and if the same shall be agreed to by a Majority of all the members elected to each of the two houses, such proposed amendment or amendments shall be entered on their respective journals, with the Yeas and Nays taken thereon, and referred to the Legislature then next to be chosen, and shall be published for three months next preceding the time of making such choice. And if in the Legislature next chosen as aforesaid, such proposed amendment or amendments shall be agreed to by a majority of all the members elected to each house, then it shall be the duty of the Legislature to submit such proposed amendment or amendments to the people, in such manner and at such time as the Legislature shall prescribe; and if the people shall approve and ratify such amendment or amendments by a majority of the electors qualified to vote for members of the Legislature voting thereon, such amendment or amendments shall, unless precluded by subsection 2 or section 2 of article 19 of this constitution, become a part of the Constitution."

[8] For example, the 2001 legislature proposed and passed that in Nev. Const. art. 2, §1 on voting rights, the words "idiot or insane person" would be replaced by "person who has been adjudicated mentally incompetent, unless restored to legal capacity," which was agreed on and passed by the 2003 legislature and approved and ratified by the people at the 2004 general election (see 2001 Statutes of Nevada page 3469 and 2003 Statutes of Nevada page 3726).

10 percent of the voters who voted at the last preceding general election, with at least one-fourth of those collected in each of the four petition districts, which match the congressional districts (Nevada Secretary of State n.d.). Then, two referendums at two successive general elections are required. Only if the voters approve the amendment twice can it be added to the Nevada Constitution (Nev. Const. art. 19, § 2).[9]

Referendum Agenda

This is a very sensitive issue as we will explain in Chapter 2. In some constitutions it is not allowed to introduce multiple issues in a referendum amending the constitution. We saw already that in Colombia the Supreme Court split one referendum into fifteen separate questions. In the **Constitution of Ireland** Article 46.4 it is specified, "A Bill containing a proposal or proposals for the amendment of this Constitution shall not contain any other proposal." A similar restriction exists in the Italian Constitution about referendums apart from when they involve constitutional amendments. Among the US states, there are twenty-six that provide for at least one type of statewide citizen-initiated measure (whether initiative, referendum, or both). Of those twenty-six states, sixteen have single-subject rules.

1.2 Conflicts among Constitutional Players

In India, the requirement for amending the constitution differs depending on the significance of the proposed amendment, with a simple majority of both the upper and lower houses required for basic issues and a two-thirds majority for more consequential ones (The Constitution of India, 1947). Since independence in 1947, there have been numerous conflicts between lawmakers and the Indian judiciary. Starting in 1950, the Supreme Court and the Indian government struggled over the issues of land rights and affirmative action for underprivileged classes. On the issue of land reform, the Indian government had passed legislation that would expropriate the zamindars, a class of landlords who had been given the right to tax small farmers in their jurisdictions during the British colonial period. To compensate the zamindars, the government would pay them future profits from the expropriated land rather than an

---

[9] For example, citizens initiated to impose term limits of twelve years on the members of assembly and senators. Article 4, § 3 and § 4 of the Nevada Constitution was amended in 1996 after the people approved and ratified it at the 1994 and 1996 general elections.

immediate lump sum. The zamindars challenged their expropriation, and several high state courts struck down the legislation on the grounds that the compensation proposed by the government was not sufficient to make up for the violation of the zamindars' rights (VanderMay 1996, Neuborne 2003, Roy and Swamy 2022).

In response, the government amended the constitution to restrict judicial review on land-reform cases like those concerning the zamindars. Although this amendment was upheld by the Supreme Court, a subsequent challenge of inadequate compensation by the zamindars in 1952 and later in 1962 led to judicial action: in the 1952 case *State of Bihar v. Kameshwar Singh*, the Supreme Court struck down "the Bihar Land Reform Act, despite the provisions ... removing it from judicial scrutiny, holding that a judicially enforceable just-compensation obligation survived the first amendment" (Neuborne 2003: 487), and in the 1962 case *Karimbil Kunhikoman v. State of Kerala*, the Supreme Court struck down Kerala's zamindari expropriation act. The government then *again* amended the constitution, further expanding the scope of agrarian reform acts that shielded it from judicial review.

On the issue of affirmative action, the government passed legislation in 1951 that would reserve slots in government-funded educational centers for "untouchables and other backward classes." These efforts were swiftly challenged by members of the upper-class Brahmins on the grounds that they "violated the fundamental right of equality protected by [the constitution]" (Neuborne 2003: 488). In *State of Madras v. Dorairajan,* the Supreme Court considered the Brahmin argument and agreed, striking down the government legislation. As in the land-reform cases, the government responded by amending the constitution to explicitly shield affirmative action legislation from judicial review.

A pattern had been established, where "a state would pass land-reform legislation; it would be challenged in a high court as violating a fundamental right; the challenge would be upheld, and the law declared unconstitutional; [and] there would be an amendment to the Constitution to protect the legislation" (Roy and Swamy 2022: 25). This pattern would persist for nearly two decades until 1967 when the Supreme Court considered *Golak Nath v. State of Punjab*. In response to the Punjab Land Reform Act, the zamindars argued that the "act violated articles 31, 19, and 14 [of the constitution], and that the provisions of the ... amendments ... purporting to shield the act from judicial review ... were themselves unconstitutional" (Neuborne 2003: 489). In a landmark decision, the Supreme Court ruled in favor of the zamindars, holding that amendments to the constitutions were technically laws and, as such, were subject to judicial review in the same way that laws were. While they did not strike down the nationalization-shielding amendments, they threatened to use their new powers to strike down constitutional amendments against any new attempts by the government to undermine fundamental rights.

Following this decision, the Supreme Court proceeded to strike down other government acts, including a bank-nationalizing act, on the grounds that they had provided inadequate compensation. Following these strikes, Indira Gandhi campaigned with the promise to weaken the Supreme Court's power. She won a super-majority, with 350 seats in the lower house, and made a series of constitutional amendments to wrest the power of judicial review from the courts. These amendments were tested in *Kesavananda Bharati v. State of Kerala*, and "by a majority of ten to three, the court overruled *Golak Nath* ... [holding that] an amendment of the Constitution was constitutional law which is to be distinguished from ordinary law" (Nanda 1974). However, the victory for Gandhi was not complete: the court also ruled that "parliament's power of constitutional amendment was not unlimited and that, through judicial review, the limits were to be enforced" (Nanda 1974: 868), arguing that certain core features of the constitution such as fundamental rights could only be revised by wholesale constitutional change. In doing so, the Indian Supreme Court effectively gave itself the power to protect the "core" of the constitution.

In Israel, on July 24, 2023, the so-called reasonableness bill passed the Knesset to limit the Israeli Supreme Court's power in general. The reasonableness bill curbs judicial review over legislation by explicitly legislating against the Supreme Court's exercise of judicial review of Basic Laws and requiring a full bench of Supreme Court justices to preside over any case in which the legality of regular legislation passed by the Knesset is evaluated. Under this bill, 80 percent of the bench is required to rule for invalidation of such legislation.

The Israeli coalition government that proposed the reform consists of seven parties – Likud, United Torah Judaism, Shas, Religious Zionist Party, Otzma Yehudit, Noam, and National Unity – and is led by Benjamin Netanyahu, who is the chairman of Likud. According to McKernan (2023), "the changes are spearheaded not by the prime minister, but by his Likud party colleague Yariv Levin, the justice minister, and the Religious Zionist party lawmaker Simcha Rothman, who chairs the Knesset's law and justice committee." McKernan continues to reason that "Levin and Rothman have a longstanding hatred of Israel's Supreme Court, which they see as too powerful and as biased against the settler movement, Israel's ultra-religious community, and the Mizrahi population, Jewish people of Middle Eastern origin. In particular, many on the Israeli right have never forgiven the Court for decisions related to Israel's unilateral withdrawal from the Gaza Strip in 2005." In 2005, the Israeli Supreme Court had ruled the plan by then–prime minister Ariel Sharon to be constitutional, pathing the way for 9,000 settlers to be evacuated from Gaza. In a ten-to-one vote, it rejected the settlers' arguments that their human rights would be violated and held that it was ultimately a political decision by stating "their removal had been mandated legally by Parliament and 'appropriate compensation' had been ensured by law" (New York Times 2005). Leaders of the right wing contended for decades that the Supreme Court is biased against the settlement movement and acted particularly contradictory when it struck down legislation as unconstitutional, such as in 2020 when the law would have allowed for the retroactive legalization of around 4,000 Jewish homes built on occupied West Bank land privately owned by Palestinians (Halbfinger and Rasgon 2020). Therefore, the reform package had initially included an "override clause," which would have allowed the Israeli Knesset to reenact laws with a simple majority that the Supreme Court had nullified, reducing the court's ability to strike down the Knesset's laws that were deemed unconstitutional. Furthermore, it involved granting the government control over judicial appointments by changing the makeup of the Judicial Selection Committee and limiting the authority of its legal advisors by giving the ministers power to appoint and dismiss them, making them subordinate directly to the ministers rather than to the Justice Ministry's professional oversight. To the government, "these moves are a legitimate way to address a longstanding power imbalance between an overactive and unelected judiciary that selects its own members and that holds unreasonable veto power over democratically chosen representatives" (Kingsley 2023b). Prime Minister Netanyahu, although not the initiator, backed the reform for supposedly two reasons. First, as he is on trial for alleged corruption, he might personally benefit from the reform "in terms of the administration of his trial" (Goldenberg 2023). He denies the charges and has "campaigned against the justice system" since the indictment in November 2019 (Debre and Federman 2023). The second strategic consideration is that he needed the support of the far-right parties to secure the survival of the coalition and, hence, his own power. Mansoor (2023) specifically mentions the national security minister, Itamar Ben-Gvir, leader of Otzma Yehudit, who "gave Netanyahu what proved to be the decisive margin." The article, published in March 2023, points out that Netanyahu agreed to delay the proposal following mass protests and "can't back away from the proposed judicial reforms entirely without risking Ben-Gvir's critical political support."

To the protestors, the reform "will undermine Israel's democracy by giving absolute power to the ruling coalition and leave minorities without protection from the will of the majority" (Lieber and Boxerman 2022). The protests in March paralyzed the nation, compelling the government to discard its initial strategy of pushing through all parts of the overhaul at once, as already mentioned (see also McKernan 2023). Instead, they are now being introduced through a series of smaller bills, with the override clause having been removed as a sign of conceding to the protesters (Lieber and Amon 2023). The reasonableness bill still triggered so much controversy – not only on the streets but among the political parties in the Knesset – that all members of the opposition left the chamber when the reasonableness bill was voted. It then passed with a sixty-four to zero vote after all members of the governing coalition voted for it. While the country was waiting for the Supreme Court to decide whether to strike down the reasonableness bill and thereby decide its own fate (Kingsley 2023a), the reform was shelved like all non-security legislation in October 2023 when Netanyahu was pressured to form an emergency unity government with his main political rival Benny Gantz, leader of the center-right National Unity party, due to the outbreak of the Israel–Hamas war (Hendrix 2023). The Supreme Court struck down the provision as unconstitutional on January 1, 2024, most likely ending the controversy because the current government cannot address the issue, and it is unlikely that a future government will be able to reintroduce it.

In Hungary, where two-thirds support from the National Assembly is required for an amendment to be approved, a number of constitutional changes followed after the election of the Fidesz party in 2010 to the Hungarian Parliament with a supermajority. Fidesz came to power in the context of the economic fallout that had followed the 2008 worldwide recession. Voters rejected the Hungarian Socialist Party, which had been in power since 2002. Although the Fidesz party won only 53 percent of the vote, this translated into a supermajority of seats in Hungary's unicameral parliament (Bánkuti et al. 2015). This disproportionate result was due to the Hungarian electoral system, which assigned 386 legislative seats using a combination of single-member districts, proportional representation-style lists, and fifty-eight compensatory seats originally designed to make up for the disproportional allotment of single-member districts (Benoit 2001). Fidesz's supermajority allocation of seats despite only winning a bare majority of votes was a result of its high degree of support in smaller, rural regions, where votes are translated to seats more efficiently, and due to the fact that because only three parties ran in the 2010 election it benefited from a relatively large proportion of the compensatory seats (Bánkuti et al. 2015).

After laying the groundwork during their first year in government,[10] Fidesz introduced a new constitution called the Fundamental Law in 2011 and proceeded to amend it significantly several times over the next few years. In June 2012, the first amendment to the Fundamental Law elevated transitional provisions to bona fide parts of the constitution in order to shield them from judicial review, ensured that the presidential salary could only be changed via the adoption of a Cardinal Law (a law whose passage requires a two-thirds supermajority), and removed a clause in the transitional provisions weakening financial oversight in response to EU criticism. The transitional provisions were a set of amendments that had not been technically ratified between the passage of the Fundamental Law in 2011 and the first round of amendments in 2012. They included clauses that guaranteed there would be no statute of limitations on crimes committed during Hungary's communist regime, that removed the chairs of the Supreme Court, National Judicial Council, and privacy ombudsman, and that guaranteed that fines levied against Hungary by the European Commission can be collected as taxes (Boros 2013, Roznai 2022).

In October 2012, the second amendment modified the transitional provisions to make voter registration in a government-controlled database prior to an election a mandatory requirement for voting. In December 2013, in response to a claim filed to the Constitutional Court that the transitional provisions were not temporary and were in fact unconstitutional attempts to amend the constitution, the Constitutional Court struck down this amendment as well as a set of other clauses from the transitional provisions that Fidesz had tried to

---

[10] Preparing to create a new constitution, Fidesz repealed the four-fifths supermajority requirement for making a new constitution and revised the formal process for selecting members of the Hungarian Constitutional Court. Prior to the amendment, each party in the National Assembly had a single vote when selecting justices, regardless of the proportion of seats each party held. As a result of the amendment, the ability of minority parties to block nominations to the Supreme Court was eliminated, and the government quickly appointed two new justices to the Constitutional Court (Uitz 2015).

elevate to Fundamental Law, such as the transitional provision that removed the statute of limitations on crimes committed during communism. This decision was made on the grounds that the transitional provisions were indeed permanent and that "their adoption exceeded the government's power under the Fundamental Law to enact transitional provisions, notwithstanding the government's clear intent to give them constitutional status" (Roznai 2022: 150).

The Fidesz government responded with the Fourth Amendment in March 2013, which sought to undermine the Constitutional Court's decision by directly incorporating the transitional provisions into the Fundamental Law itself. Critically, it removed the ability for the Constitutional Court to review constitutional amendments on substantive (rather than strictly procedural) grounds and prohibited it from referring to precedents in constitutional law from before the 2011 constitution. In addition, the amendment stipulated that political advertising during campaigns could only be broadcast over public media sources with the list of acceptable media groups to be determined by Cardinal Law, that speech which violated the "dignity of the Hungarian nation" could be criminally prosecuted, that those who received tuition grants from the government would be able to work at Hungarian companies thereafter, and that municipal governments could use the powers at their disposal to remove homeless populations from public spaces (Orange Files 2013). The effort to shield the constitution from judicial review was effective: later in the year, the Constitutional Court "rejected a challenge to various provisions of the fourth amendment ... [on the grounds] that it lack[ed] competence to conduct substantive judicial review of constitutional amendments due to explicit provisions, introduced by the Fourth Amendment, that limit[ed] its jurisdiction over constitutional amendments to formal review on procedural grounds" (Roznai 2022: 152).

In Slovakia, where a three-fifths qualified majority of legislators is needed to change the constitution, a 2014 constitutional amendment to impose restrictions on the qualifications of new and incumbent judges passed but was challenged by the Constitutional Court. If passed uncontested, the amendment would have required all new and existing judges to meet a certain degree of security clearance in order to be appointed or to retain their positions. On January 30, 2019, the court struck down the 2014 amendment on the grounds that it violated Article 1 of the Slovak Constitution, which held that the Slovak Republic was a democratic state bound by the rule of law. The court argued that it directly followed that the constitution ensured commitment to the separation of powers and the independence of the judiciary, which it considered to be "material core of the Constitution" (Domin 2019). By this ruling, the Slovakian Constitutional Court therefore gave itself the power to reject constitutional amendments that go against the "core of the constitution" (Ľalík 2020a).

The judges made the decision shortly before nine out of thirteen would leave, and it almost went unnoticed "because the political fight over the composition of the future Constitutional Court took center stage" (Ľalík 2020a: 328; see also Steuer and Láštic 2024: 248), who describe the period from 2018 to 2019 as a "gridlock in electing new judges." A few months later, the "Threema" scandal surfaced after the murder of the investigative journalist Ján Kuciak and his fiancée. Nineteen judges were accused of "delivering judgments on demand" (Čuroš 2023: 639), painting a picture of "a massive corruption scheme among the judiciary, law enforcement, politicians, and business members" (Čuroš 2022). As a result, "the outrageous crisis of legitimacy of the judiciary provided a perfect opportunity for the interference of the legislative and executive power into the judicial power. Such interventions had been attempted for years, but after the Threema scandal, the public embraced the idea of enacting significant changes in the judiciary" (Čuroš 2022). In this light, some view the reform that followed favorable, leading to more "efficiency and a better standard of delivering decisions" (Čuroš 2022), while others point toward the illegitimacy: "The passing of the amendment in question has made the parliament an unbound constitutional-maker that is neither in line with constitutionalism nor with democracy" (Ľalík 2020b).

The reform, curtailing the power of the judiciary, was passed in December 2020. Steuer and Láštic (2024) state that "the amendment can be seen as a parliamentary retaliation to the SCC's [Slovak Constitutional Court's] decision" (255). The amendment allowed for the examination of the origins of the property holdings of individual judges (purportedly to investigate corrupt dealings by judges), eased the process of judicial appointment to the Constitutional Court by allowing a simple majority of the Slovakian Parliament (rather than a three-fifths supermajority) to appoint a constitutional justice, provided the president the power to unilaterally appoint justices if the parliament fails to do so, and mandated a maximum retirement age of seventy-two years for judges on the Constitutional Court (Davala and Chudo 2021). In addition, and most critically, the amendment removed the ability of the court to review constitutional amendments and was rushed through Parliament, just barely passing the three-fifths threshold with 91 of 150 MPs voting in favor (Steuer and Láštic 2024).

In 2021, the Slovakian Supreme Court made a significant ruling under the new rules, stating that a referendum initiative on a snap election was unconstitutional. "The Court found referenda analogous, both in form and function, to constitutional amendments" (Drugda 2021), thereby reclaiming some of the power it had lost through the amendment in 2020.

This absence of a mechanism for early elections became acutely salient in 2022 when President Zuzana Caputova responded to the collection of over 380,000 signatures by three opposition parties and decided to hold a referendum, seeking approval for the early termination of the National Council of the Slovak Republic's election period either through a referendum or a resolution by the National Council. Shortly after that decision, Prime Minister Heger's coalition government faced a vote of no confidence and subsequently collapsed (Associated Press 2023a).

The referendum was held on January 21, 2023, and faced challenges due to the president stating, "I perceive this referendum as a part of a political campaign of one party . . . I am therefore not going to encourage citizens to attend, nor am I going to discourage them" (Cincurova et al. 2023). Subsequently, it resulted in a low turnout and its failure (as at least 50 percent would have been needed).

In the week prior to the referendum, President Caputova had already given parliament the deadline of the end of January to amend the constitution to make a snap election possible. Only four days after the failed referendum, ninety-two members of parliament voted for the constitutional amendment that allows a snap vote if it is approved by a three-fifths majority in the 150-seat National Council of the Slovak Republic (Associated Press 2023b).

In **Ukraine**, the Constitutional Court struck down constitutional amendments as unconstitutional years after they were made. In 2004, after the Orange Revolution, a major constitutional change was made to limit the power of the president relative to the prime minister. This amendment was proposed and passed by parliamentarians supporting the pro-Russian Viktor Yanukovych, ostensibly with the goal of weakening the power of the anti-Russian president Yushchenko. In 2010, Yanukovych regained the presidency and appointed four new members to Ukraine's Constitutional Court. Subsequently, the court ruled that the 2004 amendments to weaken the presidency were unconstitutional and ordered that they be reversed, restoring the power of the president. Following the widespread Euromaidan protests in 2013, Yanukovych fled the country, new elections were held, and the newly elected parliament repassed the 2004 amendments to weaken the presidency (Tyushka 2014).

In all of these cases, there are conflicts between the legislature and the judiciary, and in lots of them, there is an oscillation in the results: sometimes the legislature is the winner, and in others it is the courts (India and Israel are the most prominent examples). What is not obvious is the (indirect) participation of the public because, given that the constitution does not specify who should be the ultimate decisionmaker, it is the actor that will express the opinion of the public that will claim the constituent power. The following case demonstrates what happens when the carrier of the constituent power can interfere directly. It is a conflict not between legislation and constitutional interpretation (conflict within the constitutional rules) but between interpretation and constitutional amendment.

In a landmark case in October 2006, **Ireland's** high court rejected the recognition of a lesbian couple's Canadian marriage. It ruled that the constitution did not protect the rights of same-sex couples to get married, although the constitution had never defined marriage as being between a man and a woman explicitly. Instead, "[Justice Elizabeth] Dunne took the definition of marriage contained in Ireland's Civil Registration Act 2004 which defines marriage as being between a man and a woman as an indication of the 'prevailing view' as to the definition of marriage" (Tiernan 2020: 31). The plaintiffs, Katherine Zappone and Ann Louise Gilligan, had challenged an interpretation of the Taxes Consolidation Act, which provides for a husband to be assessed on his and his wife's total income and vice versa, by the Revenue Commissioners, who had denied altering their tax returns in recognition of their marriage explicitly. They had based the interpretation on the definitions of husband and wife in the Oxford English Dictionary, and Zappone and Gilligan argued to the court that it violated their constitutional rights to equal protection (Article 40.1), privacy, and dignity (Article 40.3). Justice Dunne recognized that "it is to be hoped that the legislative changes to ameliorate these difficulties will not be long in coming" (High Court 2006). Also, she delegated the responsibility for such change to happen by saying that "ultimately, it is for the legislature to determine the extent to which such changes should be made" (High Court 2006).

In response to the ruling, lower house member Brendan Howlin tabled a Private Member's Civil Union Bill on the same day that Zappone and Gilligan lost their high court case. Even though the bill was defeated in Parliament later, the introduction of (various) civic partnership bills in conjunction with this court case raised public awareness about the need for legal recognition for same-sex couples (Tiernan 2020: 39). When the Civil Partnership and Certain Rights and Obligations of Cohabitants Act was finally passed in 2010, it was clear that a constitutional amendment was needed to achieve full equality in terms of marriage and not only in terms of partnership. In 2012, a constitutional convention was established due to complex government formation negotiations between the center-right Fine Gael and the center-left Labour Party over their differing reform agendas regarding the issue of same-sex marriage, among other issues. The convention's agenda "reflected the decision of the inter-party negotiators to 'park' certain matters that were in their respective election manifestos that were unlikely to be resolved easily during their febrile and intense negotiations" (Farrell et al. 2016: 122). After the convention recommended amending the constitution, the government called a referendum.

The referendum on May 22, 2015, had a remarkably high turnout. A majority of 62 percent voted to add the following sentence to the Irish Constitution: "Marriage may be contracted in accordance with law by two persons without distinction as to their sex," making Ireland the first country in world history to extend civil marriage to same-sex couples through a popular vote. Eventually, the people overruled the court and its interpretation of the constitution. However, Doyle and Walsh (2020) emphasize that the outcome of the referendum was not particularly contentious or surprising:

> The Convention has been credited with securing "an outcome consistent with liberal value accommodation" in the same-sex marriage referendum, notwithstanding the persistence of normative opposition to same-sex marriage. Since the 1970s, however, both constitutional interpretation and constitutional amendment – reflecting changes in general society – had rendered the Constitution considerably less religious and less conservative. The same-sex marriage and abortion referendums probably marked the culmination of that process with secular/progressive forces in the ascendant. But they were not a constitutional revolution.
>
> (Doyle and Walsh 2020: 464)

In addition to this case, there were eight others in Ireland where a proposed amendment was "regarded as necessary in order to reverse statements of law resulting from unpopular judicial interpretations, or because of a judicial decision making it clear that a desired course of action would be possible only following a successful referendum to amend the Constitution" (de Londras and Morgan 2013: 182). Among the eight proposed amendments, one was on human rights (bail), two on elections, one on abortion, and four on institutions of government. Concerning bail, Raifeartaigh (1997) states that "Ireland appears to be one of the few, perhaps the only, common law jurisdiction which rejects the likelihood of further offending as a ground for pre-trial detention. In 1966, the Irish Supreme Court emphatically rejected the suggestion that one of the grounds on which bail might be refused was the likelihood that the accused might commit further offenses; again in 1989 it unhesitatingly affirmed its earlier decision. The Court's view, as we shall see, was founded on the view that such a course of action would violate the presumption of innocence" (2). What Raifeartaigh calls "a somewhat absolutist view of the presumption of innocence" led the government to hold a referendum to change the Irish legal position (Raifeartaigh 1997: 18). The new article, approved by the people in 1996, ensures that the grounds for refusal of bail by a court may be regulated in the future by the legislature so that, under the Bail Act 1997, a court can now consider whether or not a person had committed serious crimes while on bail in the past in addition to the "extraordinary circumstances" that the ruling in 1966 had implied (Raifeartaigh 1997: 18).

Two out of these eight cases failed in the respective referendum: the one on representation of rural voters and the one on parliamentary inquiries.

1.3 How Institutions Are Modified in Order to Get the Intended Outcome

In this section, I will highlight some examples from US state constitutions because they have provisions that involve referendums which, as will be explained in the next chapter, are very flexible instruments for changing the rules. The examples in this section demonstrate that modifying how easy it is to use referendums affects the facility of constitutional amendments.

The Michigan Constitution from 1850 included the provision that the voters must decide whether a constitutional convention is called automatically every sixteen years. Furthermore, the provision required that a majority of votes that are cast in the election – not just a majority of those voting on the question of the convention call – must approve all convention calls rather than only those that occur automatically. Only in 1866, pursuant to the sixteen-year requirement, and in 1906, when it was placed on the ballot by legislative action, did the voters approve the calling of a constitutional convention. In many instances, the question failed despite the majority of those voting on the question giving their approval ("CRC special report" 2010a). Five referendums failed between 1926 and 1961, and, especially during and after World War II, "a general dissatisfaction with the document created a growing desire to revise the constitution" ("CRC special report" 2010a: 2). Therefore, instead of a general constitutional revision, eighteen proposed amendments were adopted in the decade beginning in 1951, while only three were rejected ("CRC special report" 2010b). The Citizens Research Council of Michigan summarized the developments in this era as follows: "Along with 51 previous amendments, these new provisions gave the Constitution the appearance of a patchwork quilt of trivia and excessive detail, which provided for far too many executive branch agencies, excessive earmarking of taxes, and a system of legislative representation skewed toward rural interests" ("CRC special report" 2010b: 4).

As a consequence, the "long struggle for constitutional revision" (Cramton 1964: 8), amplified by the fiscal crisis in 1959, stimulated renewed efforts by a number of interest groups that had previously supported the campaigns (Sturm 1963). In January 1960, the Michigan Junior Chamber of Commerce and the Michigan League of Women Voters proposed a constitutional amendment to ease the calling of a constitutional convention. The so-called Gateway Amendment was approved by the voters later in 1960 and paved the way for a successful convention call in 1961. The referendum on April 3, 1961, did not require the majority of electors anymore, and therefore a favorable plurality on the convention question was sufficient. Michigan voters approved the proposition by a margin of only 23,421 votes (Sturm 1963). The Citizens Research Council of Michigan emphasized that "if the former constitutional requirement of a majority of those participating in the election had applied, the proposal would have failed" ("CRC special report" 2010a).

To summarize, changing the rules in 1960 was critical in allowing a convention referendum to pass in 1961 after it had been blocked on various occasions and only stepwise amendments had been possible.

In Ohio and other states, lawmakers were recently trying to achieve the opposite: They were pushing for a rule change that would make it harder for citizens to initiate and implement constitutional amendments successfully. The rule change, sought by the Republican supermajority, was specifically targeted at a citizen-led effort to put a constitutional amendment on the ballot that would prohibit banning abortion before fetal viability (Zernike and Wines 2023). The amendment that the lawmakers advanced had already passed the senate and the house. It went before voters in a special election in August 2023 and thus would have taken effect before the amendment on abortion rights advanced by citizens was on the ballot in November 2023.

First, the addition of new requirements to get proposed amendments on the ballot would have immediately hampered the citizens' effort: according to the New York Times, "proponents would have to collect signatures from at least 5 percent of the residents in all 88 counties in the state, up from the current 44" (Zernike and Wines 2023: para. 29). Additionally, they would not have been allowed to collect additional signatures to make up for those that authorities disqualified, which as of now can be done for one week (the so-called curing period) (Zernike and Wines 2023). Second, their ballot initiative would have required a 60 percent threshold once it passed the higher hurdles to appear on the ballot, rather than the current 50 percent. The Republican measure to raise this threshold, however, required support from only 50 percent of voters to pass. Furthermore, Chris Melody Fields Figueredo, executive director of the Ballot Initiative Strategy Center, which works to support progressive ballot measures, expresses suspicion in the New York Times that the new threshold was chosen strategically based on the vote for abortion rights in other red and purple states (Zernike and Wines 2023). Specifically, in Michigan, Kentucky, and Kansas the vote was between 52 and 59 percent.

However, 57 percent of the Ohio voters resoundingly rejected the amendment of the amendment rule (Ingles and Kasler 2023). Subsequently, abortion rights were enshrined into the state's constitution in the November referendum by 57 percent (so not the 60 percent that would have been necessary under the new rules), although the approval has prompted another institutional conflict over the amendment's implementation. How and when the impacts of the new constitutional protections for abortion access and other reproductive rights are felt therefore "remains unclear" (Smyth 2023b).

Similar measures have been taken in **North Dakota** in response to issues other than the abortion rights movement: "North Dakota lawmakers in recent years have grumbled about certain constitutional initiatives voters have approved, including measures for a state Ethics Commission in 2018 and for term limits on the governor and state lawmakers last year" (Dura 2023). Consequentially, the North Dakota legislature approved a bill in 2023 that makes it more challenging for constitutional initiatives to qualify for the ballot and be adopted. Voters will be asked on the 2024 ballot to approve or reject the constitutional amendment, which would (1) establish a single-subject rule for initiatives (both statutory and constitutional), (2) increase the signature requirement for constitutional amendment initiatives from 4 percent of the resident population to 5 percent of the resident population of the state, and (3) require proposed constitutional initiatives that have qualified for the ballot to win approval in both the next primary and the next general elections (Mitchell 2023).

In Arkansas, Republican lawmakers chose another route rather than amending the constitution: After voters had soundly rejected a constitutional amendment in 2022, which was proposed by the legislature to stiffen the requirements to get a measure on the ballot (increasing the required vote to approve ballot initiatives to 60 percent and applying to measures placed on the ballot via petition or by the legislature), the legislature simply passed new requirements as state law. They also aimed to increase the hurdles but targeted hurdles other than the ones that had just been rejected, picking up on a rejected amendment from 2020. Governor Huckabee Sanders signed the law in March 2023, whereby the number of counties where a minimum number of signatures from registered voters must be submitted was raised from fifteen to fifty (Smyth 2023a). The minimum is defined as "not less than one-half of the designated percentage of the electors" (Vrbin 2023), with the percentage being set at ten for proposed constitutional amendments (Smyth 2023a).

Conclusions

The goal of this chapter is to impress upon the reader two points: first, the diversity of constitutional amendments, and second, the significance of them. Section 1.1 deals with this diversity and shows how many different simple rules are used (different actors are assigned the role of a veto player, different decision-making rules are selected, intermediate elections are required, referendums may be added in the mix, or time or other constraints are imposed; then sometimes these rules are combined, and other times they are presented as alternatives). All such cases are presented in Section 1.1, with the goal to underline the diversity and complications of constitutional amendment rules.

Sections 1.2 and 1.3 focus on the significance of these rules by presenting how these rules become the objects of political conflict or the targets of modification for political reasons, making constitutional change easier or more difficult to achieve. These two sections demonstrate that the policy preferences of different actors become the source of induced institutional preferences: The actors understand that the best way to promote their policy preferences is to modify in a specific way the rules of the game (that is, alter the constitution). The conclusion of these two sections is to persuade the reader that these amendment rules matter a lot – a conclusion that may be trivial for some readers but has been disputed in the literature.

2

An Institutional Approach to Constitutional Rigidity

In the introduction, I explained that political changes come in three different levels: first, as policy changes within the constitutional equilibrium; second, as constitutional amendments moving outside the constitutional equilibrium but within the constitutional amendments rules; and third, as constitutional replacements where the whole constitution is judged inadequate and is replaced by a new one. Each of these steps is more difficult than the previous one and occurs only when the previous one is considered insufficient or inadequate.

Many analyses have dealt with the first level of changes (i.e., policy) within the constitutional equilibrium, taking the constitution of a country for granted (Shepsle and Weingast 1987, Krehbiel 1998, Strøm et al. 2003, Thomson et al. 2006, Eldes et al. 2024). This book moves to the second level and addresses the movements outside the constitutional equilibria, which take place within the rules specified by the amendment rules of the constitution itself. These amendment rules specify veto players (that is, actors whose agreement is necessary for a change of the constitutional status quo) who are different from the legislative ones. They may require different (more stringent) majorities or involve more actors. Often, the people of a country have understood that the current rules as specified by their constitution are not helpful in addressing some particular problems, so a more difficult modification of the constitution itself is in order. This is why we will be studying the constitutional amendment rules and the outcomes that they produce – that is, the constitutional changes that they enable.

This chapter is presented in four sections. In Section 2.1, I define the basic concept for the analysis, the *constitutional core,* and explain why I use this concept and how I can understand constitutional change on the basis of it by using the simplest example of a one-dimensional space. Section 2.2 calculates the core in a more complicated two-dimensional space and covers all the different provisions of existing constitutions. Section 2.3 deals with one particular set of rules, which is the use of constitutions for the final approval of a constitutional text. There, the concept of the constitutional core is not useful for reasons that I will explain, so we will instead use another way to understand the institutional provisions. Finally, Section 2.4 will use all the theoretical analyses of the previous sections as well as a series of simplifications in order to create an indicator of constitutional rigidity. This indicator will be simple and rigid in order to be applicable in the comparative statistical analyses presented in this book.

2.1 The Core in a Single Dimension and the Use of It in the Analysis of Constitutional Change

The definition of a "core" that I will use here is different from the one in the law literature, which considers a "core" as being only the constitutional provisions that are not allowed to be modified at all (Albert 2015d). I will instead adopt the definition of the rational choice literature, which is that the core of the constitution is the set of provisions that cannot be amended *given* the prevailing rules *and* the preferences of the actors involved. The reader should notice that I use a combination of the constitutional rules *and* the preferences of the political actors to define "core." For example, if a constitution requires a two-thirds majority of parliament for an amendment and such a majority is impossible to achieve, then, under the current circumstances, we find ourselves within the core. Under different circumstances (such as if the parties were less polarized or if the institutional requirements were less stringent), it would be possible to modify the constitution (so we would be outside the core). Similarly, consider a scenario with a constitution that requires a simple majority and three political parties, none of which has the majority. When they cannot agree, then, again, the core of the constitution has been achieved despite the fact that if coalitions were possible the constitution would have otherwise been amended. On the other hand, if a party has a qualified majority (like the PRI had in Mexico before 1994), any point not preferred by this party is outside the core and the constitution can be modified at will.

This concept of "core" is part of cooperative game theory. The fundamental assumption of this branch of game theory is the enforceability of agreements. Because agreements are assumed to be enforceable, anything permitted by the institutions will be undertaken in order to achieve the agreed outcome. It does not matter what the preferences of the actors were before the agreement (they may have negotiated a necessary

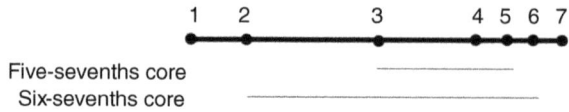

Figure 2.1 Five-sevenths and six-sevenths cores in one dimension

convergence), and it does not matter what the specific strategies are that lead to the outcome. Therefore, this theory provides an outline of the feasible solutions, but not a prediction about which one will prevail.[1]

Let us calculate the core in the simple case of a one-dimensional policy space. Assume that we have seven legislators with preferences 1 to 7 as depicted in Figure 2.1. Let us assume that this legislature is requested to modify the constitution under two different sets of amendment rules: first by a qualified majority of five-sevenths and second by six-sevenths. We can calculate the qualified-majority cores of this legislature as follows. First, if the required majority is five-sevenths, the constitutional core lies in the interval between Point 3 and Point 5 in Figure 2.1. Indeed, a status quo provision that lies between Player 3 and Player 5 cannot be altered with a three-fifths majority. For any point inside this interval, a blocking minority will always prevent movement away from it. If one considers Point 3, for example, it cannot be moved to the left because 3, 4, 5, 6, and 7 will object; similarly, it cannot be moved to the right because 1, 2, and 3 will object. If the constitution requires a six-sevenths majority for revision instead of five-sevenths, the core grows, now ranging from Point 2 to Point 6. In this case, moving to the right of Point 2 or to the left of Point 6 will raise objections from 2 out of the 7 members, so the required six-sevenths majority would not be reached. As one might expect, increasing the size of the required supermajority renders it more difficult to revise a constitution. Indeed, under the six-sevenths case, a larger number of provisions become unalterable in this seven-person legislature.

Let us now modify the preferences of the actors while preserving the amendment rules. This will likely happen when a country tries to revise its constitution. Figure 2.2 replicates the five-sevenths and six-sevenths core arguments under two different preferences of the seven legislators. The "old" preferences are represented by the gray numbers 1 to 7, and the "new" preferences are represented by the black numbers 1' to 7'. Note

---

[1] This is similar to the concept of "equilibrium" in non-cooperative game theory.

2.1 THE CORE IN A SINGLE DIMENSION   57

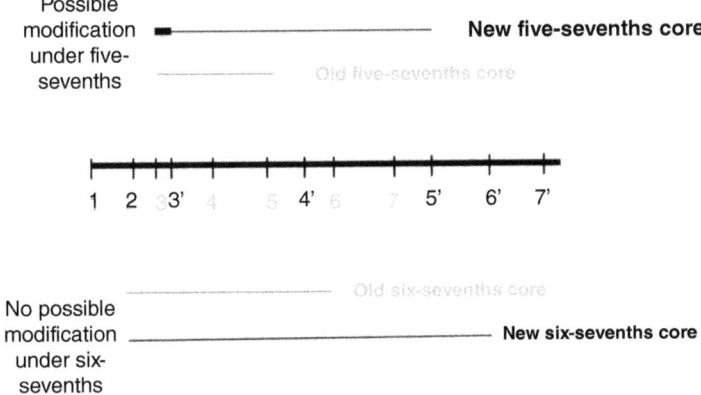

Figure 2.2 Change of core in one dimension under five-sevenths and six-sevenths majority

that the political change that occurred in this country was a shift to the "right" of monumental proportions, where three of the seven actors (5, 6, and 7) have changed their opinions so much that their positions did not exist in the political spectrum of the past, while two of them (1 and 2) have kept their preferences unchanged. Given such a policy change, it is reasonable to assume that the political system would want to modify the constitution accordingly. The concept of the core identified before will help us understand the magnitude of constitutional change.

In this simplified one-dimensional representation, the old five-sevenths constitutional core would be indicated by the gray line at the top of the picture, while the new five-sevenths constitutional core would be indicated by the black line. The feasible difference between the two lines, corresponding to the possible constitutional change, would be the tiny segment in red. This is the *only* possible constitutional change. If the constitution happened to be located anywhere in the 3–3' segment of the line, it would be modified to go to 3'. Otherwise, it will remain unmodified. The reason for this is that for a five-sevenths majority the outcome is to be within the new core; consequently, the approval of Player 3 (now 3') is necessary.

Let us now look at the bottom of the figure, which assumes a six-sevenths qualified majority for modification of the constitution (that is, it addresses the issue of a six-sevenths constitutional core). Now, constitutional change is impossible because Legislator 2 has to approve it and they have not changed their opinion.

58   CONSTITUTIONAL RIGIDITY: INSTITUTIONAL APPROACH

In both cases, the part of the constitution that can be modified is the difference between the new and the old core – that is, anything that happens to be in the old core and is not in the new one. This difference is very small in the case of amendment rules requiring five-sevenths and is non-existent in the case of amendment rules needing a six-sevenths majority. This makes it clear why different amendment rules have very different outcomes. Consequently, the Burgess (1890) argument, which states that amendment rules are the most important part of the constitution (and is an argument shared by many researchers, as we saw in the Introduction), is not an idiosyncratic statement based on his preferences but a belief based on the way institutions work.

The astute reader will understand that the larger the core of the constitution (I remind them, this depends not only on amendment rules but also on the actors' preferences), the less frequent and/or significant amendments will become. A more accurate argument, though, is that a large constitutional core is incompatible with significant amendments. However, one should be uneasy about the simplicity of the one-dimensional space I used to make my analysis. A very reasonable objection is that constitutions are much more complicated objects. However, the advantage of theory is that it allows one to see the consequences of bare-bones arguments and then complicate them. We will now move to a two-dimensional space of constitutional cores.

2.2 Two-Dimensional Cores Generated by Complicated Amendment Rules

Let us assume that we have a single congress with seven legislators (for reasons of simplicity) that requires a two-thirds majority to amend the constitution, as in Figure 2.3. If we assume that each one of these seven legislators has their own preferences (depicted by the location of Points 1 to 7) and that each one of them prefers outcomes that are closer to their preference over outcomes that are further away, then we can calculate the qualified majority core of this "legislature" as follows. Given that the constitution specifies a two-thirds majority for successful amendments, it requires that five of the seven members vote in favor of revisions in order for them to pass. Figure 2.3a presents a five-sevenths core by drawing a line between two players such that there are two points to one side of the line and five points either on the line or to the opposite side of the line (as with lines C1C4, C2C5, C3C6, etc.). The core, for example, cannot be north of line C2C6 because five group members (C2, C3, C4, C5, C6) will

2.2 TWO-DIMENSIONAL CORES

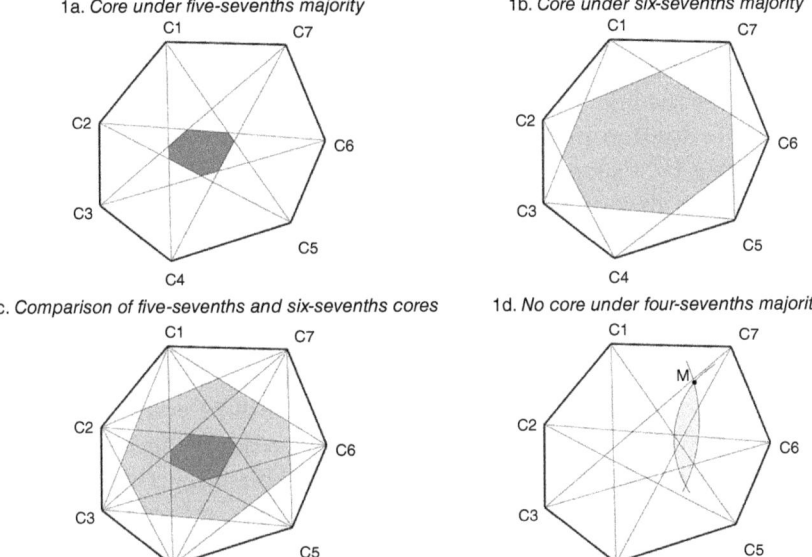

Figure 2.3 Core of a unicameral legislature under qualified majorities and lack of core under simple majority

replace such a point by its projection on the line itself (which they prefer). Similarly, the core cannot be south of line C2C5 because five members (C1, C2, C5, C6, C7) will pull this point down on line C2C5. Once all such possible lines are drawn, the core is formed at the intersection of all the preferences of five points (Figure 2.3a). A similar process is followed to generate the six-sevenths core depicted in Figure 2.3b. Here, lines are drawn to exclude just one point instead of two. The resulting intersection is larger than in the five-sevenths case, indicating a larger core. Here again, under the six-sevenths arrangement, one should expect less constitutional revision over time. Figure 2.3c indicates that the five-sevenths core is included in the six-sevenths core.

What is more interesting, however, is that if the required majority is a simple majority or less, the core ceases to exist. Indeed, if we draw a *median* line that has a simple (not qualified) majority on one side of it, it will also have a simple majority on the other side: The line C2C6 in Figure 2.3d, for example, is such a median line since it has four points either on it or on one side of it (C1, C2, C6, C7) and five points (C2, C3, C4, C5, C6) either on it or on the other side of it. Consequently, the line has a majority on both sides of the line, leading to the situation that any point in this two-dimensional space can be defeated by a simple majority – or, in other words, that the core is empty. Let us now consider Point M north of the line C2C6. We show that this point cannot be within the core if the decision-making rule is a simple majority – that is, that it can be defeated by a simple majority. If we draw the circles C2M and C6M, any point in their intersection defeats M by a simple majority. Indeed, any point north of the line C2C6 is preferred over M by points C1, C2, C6, and C7, and any point south of the line is preferred by points C2, C3, C4, C5, and C6. Consequently, Point M can always be defeated by a simple majority. By moving Point M to different locations, we can prove that there cannot be any point that is undefeated, and, therefore, the simple majority core is empty. This condition will be even more true if the required majority is smaller than a simple majority (such as 40 or 45 percent). I could make the same argument with respect to any other median line, and I could complicate the picture by creating what is called the win-set of Point M – a flowerlike pattern that identifies all the points that can defeat Point M by a simple majority of the members of congress C1C7. I will present a simpler picture in Section 2.3.

Let us now assume that we have a bicameral congress (like one-third of the countries in the world) that requires specifically a two-thirds majority in both chambers in order to amend the constitution (this is the requirement in the US and Mexico). Figure 2.4a replicates the argument presented above in each one of the thirteen-member chambers by excluding five members and creating different majorities with eight out of thirteen members. Figure 2.4b connects the two separate cores and creates the bicameral two-thirds core of the legislature. In this case, the constitutional core expands significantly. Indeed, if we connect the core of one chamber with the core of the other, the whole composite area becomes the constitutional core of the country. Any point inside this area cannot be defeated by a concurrent two-thirds majority because it can be moved neither up or down (at least five members of one chamber would object) nor left or right (the whole upper or lower chamber would object).

The major additional point that Figure 2.4 makes over Figure 2.3 is that the conjunction of two different bodies significantly expands the core of a constitution. Further, the argument is not restricted to two bodies. Figure 2.5 adds to the bicameral legislature an additional body that is required to agree by simple majority (this is the case for the Mexican constitution that requires two-thirds majorities of both chambers and a majority of the states).

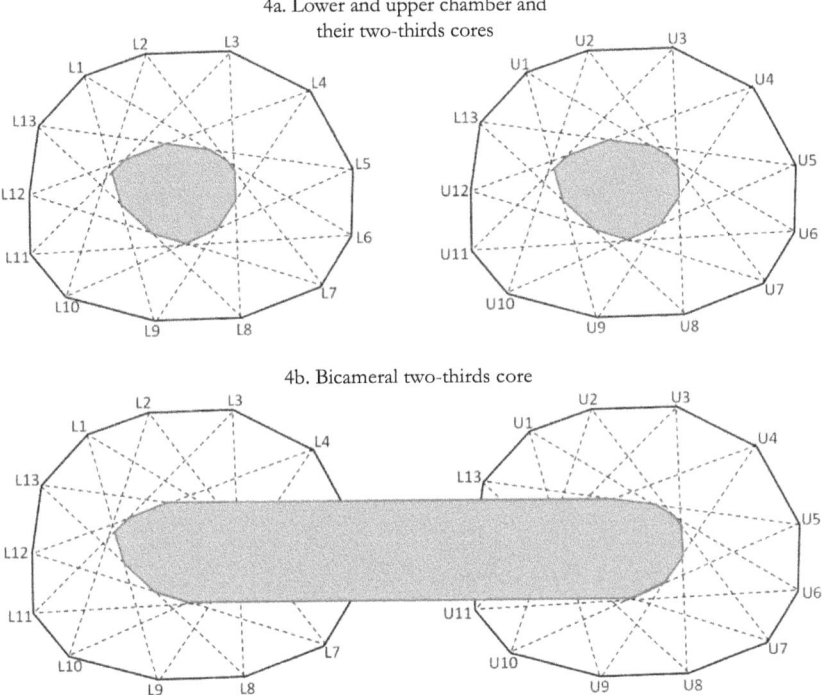

Figure 2.4 Constitutional core of a bicameral legislature

Now, with three different bodies, the core of the constitution expands even further. Any point inside the shaded area cannot be defeated on the basis of the existing rules because at least one of the conditions will be missing.

There is one more complication in the amendment rules of some countries. What happens if the constitution adds alternate methods of revision rather than adding constraints? Figure 2.6 presents such a situation. Consider that in addition to a three-fourths majority required for approval by a bicameral legislature, represented by chambers $A_1A_2A_3$ and $B_1B_2B_3$, the constitution requires either approval by a referendum, represented by Player P, or by an elected president of the republic, represented by Player Q. Based on the previous analysis, the bicameral core would be the whole area $A_1A_2A_3B_3B_2B_1$. The additional requirement of a referendum would expand the core to the area $A_1A_2A_3PB_2B_1$, while the alternative route of asking for the approval of the president of the republic would generate the core $A_1A_2A_3QB_2B_1$. However, the dotted

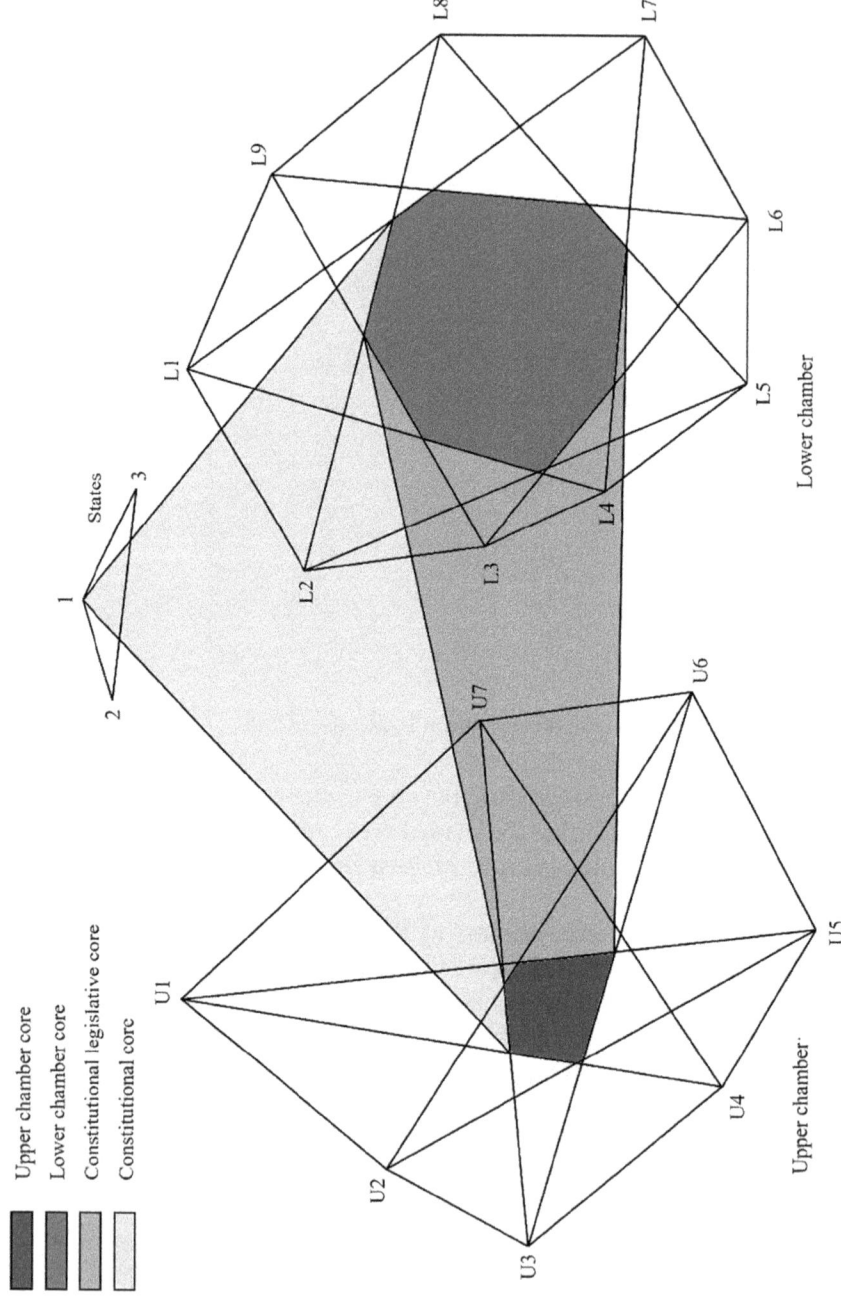

Figure 2.5 Constitutional core with two-thirds majority in both chambers and a majority of states (Mexico)

2.2 TWO-DIMENSIONAL CORES

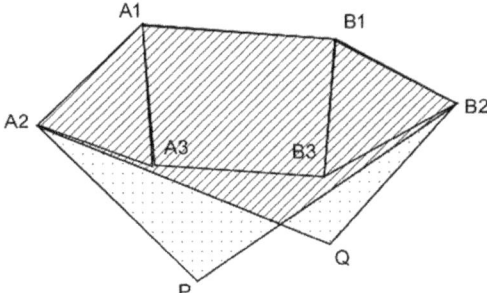

Figure 2.6 Core with alternative constitutional provisions

areas in the picture are not parts of the constitutional core of the country. The points in the dotted areas can be modified by *one* of the two permissible mechanisms – either the referendum or the president. The constitutional core will be the intersection of the two possible cores, represented by the shaded area in Figure 2.6.

Figures 2.5 and 2.6 demonstrate the logic of constitutional revisions. Their extent depends not only on the institutional provisions but also on the positions of the actors involved. For example, in Figure 2.5 the constitutional cores of the two chambers could be smaller or overlap, leading to a reduction of the size of the constitutional core. On the other hand, they could be larger and further away from each other, leading to an expansion of the core. Similarly, in Figure 2.6, one of the two procedures could become easier than the other. For example, if Q is inside the triangle PA_2B_2, then the approval of Q will be easier than that of P, and P will become irrelevant (all other players would prefer the approval of Q instead of P).

There are two rules that will produce stable effects on constitutional cores. The first is that *adding constraints will never reduce a constitutional core, although it may not affect it, depending on the positions of the actors.* The second is that *adding alternatives will never expand the constitutional core, although, again, depending on the position of the actors, it may result in no change.* I will use these two rules extensively in the calculation of constitutional cores for the sample of countries in this analysis. I will discuss the issue of dependence on actors' preference on the core in the conclusions of this chapter.

Finally, another result of my analysis of the constitutional core as a condition for constitutional amendments is that *the small size of the core is a necessary but not sufficient condition for constitutional amendments.* Here are the reasons why.

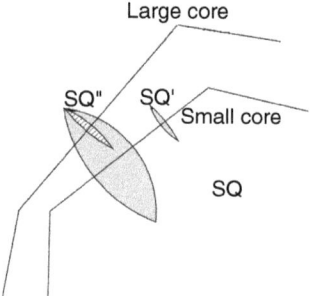

Figure 2.7 Large core produces smaller win-set, no matter where the status quo (SQ) is

Figure 2.7 presents two different constitutional cores, one large and one small (which is a subset of the large core). This configuration occurs when one removes restrictions from the amendment rule – for instance, when moving from a three-fourths to a three-fifths majority, or if only one chamber of a bicameral legislature is required to approve some constitutional revisions (as in the case of Austria). This configuration presents three different potential positions of the status quo. In the first case, the status quo SQ is located inside the small core (that is, inside both cores), and, therefore, no constitutional revision is possible. In the second case, the status quo SQ' is located outside the small core but inside the large core, so constitutional revisions are possible if the core is small, but impossible if the core is large. In the third case, the status quo SQ" is located outside both cores, and, while constitutional revisions are possible, the set of possible revisions is larger than in the case with the small constitutional core. All of these statements are true regardless of the position of the status quo in each one of the three areas.

There are several conclusions from this analysis. First, regarding the *frequency* of amendments, the larger the core, the fewer constitutional amendments are possible (e.g., SQ' can be modified with a small core, but not with a large one).

Second, the importance of the potential amendments is correlated with the size of the core. In Figure 2.7, SQ" has a large distance from the small core (but not from the large one). Consequently, a large constitutional revision is possible if the core is small. Figure 2.7 also demonstrates that this change is not possible with a large core.

Third, the arguments above produce necessary but not sufficient conditions for constitutional amendments. Constitutional amendments are impossible when the status quo is inside the core, but they are just possible (though not necessary) in cases where the status quo is outside the core. This has implications for the variance of the relationship between the size of the core (constitutional rigidity) and the frequency of amendments: Lower constitutional rigidity will present higher variance because more constitutional amendments become possible (but, again, not necessary). Consequently, my analysis predicts that constitutional rigidity will have a double impact on the frequency of amendments: Higher rigidity will produce both a lower frequency of amendments and a lower variance of amendments.[2]

2.3 Referendums as Agents of Constitutional Modification (and Replacement)

In Chapter 1, we saw that referendums are used by either individual (in France, the president) or collective (in Ireland, the government) agents for confirmation of their constitutional amendment proposals. More frequently, particularly in Latin American countries, they are used as the final institution of approval of a change of the whole constitution. This is a subject that we do not fully address in this book, but we do slightly touch on it in Chapter 4 because in Chile the failure of a process of constitutional amendment led to a process of constitutional replacement (which was also a double failure).

Referendums may or may not have some participation requirements for the validity of results, but the decision is made by simple majority rule. In Section 2.2, we saw that simple majority rule decisions do not have a core. Consequently, the fundamental concept of this chapter (the constitutional core) cannot be of any further use.[3] We will use another concept instead: *the win-set of the status quo* – that is, *the set of points that can defeat the status quo by majority rule*. The core is actually a derivative of this concept, since it can be defined as the set of points for which the win-set of the status quo is empty. In addition, the core is a more partial concept (sometimes it exists, sometimes it does not), while the win-set of the status quo is a universal concept (it rarely does not exist). The outcome of these definitions is twofold: first, analyses on the

---

[2] In formal terms, the relationship between rigidity and amendment frequency is heteroskedastic.
[3] Actually, this statement is not always correct as we will see in Chapter 4 in the case of Italy. There, we will calculate the core of a bicameral parliament that decides by majority rule.

basis of the core are simpler (there is no reference to the status quo; this is why I used it as much as possible); second, analyses on the basis of the core and analyses on the basis of the win-set are consistent with each other because when the core shrinks the win-set of the status quo expands, and when the core is empty the win-set of the status quo expands even more. In other words, both concepts are related to constitutional rigidity in inverse ways.

Let me revisit the fundamental conclusions of Sections 2.1 and 2.2 on the basis of the win-set concept and, consequently, generalize them (in case there is no core).

Proposition 1: For any SQ, an additional constitutional amendment constraint does not increase the win-set of the SQ.

The reason for Proposition 1 is that any constraint will be either operational, in which case it will exclude some outcomes and decrease the win-set of the SQ, or not, in which case it will leave it unchanged.

Proposition 2: For any SQ, an alternative constitutional amendment procedure does not decrease the win-set of the SQ.

The reason for Proposition 2 is that any alternative procedure will be either easier, in which case it increases the win-set of the SQ, or more difficult, in which case it leaves it the same.

Proposition 3: A large win-set of the SQ is a necessary but not sufficient condition for significant constitutional amendments.

The reason for Proposition 3 is that a large win-set of the SQ provides the possibility of significant amendments but does not guarantee them.

I will now describe the win-set of the status quo of a single actor and then expand it in the case of a referendum. Figure 2.8 presents an individual Y and the status quo in a two-dimensional policy space. This actor would prefer any point that is closer to their preferences over the status quo, so Policies 1, 2, and 3 but not Point A would replace the status quo. Another way of describing the situation is that Points 1, 2, and 3 are inside the win-set of the status quo, but Point A is not. The conclusion from this discussion is that what belongs in the win-set of the status quo depends on the position of Y and the position of the status quo (or either of them along with their distance).

Now let us consider a collective actor like a whole population and the status quo. In order to calculate the win-set of the status quo, we should draw as many circles as the members of the population (most likely in the

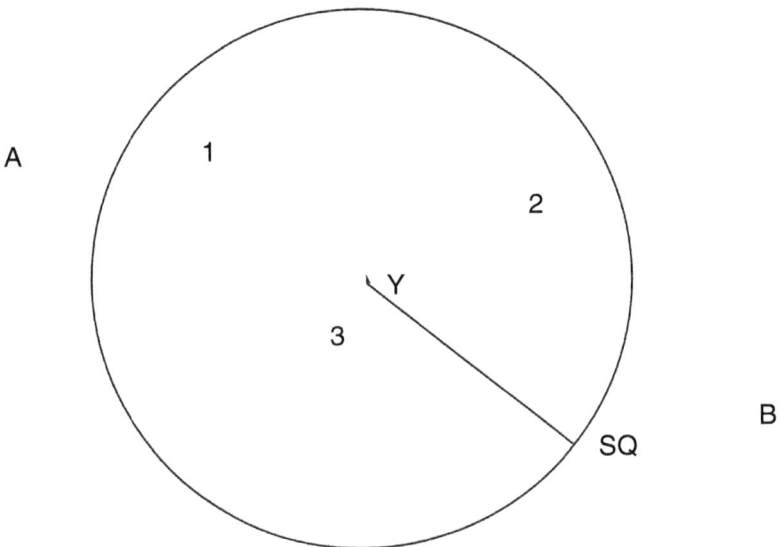

Outcomes 1, 2, 3 can prevail; outcomes a and b will be rejected.

Figure 2.8 Outcomes of a referendum

millions), consider the intersection of these circles, and select a point in any of the possible intersections of a majority of these circles. This appears to be a daunting enterprise. However, appearances are deceiving. Ferejohn et al. (1984) have proven that the situation in a referendum is not very different from the one described in Figure 2.8. The win-set of the status quo of a collective player can be included inside a circle and includes another circle, both with the same center. The larger the population, the more these two circles approximate each other in size (Tsebelis 2002: Ch. 5), and, consequently, the analysis of the outcomes of a referendum can be done in Figure 2.9.[4] The win-set of the status quo will be located again inside the circle YSQ, and any point inside this circle would defeat SQ while any point outside would be defeated by SQ.

---

[4] Technically, the point Y is uniquely defined and is called the center of the yolk. Further, the win-set includes a circle with radius $d - 2r$ and is included in a circle with radius $d + 2r$ where d is the distance YSQ and r is the radius of the yolk. Because r decreases in size with the number of the members of the population, when there are millions of members r tends to equal zero and the two circles almost coincide.

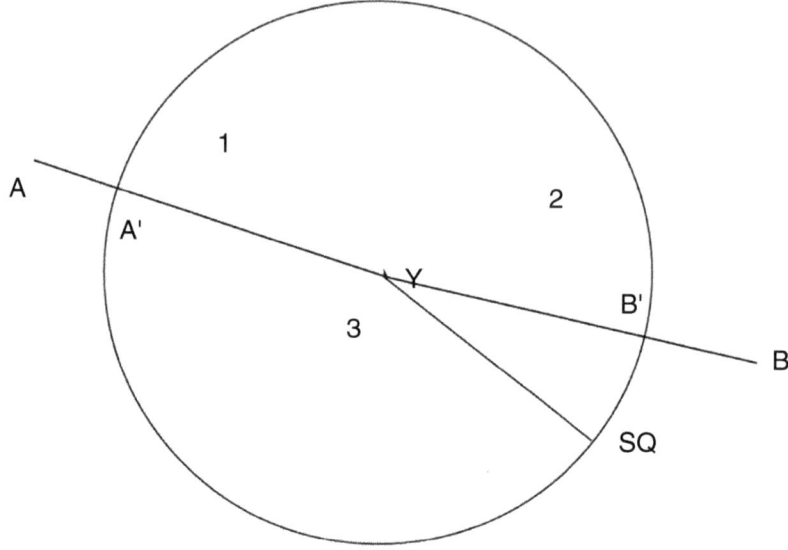

1. Outcome depends on position of sq
2. Agenda setters further away from sq (a and b) make proposals a' and b' inside the circle (y, sq)
3. Competition among agenda setters (1, 2, and 3) approximates better preferences of the public

Figure 2.9   Referendum outcomes as a function of agenda setter

Let us use this picture to help our analysis of constitutional amendments. As we said, there is an additional actor (individual or collective) who proposes the amendments to the population. If this actor is inside the circle YSQ (such as Points 1, 2, or 3), they can propose their own preferences, which will be adopted. If they are outside the circle YSQ (such as A or B), their proposals will be rejected, unless they select a point inside the circle. So, rational actors would select the points A' or B'.

One additional point (although it does not address, to my knowledge, constitutional revisions) is that if we do not have a single agenda setter but several that compete with each other, such as several proposals presented to the people as is the case with popular initiatives, then these agenda setters will make proposals approaching closer to the ideal point Y of the population in the hope that they will attract more votes and win.

The fact that there is no core in a referendum and, therefore, constitutional change is easier to make happen is the reason for the frequent use of referendum procedures for adopting constitutional amendments – or even for replacing whole constitutions, as we will see in the next chapter. There are even situations where agenda setters deviate from the constitution and try to enshrine their preferences through a ratification by referendum – a process against which the Venice Commission guards:

> The Commission also wishes to stress that recourse to a referendum should not be used by the executive in order to circumvent parliamentary amendment procedures. The danger and potential temptation is that while constitutional amendment in parliament in most countries requires a qualified majority, it is usually enough with simple majority in a referendum. Thus, for a government lacking the necessary qualified majority in parliament, it might be tempting instead to put the issue directly to the electorate. On several occasions the Venice Commission has emphasized the danger that this may have the effect of circumventing the correct constitutional amendment procedures. It has insisted on the fact that it is expedient in a democratic system upholding the separation of powers that the legislature should always retain power to review the executive's legislative output and to decide on the extent of its powers in that respect. (European Commission for Democracy through Law 2010: 37)

2.4 Computing Constitutional Rigidity

It is now time to use all these analyses to produce a means to consistently assess the constitutional rigidity of different countries. Sections 2.1 and 2.2 calculated the core of a constitution as a function of the actors required to agree and the majorities required for valid decisions in each one of them. Section 2.3 analyzed the case when one of them is a referendum, when all the other relevant actors will be the agenda setters and they have to produce a constitutional solution acceptable to the majority of voters (that is, a solution within the win-set of the SQ of the population). This method is based on the interaction between the institutions specified in the amendment provisions of the constitution and the preferences of the relevant actors. However, the preferences depend on the subject matter of the constitutional review and cannot be assessed a priori and in comparative perspective. Instead, I use the arguments to construct a simplified index based only on the amendment provisions. I will return to this issue in the conclusions of this chapter.

Now, I will calculate the index by summing the approval thresholds of different elected institutions. This combines the veto players who are required by the founders of the constitution with the qualified majorities included to protect it. For all countries, the formula includes the threshold that must be reached for approval in any popularly elected body that must approve a constitutional amendment (any constitutional veto player). If applicable, this formula includes the executive (in presidential systems), the legislative, the people (referendums), and regional governments. For example, if a legislative body must pass an amendment by a simple majority, 0.5 is added to the formula. If an intervening election is required between two rounds of majority approval, 0.5 + 0.5 is added. For example, in Greece, two votes are required by two successive parliaments (with an intervening election). One of the two majorities is three-fifths, and the other is a simple majority. As a result, the basic score for constitutional rigidity in Greece is (3 / 5 + 0.5) = 1.10 (see Appendix II).

For my analysis, I focus on the constitutions of countries included in the Constitute Project in effect in 2013 (www.constituteproject.org/). I restrict my analysis to only "democratic" countries, which I will operationalize as countries ranking five or above in the POLITY2 Index.[5]

Some constitutions provide alternate paths to revision. When there are several alternative procedures, I measure only the one that is first presented in the constitution. This first path is the one that the founders intended to be the primary process. We will look at such procedures in Chapter 4, where we will study amendments in Italy and Chile in detail. If there are subsequent alternative methods,[6] my index (which is calculated a priori) will include them with a small reduction of rigidity as calculated by the first method. Finally, if there are different procedures for explicitly enumerated articles of the constitution, they will be ignored (as different amendment procedures would generate different indexes in many countries). That would mean that analyses that deal with specific subjects which have different amendment rules, such as budget

---

[5] These restrictions yield 101 countries. To these, I added Israel and the UK, bringing the number of countries to 103 (they are not included in the Constitute Project because they do not have a written constitution, but they do have fundamental documents that are functionally equivalent). The choice of cutoff point is arbitrary (although six is usually used in the literature). I replicated my calculations using all the higher cut off points (six through ten), and the results are robust to this change. Also, three of the countries I cover – the UK, Turkey, and Taiwan – modified their amendment rule during the time covered by my study. Given that their constitution changed in the dimension I am examining here, I considered only the more recent part of their amendment history. The alternative would have been to consider these three countries as two observations each, bringing the total number to 106 instead of 103.

[6] The actual political actors in such a case will select the "easier" method, or the one that is more likely to produce the constitutional revision. The choice will depend on the policy positions of the actors involved and cannot be included in my index.

amendments or human rights, should calculate new constitutional rigidity indexes on the basis of these rules.

2.4.1 Measure of Bicameral Legislatures

I will now turn to the second chamber of a bicameral legislature. A second chamber can have a majority independent from the lower chamber. Most of the time, the founders of a constitution designate the legislature as a required veto player in addition to specifying the required majority for approval. If the legislature is composed of two chambers, they are usually both designated as veto players.[7] I use the Euclidean distance between the two chambers as a measure of their disparity: if one legislature is composed of parties with proportions $x_1, x_2, x_3, \cdots, x_n$, while in the second legislature the same parties have percentages $x'_1, x'_2, x'_3, \cdots, x'_n$, the compositional distance between the two chambers is $\left[(x_1 - x'_1)^2 + (x_2 - x'_2)^2 + (x_3 - x'_3)^2 \cdots (x_n - x'_n)^2\right]^{0.5}$, which increases as a function of the difference in the percentage that each party wins in each chamber. If the two chambers have identical composition, which is what Lijphart (2012: 99) calls "congruent," then this indicator counts them as a single unicameral legislature. According to this index, as the difference in the composition of the two chambers increases, constitutional revisions become significantly more difficult.[8] This calculation of the difference in the composition was done at the end of 2013. My choice implies that this difference approximates the average difference over the whole period of democratic rule in a country, which would have been a more accurate measure. One example for how this measure

---

[7] Austria is an exception, and the upper chamber participates only in constitutional revisions related to Federalism. South Africa's upper chamber functions similarly. Burundi requires different majorities for each of its chambers (four-fifths for the lower and two-thirds for the upper).

[8] I have also calculated two alternative measures. One considers (weighs) all bicameral legislatures as 1.5 of unicameral ones, and the other considers the chi-squared distance in the composition of the two chambers. The correlations among these indices are extremely high, so I report the results of Euclidean distances alone. This method is close to Negretto's (2012) approach. He considers the effective number of parties in each legislature as creating an obstacle to the passage of constitutional reforms. All these methods use numeric approximations to spatial distributions; hence, they rely on strong ceteris paribus assumptions. For Negretto, such assumptions rely on the similarity of Latin American countries. In this book, the comparison is only between the two legislatures of the same country.

of bicameral legislatures is applied can be found in Germany. In this country, both chambers of a bicameral legislature have to agree on a constitutional revision with a two-thirds majority. The Euclidian distance of the two chambers is 0.281. Consequently, I calculate the constitutional rigidity in the German Federal Republic as $2/3 \times 1.281 = 0.854$ (actually, in Appendix II I add 0.01 and report 0.864 for reasons that will become clear later in this chapter). My approach does not address the question of whether the political majorities in both chambers are the same or not, which is an issue that would be complicated to calculate comparatively but would have significant effects in single-country studies.

2.4.2 The Epsilon Rule

To account for any modifications of the rules that make constitutional amendments more or less difficult than specified in the fundamental method, I add or subtract an epsilon (i.e., a small number – in this case, 0.01). This is done for any provision that would increase or decrease rigidity. Examples of such modifications – and, therefore, an addition or subtraction of an epsilon – may include a provision outlining the percentage of members required for a quorum, a requirement that a revision be passed twice, or a delay from one passage to the next. If an alternative procedure is specified, I will subtract an epsilon (see Appendix II).

This method ensures that *every single rule* that addresses constitutional revisions is incorporated into my measure, including any compositional differences between the two legislative chambers. What is missing, though, is the actual ideological distance of the different parties or other institutional veto players.[9]

While these rules are applied in a consistent way, they are not the only ones possible. For example, under the current assumptions, it makes no difference for the constitutional rigidity of a country if the parliament votes by simple majority for the amendments followed by a referendum or if there is a new election and the new parliament approves the

---

[9] It is possible that, in a country that requires approval by a bicameral legislature and a referendum, the position of the electorate is between those of the house and the senate; hence, the electorate should not be included in the calculations since it would be absorbed as a constitutional veto player (Tsebelis 2002). However, the formula here would include the referendum as an additional constraint despite the fact that if the measures are approved by the two houses, they would not be rejected by the referendum.

2.4 COMPUTING CONSTITUTIONAL RIGIDITY

amended provisions, provided simple majorities are required in parliament and the referendum. Some might object to this simplification. The voters may have different preferences than a subsequent parliament, and it is not obvious which one of them is closer to the positions of the initial parliament. However, the constitutional rigidity index calculation would be $0.5 + 0.5 = 1$ in both cases. Similarly, it makes no difference in the index if a double passage by the same parliament is required or if there is a quorum requirement. Both cases result in adding an epsilon to the indicator. For more clarification, the reader can refer to Greece and Germany in Appendix II. For Greece, an epsilon is added because of two votes required in the first reading, and an epsilon is subtracted because of the two alternative procedures. This leaves the index unchanged **at 1.10**. For Germany, I add an epsilon to represent the requirement of two-thirds of the total number of members of the chambers (and not of the members present); the final result for Germany is 0.864. These choices are the simple application of the rules outlined earlier.[10]

I only consider the constitutions in effect in 2013 and the constitutional history of countries only when they are democratic. If a country falls below five in the POLITY2 index, the corresponding years are eliminated. Given that I use the rate of amendment years over the total democratic years, the elimination of a year may affect the numerator of my variable (which is the number of amendment years) but will certainly affect the denominator (which is the total number of democratic years).[11] These restrictions leave a sample with a wide range of both constitutional rigidity and constitutional amendment frequency. The range of the constitutional rigidity scale extends from 0.5 to 1.85, with a standard deviation of 0.29. These numbers roughly correspond to one to three different veto players with simple or qualified majorities. An intuitive way of understanding this measure is to say that a change of two

---

[10] For the researchers who do not share my assumptions and simplifications, Appendix II provides the necessary information to alter them and produce a different indicator of constitutional rigidity.

[11] I also drop amendments from the sample if the individuals coding the significance of these amendments agreed that there was no amendment in a given year. This occurred in the following cases: Austria in 1954, Cape Verde in 1992, the Czech Republic in 2013, El Salvador in 2003, Guatemala in 1986, Honduras in 2012 and 2013, Latvia in 2013, Luxembourg in 1988, Malaysia in 1959 and 1961, Nicaragua in 1994, and Switzerland in 2007 and 2011. In Nepal, there was an amendment in 2012 that was missing from the data. Given that out of 866 classified amendments only 15 cases of disagreement were identified, the Ginsburg and Melton (2015) amendment data are very reliable. The reader can consult Appendix I for a complete list of amendments.

standard deviations is roughly equivalent to adding a referendum or the approval of a popularly elected president as a requirement for the validity of a constitutional amendment. With respect to amendment frequency, the range is from zero (no amendments in any democratic year) to one (amendments passed in every democratic year). The average constitutional rigidity in the sample is 0.89, and the average amendment frequency is 0.25 amendments per year (that is, one amendment every four years). The empirical analysis in Chapter 6 will demonstrate the empirical relevance of this chapter.

I will call the index generated in this book the veto players rigidity index because the analysis presented in this chapter is based on the theory of veto players (Tsebelis 2002).

Conclusions

There is one significant difference between the theoretical approach in Sections 2.1, 2.2, and 2.3 of this chapter as well as the empirical indicator I generated in Section 2.4. In the theoretical analysis, I rely on both the preferences of the actors and the amendment rules of the constitution for the calculation of the core or the win-set of the status quo. In the calculation of the index, I rely only on the amendment rules. This is a significant and unfortunate modification that I would have preferred to avoid. Therefore, I must explain why I could not do so.

The arguments in the first three sections depend on the relevant positions of the actors. For example, the core of the constitution will be significantly reduced if the preferences of the actors approach each other. However, these preferences will change over time. Such changes could occur because of political conditions (a shift in coalitions, polarization because of upcoming elections, etc.) or changes in the opinion of the voters. Similarly, the position of the status quo will change over time. The obvious reason for this would be a legislative change, but I want to underline one additional, less obvious reason for change. Consider legislation on social security or unemployment – the same legislation can have completely different effects several years later when different generations come to retirement age or when there are different economic conditions. Such exogenous changes to the status quo may require not only policy changes but even constitutional ones. I do not know how to take into account such changes in a comparative analysis. Some researchers approximate it by the number of parties (Negretto 2012). However, as I will show in Chapter 5, the case of Mexico where multiple parties sign agreements and behave as a single party does not support the approach in comparative perspective. Others that attempt to incorporate preferences at the comparative level have not been successful in my judgment, as I will demonstrate in Chapter 3.

In my analysis, a very promising step forward could be made by operationalizing the concept of polarization. Highly polarized countries would have larger cores and smaller win-sets of the SQ than more consensual ones. Consequently, amending the constitution should be easier in such countries. I do not know of any indicator of cross-national polarization. However, even if such an indicator existed, it should be differentiated across policy dimensions. For example, differentiation along the environmental policy dimensions today should be significantly lower than twenty years ago, and constitutional changes on environmental issues (such as including constitutional provisions about environmental assessment of policy measures) should be easier. The fact that such a comparative analysis is not possible today does not mean we should not assess the effects of amendment rules at all. As the reader will verify, I make such an assessment of the institutions as a necessary but not sufficient condition for change and leave it open for any additional variables that we will be able to convincingly generate in the future.

3

Cultural Theories of Constitutional Amendments

In the previous chapter, we did what all institutional political science literature does by tracing the constitutional amendment decisions in order to understand the constitutional amendment properties (that is, the content of successful amendments). However, we did not deal with the distribution of preferences of the different actors. In the conclusion of Chapter 2, we made it clear that if these preferences were located close to each other, more frequent and more significant constitutional amendments would be possible, but we did not establish a theory about when preferences would be less polarized.

In this chapter, we will now look at the literature and discuss the argument that some principles of preference organization affect the constitutional amendments as well as or even instead of the amendment rules included in the constitutions. Indeed, a series of authors have identified constitutional "cultures" – that is, "shared attitudes about the desirability of amendment," as Ginsburg and Melton (2015: 699) define it.

Culture is a very general concept referring to the way of life, behaviors, beliefs, values, and symbols of a group of people. Students of comparative politics have used cultural differences to explain observed variation across political units for over a century (or even further if one considers Aristotle, Plato, or Thomas Aquinas). One might call Weber's analysis of the Protestant Ethic and the rise of capitalism in Europe the birth of cultural theory in political science. His understanding of culture was the coherence of clusters of attitudes and values in the population, determined by the relative size of the Protestant population. Systematic empirical analyses of the phenomenon took off in the 1960s with Almond and Verba's *The Civic Culture* and were reintroduced by Inglehart's *Culture Shift* and Putnam's *Making Democracy Work* in the 1990s. The methods for measuring civic engagement, civic community, or civic virtue vary: Almond and Verba along with Inglehart survey citizens in different countries, while Putnam compiles an extensive data set that goes beyond the individual level concerning a wide variety of social, economic, and political attributes of each region in Italy. They are united in aiming to explain outcomes on the macro level, focusing on democracy (Almond and Verba), economic performance and democratic stability (Inglehart), and regional government performance (Putnam et al. 1993).

Concerning political culture in the US, Elazar (1984) in *American Federalism* uses an inductive approach to classify the culture of the forty-eight mainland US states. His theory of moralistic, individualistic, and traditionalistic subcultures was used to develop measures of culture (Sharkansky, for example, recoded his data to construct a numerical estimate of each state's position) and linked to other concepts such as female representation in state legislatures (Hill 1981), utilization of corporal punishment in public schools (Vandenbosch 1991), and personality traits (Mondak and Canache 2014). Taking up Putnam's ideas, Rice and Sumberg (1997) developed civic culture estimates for the US states and demonstrated the relationship between their measure and Elazar's. A more recent conceptual development stems from Oliver and Wood (2014), who study the support of conspiracy theories as part of American political culture.

Turning to legal and, more specifically, constitutional cultures, Gardbaum (2018) argues that a legal culture, which includes "(1) the status of judges, (2) their historical degree of independence, and (3) cultural adherence to rule of law norms within a system" (22), may enhance or detract from the ability of courts to increase their own powers beyond those originally bestowed. He does not measure culture quantitatively; however, the theoretical insights are valuable, as are Dixon and Landau's (2018) in their proposal of a third model of constitutionalism besides the short, abstract, and rigid model and the lengthy, detailed, and flexible one. They highlight that realizing the goals of constitutionalism, such as stability and the realization of the objectives enshrined in the constitution, may be influenced by the citizens' identification with their constitutional text as it makes "replacement less likely; popular buy-in of existing constitutions will increase resistance to attempts to scrap the existing constitutional text" (Dixon and Landau 2018: 467). Further, it will also increase "support for those objectives and thus [place] pressure on politicians to achieve them" (Dixon and Landau 2018: 468).

In this chapter, I will not speak about culture in general or constitutional culture in an abstract sense. I will focus on studies that are using "constitutional culture" in order to explain the frequency of constitutional amendments – that is, which are using "constitutional culture" as their explanatory variable and are using the frequency of amendments as the variable to be explained. I will show that different authors understand and use this concept of constitutional culture in three distinct ways, which I will discuss sequentially as (1) "culture" as a random element, (2) "culture" as a systematically omitted variable, and (3) "culture" as an independent variable.

3.1 "Culture" as a Random Element

Richard Albert has produced an extensive body of writings on constitutional amendment rules (e.g., Albert 2010, 2015a, 2015b, 2015c, 2018, Albert et al. 2018) which culminate in a very important book, *Constitutional Amendments: Making, Breaking, and Changing Constitutions* (Albert 2019). He argues the following:

> Rankings of comparative amendment difficulty [what this book did in Chapter 2] have a fatal flaw: they either ignore or fail to account for sources of amendment ease or difficulty. These non-textual sources include uncodified changes to formal amendment rules, popular veneration for the constitution, temporal variability in amendment difficulty, and prevailing cultures of amendment. I moreover define and illustrate three different cultures of amendment—each of which has the effect of either exacerbating or assuaging amendment difficulty: amendment culture as an accelerator of change, as a redirector of change, and as an incapacitator of change. I ultimately arrive at two conclusions: first, that studies of amendment difficulty are doomed to failure; and second, that in any case they may not be worth the effort. (Albert 2019: 32)

One may infer from this quote, which in essence is replicated multiple times throughout the book, that Albert is neglecting the significance of the written text. However, Albert extensively argues in favor of "writtenness":

> Modern constitutionalism has given us good reason to celebrate the written tradition in which the rules of formal amendment are anchored. Writtenness is deeply interconnected with the rule of law and indeed serves its democratic values, namely predictability, transparency, and publicity. The written tradition gives political actors and the people notice about the rules to which they will be held, it allows the governed to hold their governors to account, and it creates a textual referent for challengers to contest the conduct of incumbents. The uses of writtenness moreover extend well beyond these proceduralist functions: it also holds promise for cultivating a culture of public-oriented citizens who come to know, understand, and respect the codified constitution and the moral commitments it entrenches. (Albert 2019: 137)

3.1 "CULTURE" AS A RANDOM ELEMENT

In this respect, he is repeating the arguments of authors like Aristotle (in *Rhetoric*), Locke (in *Two Treaties on Government*), and Montesquieu (in *The Spirit of Laws*), to mention only a few (see also my discussion in the Introduction).

However, Albert's argument is that the articles that specify the rules of constitutional amendment are only part of the story and that the constitutional culture, which facilitates or obstructs the facility of amendments as specified by the text, is so complex that it makes the assessment of amendment difficulty on the basis of the text doubtful, to say the least. In his approach, "*Amendment culture can accelerate, redirect, or incapacitate formal amendment in a given jurisdiction*" (Albert 2019: 111; emphasis mine). The result is that, "If only this thin and quite unsatisfactory measurement of amendment difficulty is possible, we confront again the question we continue to encounter: Why measure amendment difficulty at all? It is far from clear that this question has a good answer" (Albert 2019: 172).

According to Albert, the situation provides layers of complication:

> For decades, codified rules of formal amendment have been modified in circumvention of those very rules and sometimes in direct violation of them. In other words, codified amendment rules have been altered without a corresponding codification. One implication of this trend involves text-based studies of formal amendment difficulty: How can we measure comparative amendment difficulty with any reliability if formal amendment occurs according to rules unseen in the codified text? This is a further quite devastating reason to doubt rankings of amendment difficulty that focus exclusively on a narrow textual analysis of the codified rules of change. (Albert 2019: 127).

I do not want to contradict Albert's arguments – particularly his thorough analysis of the Canadian Constitution. What I will argue, however, is that his analysis is on the relative significance of written and unwritten rules in each *individual* constitution. Further, for a given individual constitution, the better we understand the unwritten rules, the better we will understand the constitutional revision process. But, as Albert says, these unwritten rules sometimes increase and other times decrease the ease of amendment. If we knew the conditions under which a "culture" or "norm" would operate one way or the other, we should include it in our analysis. Such a rule is not provided, however, and neither do we know whether different researchers would identify the same norms across constitutions or whether they would classify them in the facilitating category or the opposite group. From a comparative

Table 3.1 *Difference between actual and formal rigidity: As n increases, the error term (difference) approaches zero*

	Number of countries			
	1	5	10	100
Actual rigidity (mean)	3.9	4.31	3.5	4.82
Formal rigidity (mean)	5.36	5.19	5.5	4.79
Error (mean)	−1.46	−0.89	−2	0.03

Note: The formal rigidity variable is drawn from a normal distribution with a mean of five and a standard deviation of two. The error is also distributed normally with a mean of zero and a standard deviation of five. The actual rigidity is constructed as the sum of the estimated rigidity and error.

perspective, we have to classify all these "cultural" factors as a random error, while the written text provides the systematic basis for the analysis.

My argument is that the written text of the amendment provisions is the systematic component of the analysis and the nonwritten text is the random error of my analysis. I may also agree that this random component may be very significant at times (Albert's analysis of the Canadian constitutional text and amendments is a very good example of this). However, when we compare constitutions, we have to base our judgment on the systematic elements and leave the error term aside.

Let me provide the statistical argument which draws conclusions from a set of constitutions rather than just from one. In Table 3.1, I present a computer simulation of constitutional rigidity measures, with *formal* being measured by the written rules and *actual* being measured considering both formal and informal rules. The formal rules have an average of five units and a standard deviation of two, while the random element (informal rules) has an average of zero units and a much more significant standard deviation of five. The reason I am making this choice is to replicate Albert's argument that informal rules may contribute more than the formal ones to the final outcome. Table 3.1 presents the comparison between formal rigidity and actual rigidity when we include 1, 5, 10, or 100 countries. The reader can verify that this difference between formal and actual practically disappears when we take the average of 100 countries.

However, the reader may object to this as we are not going to measure an average country. Instead, we are going to measure the effect of constitutional rigidity (measured textually as in Chapter 2) on another variable: the frequency of amendments. This is the subject of Table 3.2, which is a

Table 3.2 *Effect of formal rigidity on another variable (constitutional amendments): As n increases, the coefficient approximates the true value*

	Constitutional amendments			True value
n	5	10	100	
(Intercept)	3.395	5.760	0.707	
	(3.117)	(2.990)	(1.378)	
Formal rigidity	−1.385	−1.553 *	−0.616 *	−0.6
	(0.575)	(0.505)	(0.254)	
R^2	0.659	0.542	0.057	

* $p < 0.05$.
Note: The formal rigidity variable is drawn from a normal distribution with a mean of five and a variance of two. The error is also distributed normally with a mean of zero and a variance of five. The constitutional amendments variable is constructed as the sum of the estimated rigidity multiplied by a coefficient with the value −0.6 and the error.

precursor of what will come later in this book: we will use the approximation of constitutional rigidity generated in Chapter 2 to estimate the frequency of constitutional amendments in different countries (Chapter 6).

Here, we give a summary of the statistical argument that will follow. We create a frequency of amendments variable that is as follows: (Amendment frequency) = −0.6 × (real rigidity) when, as before, (real rigidity) = (formal rigidity) + (error term).

Table 3.2 is slightly more complicated than Table 3.1 in the sense that it will help us assess the relationship between two variables. Formal rigidity is again constructed to have an average of five and a standard deviation of two, while the error term is constructed to have an average of zero and a standard deviation of five (just like in the previous example). The reader can verify that if we are fortunate to have 100 countries in our sample, the actual estimated coefficient will differ very little from the real one.

In conclusion, as long as "culture" is not systematic but can be assimilated as a random error, it can be ignored in a comparative approach, and the results of the analysis will not be affected. It seems to me that there is a way to systematize Albert's analysis. On the basis of his arguments, there should be a difference in the analysis of specific constitutional articles before and after the nonwritten modifications. One can compare the textual analysis of these articles before and after and assess whether the changes were strengthening or weakening the restrictive nature of the articles and, as a result, identify the systematic nature of these nontextual amendments. If one identifies specific indicators reflecting more and less restrictive effects, then we would be able to assess systematic forces at the cross-national level and include Albert's understanding of "culture" in the analysis. However, is there any other way to include "culture" as a systematic force? We will now turn to this question.

3.2 "Culture" as a Systematic Omission

A different analysis of constitutional "culture" is provided by Ginsburg and Melton (2015) in their very influential article: "Does the Constitutional Amendment Rule Matter at All? Amendment Cultures and the Challenges of Measuring Amendment Difficulty." Ginsburg and Melton's analysis begins with the fact that many attempts to measure constitutional rigidity did not find a very strong relationship with constitutional amendment frequency. They propose "an alternative theory of amendment difficulty," stating, "We articulate the idea of an *amendment culture* which we argue is implicit in many accounts of constitutionalism more generally" (Ginsburg and Melton 2015: 215, 687). Their indicator is presented as an "alternative to institutional factors that constrain amendment" (Ginsburg and Melton 2015: 691). Looking at the literature, they have not been able to identify a cross-national measure of amendment culture, so they generate their own, using the amendment rate of the previous constitution as "amendment culture." Their argument is that if the amendment rate does not depend on the institutions, then high amendment rates in the previous constitution would be due to a permissive amendment culture and low rates would be due to a restrictive culture. The persistence of this amendment culture would lead to high or low amendment rates for the current constitution as well.

Ginsburg and Melton proceed to an empirical test of their argument, and they regress the number of years an amendment was performed in different countries on their institutional factors (amendment threshold, number of proposers, number of approvers, multiple sessions required, judicial review, political constraints, ln of length in words, scope, age of constitution) as well as on their "amendment culture," defined as the frequency of amendments in the previous constitution. Their result is that most of the institutional variables lack significance and sometimes even have the wrong sign, while the only significant variable is

3.2 "CULTURE" AS A SYSTEMATIC OMISSION

"amendment culture."[1] Some of their results are that "large vote thresholds are positively correlated with the amendment rate, suggesting that higher vote thresholds actually yield higher amendment rates. Similarly, requiring votes in multiple parliamentary sessions is associated with higher amendment rates. The only procedural variable with the correct sign is the one indicating the number of approving actors... In short, amendment culture is more important than institutional constraints in explaining amendment practices" (Ginsburg and Melton 2015: 711).

Ginsburg and Melton created an *acquis communautaire* (or "acquired by the community") among students of constitutional law. Contiades and Fotiadou (2016) consider this finding to be a correction to Ginsburg and Melton's previous analyses. They argue, "By articulating this indicator of amendment culture, [Ginsburg and Melton] remedy the flaws of their earlier work and allegedly add a new parameter to constitutional scholarship" (Contiades and Fotiadou 2016: 198). Bucur and Rasch (2019) summarize the literature as follows: "A growing body of literature challenges the purely institutional understanding of constitutional change. Probably the best example of this position is the 'amendment culture' argument put forward by Ginsburg and Melton (2015), according to which norms and habits are better predictors of constitutional change than the choice of amendment rules" (171).

Marshfield (2018: 80) argues that we should abandon institutional measures, and Versteeg and Zackin (2016: 661) echo this sentiment. Marshfield (2018) writes, "A better measure of constitutional flexibility is a constitution's actual amendment rate because this presumably captures both the formal barriers to amendment contained in the amendment rules as well as cultural attitudes regarding formal amendment" (80). Versteeg and Zackin (2016) agree, saying, "The measure [of constitutional entrenchment] does not rely on formal amendment rules because these rules are mediated so dramatically by political norms (Ginsburg and Melton 2015, Klug 2015)" (661). Hayo and Voigt (2016) would have liked to use constitutional rigidity to calculate judicial independence but avoided it because of the Ginsburg and Melton analysis: "Ideally, we would include a variable controlling for the formal difficulty of amending constitutions. Although some attempts to measure this difficulty have been undertaken, none of them have been completely successful. Ginsburg and Melton (2015) even propose abandoning all

---

[1] In statistical terms, what there are doing is using the lagged dependent variable as a regressor.

such attempts and looking at what they call 'amendment cultures' instead" (6). Given the impact of the Ginsburg and Melton analysis, we have to consider it very seriously indeed. I have three critical remarks: the first is theoretical, the second empirical, and the third statistical.

The theoretical objection stems from two sources: the first is epistemological, and the second logical. The epistemological objection originates from Lakatos' (1978) "The Methodology of Scientific Research Programs," where he argues that each scientific research program includes a positive (what the researchers should be doing) and a negative (what they should never do) heuristic. The negative heuristic cannot be abandoned any time that an empirical test does not corroborate the theory because, in reality, an empirical test points out an *inconsistency* among many assumptions, and it is for the researcher to identify which one of them that was produced is causing the problem. In Lakatos' (1978) terms (and notation): "It is not that we propose a theory and Nature may shout NO; rather, we propose a maze of theories, and Nature may shout INCONSISTENT" (45). In the case of constitutional amendments, the "maze" of theories involves the assumption that all amendments are of the same significance, that cultural variables matter and can be approximated by the frequency of amendments in the previous constitution, that linear regression is the appropriate methodology for the analysis, and so on. All these assumptions are part of the Ginsburg and Melton analysis, and we will discuss (dispute) them in detail later in this chapter. The "negative heuristic" for an institutional research program is the significance of institutions, and it cannot be disputed as long as we stay within this research program. If all other assumptions cannot be disputed, then the research program will have run its course.[2]

The logical objection comes from equilibrium analysis. Ginsburg and Melton are using the decision-making procedure of the previous constitution in order to understand what is happening under the current one. Why would it be relevant? Why would the decisions to amend today's constitution depend on the frequency of amendments of the past? Instead of tracing the actual decisions, Ginsburg and Melton use an inertia factor, claiming that it is more important than the current problems or the current conditions. This analysis would require a serious explanatory argument, which is missing, but, in my opinion, it would be untenable. However, I understand that many readers would not give

---

[2] Lakatos presents a more plausible mechanism for a scientific research program to be replaced so that an alternative one with "excess content" emerges.

rationality arguments the same weight as I would, so I will not stop my criticism here.

The empirical objection is the following. For the amendment rules to be irrelevant and for the amendment culture instead to be significant, amendment frequency must remain the same *despite* amendment rules changing. If amendment rules remain the same, then the argument is not only invalid but could instead be an argument in favor of institutionalism. So, if constitutional replacement is not accompanied by a change of amendment rules, then the argument is in favor of an institutional, not cultural, explanation. This is exactly the case. I examined the previous constitutions of the countries I include in my sample (which are the democratic countries in 2013, excluding the ones without a previous constitution like the US; see Chapter 2) and divided them into two groups: the ones that changed their constitution while remaining democratic, and the ones that moved from a dictatorship to a democracy. One would expect that the constitutional changes would be more significant in the second category. This expectation is correct, but the amendment rules of the different constitutions changed very little. As Figure 3.1 indicates, in democracies there are very few changes in the index of constitutional rigidity as calculated in the previous chapter, but, in most cases, the difference is zero, indicating that the actual amendment institutions remain identical from one constitution to the next.

Figure 3.2 provides a bird's-eye view of the situation: In democracies, the overwhelming majority of countries changed their constitution without modifying the amendment rules, but this is not true of transitions from dictatorships to democracies (although, still, the majority of countries concerned do not modify constitutional rigidity). The conclusion is that a significant majority of the countries I checked[3] did not modify their constitutional rigidity despite constitutional change. Ginsburg and Melton deal with many more constitutions since they examine the history of all countries, not just the more recent past, and they do not restrict their study to democracies. However, my analysis indicates that the high significance of the "amendment culture" coefficients in the Ginsburg and Melton regressions is more likely to be the effect of the same institutions, not the same culture.

Last but not least is **the statistical argument**. Let us forget the previous two arguments – that is, that the current institutions do not matter (theoretical argument) and that the reason that the frequency of

---

[3] I remind the reader that I deal with countries that had a democratic constitution in 2013.

86 CULTURAL THEORIES OF CONSTITUTIONAL AMENDMENTS

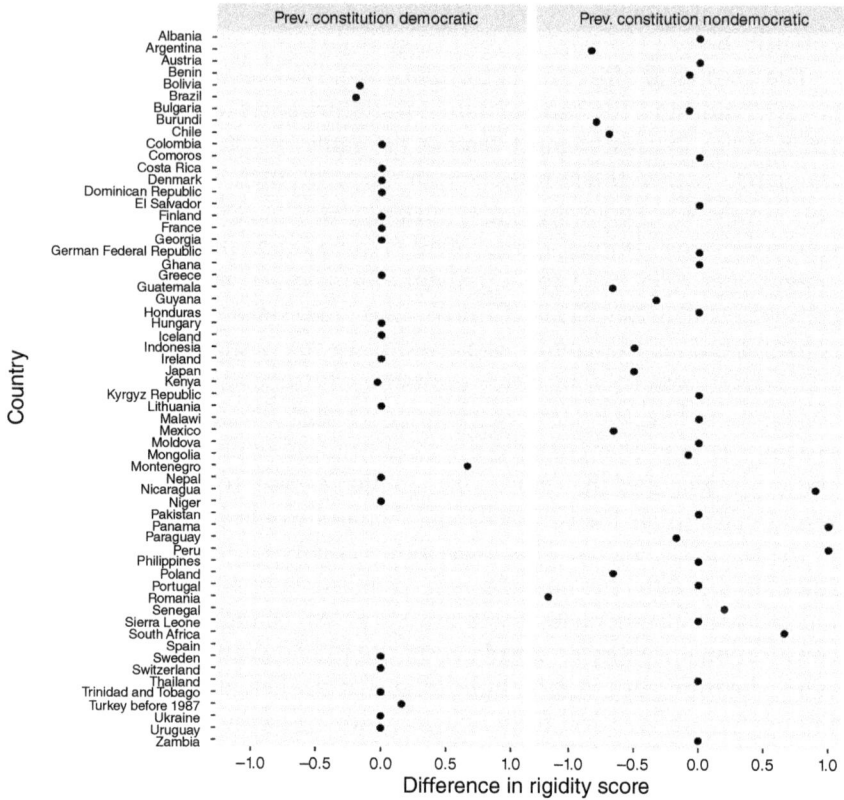

Figure 3.1 New constitutions do not come with new levels of constitutional rigidity

amendments remains the same is because the amendment rules are the same (empirical argument) – and now look at the statistical validity of the procedure where the lagged dependent variable is included in the regressors. As Achen (2000) argues, "When one or more lagged values of the dependent variable are added 'as a control' ... in many instances the autoregressive terms are strongly significant, and the fit improves sharply, but the original sensible substantive effects of other variables disappear. This pattern frequently occurs even when the lagged variables have no plausible causal interpretation" (1).[4] This result (as Achen demonstrates) occurs because, if there is a time trend, the inclusion of the lagged dependent variable picks the time trend up not only from the omitted variables *but also from the included ones.*

---

[4] This is exactly what I argued in the end of Section 3.1.

3.2 "CULTURE" AS A SYSTEMATIC OMISSION

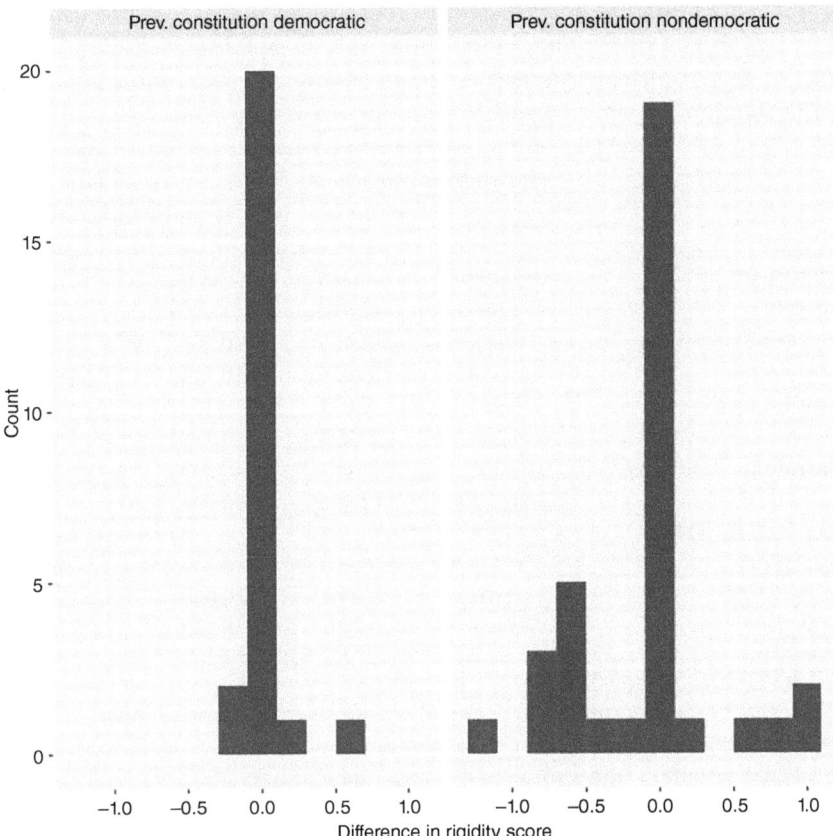

Figure 3.2 Summary of the number of countries that changed their constitution and the difference in rigidity scores

Ginsburg and Melton (2015) do not have a whole time series analysis – just one step. However, (as argued in Section 3.2) the amendment rules of the current constitution will be dependent on the ones of the previous constitution, particularly if these rules are finely defined like what Ginsburg and Melton have done (who state that amendment threshold, number of proposers, number of approvers, multiple sessions required, and judicial review are all independent variables).[5] It is this serial dependence that is picked up by the amendment frequency of the

---

[5] For example, with respect to institutional provisions, Cheibub et al. (2014) do find serial correlations among constitutions.

Table 3.3 *Estimation of coefficient of "culture" as a lagged dependent variable: When institutional data are serially correlated, including a lagged dependent variable will inflate its estimated effect and lead to misestimation of other variables including the wrong sign*

	Amendment frequency			True value
n	10	50	100	
(Intercept)	−2.159	−0.255	0.602	1
	(1.767)	(2.442)	(1.249)	
Institutional dummy A	4.071 *	−2.455 *	−0.584	0.1
	(1.314)	(0.979)	(0.511)	
Institutional dummy B	5.191	0.831	0.102	0.8
	(2.210)	(0.996)	(0.799)	
Institutional dummy C	−5.358 *	0.961	−0.013	0.3
	(1.571)	(2.490)	(0.944)	
Omitted variable				0.4
Lag DV	0.775 ***	0.993 ***	0.975 ***	0.8
	(0.101)	(0.064)	(0.041)	
R^2	0.948	0.871	0.882	

*** $p < 0.001$; * $p < 0.05$.
Note: Institutional dummies A, B, and C are drawn from Bernoulli distributions with probabilities 0.5, 0.8, and 0.9, respectively. Additionally, O is drawn from a normal distribution with a mean of two and a standard deviation of five. The error is also normally distributed with a mean of zero and a standard deviation of one. All independent variables are serially correlated by a factor of 0.3. The dependent variable is constructed as
$y[t] = 1 + 0.1 * A[t] + 0.8 * B[t] + 0.3 * C[t] + 0.4 * O[t] + 0.8 * y[t-1] + e[t]$.

previous constitution as well as other omitted variables (such as economic development, ethnic divisions, etc.).

I simulated a model like the one Ginsburg and Melton present in Table 4 of their article in Table 3.3. I created a dependent variable y, which was a function of a series of dummy variables A, B, and C (expressing different components of rigidity like a vote by one chamber, a referendum, etc.), an omitted variable O, and the lagged dependent variable. This equation is as follows:

$$y[t] = 1 + 0.1 * A[t] + 0.8 * B[t] + 0.3 * C[t] + 0.4 * O[t] + 0.8 * y[t-1] + e[t].$$

Then, I estimated the (known by construction) coefficients. The results are presented in Table 3.3. They all confirm Achen's expectations.

Actually, most of the institutional dummies lack significance or even have the wrong coefficient, and the only significant variable is the lagged dependent one, which is overestimated compared to its real value. So, Achen's expectations are confirmed, and the results of Ginsburg and Melton's Table 4 are replicated. The arguments of "amendment culture" as an inertial approach are not valid theoretically (out of equilibrium), empirically (what appears to be inertia is determined by the same institutions), or statistically (the method of approach leads to biased conclusions).

Let us now move to the third kind of "cultural" approach.

3.3 Culture as an Independent Variable

The methodology of this third kind of cultural approach is the appropriate one: instead of adding a random variable or the lagged dependent variable, researchers identify a new independent variable of "cultural" nature and include it in the analysis. They argue that the frequency of amendments does not depend exclusively on institutions but also on the preferences of the involved actors. In addition, they proceed one step further, and instead of arguing (as I did in Chapter 2) that we cannot make any prediction about the preferences of these actors, they claim that some particular cultural variables characterize in a significant way the population of each country, and, as a result, the whole country will adopt institutions in agreement with these characteristics, or at least as frequently as these characteristics impose.

There is one important weak point of this argument. The conceptual distance between any variation of "culture" and the frequency of constitutional amendments is very big, and, consequently, a series of empirical arguments will be necessary to lead from one to the other. Each step in this road will be an argument to be corroborated by empirical evidence, and the more steps that are necessary will result in a less reliable final conclusion. This is the essential objection that I will raise at the end of this section, urging for convincing and empirically relevant arguments.

To my knowledge, there are two analyses that deal with constitutional amendments as the dependent variable.

The first approach is "what constitutes a constitutional culture" (Tarabar and Young 2021), which uses the cultural indexes from Hofstede (2001) and Hofstede et al. (2010) to estimate amendment frequencies. These indexes, which are based on surveys, identify six broad cultural attitudes, four of which are used to assess amendment frequency: *individualism, power distance, uncertainty avoidance,* and *long-term* *orientation*. Out of these four characteristics, two turn out to be of (statistical) significance: individualism and uncertainty avoidance. In addition, when used along with the lagged amendment rate introduced by Ginsburg and Melton (2015), they eliminate its statistical significance.[6]

The argument for why these cultural features will be associated with amendment rates is as follows: "In a more individualistic society, people emphasize their own particular interests over general ones... In the constitutional context, this can lead people to view amendments as desirable whenever they serve their particular interests. By not insisting on a generality norm, individualistic societies may have higher amendment rates, all else equal" (Ginsburg and Milton 2015: 2). They go on to say, "Uncertainty avoidance measures extent to which people are comfortable in unstructured versus controlled and predictable environments. Individuals with high uncertainty avoidance may favour the predictability of governance under an entrenched constitution; as such, they perceive amendments to be generally undesirable" (Ginsburg and Milton 2015).

My objection to the argument that individualism and/or uncertainty avoidance would have a determinant impact on constitutional amendment frequency is that they should first have an impact on other more direct variables. For example, in my mind, the most direct effect of individualism would be on taxes: Individualists would not like to pay money to the government because their own money would be used by the government to promote its own preferences and even give subsidies to people other than the ones paying the taxes. Therefore, individualism should lead to lower tax rates in the corresponding countries. Similarly, uncertainty avoidance would have a much more direct impact on the desirability of income fluctuations than on constitutional amendments. Further, if one would raise the objection that people cannot shape these policies according to their preferences, I would answer that this argument applies even more to constitutions than policies. Table 3.4 demonstrates that these cultural variables have either the opposite than expected effect or no effect on these more directly relevant policies.

Individualism is significantly positively associated with taxes, while we expected the sign to be negative. Uncertainty avoidance is not significantly associated with the volatility of GDP (measured for the period of 1980–2014 as the mean of the absolute values of the annual change of

---

[6] In this respect, they reach the same conclusion as in Section 3.2.

Table 3.4 *Association of indicators of culture from Tarabar and Young (2021) with economic outcomes (based on IMF data) are not as expected*

	(1) Individual income tax revenue in percent of GDP in democracies	(2) Volatility of GDP in democracies
n	28	28
(Intercept)	0.272	−0.380 ***
	(0.178)	(0.080)
Individualism	0.637 ***	
	(0.157)	
Uncertainty avoidance		0.017
		(0.080)
R²	0.388	0.002
Adj. R²	0.365	−0.037

*** $p < 0.001$.

GDP in one year subtracted from the annual change of GDP in the following year).

I do not know what the reason is for these discrepancies, but they are sufficient to take us back to the drawing board. However, researchers raise more significant, sustained, and systematic objections, saying that "the validity of the VSM 2013 [the dataset used by Tarabar and Young] is in doubt, and the internal consistency of the VSM 2013 scales was overall poor" (Gerlach and Eriksson 2021). To go back to Lakatos' terminology, it looks like the VSM is the prime suspect for "inconsistency."

The second approach deals with a concept relevant to culture: social capital and its relation to constitutional amendment rates (Blake et al. 2023). The argument is that social capital will be positively correlated with the frequency of amendments, and it is made in two steps: first, in a comparative way, including the amendment rules of different countries and finding that social capital matters at a 90 percent level (along with constitutional rigidity); and second, in a time series way, finding that in each country periods of higher social capital lead to higher frequency of amendment.

I consider the second part of the argument a very productive application of cultural or social capital arguments because, by definition, it controls for institutions and looks at how social capital and behaviors covary. Here, I will focus on the first part of the argument because I want to compare their argument and findings with what will follow in this book, and the time series effects cannot be addressed with my approach. I do not disagree with the methodology of the approach; if one believes that social capital affects constitutional amendments, this is the way to investigate the argument empirically. But why would one entertain this belief? Here is Blake et al.'s explanation:

> While social capital does not directly measure amendment attitudes, trust and activism may be factors that shape a constitutional culture. Scholars have found that social capital affects policy innovation (Putnam et al. 1993: 82–120, Putnam 2001: 346–347), and we extend this insight to constitutional innovation. Constitutional rules impose transaction costs (Buchanan and Tullock 1965), and, in general, social capital reduces transaction costs (Fukuyama 1995). Thus, we predict that amendments will be adopted more frequently in polities with higher levels of social capital or at times within a polity's history when social capital is comparatively higher. (Blake et al. 2023: 2)

This quote is the whole argument they provide and includes two branches, but, as I said, I focus only on the first which is relevant to my analysis.[7]

The reference to Putnam comes from *Bowling Alone* (Putnam 2001) and is elevated to the status of universal truth, which supports generalizations. The original quote is much more modest and involves an operational mechanism which includes governments: "Preliminary studies suggest that states high in social capital sustain governments that are more effective and innovative" (Putnam 2001: 361).[8] In the Blake et al. (2023) article, social capital affects policy innovation directly. We will see in Appendix 3.A that different meanings of social capital will support different constitutional amendment results.

The second part of the argument (the "extension") makes use of what Sartori (1970) calls the "concept stretching" strategy by introducing the claim that constitutional innovations (which is implicitly equivalent to constitutional amendments)[9] are an extension of policy innovations. I take issue with this claim because the element of surprise, originality, or unexpectedness implied in the term "innovation" does not exist in constitutional amendments. As I argued in the Introduction,

---

[7] The second branch does not make any reference to constitutional amendments: It connects constitutional rules (existing ones I presume), transaction costs, and social capital, but it does not lead in any discernible way to constitutional amendments.
[8] This text is supported by a footnote providing references to works that do not seem relevant to our subject.
[9] One could very well consider constitutional court interpretations as innovations too.

constitutional amendments are Level 2 amendments – that is, they occur when legislation or judicial interpretations (strategies within the constitutional equilibrium) cannot achieve the desired outcomes. In this case, the only possible path is a constitutional amendment (Level 2 changes or modifications outside the constitutional equilibrium, as I explain in Table I.2). Constitutional amendments are institutional changes that are very well studied and discussed in order to achieve the necessary majorities (specified by the constitutional amendment rules). As I argued in Chapter 1 (Sections 1.2 and 1.3), some of them were submitted several times and failed before they could be adopted, others remained on the back burner for years before they were introduced precisely for fear of rejection, and others even required a change of the amendment rules precisely because the existing rules made them impossible to be adopted. Consequently, the claim of "innovation" when applied to constitutional amendments is an unfounded one.

It is well known that a causal chain is as strong as its weakest link, so the first part of the argument, being the mixture of a concept stretching and a false argument, is not supported. In my mind, this is sufficient not to test the empirical expectation. However, if we go ahead and observe the existing correlations, the ones reported in the first part of Blake et al.'s (2023) article are not sufficient (even the authors report that they are at the level of 90 percent one-sided). In addition, the variables used do not eliminate the constitutional rigidity arguments despite the verbal arguments that "group membership, civic activism, and political trust can offset the effect of amendment rules" (Blake et al. 2023: 1). This statement is not only not corroborated in the article but is not even tested.[10]

---

[10] This would require an interactive use of the variables so that the cultural ones would be more influential with rigid constitutions, yet there is no such test. Both kinds of variables are operating independently of each other in the Blake et al. (2023) article. This finding leads to the conclusion that social capital variables increase amendments (always) and amendment rules reduce them (always). In my own replications of the fifty-seven countries (the intersection of my own dataset with the fifty-seven countries included in the Blake et al. [2023] data), while constitutional rigidity is always negative and significant as expected, the only variable that retains significance when tested at the same time is not groups or political trust but civic activism. In case the lack of significance was due to the small number of countries, I increased the countries I examined to sixty-seven (the intersection of my dataset with the World Values Survey [WVS], which are the countries examined in Appendix 3.A). While the variable "trust" remained insignificant, the "groups" became significant but with the opposite sign from what was expected. The results are replicated if one uses the cultural variables with each one alone vs. constitutional rigidity or all together. The results were also nonsignificant for the human capital variables of the second part of the Blake et al. article, whether I used fifty-seven or sixty-

In Figure 3.3, I demonstrate the variety of social capital or cultural indicators included in the datasets used in the Blake et al. (2023) article (the WVS and V-Dem).[11] It is to be expected that, among all these indicators, some could be of high correlation with the frequency of constitutional amendments (or any other variable for that matter). It turns out that the highest correlation with the frequency of constitutional amendments is provided by one of the components of "civic activism" (signatures to petitions), which lifts the correlation between "civic activism" and frequency of amendments to high levels – higher than any of the other variables among these two datasets either included in the Blake et al. (2023) article (like "trust"[12] and "groups") or excluded from it. In addition, as Figure 3.3 demonstrates had group membership, mass mobilizations, or trade union participation been included (instead of signatures to petitions) as an indicator of social capital the argument would have to be a negative relation with constitutional amendments. The interested reader can find in Appendix 3.A the set of countries that provided the data.

seven countries. Appendix 3.A indicates the low correlation of groups and trust with frequency of constitutional amendments in a simpler way. Actually, the table in Appendix 3.A shows that out of all the cultural variables of both the WVS and V-Dem datasets, the only one with some correlation with constitutional amendment frequency is civic activism (more accurately, signing petitions). We will test the combination of the cultural and institutional approach in Appendix 6.A.2.

[11] I could have extended the argument to search for correlations by extending the datasets used to include modules from the International Social Survey Program, or ISSP (especially the Social Networks and Citizenship modules). The questionnaires for the three social networks modules from 1986, 2001, and 2017 include questions such as "How often do you see or visit your father?", which in 2017 was amended to "Please think about the parent you have contact with most frequently: How often do you have contact with that parent, either face to face, by phone, internet or any other communication device?" and "How often do you see or visit your friend (the friend you feel closest to)?", which is the 2002 version and was slightly different in the two other waves. The questionnaires for the citizenship modules contain questions on what it takes to be good citizen and how important the respondents find "Always to vote in elections," "Never to try to evade taxes," and "To be active in social or political associations." Furthermore, the Valued Living Questionnaire (Wilson et al. 2010) which estimates the domains of life values that govern our actions, one of them being community life, the Schwartz Value Survey (Schwartz 1992), social network data from Facebook (e.g., Chetty et al. 2022), or Elazar's (1984) political culture typology provide even more approaches to measuring social capital, although they cover only one country or one point in time, unlike the WVS, V-Dem, or ISSP.

[12] The variables from the WVS that Blake et al. (2023) use to build their political trust variable all utilize the term "confidence" (in government, political parties, and courts, respectively). In line with them, however, I use the term "trust" instead of "confidence."

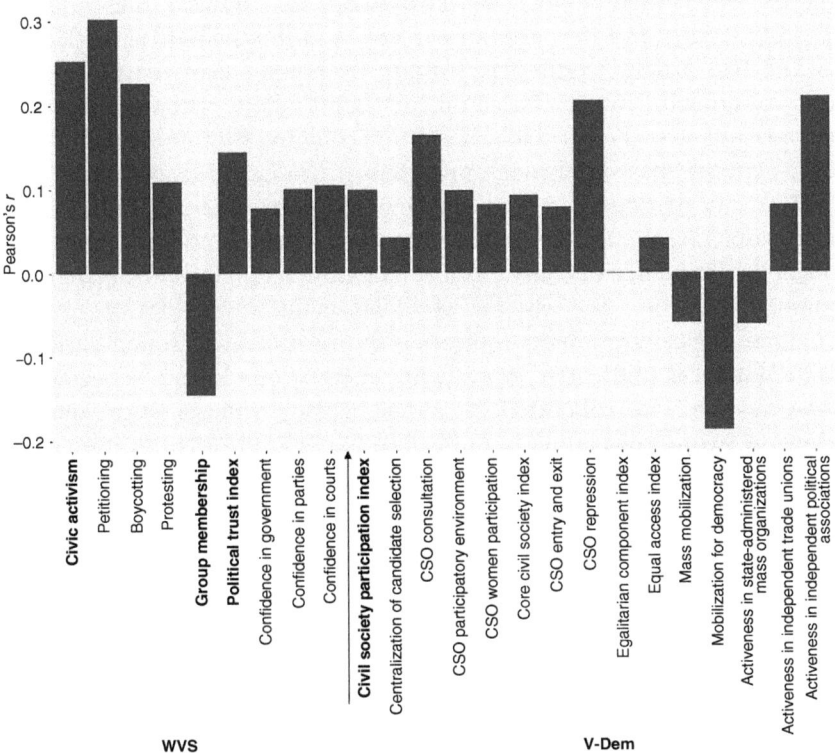

Figure 3.3 Correlations between amendment frequencies and the World Values Survey (WVS) and V-Dem Variables (variables used by Blake et al. [2023] in bold)

The question that remains in my mind after reading Blake et al.'s (2023) article is this: Even if the argument that constitutional amendments are some form of innovation was not false, how would that argument explain how signatures of petitions would increase the frequency of constitutional amendments? Again, the finding, if it was (inappropriately) taken for granted, should lead us back to the drawing board.

Conclusions

In this chapter, I described three different ways that culture has been used in assessing the impact of constitutional amendment rules on the frequency of constitutional amendments. The first was as a random variable, the second was as a constant (lagged dependent variable), and the third was as an independent variable. Out of these three ways, only the last one is methodologically tenable, but, as I showed, there are few existing studies and they are not persuasive at the theoretical level.

The two articles connecting culture or human capital with constitutional amendments are based on correlations alone without presenting any reasons why the particular indicators (ranging from individualism to civic activism, passing through uncertainty avoidance, groups, trust, and civil society participation, and omitting countless others as indicated in Appendix 3.A) should be selected (that is, why they should be expected to affect the frequency of constitutional amendments). However, if we want to understand how and why the world works the way it does, we need to combine logical arguments indicating the relationship among variables with statistical ones used to evaluate whether our logical expectations (theories) were corroborated. It cannot happen with statistical analysis alone. A strong correlation is, in the best of cases, the identification of an interesting puzzle, not an answer.

As I argued at the end of Chapter 2, this book does not offer any way of assessing the distribution of preferences of the actors involved. Cultural theories make the implicit argument that there is a uniform force operating in societies that will affect outcomes in a similar way (much like individualism will affect constitutional amendments). I have argued that there are two reasons that undermine such claims. The first is the dimensionality of the underlying space: It may be that the expectation is correct in some dimensions but not in others. This would undermine the uniformity of results. The second is the role of institutions. It may be that institutions interfere and disallow the adoption of outcomes preferred by majorities, even in democracies (constitutional rigidity is clearly one of them). In other words, there is *no direct effect* of public opinion, attitudes, or culture on political outcomes or events, and certainly not on constitutional ones. They may or may not work – the example of the conflict between legislature and courts in Israel or the conflict between the values and policies indicated in Table 3.4 indicate cases of discrepancies.[13] Further, in the Appendix of Chapter 6, the reader can verify that when the human capital variables of Blake et al. (2023) are introduced along with constitutional rigidity, they almost always lose their significance.

These arguments are antagonistic to theories of culture at the empirical level. Even more, though, at the theoretical level, I have serious doubts about whether we will be able to offer a theory of preferences

---

[13] A more vivid example may be that the American public opinion wants gun restrictions, but such a policy is not implemented.

where we will be able to understand how the tastes of different individuals evolve and what they depend on. All these reasons do not imply that we should give up and not try to formulate rules of thumb about what kind of preferences will affect what kind of outcomes. In this chapter, I argue that we will need many more efforts in this direction.

Of all the different ways of understanding the effect of "culture" on the frequency of constitutional amendments presented in this chapter, I think the most fruitful would be the first if we are able to systematize the permissive and restrictive processes over constitutional rules. This would be a monumental task since it would involve written texts (other than the constitution).

In the remainder of this book, I will be focusing on constitutional amendment rules alone in a comparative way (which, as I have argued, are the necessary conditions). When theories of culture are sufficiently developed in a comparative way, they will be "graftable" to the constitutional analysis I provide.

Appendix 3.A

As in Blake et al. (2023), the WVS variables are constructed by creating a country-wave average and then a cross-wave, national average for countries surveyed in multiple waves. The three indices used in Blake et al. (2023) are included, as well as the variables that make up civic activism (past petitioning, boycotting, and protesting experience of the respondents) and political trust (confidence in government, political parties, and courts).

The variables from V-Dem are constructed as country averages from 1981 to 2022, the same timespan as the WVS. In addition to the Civil Society Participation Index that Blake et al. (2023) use, Figure 3.3 includes the Core Civil Society Index as well as the variables that constitute both of these indices: centralization of legislative candidate selection within the parties, consultation of civil society organizations by policy makers on policies relevant to their members, degree of voluntary participation and popular involvement in civil society organizations, prevention of women participation in civil society organizations, control of government over entry and exit of civil society organizations into public life, repression of civil society organizations. Moreover Figure 3.3 incorporates other variables from V-Dem that potentially reflect social capital: the egalitarian component index on achieving the egalitarian principle of democracy among social groups, the equal access to power index on de facto capabilities to participate, frequency and size of events of mass mobilization, frequency and size of events of mass mobilization for prodemocratic aims, share of the population active in state-administered mass organizations, share of the population active in independent trade unions, share of the population active in independent political associations.

All countries were included that are present in Tsebelis (2022) and have data on all the variables, leading to 67 countries: Albania, Argentina, Armenia, Australia, Bolivia, Brazil, Bulgaria, Canada, Chile, Colombia, Croatia, Cyprus, Czech Republic, Dominican Republic, Ecuador, Estonia, Finland, France, Georgia, Germany, Ghana, Greece, Guatemala, Hungary, India, Indonesia, Italy, Japan, Kenya, Kyrgyz Republic, Latvia, Lebanon, Lithuania, Macedonia, Malaysia, Mali, Mexico, Moldova, Mongolia, Montenegro, Netherlands, New Zealand, Nicaragua, Norway, Pakistan, Peru, Philippines, Poland, Romania, Slovak Republic, Slovenia, South Africa, South Korea, Spain, Sweden, Switzerland, Taiwan, Thailand, Trinidad and Tobago, Tunisia, Turkey, Ukraine, United Kingdom, United States, Uruguay, Serbia, and Zambia.

4

Cases of Failed Amendments: Italy and Chile

This chapter examines in detail the cases of failed amendments in two countries, Italy and Chile. On the basis of Chapter 2, these failures were primarily due to the rigid rules of constitutional amendments. However, a closer examination will reveal more institutional reasons. This chapter is divided into three parts. Section 4.1 describes the core of the constitutions of both countries. Italy has two alternative amendment procedures, while Chile has three. We will calculate the core of each one of these countries as specific examples of how the arguments made in Chapter 2 can be applied in single-country analyses. In addition, because the institutions of Chile are quite unusual (in a comparative sense), we will describe the historical conditions of their adoption. Section 4.2 describes the history of the failed amendments. Here, there are similarities (both amendments failed) and differences (in Italy, the result was accepted; in Chile, a series of failed attempts to replace the constitution itself followed). Section 4.3 will deal with another similarity between the two countries, focusing on how they both used referendums in their constitutional procedures. The reason for this was that they were expecting an easy approval of the proposed amendments (Italy) or constitutions (two different attempts at a new constitution in Chile), as we argued in Chapter 2. However, unlike the argument in that chapter, in both countries the referendums led to a NO result (actually in Chile this happened twice!). Because of this, we will explain in Section 4.3 what was mistaken in Chapter 2's analysis regarding the argument that referendums have no core which, consequently, makes it easier to make amendments (or replacements) through this procedure. We will use examples from EU referendums in order to have a broader understanding of how this institution works.

4.1 Calculating the Core of Two Constitutions

4.1.1 Italy

According to the Italian Constitution (Part II, Title VI, Section II, Article 138), amendments require the following:

> Laws amending the Constitution and other constitutional laws shall be adopted by each House after two successive debates at intervals of not less than three months, and shall be approved by an absolute majority of the members of each House in the second voting. Said laws are then submitted to a popular referendum when, within three months of their publication, such request is made by one-fifth of the members of a House or five hundred thousand voters or five Regional Councils. The law submitted to referendum shall not be promulgated if not approved by a majority of valid votes. A referendum shall not be held if the law has been approved in the second voting by each of the Houses by a majority of two-thirds of the members.

Figure 4.1 helps us visualize the situation. The set of provisions of Article 138 specifies two alternative procedures for constitutional revision: revisions may occur via a two-thirds majority in both chambers of the legislature or by simple majorities plus a referendum.[1]

Figure 4.1a demonstrates the core of the first procedure for revision, which is a two-thirds majority in both chambers. I represent each chamber with five members (L1–5 and U1–5) and look for agreement from four of the five members in each chamber, as four out of five most closely approximates the two-thirds majority required to pass constitutional reforms under the first procedure. Under this arrangement, the pentagon CL represents the core of the lower chamber: any point outside this pentagon can be defeated by its projection on the pentagon since four out of the five members of the lower chamber would prefer this solution. Similarly, the pentagon CU depicts the core of the upper chamber. The bicameral constitutional core, in this case, is comprised not only of both CL and CU but also of the area between them (the shaded area in Figure 4.1a).[2]

Figure 4.1b captures the second possible procedure for constitutional revision: concurrent simple majorities in both chambers plus a

---

[1] For each one of these procedures, there are some additional constraints (i.e., double passage by the same legislature after a time interval), but these are the most important features of the two alternatives.
[2] In this figure, I have deliberately selected two chambers with preferences that do not overlap in order to have a clear picture. If the preferences were overlapping, the two pentagons would come closer, and the bicameral core would shrink.

4.1 CALCULATING THE CORE OF TWO CONSTITUTIONS 101

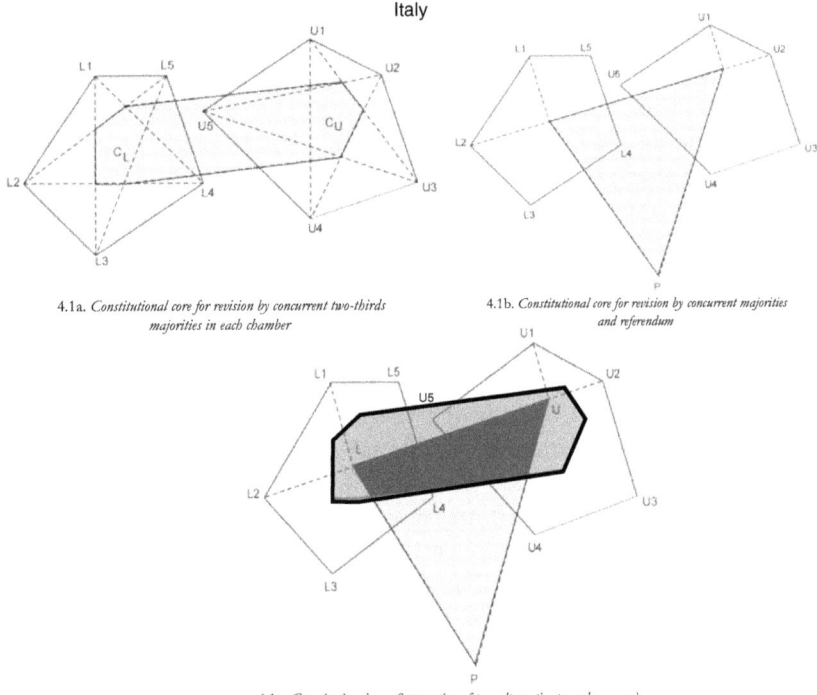

4.1a. *Constitutional core for revision by concurrent two-thirds majorities in each chamber*

4.1b. *Constitutional core for revision by concurrent majorities and referendum*

4.1c. *Constitutional core (intersection of two alternative procedure cores)*

Figure 4.1 Constitutional core of Italy under Article 138

referendum. In this case, the bicameral core by simple majority is located along the line segment L2U2. Indeed, this line is a "bicameral median" – that is, it has a majority of members of both houses on either side of it. It follows that there is a majority in both houses that would prefer, over any point outside this line, its projection on the line itself. The bicameral core, however, does not extend beyond point L2 and U2: Anything outside the solid line in the figure does not command a majority in one of the chambers. Therefore, the bicameral core is the solid line between L2 and U2. In order to calculate the whole constitutional core, including the referendum requirement, one must factor in the voters (Point P) and expand the core. The shaded triangle depicts that addition.[3]

---

[3] Again, I have selected the points on purpose to consider distinct preferences. If the two houses come closer to each other, or if the voters have preferences similar to one of the houses, the triangle will shrink, but it will not affect the logic of the argument.

The core of the Italian Constitution exists at the intersection of the cores of the two procedures delineated in Figure 4.1a and Figure 4.1b. Indeed, any point that belongs to *only one* of the procedural cores can be changed by using the alternative procedure. This intersection is represented by the darkly shaded area in Figure 4.1c. It cannot be assessed a priori which one of the two procedures is easier to use. Indeed, this depends not only on the institutional rules but also on the actual preferences of the actors. However, the system does behave in predictable ways. For example, if the preferences of the people are much closer to both houses than Figure 4.1 indicates, then it is easier to make a constitutional revision with a referendum than it would be with two-thirds of both chambers. This seems to be the case for the amendment we will discuss in Section 4.2.1 because it prescribed the reduction of the powers of the senate and consequently would make it difficult to get a two-thirds majority of votes in the senate. Similarly, if the two houses drift apart, the segment LU in Figure 4.1 will become longer, and the core will expand. Indeed, all three cores in Figures 4.1a, 4.1b, and 4.1c will become larger, and constitutional revision will become more difficult. This would be the case under the electoral system for the senate created by the proposed constitutional reforms. The proposed electoral law would have the senate elected *indirectly* through *regional councils*. This reform would result in a significantly different composition of the senate from the national assembly. That would generate more disagreements between the house and the senate, but the senate would have lost political significance except on constitutional issues.

4.1.2 Chile

The Chilean constitution provides for two different paths to constitutional amendment. The first, requiring cooperation between the legislature and the executive, is detailed in Article 127: "The Bill of reform will require for its approval in each Chamber the confirming vote of three-fifths of the Deputies and Senators in office."[4]

---

[4] Article 127 also states: "If the reform concerns Chapters I, III, VIII, XI, XII or XV it will require the approval of two-thirds of the Deputies and Senators in office. Concerning [matters] not provided for in this chapter, the norms concerning the formation of the law shall be applicable to the process of the Bills of constitutional reform, the quorums specified in the previous paragraph always being respected." According to Chapter 2, one would need a different analysis in order to study amendments of these chapters.

4.1 CALCULATING THE CORE OF TWO CONSTITUTIONS

Article 128 adds an additional requirement to the three-fifths majority: "The Bill which both Chambers approve will be transmitted to the President of the Republic... If the President of the Republic totally rejects a Bill of reform approved by both Chambers and it insists on its totality by two-thirds of the members in office of each Chamber, the President must promulgate that Bill." Figure 4.2 depicts the core resulting from this revision procedure, as discussed in Chapter 2. Figure 4.2a presents these cores in two thirteen-member legislatures, as created by the three-fifths majority requirement. Next, Figure 4.2b presents the joint bicameral core with a three-fifths majority in each chamber. Since revision requires approval by both chambers concurrently, the core must grow to include all points located between the two legislative cores. Indeed, any point in this area cannot be defeated by the required three-fifths bicameral majorities: it cannot be moved up or down because such a movement does not get endorsed by three-fifths, and it cannot be moved left or right because one of the two chambers will disagree. Thus, in Figure 4.2b, the core stretches between the cores depicted in Figure 4.2a. Finally, I incorporate the president into the core. Here, because the president's approval is required alongside both chambers, the core must expand, this time to include all points between the region in Figure 4.2b and the president's ideal point, P. This generates the triangle-shaped core found in Figure 4.2c.

However, according to Article 128, if there is disagreement between Congress and the president, the president's opinion can be overruled by a two-thirds majority of both chambers. Chile's constitution, therefore, allows for an alternate route to constitutional revision that bypasses the president. Indeed, if the president decides against proposed revisions, the legislature can overrule their decision via concurrent two-thirds majorities in each chamber of the legislature. Figure 4.3a presents the two-thirds core of each chamber (created using the same procedure presented in Figure 4.2), and Figure 4.3b depicts the bicameral core of this alternative procedure. Figure 4.3b connects the cores of each chamber (just like in Figure 4.2) to account for the concurrent majority requirement. This shaded region is the core of the two-thirds concurrent majority alternative for constitutional revision.

As explained in Chapter 2, the final constitutional core is the intersection of these two cores (just like in Italy). Figure 4.4a thus depicts this final, smaller core.

However, Chile's constitution introduces an additional wrinkle into its constitution revision process: If the president is overridden, they can

CASES OF FAILED AMENDMENTS: ITALY AND CHILE

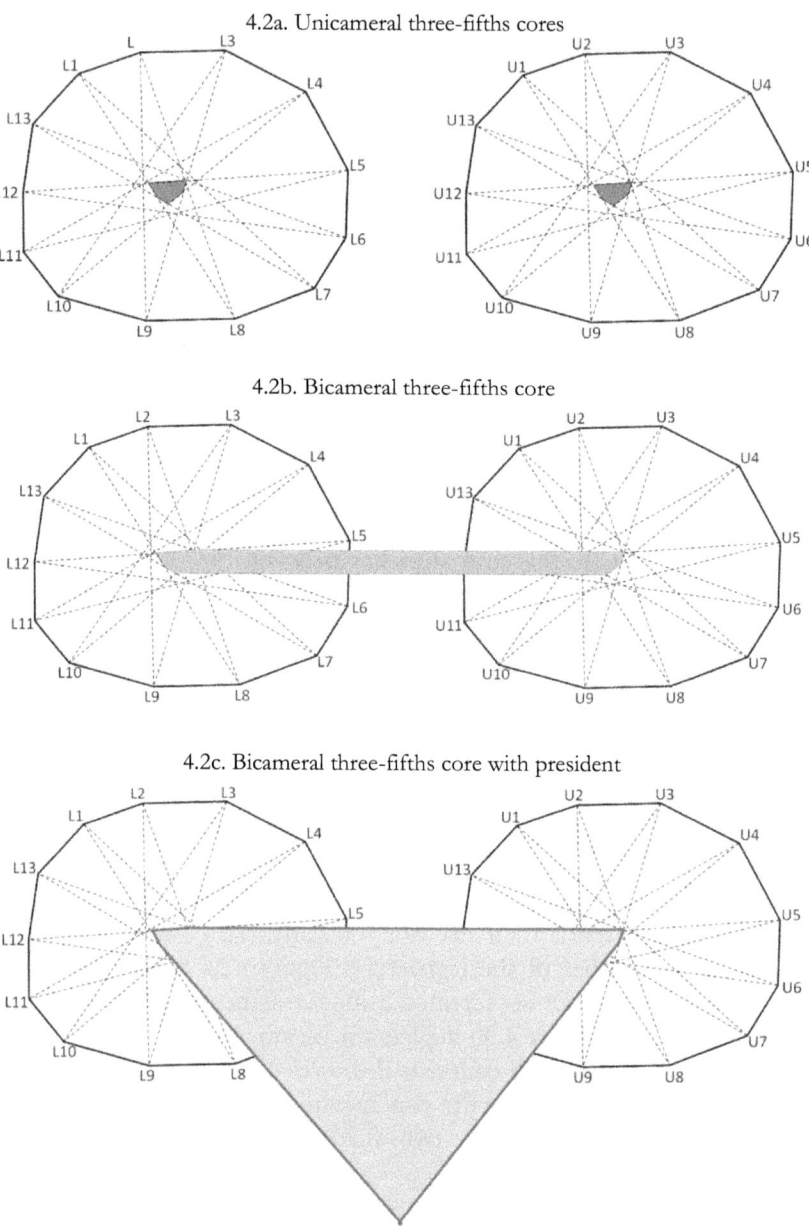

Figure 4.2 Constitutional core of Chile, three-fifths, and president

4.1 CALCULATING THE CORE OF TWO CONSTITUTIONS 105

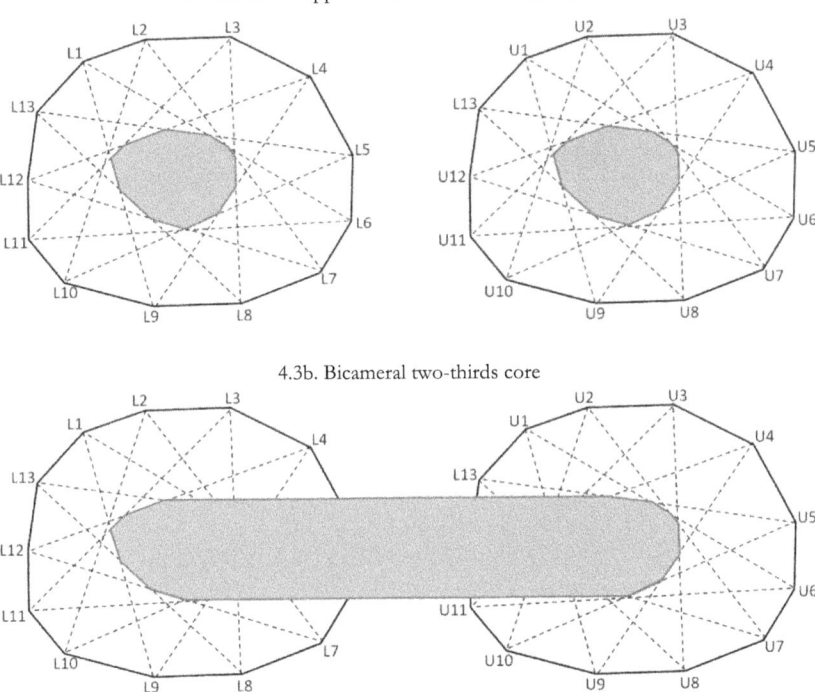

Figure 4.3 Constitutional core of Chile and two-thirds without president

overcome the override through a plebiscite. According to Article 129, the "consultation" of the people through "plebiscite" must proceed as follows:

> The convocation to [the] plebiscite must be effected within thirty days following that on which both Chambers insist on the Bill approved by them, and it will be ordered by supreme decree which will establish the date of the plebiscitary voting, which shall be held one hundred twenty days from the publication of the decree if that day corresponds to a Sunday. If this should not be so, it will be held on the Sunday immediately following. If the President has not convoked a plebiscite within such period of time, the Bill approved by the Congress will be promulgated.
>
> The decree of convocation will contain, as it may correspond, the Bill approved by the Plenary Congress and totally vetoed by the President of the Republic, or the questions of the Bill on which the Congress has insisted. In this latter case, each one of the questions in disagreement must be voted [on] separately in the plebiscite.

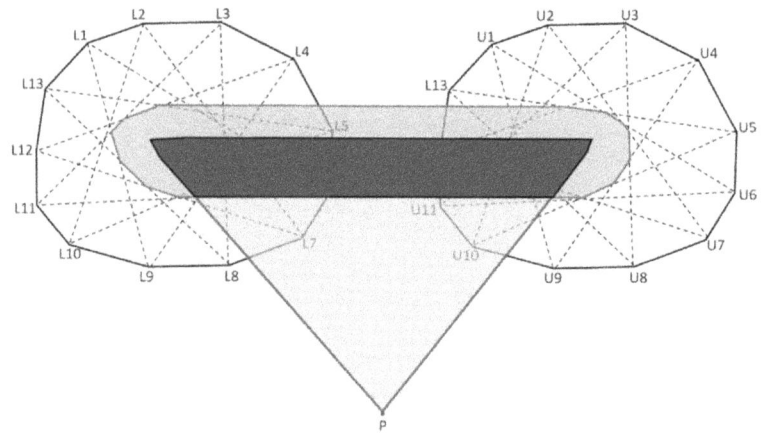

4.4a. *Constitutional core without plebiscite*

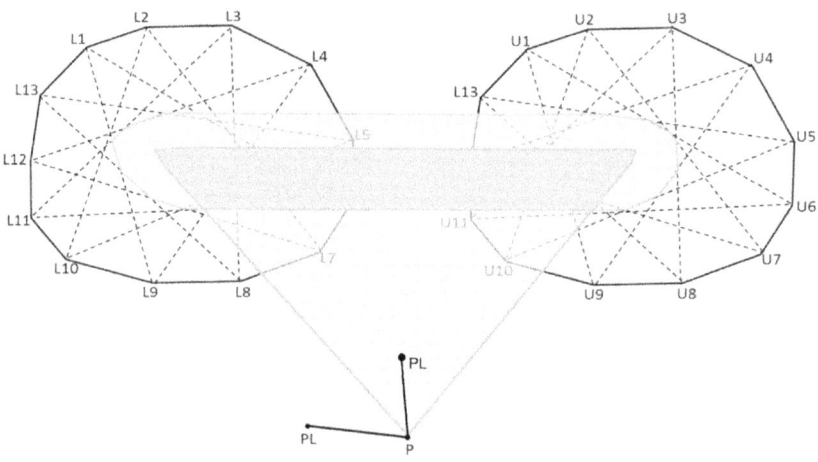

4.4b. *Constitutional core without plebiscite*

Figure 4.4 Constitutional core of Chile with all alternatives

If the president opts to put constitutional changes up for popular vote, such a choice drastically alters the constitutional core. Because the plebiscite can override any decision made by the legislature, the previous core becomes irrelevant, and the new core now lies along a straight line connecting the president's and the public's ideal points. Figure 4.4b presents the new core, which replaces the old one.

4.1 CALCULATING THE CORE OF TWO CONSTITUTIONS 107

The constitutional provision found in Article 129 is completely unique from a comparative perspective and, therefore, merits additional attention. According to my analysis, the third alternative (plebiscite) seems to overrule the previous two, and, consequently, the actual intersection of all three cores is the *empty set*. Indeed, given that the intersection of the cores of the first two procedures does not include the president, the intersection of the three cores is empty whether the people are located outside the initial triangular core (three-fifths and the president) in the position PL or inside it in the position PL'. An empty constitutional core implies that there is *nothing* immune to change inside the Pinochet Constitution. If the president is willing to use the plebiscite specified by Article 129, anything can change, and the agreement between the president and the people will become the new constitution. There is one exception to this rule: If the president and the congress want to modify the status quo in opposite directions, but the status quo is the second-best option for both of them (that is, if each one of them prefers the status quo over the other's proposal), then the status quo will prevail. Here is the description of this rule according to Article 128: "In the case that the Chambers do not approve all or some of the observations of the President, there shall be no constitutional reform of the points in dispute, unless both Chambers insist by two thirds of their members in exercise on the part of the project approved by them."[5]

The combination of all these constitutional revision articles provides the following synthesis. For an amendment to be successful, it requires a three-fifths majority in both chambers and the president's approval (two-thirds for articles in Chapters I, III, VIII, XI, XII, or XV of the constitution). In addition, the president can be overruled by concurrent majorities of two-thirds in both chambers. In case of disagreement between Congress and the president, Congress can either opt for the status quo (by not approving the president's proposals) or for a confrontation (by overruling by two thirds) – in which case, the president can send his proposal to a referendum. In the case of disagreement without confrontation, there is no modification of the constitution; in the case of confrontation, the plebiscite becomes the president's nuclear option.

The Chilean Constitution provides the president with extraordinary legislative powers. They can introduce amendatory observations in legislation, and the congress can overrule their amendments only by a two-

---

[5] I thank Eduardo Alemán for pointing this point out to me.

thirds majority. In comparative perspective, these powers do not exist in other Latin American constitutions except for Uruguay and Ecuador (Tsebelis and Alemán 2005).

However, in terms of constitutional revisions, there is no other constitution in the world that provides one individual with so much power. The president both controls the question that will be asked and can decide whether to trigger the referendum or not. Consequently, they have complete control of the agenda.

It is surprising that such a provision exists in a democratic constitution and has not been removed after so many years of democratic rule. To understand this peculiarity, we need to explore its genesis in the history of Chile's constitution and its amendment provision.

4.1.3 History of Chilean Article 129

Chile's modern constitutional history – and its unique plebiscitary provision for constitutional amendment – began with the 1924 efforts to reform the 1833 constitution. Prior to the 1920s reform efforts, the Chilean government had become mired in a struggle for power between the legislative and executive branches. For years, Chile was regarded as a "parliamentary republic" (Valenzuela 1977), but. in response to social and economic challenges, their newly elected president Arturo Alessandri had attempted to wrest power from the legislature. This struggle stalemated the Chilean government (in spite of many urgent challenges facing the country), leading the military to form a junta to demand a resolution to the stalemate. After an internal struggle for control within the military itself, political reform efforts began in earnest in 1925 (Stanton 1997b: 134).

Military officers placed President Alessandri in charge of reforming the constitution. This created institutional tension, however, because the 1833 constitution made it clear that constitutional reforms lay within the purview of the legislature's powers. In response, President Alessandri assembled a consultative commission by decree, which would be made up largely of democratically elected representatives. The commission was to be made up of two subcommissions: one would be in charge of overseeing the constitutional amendment process (and ensuring its popular legitimacy), and the other would decide on the content of the reforms. The commission met for the first time on April 4, 1925 (Stanton 1997b: 135).

From the time of the commission's first meeting, Alessandri expressed doubts about its efficacy and usefulness. According to Alessandri, political reform via the constituent assembly was not likely to happen, nor was the result likely to match his own vision for constitutional reform. After all, conservatives had not yet submitted to the idea that the "parliamentary republic" needed to be done away with. In his own words, "[I] had contracted a commitment with the country that it was necessary to fulfill; but, that same public opinion would have to come to realize that it was not possible to be successful and to achieve that which it desired" (Alessandri 1967: 166). Thus, instead of moving forward with the popularly elected constituent assembly, Alessandri concentrated reform efforts in a subcommittee of the commission, called the "Subcommission of Constitutional Reforms" (Alessandri 1967: 142).

Unlike the constituent assembly in the consultative commission, the subcommission was filled with politicians and other political operatives – particularly representatives of the major political parties in Chile. Thus, while Alessandri seemingly had greater faith in the efficacy of the subcommission, it was not without its own challenges. In fact, following pro-legislature remarks by one conservative party representative, Alessandri reportedly stormed out of a subcommission meeting and was ready to halt reform talks altogether. However, according to historians, a number of factors contributed to the ability of the subcommission to remain intact. First, military leaders arose early in the process as opponents of any return to the "parliamentary republic." Figures such as General Mariano Navarrete reminded the subcommission throughout the deliberation process that the military junta itself materialized because of public dissatisfaction with parliamentary predominance. General Navarrete stated that "the Army ... is horrified at politics ... but nor will it look on with indifference as the slate is wiped clean of the ideals of national purification, ... as the ends of the revolutions of the 5th of September and the 23rd of January are forgotten in a return to the political orgy that gave life to those movements" (Ministerio del Interior 1925: 454–455). Constitutional reforms, then, should reflect this public desire to roll back the powers of the legislature. Given that the military junta had organized efforts for constitutional reform in the first place, the presence of military officials at the meetings helped to keep conservative and radical party members at the negotiating table. Additionally, the small size and frequent meetings of the subcommission allowed factions to reach a consensus on difficult issues (Stanton 1997a: 13–17).

While the subcommission provided Alessandri with a more favorable venue through which to enact constitutional reform, the president encountered a problem with his new focus on the subcommission:

Unlike the constituent assembly, the subcommission lacked popular legitimacy. In response to this problem, Alessandri announced his intention in a manifesto on May 28, 1925, to subject the subcommission's proposal to the plebiscite. Such a move was not expected by practically any political actor at the time. Indeed, even Alessandri himself did not seem to indicate that a plebiscite was a possibility when he initially convened the consultation commission. Opponents, too, seemed to doubt whether Alessandri was serious about holding a plebiscite: Rather than actually drafting an alternative proposal for a plebiscite, Alessandri's opponents instead focused their energy on public messaging about the constitutional reform process.

However, while the plebiscite did not appear as part of Alessandri's original plan, the arrangement ultimately benefited his view of reform quite well. First and foremost, it was not until July 22, 1925, that Alessandri made it explicit that the constituent assembly would have nothing to do with the constitutional reform efforts – an announcement he made by angrily "declaring" at a sub commission meeting that the constituent assembly "has ended." Alessandri said, "It is time to finish for once and for all the political comedy, it is time for the President of the Republic to stop being the whipping boy" (Ministerio del Interior 1925). The subcommission subsequently voted in favor of holding a plebiscite. Given that the plebiscite occurred in August, this gave opposition reformers only a month to draft an alternative constitution proposal. Unsurprisingly, their proposal was short and unimpressive in comparison to the subcommission's. In fact, many reformers advocated for a boycott of the plebiscite altogether rather than submit a hasty proposal (Stanton 1997b: 161). Moreover, because President Alessandri's administration was in charge of executing the plebiscite, Alessandri could (reportedly) further influence the process via biased language in the plebiscite and even police interference (Vial 1987: 548). Taken together, in spite of the low turnout resulting from the aforementioned calls for boycott, the subcommission's constitution was accepted by a count of 127,483 votes to 5,448 (Bernaschina 1956: 49).

Ultimately, the ad hoc and combative nature of Chile's constitutional reform in 1925 led the system to collapse shortly after in 1927. However, its nonlinear development also resulted in the peculiar plebiscitary provision that remains in Chile's constitution today. Indeed, because Alessandri resorted to an extra-constitutional means of "legitimizing" his subcommission's constitutional proposal, the plebiscitary provision found its way into the new constitution retroactively. Pinochet retained the provision in his constitutional revisions in 1980, and the provision persists to the present day.

Be that as it may, it is understandable why any elected president would not even think of using this plebiscitary provision: A constitutional revision with the use of Article 129 would be an official admission of war between president and Congress, and the president (if not impeached) would not be able to make any policy decision for the remainder of their term.[6]

4.2 History of Failed Amendments

Having studied the constitutional core of Italy and Chile, let's now turn to the history of the political events that revolve around the amendments.

4.2.1 Italy

Italy is a country with "symmetric bicameralism" – that is, perfectly equal powers for the House and Senate. Actually, the constitution does not differentiate between the two chambers and uses the expressions "either chamber" or "both chambers" to refer to them. For much of Italy's history under the 1947 constitution, the Senate did not restrict the set of feasible outcomes (the win-set of the status quo) because of its ideological makeup per se – after all, it had the same composition as the Camera dei Deputati. Instead, lack of political alteration led to "immobilismo," or immobility. The electoral reforms in 1993 and 2005 created ambiguous results. On the one hand, alternation in the Italian political system turned Italy into a two-coalition (center-left or center-right) system. On the other hand, in the 2005 electoral reform, the bonus distribution at the national level for the House of Deputies and at the regional level for the Senate increased the ideological distance between the National Assembly and the Senate. The resulting complication was compounded by the intervention of the Constitutional Court, which declared the electoral reforms unconstitutional.

The combination of perfect bicameralism and different composition of the two chambers created (in Lijphart's [2012] terms) a "strong bicameralism" in Italy, which reduced the ability of governments to legislate. The government of Enrico Letta (April 2013–January 2014) followed a

---

[6] This is the reason I have not included Article 129 in the empirical analysis of Chapter 6.

strategy of "inclusion" and had ministers from parties of both the Left and the Right, but it still could not overcome the problem of political divisions and create policies. Letta resigned when the Democratic Party led by Matteo Renzi withdrew its support to the government.

Renzi was appointed prime minister of Italy, and because his strategy of policy adoption was impossible under the current institutional structures, he had to modify the structures first. He continued a long-standing discussion about the constitutional amendments necessary to alleviate Italy's problems and proposed amendments that would reduce the policy impact of the Senate (in his plan, he gave the Senate jurisdiction only on regional issues but preserved the perfect bicameralism on constitutional amendment issues).

Given the content of the amendments (including reduction of the power of the Senate), it is obvious that Renzi could not expect a two-thirds approval by the Senate. Therefore, he had to select the alternative procedure of achieving simple majorities in both chambers and being ratified by a referendum. Still, even this procedure could not be considered an easy task. Renzi had made an agreement with Berlusconi to support his amendment, but the latter changed his opinion in the middle of the process.[7] The procedure was finally aborted, but not from the most obvious obstacle (the Senate).

In October 2015, the Italian Senate voted 179–10 in favor of the largest constitutional reforms since its ratification in 1947. Amid a boycott by over a hundred senators, the vote approved measures that would drastically weaken bicameralism in Italy, stripping the Italian Senate of its ability to veto most types of legislation. Although it was only one step in the constitutional amendment process, the vote represented a key victory for proponents of the reforms who believed the changes would finally address the legislative gridlock and governmental instability that has long beleaguered Italy's political system. Prime Minister Renzi said of the successful vote, "You can agree or not with what we're doing, but we're doing it: the long season of inconclusive politics is over" (Follain 2015). Minister of Reform Maria Elena Boschi took it a step further, calling the reforms a "Copernican revolution" for Italy (Economist 2015).

These assessments would be correct for a successful amendment, but the main hurdle turned out to be the last step of the process. Poll information did not indicate popular support for the referendum, particularly after Berlusconi's reversal. Renzi, in trying to support the

---

[7] Berlusconi's stated reason was that he considered Renzi's choice of Mattarella for president to be a rupture of the pact.

reforms, repeatedly declared, "If I lose the referendum, I will go home" (Ansa 2016). (Actually, he made an even more unambiguous statement about abandoning politics altogether and matters of honor.) As we will see in Section 4.3, these statements undermined his chances rather than help him. On December 4, 2016, the referendum rejected the amendments by a decisive 59.12 percent majority.

4.2.2 Chile

The Chilean constitution was introduced in 1980 under the dictatorship of Augusto Pinochet and was approved by a referendum which, to say the least, had no democratic credentials. As such, it included a series of undemocratic provisions which were considered unacceptable by parties both of the Left and the Right. As a result, the constitution was amended many times, but the most significant revisions (in 1989 and 2005) involved long-negotiated agreements among the political parties in order to achieve the high thresholds specified by the constitution and described in Section 4.1. When major reforms lacked the support of the Right, they failed to get the required majorities (in 1992, 1994, and 1995).

It is interesting to see how this consensus agreement was achieved. According to Fuentes (2006) regarding the 1989 agreement:

> The then-opposition leaders saw that they should focus their efforts on *ensuring opportunities for future constitutional reform*. In this sense, the strategic calculation of the negotiators was not to seek reform of all the negative aspects of the 1980 constitution, but rather simply to try to maximize the opportunities for future efforts at reform. This they did in two ways: by reducing the quorums necessary for introducing reforms and increasing the number of senators in order to reduce the relative strength of the non-elected senators (Andrade 1991, Heiss and Navia 2007). This was clear in April 1989, when the then-Interior Minister Carlos Cáceres presented the reform package that would be put up for the plebiscite once negotiations with the opposition concluded. (Fuentes 2006: 18; emphasis mine)

The second major amendment enterprise began in 2000 and ended in 2005, covering fifty-eight topics of the constitution (Fuentes 2015: 111). These involved the following:

> Repeal of the institution of designated and life senators, a change in the composition of the National Security Council and a reduction in its powers, restoration of the president of Chile's power to remove commanders-in-chief of the armed forces and the director of the *Carabineros*

(the uniformed national police force), a modification of the composition of the Constitutional Tribunal, an increase in the powers of the Chamber of Deputies to supervise the executive, a reduction in the presidential term of office from six to four years without consecutive re-election, a reform of the constitutional states of exception in order better to protect rights, and the elimination of special sessions of Congress. (Fuentes 2015: 100)

By 2015, the constitution was locked (as described in Section 4.1). It still had a serious congenital defect, but it had been significantly improved compared to the initial document. It is interesting to note that in an academic debate in the political science journal *Politica y Gobierno* one position supported the preservation of the constitution and incremental changes (Navia 2018), one its total replacement (Fuentes 2018), and a third its replacement with incremental changes (Tsebelis 2018a).

In October 2015, President Michelle Bachelet proposed on television a constitutional reform process that included four phases and would be completed by 2017. It involved popular education first; a second stage of participation controlled by a committee selected by the president herself; a third stage which specified the submission of a constitutional amendment accepted by a two-thirds majority in both chambers (note that she *increased* the required majority from three-fifths according to the constitution to a higher threshold); and finally a discussion of this amendment by a specific body and the ratification by a referendum (Garcia 2023).

On the basis of the analysis of Section 4.1, this project was doomed to failure. Actually, I had predicted this outcome in writing before the end of Bachelet's term (Tsebelis 2018c). Bachelet did not even propose an amendment, she was replaced in the middle of this process, and her successor refused to continue it. As Fuentes accurately put it:

> In the case of Chile, we need to explain the following paradox: knowing the institutional and political difficulties properly described by Tsebelis, President Bachelet nonetheless sought to replace the Constitution through a totally impracticable path. Despite not having a large enough majority in Congress and despite the massive existing legal barriers, her administration tried the apparent "political suicide" of promising a constitutional change that would not happen. Why? (Fuentes 2018: 473)

I agree with Fuentes' analysis,[8] but there are other analyses that find Bachelet's process "useful" (Garcia 2023). In fact, after its failure, a formal constitutional revision succeeded. While Bachelet was aiming at an

---

[8] I have provided my answer to his question in the *Politica y Gobierno* discussion.

amendment (although the process she adopted would have led to a multiple-screening constitutional revision), Chile chose a series of formal constitutional revisions this next time. In fact, there were two revisions, and both of them failed. Here, I will summarize these "current events" in order to lead into Section 4.3, which analyzes the mode of failure: the referendum process.

In 2020, the people of Chile decided by a majority of 72 percent in a referendum to replace the Pinochet Constitution. As I said before, despite the multiple revisions, the document has a congenital defect. There was a complicated process with a constituent assembly that required a two-thirds majority for successful proposals, wherein the Left cleared this threshold and ignored the objections of the Right. This process led to one of the most progressive constitutional drafts in the world (Harrison 2022). Others have called it "Utopian Constitutionalism" (Landau and Dixon 2023). The referendum of September 4, 2022, rejected it by 62 percent. A new process was initiated immediately following the rejection. It also required approval by two-thirds of the constituent assembly, but this time the Right cleared the threshold and created a draft constitution that was more conservative than the Pinochet Constitution (after the amendments).[9] The referendum of December 17, 2023, rejected this one by 56 percent. At the time of writing this book, we do not know what the next step of the process will be. President Gabriel Boric has announced that he will not repeat the process for a third time.

What we see in this section is that in both Italy and Chile the amendment provisions are stringent but provide alternatives, and, consequently, the actors opt for the less stringent path (which, according to Chapter 2, is the referendum). Renzi was not able to get the two-thirds majority and had to go to a referendum; Bachelet failed even to design her amendments, and the new procedure involved new constitution drafting and a referendum for approval. Technically speaking, the Italian case falls within the constitutional amendment scope of the book, while the Chilean one starts as an amendment and develops as a constitutional

---

[9] For example, Mr. Gatica, who was blinded by rubber bullets shot by police in 2019 and was one of the reasons for the mobilization against the Pinochet Constitution, is now considering voting in favor of it because, as he says, "Unexpectedly, they managed to write an even worse constitution" (Nicas 2023). Actually, the argument can be made that both constitutions were further away from the preferences of the median voter (one to the Left and one to the Right) than the Pinochet Constitution as amended over the years. Points A and B in Figure 2.8 in Chapter 2 illustrate exactly this possibility.

replacement. However, they both deal with one or two referendum processes, and they both raise questions about the arguments made on referendums in Chapter 2 where they were presented as procedures without a core, consequently facilitating change. Here, we see amendments failing. Of course, it could still be the case that they were the most likely procedures to succeed, and all the others would have led to more patent failures. Nevertheless, it is a serious problem that we need to address, which will be the subject of the next section. There, I will bring more empirical examples in order to buttress my arguments.

4.3 Why So Many Failed Referendums?

We treated referendums in a separate section in Chapter 2 for two reasons. The first was theoretical: Because they are decided by simple majority, there is no core and, consequently, changes are easier to achieve. In addition, the win-set of the status quo (which was the concept we used for the investigation) is simply larger the bigger the size of the electoral body. The second reason was empirical because referendums are often mentioned or used on constitutional issues, whether they are amendments (like in Italy and Chile) or even replacements (like in Chile).

In our theoretical investigation, a fundamental assumption was the comparison of the amendment with the status quo. Indeed, the one investigative concept was the win-set of the status quo – that is, all the solutions that can defeat it – or the core, which is the set of points that cannot be defeated (that is, any invulnerable status quo). This comparison between the status quo and the amendment is legally guaranteed when the decision is made by a parliament or by a convention (which would adopt parliamentary procedures). As Rasch (2000: 15) argues, in an overwhelming majority of European countries, the most extreme alternatives are introduced first, which leads to the selection of the most central alternative as the final outcome,[10] or the status quo is formally voted last and compared with the predominant alternative (like in the

---

[10] In this latter procedure of successive voting (in Rasch's terms), the status quo survives over a series of the first alternatives (the more extreme ones) and possibly gets defeated early in the process, but the final outcome will be either this particular alternative or one that defeats it, which in one dimension means that both candidates are in the win-set of the status quo.

4.3 WHY SO MANY FAILED REFERENDUMS?

US). In both procedures, the winner is included in the win-set of the status quo.

Such a provision is not guaranteed to exist in referendums. It is possible that people prefer to modify or replace the constitution yet vote against the amendment or replacement. This is not necessarily a contradictory set of choices. Assume for one individual Voter I that there are four alternatives: The status quo (SQ), the amendment (A) as proposed, the amendment without some negative points according to his judgment (A¯i), and his own ideal choice (Ii). There are three different kinds of voters, all of them having their own ideal constitution (Ii) as their first choice and preferring the amendment without their objections (A¯i) over the amendment (A):

(1) The ones with the preferences A < SQ < A¯i < Ii
(2) The ones with the preferences A < A¯i < SQ < Ii
(3) The ones with the preferences SQ < A < A¯i < Ii

The differences among these three types are in respect to their evaluation of the status quo. Type (1) considers the status quo to be better than the amendment, and Type (2) prefers the status quo even after embellishments of the amendment. As a result, these two types will vote NO in a referendum. Type (3) voters would vote YES if they compare SQ and A, but NO if they compare A with A¯i or Ii.

Type (3) voters, if asked, would answer YES, that they want to amend (or replace) the constitution. If asked if they approve the amendment, they may reply NO if they compare it with A¯i or with Ii. Of course, there is no reason to believe that the different voters would have the same ideas about what these projects (A¯i or Ii) would be.

Political parties objecting to the referendum would try to make use of these popular preferences and persuade voters that the proposal includes all the negative points they are afraid of or that it does not include the things they desire. In particular, it is easy to make such arguments when the proposal involves over 50 (if it is an amendment) or 200 (if it is a whole constitution) articles. Voters often declare that they would like to know the content of the alternative but do not have time to read it.

The situation I just described would lead to an outcome like the ones we saw in Italy or in Chile: The people have explicitly asked for or are assumed to approve a replacement or a revision, but when this alternative is presented, it is voted down (in Chile, even twice!). The necessary condition for this development is that voters do not compare the alternative to the status quo but respond to different dilemmas prevailing in their own minds. Is there any evidence that this is the case?

The analytical tradition of "retrospective voting" created by V. O. Key is based exactly on the evaluation of one alternative: the incumbent alone. It is a well-known strategy among political strategists of the challenger to turn elections into a referendum on the incumbent. This way, they will turn all the voters who are dissatisfied with the incumbent in their favor. Further, it is the incumbent's strategy to bring the challenger's features into focus. President Biden expressed it most forcefully when journalists asked him about his low approval in the polls, responding, "Don't compare me to the almighty; compare me to the alternative" (White House 2023).

Other people argue about electoral competitions, claiming that they are not referendums. In all these arguments, referendums (and sometimes elections, too) are assumed to be simple one-issue evaluations. Is this true? In order to answer this question, we have to study the voters in the different referendums we spoke about in this chapter and understand their motives.

There are sparse poll data in Italy about why the Italian voters voted NO in their referendum. At the time of the vote, all political parties (including Berlusconi, who initially supported the amendment) advocated a NO vote. A series of research articles mention post-referendum polls by the Italian National Elections Studies Association, but all of them discuss the data without making a specific reference to how the data can be retrieved. Bergman (2019: 185) analyzes these data and finds that there are three factors that have a statistically significant impact on the NO vote: EU discontent (positive association), government performance (negative association), and referendum-specific (negative association). He explains that this referendum-specific variable is composed of four variables included in the amendment proposal (reduced number of senators, reduced power of the senate, centralization of infrastructure, and reduced quorum requirements for future referendums) which are analyzed by principal components (Bergman 2019: 182). This is not direct evidence but is corroborated by other articles that claim that the NO in the referendum was a decision against Renzi (I remind the reader that the prime minister had placed a target on him by declaring that he would leave if the amendments were rejected). Di Mauro and Memoli (2018) entitle their article "Targeting the Government in the Referendum: The Aborted 2016 Italian Constitutional Reform." Ceccarini and Bordignon (2017) in "Referendum on Renzi: The 2016 Vote on the Italian Constitutional Revision" summarize their point as follows: "The referendum turned into a vote on Renzi himself." Other analysts like Negri and Rebessi (2018) go

Table 4.1 *Reasons for "NO" vote of Chilean referendum in September 2022*

	First reason	Overall mentioned
Because the process that the constituents carried out was very bad/distrustful	21	40
Because of multinationalism and indigenous autonomy	16	35
Because I disapprove of President Boric's government	12	39
Due to the instability and political and economic uncertainty that generates fear and concern	12	24
Due to restrictions on freedom and private property in health, education, pensions, and housing	11	13
Because the country is on the wrong path in terms of economy, crime, and Mapuche conflict	9	13
It is not necessary to make a new constitution; it must be reformed	7	12
For value issues such as abortion, regionalism, feminism, and environmentalism	6	8
Due to changes to the political system	6	8

one step further and explain the reversal of Berlusconi's position, which was fatal for the amendment because of Renzi's support of Mattarella for president of the republic. All of these analysts argue that the political game and the support for the government were significant factors for the vote, but none of them focus on the reasons that the voters themselves would give.

The Chilean evidence is more to the point.[11] Cadem (2022) runs a survey immediately after the NO vote in September 2022. The results are presented in Table 4.1.

The reader can verify some policy evaluations about the role of the referendum – for example, the disagreement with the recognition of multinationalism and indigenous autonomy, the restrictions of freedom and private property, and objections to value issues like abortion. I remind the reader that this is a very progressive constitution, and these are right-wing objections. However, most objections are contextual: the

---

[11] This argument is an alternative to the one that states both proposals were extreme and rightfully rejected by the voters. Actually, each one of the explanations is sufficient for the NO vote (in this sense, they are competing, and further research will show which one is true).

Table 4.2 *Reasons for "NO" vote of Chilean referendum in December 2023*

	Most important reason
Don't like the proposal; many setbacks especially with abortion and women	55
Disapproves of the work of conventional Republicans, a right-wing constitution	28
Rejection or distrust of politicians and everything they propose	27
Constitution does not resolve the issues important for security, inflation, and health	18
Not informed, he was not interested	8
Supports of President Boric's government	7
Rejects of José Antonio Kast and Evelyn Matthei	5

process was inappropriate, the government is wrong, political and economic uncertainty, and so on.

More to the point, González-Ocantos and Meléndez (2024), based on data collected during this referendum, performed an "innovative conjoint experiment ... to estimate if different elements of the constitution sunk the proposal." Their conclusion is that "the incumbent's popularity significantly affected vote choice."

With respect to the second referendum, the rejection reasons according to the Cadem (2022) poll are presented in Table 4.2.

I will provide some more-to-the-point evidence from the EU because, after the European convention and a series of adjustments to the constitutional document[12] it produced, several EU countries chose to submit the constitutional document for evaluation by referendums. This process is exactly equivalent to a series of constitutional ratifications. While some of the countries who had selected the referendum process approved the document, two of the founding countries of the EU, France and the Netherlands, rejected it. The rejection produced a high level of anxiety across the EU first because of the status of the founding countries (particularly France) and second because it was not clear what the

---

[12] I use this term because, given that the EU is not a country, the term constitution would be inappropriate; however, for all practical purposes it works like a constitution of a federalist country.

implication of a NO vote was. While it was clear that the previous institutions would remain in place, it was not clear how the apparent impact would be overcome. The European Commission declared a six-month period of reflection, and all the European elites were extremely interested in the course of action to overcome the situation. In this context, the commission requested polls in the countries that rejected the constitutional document. The way these polls were performed was by asking open-ended questions and classifying the answers after the fact. The reason they chose this procedure was that the commission wanted to genuinely hear and study the opinion of the people who had rejected the new document. Among other things, this document was a significant simplification and replacement of all the past intergovernmental agreements of the EU countries, which were kept in place and altered by more recent documents.[13]

Table 4.3 presents the reasons why the two peoples voted NO in the referendum. From the differences in the answers, one can understand the superiority of the method selected (codifying the answers a posteriori). Focusing on the specific reasons, the factual irrelevance of the answers is quite impressive. For example, employment and economic conditions (in France) are irrelevant to the constitution. Opposition to national government is not an issue of European jurisdiction (in both countries) but of national electoral politics. The issue of the reduction of national sovereignty had already been materialized. Finally, the original irrelevance of the anti-Turkish feelings in France would have never been captured by a closed questionnaire.

After evaluating the situation the referendums created, the leaders of the EU decided not to use any referendums for the continuation of the process. In order to facilitate this decision, they removed the European flag (blue with twelve yellow stars) and the EU anthem (Beethoven's "Ode to Joy") so that there would not be reasons like abdication of national sovereignty that would justify the use of referendums. The commitment was firm and was followed in all countries except for Ireland, where it is constitutionally mandated.

According to my analysis, the vote of NO may depend on the number of voters of Type (3).[14] There were many such voters in the two reported

---

[13] This process has been studied in Finke et al. (2013) and, among other things, explains how the new institutions were created in the European convention (a remarkable success) and how the modification of EU institutions from the Nice Treaty of 2000 to the Lisbon Treaty of 2007 took almost a decade to be completed.

[14] See the start of Section 4.3.

Table 4.3 *What are all the reasons why you voted "NO" at the referendum on the European Constitution?*

a.	
France	
It will have negative effects on the employment situation in France/relocation of French enterprises/loss of jobs	31%
The economic situation in France is too weak/there is too much unemployment in France	26%
Economically speaking, the draft is too liberal	19%
Opposes the president of the republic/the national government/certain political parties	18%
Not enough social Europe	16%
Too complex	12%
Does not want Turkey in the European Union	6%
Loss of national sovereignty	5%
Lack of information	5%
I am against Europe/European construction/European integration	4%
I do not see what is positive in this text	4%
The draft goes too far/advances too quickly	3%
Opposition to further enlargement	3%
Not democratic enough	3%
Too technocratic/juridical/too much regulation	2%
I am against the Bolkestein directive	2%
I do not want a European political union/a European federal state/the "United States" of Europe	2%
The draft does not go far enough	1%
Other (SPECIFY)	21%
DK/NA	3%

b.	
The Netherlands	
Lack of information	32%
Loss of national sovereignty	19%
Opposes the national government/certain political parties	14%
Europe is too expensive	13%
I am against Europe/European construction/European integration	8%
It will have negative effects on the employment situation in the Netherlands/relocation of Dutch enterprises/loss of jobs	7%
I do not see what is positive in this text	6%

Table 4.3 (cont.)

b.	
The Netherlands	
The draft goes too far/advances too quickly	6%
Too technocratic/juridical/too much regulation	6%
Opposition to further enlargement	6%
Not democratic enough	5%
Too complex	5%
Economically speaking, the draft is too liberal	5%
The economic situation in the Netherlands is too weak/there is too much unemployment in the Netherlands	5%
I do not want a European political union/a European federal state/the "United States" of Europe	5%
Europe is evolving too fast	5%
The "Yes" campaign was not convincing enough	5%
This constitution is imposed on us	5%
The Netherlands must first settle its own problems	4%
I do not trust Brussels	4%
Does not want Turkey in the European Union	3%
Loss of Dutch identity	3%
Not enough social Europe	2%
There is nothing on human rights or on animal rights	2%
Influenced by the "No" campaign	2%
Other	7%
DK/NA	2%

referendums in the EU, fewer in Italy, and perhaps an insufficient number to be pivotal in Chile.

Conclusions

This chapter started with the presentation of complicated amendment provisions, which led us to the calculation of the core of the Italian case and the absence of it in the Chilean case. However, I explained why Article 129 in the Chilean case, which eliminates the core, will never be applied in a democratic country; consequently, in the empirical analysis that I perform in Chapter 6, I will use the combination of Articles 127 and 128 of the their constitution (but not Article 129). In both cases, the cores of the constitutions of these countries are large enough that successful constitutional amendment requires lots of preparation and successful coalition formation. In Chile, we saw that significant amendments required five years of negotiations to be successful.

I described the conditions of amendment (or replacement) failure in both countries, which were unanticipated referendum rejections. Although referendums were analyzed in Chapter 2 and were found to be malleable institutions, there were two reasons for these failures. In both cases, the agenda-setting institution was a partial reason. In Italy, the referendum was driven by Renzi's party alone. As I argued, it was a very reasonable amendment that would have improved the way Italian institutions function. In Chile, the first referendum was drafted by a left-wing coalition ignoring the preferences of the right-wing parties, and the second was the opposite. One can argue that what the Chilean people did was the only reasonable option against runaway elites who wanted to weaponize the constitution. The constitutional document of the EU did not provide any reasonable reasons for a return to the status quo. Lupia (1994, 2006) has argued that people use shortcuts in order to guess the reasonable answers to different political dilemmas that they face. With respect to the examples I gave in this chapter, one can argue that they did a very good job in Chile, a questionable one in Italy, and a bad one in the EU. However, one particular modification of institutions would help the popular decision-making. I demonstrated that a plausible reason for the failures was that people – specifically Type (3) voters – very often do not seem to focus on the actual question, which is the comparison of the amendment to the status quo.

Cancellation of constitutional referendums (as they did in the EU) would produce the results desired by the political elites by moving the power to make decisions on complicated issues from the masses back to them. However, an alternative procedure would be to make sure that coalition building is necessary for the constitutional design phase – that is, the constituent assembly (a proportional electoral system and qualified majority bigger than anticipated splits would achieve that result).[15]

---

[15] In Chile, the threshold was placed at two-thirds, which is reasonable, but the Left (the first time) and the Right (the second time) managed to clear this threshold. The electoral system was not the same, and while the public may have changed its opinion from one election to the next, the fact that in the first convention there were 17 out of 155 members of the indigenous population while in the second there were 1 out of 51 indicates at least a lack of proportionality of at least one of the electoral systems.

Further, a modification of the question of the referendum so that it would include the status quo would extend the courtesy of making the actual question apparent not only to the elites (as it is done by parliamentary procedures) but to the people as well. So, instead of "Do you want this amendment (or this constitution), yes or no?", the question should be: "Do you prefer this amendment (or this constitution) to the current one?". These institutional modifications make a proposal more difficult to emerge, but, when it does, it is more likely to be accepted because it will be supported by the consensus of parties that contributed to its design and, consequently, amendments will be more durable.

The rewording of the question I am proposing may be an issue involving serious political debate. In order to make sure that the process is not hijacked politically, the summary of the question (once the amendment or the alternative is finished) may be delegated to the judiciary or to a specially appointed committee of experts selected by a supermajority.

As we saw in Chapter 1, there is an aversion of political elites toward referendums. The reason is that referendums supersede their legislative authority. However, there are cases where referendums are the only way to respect the popular will. In Chapter 1, we showed examples of simple questions like abortion or the electoral system where the legislature disagrees with the public and tries to reduce the applicability of referendums in order to have its preferences prevail. There are cases in which referendums are excluded as a means to make decisions – for example, on taxes in several jurisdictions. There are cases in which the question is evaluated by the judiciary and the referendum may be aborted. In Italy, unconstitutional referendums have to be approved by the Constitutional Court, which evaluates if the issue is simple enough to have a YES or NO answer.

Briefly, I proposed two amendments to the referendum process. At the level of agenda setting, I proposed a competitive (among potential agenda setters) and/or restrictive (with involvement of the judiciary) process which eliminates unconstitutional or extreme proposals. At the level of voting, I proposed institutional solutions that "turn the referendum into an election" – that is, identify the issue precisely.[16] The amendments I am proposing are simple and less restrictive than the existing practices and are designed to preserve referendums rather than eliminate them.

---

[16] In elections, the different parties try to focus against their opponent and "turn the election to a referendum" on this opponent. I am making an institutional proposal for the reverse in referendums.

5

A Case of Successful Amendments: Mexico

Most scholars examining the amendment provisions of the Mexican Constitution commonly view it as rigid, anticipating infrequent amendments (Lutz 1994, Lorenz 2005, Lijphart 2012, Anckar and Karvonen 2015, Velasco-Rivera 2019, Velasco-Rivera 2021). However, despite the stringent requirements for approval, which entail a two-thirds majority in both the House and the Senate along with the support of a majority of the states of the Mexican federation, the actual frequency of amendments is remarkably high (amended over 700 times since 1917 [Cámara de Diputados 2023]). While most of this period was under a single-party government, in which case this party could make as many amendments as it wanted, it later became a multiparty government. Despite that, though, the frequency of amendments has actually increased (this is the period I cover in the comparative part of this book). In the period from 2000 to 2015, there have been 4,026 amendment attempts, 326 of which succeeded. This amendment rate of (326 / 16 =) 20.31 amendments per year presents a puzzle, which is the focus of this chapter.

Some scholarship attributes the frequency of changes to a form of name-calling, exemplified by the term "constitutional fetishism" as described by Velasco-Rivera (2021: 1049), which suggests a belief among reformers that altering the constitutional text will solve real-life problems. Alternatively, others perceive the increasing amendment rate as a product of a "national culture" that exhibits minimal respect for their constitution (Ibarra Palafox 2016). The "national culture" argument is explained by Ginsburg and Melton (2015) who state that in Mexico "stakes of amendment are lower, and so cultural resistance to amend is less than in societies where it is infrequent" (689).

On the other hand, other researchers attribute the frequency of amendments to the political game superseding the institutions (Negretto 2012, Velasco-Rivera 2021). Negretto (2012) posits the argument that "the most rigid amendment procedure can become flexible in a dominant party system, as under the hegemony of the Institutional

Revolutionary Party (Partido Revolucionario Institucional, PRI) in Mexico. By contrast, a flexible amendment procedure may become rigid in practice if party system fragmentation becomes very high, as has been the case in Ecuador since 1979" (760). These arguments are consistent with the analysis in Chapter 2 of this book.

Here, I will add a third component to Negretto's argument, suggesting that even within a fragmented party system a consensus mode can enable parties to achieve more power and overcome institutional constraints. I will also explain why the Mexican Constitution is not as rigid as some researchers contend as well as how its length and inconsistencies generate the need for amendments.

I will analyze the amendment provisions of the Mexican Constitution by identifying its core and providing institutional reasons that explain why the actual amendment provisions are not as formidable as commonly perceived (Section 5.1). Then, I will provide textual reasons that indicate the Constitution's exceptionally lengthy and contradictory nature (Section 5.2). I will next give political reasons that demonstrate that qualified majorities, as required by the Constitution, are the norm in Mexican politics, which is evident not only during the Revolutionary Institutional Party's (PRI's) dominance but also in the current context of multipartyism (Section 5.3). Finally, I will scrutinize successful amendments during the period of 2000–2013 and assess the significance of the reasons discussed in Sections 5.1 and 5.3 (Section 5.4).[1]

5.1 Is the Mexican Constitution Rigid?

Article 135 of the Mexican Constitution states these requirements: "The vote of two-thirds of the present members of the Congress of the Union is required to make amendments or additions to the Constitution. Once the Congress agrees on the amendments or additions, these must be approved by the majority of state legislatures." These requirements are visualized in Figure 2.5 of Chapter 2 which presents a constitutional core that is significant in size.

Some researchers consider the amendment mechanism of the Mexican Constitution to be quite similar to the US Constitution. For example, Velasco-Rivera (2021) argues that "the constitutional amendment mechanism of the Mexican Constitution of 1857 (reproduced in the

---

[1] The length and inconsistency of the Constitution (Section 5.2) are always present.

Constitution of 1917) and Article V of the U.S. Constitution are very similar in design" (1042). Actually, the only textual difference between Article V (US) and Article 135 (Mexico) is that a three-fourths majority of the states is required in the US while a simple majority of the states is required in Mexico. When I examine the Mexican institutions more closely, I will show that the differences are wide.

The most important difference between the US and Mexican reform procedures is that in Mexico Article 63 establishes that "neither the Chamber of Deputies nor the Chamber of Senators shall be allowed to open their sessions or perform their duties without the presence of at least half plus one of their respective members." The result of the combination of Articles 63 and 135 is that in order to modify the Mexican Constitution one-third of the members of the House and the Senate is required (if it happens that almost half of them are not present). Reexamining the arguments in Chapter 2, it becomes clear that under those conditions there is no constitutional core, and any provision can be changed (if members of the two chambers decide not to be present in the discussion and vote). So, with less than three-fourths of the members present, there is no constitutional core in Mexico.[2]

There is, however, a second and almost as important difference between the two countries: the distribution of preferences in the states. In Mexico, because of the electoral system of the country (which until the electoral reform of 2014 did not permit any elected representative to stand for immediate reelection in the same position), all the party representatives had a serious allegiance to their party, which was responsible for their political career. Indeed, the faithful representatives could be moved from one position to another, while the problematic ones would lose their party favors. This means that state representatives would vote the way their parties instructed, not the way their constituents wanted. In contrast, US state representatives will faithfully represent their constituencies because of individual electoral competition. As a result, the diversity among US states is significantly higher than that of Mexican ones. So, to get three-fourths of the states in the US to agree is a herculean task, as the failure of the Equal Rights Amendment to recognize equality between the genders demonstrates. By contrast, no Mexican

---

[2] The number three-fourths is calculated so that if that many people are present, two-thirds of the present members are a simple majority the whole chamber: two-thirds × three-fourths = one-half.

constitutional amendment cleared the other obstacles but got aborted by the states.

Empirical evidence corroborates these statements: The success rate of proposed amendments is much higher in Mexico than in the US. Between 1997 and 2015, spanning six legislative periods, there were 4,034 constitutional reform initiatives proposed and 326 adopted in Mexico, which means that there was a success rate of 8.08 percent.[3] By contrast, in the US, the number of submitted amendments was 11,969, while the actual amendments adopted were 27. The success rate was 0.0022 (Stohler et al. 2022). These results are consistent with the argument that constitutional rigidity in Mexico is much lower than in the US.[4]

5.2 Length and Inconsistencies of the Mexican Constitution

The first argument I will make is that the Mexican Constitution requires many changes – that is, the constant amendments of the Constitution are an equilibrium phenomenon where the different actors behave the way they are expected to. There are two reasons for this: first, the Constitution is long, and second, it is inconsistent.

5.2.1 Length of Mexican Constitution

All comparative constitutional analyses lead to the conclusion that the length of a constitution is positively correlated with the frequency of amendments (see Chapter 7). Along with all of the references mentioned in the introduction of this chapter, other analyses that do not find any relationship between constitutional rigidity and frequency of amendments still find a relationship between length and frequency of amendments. For example, Ginsburg and Melton (2015) dispute whether the

---

[3] The number of initiatives increased dramatically from the one-party dominance to the multiparty system in Mexico.

[4] It is interesting to investigate why there have been so many amendments with such a low success rate in the US. All the analyses refer to reasons that are nonrelevant to the Constitution. For example, Bárcena Juárez (2017) argues that in the absence of immediate reelection during the period under review, legislators intending to prolong their political careers must find a way to position themselves to transition to the next political position outside the legislature. Brunner (2013) argues that a high proportion of amendments are introduced by minority party legislators in order to promote out of legislature careers (Brunner 2013, Bárcena Juárez 2017). A similar analysis of non-constitutionally relevant reasons regarding the US can be found in Stohler et al. (2022).

amendment rules matter at all and "go on to develop a measure of amendment culture as an alternative to institutional factors that constrain amendment" (691). However, they do find a positive correlation with length, and they also argue:

> Along with our co-author Zachary Elkins, we have celebrated the virtues of what we might call statutory constitutions: those with flexible amendment thresholds that are fairly detailed. The constitutions of India, Mexico, and Brazil, to take three prominent examples, are amended nearly every year. Such constitutions have the virtue of being frequently changed through internal mechanisms, avoiding the costly route of a total replacement. In such countries, we argue that the stakes of amendment are lower, and so cultural resistance to amend is less than in societies where it is infrequent. (Ginsburg and Melton 2015: 689)

Similarly, Versteeg and Zackin (2016) claim that "the measure [of constitutional entrenchment] does not rely on formal amendment rules because these rules are mediated so dramatically by political norms" (661) and find a correlation between length and frequency of amendments.

Consequently, according to all researchers, the length of a constitution is correlated with the frequency of amendments, and thus the high frequency of constitutional amendments in Mexico is consistent with the 62,612 words it contains (Constitute Project 2015). However, the size of the Mexican Constitution has not been the same over the years. According to the Belisario Domínguez Institute, it started as a 21,382-word document, and over the years it kept expanding (Giles Navarro 2018). According to Rivera León (2017),

> A good example is the case of Article 41. Originally, Article 41 consisted of a single, 7-line paragraph. Those 7 lines contained 63 words. Currently, Article 41 has more than 70 paragraphs with nearly 5000 words. The level of detail in Article 41 (which currently regulates political parties and electoral administration) is truly surprising. It defines political parties and their creation, mathematical formulas for calculating public financing for political parties, percentages, and differentiations of the financing depending on the type of election. It also sets rules for precampaigns, specifies the number of minutes (honestly, the number of minutes!) political parties are entitled to on television and in the media during campaigns, describes the complete organization of the National Electoral Institute, sets up a complex network outlining the powers of the National Electoral Institute and local electoral institutes, etc. In conclusion, Article 41 is clearly set up as an Electoral Code. (Rivera León 2017: 24)

The consequence of including such an extensive Article 41 is that any time a modification is necessary, the required procedure is a constitutional amendment.

Similarly, according to Orozco Pulido (2020), "The original constitution of February 5th, 1917, had only nineteen transitory articles. Considering that the Constitution was written during a transitional period following a revolution, this seems to be a coherent number. The education reform of May 15th, 2019, includes eighteen transitory articles and sets complex rules related to the contents and implementation of the reform" (209). Also, Orozco Pulido (2020) argues that the Mexican Constitution has not respected the golden rules of writing with precision, clarity, and without ambiguity as they do not practice "writing in the active voice, in the present tense, preferring shorter sentences rather than longer ones, careful wording, and using positive statements instead of negative ones" (206).[5]

5.2.2 Inconsistencies of the Mexican Constitution

In principle, inconsistencies should not exist inside a legal text for the simple reason that the different parts of an inconsistent statement may become the basis of different arguments. This will lead to contradictory conclusions, and it will not be clear which one of these conclusions should prevail. However, a constitution is not just a legal document but also a political one, and it reflects the conditions that prevailed at the moment of its adoption (or the adoption of its amendments). It is possible that at the moment of the adoption of a constitution, or even an amendment of a constitution, different participating groups had different opinions, and they tried to resolve their differences. According to the literature, the Mexican Constitution is full of inconsistencies. Our goal, though, is not to identify whether they were due to political compromises or to lack of care.

Fix-Fierro and Valadés (2015) have collaboratively overseen a scholarly endeavor concerning the structural organization and fortification of the Mexican Constitution. The study delineates several noteworthy observations:

(1) Some constitutional provisions are redundant.
(2) The Constitution exhibits an irregularity in the application of terminology.

---

[5] This statement is in reference to Bowman (2006).

(3) There exists a pronounced variance in the extent of discourse on diverse subjects.
(4) The Constitution manifests an evident disarray in the thematic categorization of its articles.
(5) The Constitution presents suboptimal positioning of certain provisions.
(6) The constitutional manuscript contains terminological inaccuracies.
(7) Some articles, intrinsically regulatory in nature, operate akin to subsidiary directives across various domains.

Overall, it can be observed that the Mexican Constitution has several issues in terms of legal inconsistencies (Fix-Fierro and Valadés 2015).

Pozas-Loyo et al. (2022) have identified another dimension of the Mexican Constitution that is generated by these inconsistencies: "A strong and creative judicial interpretation was made necessary by the effects hyper-reformism had on the Constitution: it made it a very long, complex, and at times inconsistent text. Under this constitution creative judicial interpretation was required for solving the many conflicts created by the very nature of the text" (3). The result of their analysis is that, unlike in other countries, in Mexico there is a positive correlation between constitutional amendments (i.e., changes to the constitution generated by the political system) and judicial interpretation (i.e., changes to the legal systems performed by the judiciary).[6] Pozas-Loyo et al. (2022) base their analysis on the contradictions of the Mexican Constitution (a term they use eight times in their article), but they are not the only ones who do so; other analyses share the same basis (Pou Giménez 2018, Pozas-Loyo and Saavedra-Herrera 2021).

Arguments have been presented suggesting that the inconsistencies generated by constitutional reforms are so severe that a transition towards a new constitutional pact is necessary. For instance, Cárdenas Gracia (1994, 1998) suggests that the Constitution has a nondemocratic design and that the rules of political processes are influenced by meta-constitutional factors. Similarly, González Oropeza (1998) maintains that the Mexican president has been the sole reformer of the Constitution, leading to the constitutional text becoming a government agenda for the incumbent president.

---

[6] In other countries, high constitutional rigidity leads to low amendment frequency and high judicial independence (Lutz 1994, Tsebelis 2022).

In conclusion, the Mexican Constitution was not long and contradictory from the beginning and did not need to become as such. However, once it developed these characteristics, it had to be amended often, and the amendments had to be interpreted by the Supreme Court frequently in order to address the problems generated.

5.3 Constitutional Coalitions

In Mexican politics, broad coalitions in the legislative arena are very frequent. Originally, in 1988, this phenomenon of convergence and exchange among the political parties was named "concertacesiónes." Ortiz Gallegos (2007) contends that the neologism "concertacesión" implies a scenario where one side gives up something in exchange for an advantage provided by the other party. There are three different ways of eliminating differences (Tsebelis and Hahm 2014): (1) by finding some middle way between the different points of view (some kind of weighted average); (2) by eliminating or obscuring the differences between the different points (so that different behaviors would be consistent with the text); or (3) by separating the issues and permitting one side to prevail in one issue and another in a different issue. In Tsebelis and Hahm's empirical analysis of the European Fiscal Compact, the method most often used was the elimination of differences (Method 2), while "concertacesión" is clearly the trading across issues method (Method 3). This phenomenon has been widely studied, and different explanations have been provided. Because of this, in this section I analyze the political reasons for why parties decide to take their agreements to the constitutional level through broad coalitions. I argue that an explanation for this phenomenon must address the political issue along with the institutional one. I explore different episodes of convergence of political parties to carry out constitutional reforms. My aim in this section is to emphasize the need to incorporate political behavior to understand constitutional reforms. I demonstrate why it is rational to amend the constitution once political agreements have been reached.

Mexico was dominated in the twentieth century by the PRI (Revolutionary Institutional Party) which was the only party at the time and controlled all three institutions (presidency, House, and Senate) for most of the century. The fact that it was a "dominant party system" explains why it could make any decision it wanted and include it in the Constitution. This is why I begin my study of constitutional amendments at the year 2000 when the presidency was occupied by another party, the right-wing PAN (National Action Party). During the period of sole rule, the PRI was a corporatist party that included leftist elements. However, beginning in the 1980s there was a shift in the policy positions of the PRI towards free markets, and this shift was officialized with the modification of Article 27 of the Constitution in coalition with PAN in 1992. In addition, in 1988 there was a political shift, and an agreement was made with the PAN. Later, there was a (successful) attempt to add the left-wing party (the Party of the Democratic Revolution, or the PRD) to the coalition. I will analyze two significant achievements of the periods under study, the multiple modifications of Article 73, and the Pact for Mexico. Given the existence of this three-party coalition during the period I am covering, enshrining party agreements inside the Constitution is a dominant strategy for all the actors involved. Therefore, one of the reasons for the high frequency of constitutional amendments is the wide agreement among Mexican political parties.

5.3.1 The Reform of Article 27 of the Constitution and NAFTA

Beginning in 1982, the federal government, led by Miguel de la Madrid (of the PRI), initiated a shift in the country's economic direction. The administration started to distance itself from nationalist economic policies and embarked on a process of economic liberalization (Soederberg 2005, Escalante Gonzalbo 2015). Subsequently, in the early years of Carlos Salinas de Gortari's administration, a process of deepening economic liberalization commenced which would culminate in the North American Free Trade Agreement (NAFTA). However, the Mexican Constitution did not allow foreign investment in the exploitation of natural resources, necessitating its amendment. The passage of the constitutional reforms in Mexico to facilitate the ratification of NAFTA represents a pivotal moment where economic imperatives catalyzed political collaboration, transcending typical partisan boundaries. Acknowledging the paramount importance of NAFTA for Mexico's economic growth, the PRI and the PAN engaged in strategic alliances not out of institutional necessity but because of a shared recognition of the treaty's significance in enhancing the country's economic stature vis-à-vis its North American counterparts, the US and Canada.

This political calculus was predicated on the understanding that NAFTA was not merely a trade agreement but a critical lever for Mexico's economic development and modernization. The constitutional impediments, specifically those within Article 27 that restricted private and foreign investment in land and natural resources, were at odds with NAFTA's liberalizing agenda (Zamora 1992, Arellanes Jiménez 2014). As such, a political agreement was essential for amending these provisions to align with the requirements of free trade and the attraction of foreign investment.

The political will to forge expansive legislative coalitions was evident in the overwhelming majorities that voted in favor of the amendments: a unanimous vote in the Senate (fifty votes in favor and zero against) and a significant majority in the Chamber of Deputies (387 votes in favor and 50 against). This was a strategic and deliberate political maneuvering by the PRI and the PAN, underlining the treaty's crucial role in Mexico's economic trajectory, and their substantial agreement signaled a momentous shift towards economic integration with the global market. It was this pursuit of economic prosperity through free trade that necessitated and justified the creation of such broad legislative alliances, emphasizing the role of NAFTA as a catalyst for cross-party cooperation in the Mexican political landscape. This analysis focuses on the economic policy positions of the two parties. The political dimension follows.

5.3.2 The Birth of Multipartyism in Mexico

Before 1988, the PRI had no need to negotiate with any opposition parties since it controlled both chambers of the federal Congress and all the governorships. It was the textbook example of a hegemonic party (Magaloni 2006). However, by 1988, the landscape was altered significantly as the PRI found itself compelled to negotiate with opposition parties following the presidential election in which the PRI candidate Carlos Salinas de Gortari assumed power amid widespread illegitimacy accusations (Becerra et al. 2011, Woldenberg 2012) and allegations of electoral fraud (Cantú 2019). This led to a political process of interparty bargaining known as "concertacesiónes." Arguably, the most memorable "concertacesión" took place between the PRI and the PAN in 1988.

Given that Carlos Salinas assumed the presidency with a broad shadow of illegitimacy, he had to negotiate with the PAN to have them accept his mandate and approve a series of reforms (Ortiz Gallegos 2007). Part of the arrangements that the PAN set with Carlos Salinas was that the PRI and Salinas himself would recognize and respect their electoral victories at the gubernatorial level. This moment marked a significant turning point in negotiation strategies as a behavior rooted in compensation

Table 5.1 *Congressional seats of main parties in Mexico (1997–2015)*

Number of seats in House from 1997 to 2015

Legislature	Period	PAN	PRI	PRD	REST	PRI + PAN	PRI + PAN percent
LVII	1997–2000	122	239	125	14	361	72.2
LVIII	2000–2003	206	211	50	33	417	83.4
LIX	2003–2006	152	224	96	28	376	75.2
LX	2006–2009	206	106	127	61	312	62.4
LXI	2009–2012	143	237	69	51	380	76
LXII	2012–2015	114	213	101	72	327	65.4

Number of seats in Senate from 1997 to 2015

Legislature	Period	PAN	PRI	PRD	REST		
LVII	1997–2000	33	77	16	2	110	85.9
LVIII–LIX	2000–2006	46	60	16	6	106	82.8
LX–LXI	2006–2012	52	33	26	17	85	66.4
LXII	2012–2015	38	52	22	16	90	70.3

mechanisms began, which still persists to this day. This moment was the birth of multipartyism in Mexico.

This political exchange of mutual recognition (presidency vs. governors) had significant legislative and constitutional implications because the PRI was the median party in both chambers of Congress. Because of this, it needed to approve any piece of legislation to clear Congress, and from 2000 onward it alternated in the presidential position with the PAN. As a result, an agreement of these two parties was necessary for any political solution in Mexico. However, as Table 5.1 demonstrates, this PRI–PAN agreement was also sufficient for any constitutional amendment. The last column of the table shows the percentage of votes that the PRI and the PAN represented with respect to the total membership of the Chamber of Deputies and the Senate. It is evident that most of the time the percentages were above two-thirds of the total number of members of the corresponding chamber. For the few cases that this was not the case, a few abstentions in the corresponding chamber would clear the two-thirds majority of the members present that was specified by the

Constitution.[7] Therefore, the bipartisan agreement which was necessary for legislative action was also sufficient for constitutional decisions. Nevertheless, as I show in Section 5.4, the PRI and the PAN expanded their coalition to the successfully left-wing PRD.

5.3.3 Centralization Through Article 73

The unanimous pattern of amendments to Article 73 of the Mexican Constitution by the three principal political parties of the study period – the PRI, the PAN, and the PRD – serve as a paradigmatic example of strategic consensus-building aimed at the recalibration of power dynamics within the federation. Article 73 serves as a delineation of congressional functions and is composed of a multitude of sections, each detailing specific legislative competencies. It is pertinent to note that the Mexican constitutional framework, specifically Article 124, bestows residual powers to the states akin to the Tenth Amendment of the US Constitution (Serna de la Garza 2016). Thus, any expansion of Article 73 inherently signifies a centralization of authority; it systematically extracts governance on specific issues from the purview of state jurisdictions and incorporates them into the federal legislative domain.

The amendment of Article 73, and, consequently, the centralization of functions, represents a confluence of political objectives across the PRI, the PAN, and the PRD. This strategic alignment reflects a collective pursuit of enhancing federal legislative power – a move that invariably consolidates the roles and influence of these major parties within the national governance architecture. Such a concerted approach underscores a shared political agreement among Mexico's dominant parties: that the fortification of federal power is instrumental to their broader political aspirations.

Article 73 is the most frequently amended article in the history of the 1917 Constitution during the period being studied and is one which the political parties almost unanimously agreed to amend. Between 2000 and 2013, Article 73 was modified twenty-seven times, accounting for 39.71 percent of the sixty-eight constitutional reforms observed during that period. Generally, amendments to Article 73 are instrumental in bringing about significant changes to the political system as legislators seek to equip themselves with the requisite authority to legislate on various

---

[7] See Article 63 in Section 5.1.

domains that were not explicitly addressed in the original wording of the Constitution.

The modifications of Article 73 can be classified either as direct or indirect (aimed at bestowing additional powers to Congress by making changes to other articles of the Constitution). Out of the total reforms observed from 2000 to 2013, there were twelve direct amendments made to Article 73, constituting 44.44 percent of all reforms to this article. In each of these cases, Congress expanded its powers. Notably, all twelve direct amendments were approved by the PRI–PAN–PRD coalition.

Additionally, there were fifteen indirect reforms, making up 55.56 percent of all reforms to Article 73. It is significant to note that fourteen of these fifteen modifications were approved by the PRI–PAN–PRD coalition.[8] An illustrative example of indirect modification of Article 73 is the establishment of ordinary legislation on national security, which necessitated the modification of Article 89 of the Constitution as well as Article 73. Similarly, the constitutional autonomy of the National Institute of Statistics and Geography (INEGI) required a concurrent amendment to Article 26 and Article 73. Furthermore, during a major political-electoral reform in 2013, which involved various aspects of the political regime, Congress was granted the power to ratify different secretaries of state. Consequently, Article 73 had to be amended to empower the legislative branch to perform these new functions.

As can be observed, there was an agreement to reform this article by the most relevant political parties of the period in twenty-six out of twenty-seven reforms, implying a convergence of the three political forces in 96.3 percent of the cases. These episodes of convergence can be explained by the fact that the reforms to Article 73 involve the centralization of powers in the federal Congress. In this sense, parties can generate broad agreements because the reforms to Article 73 grant more powers to political parties represented at the federal level.

5.3.4 The Pact for Mexico

The Pact for Mexico marked a seminal political accord that was consummated by the collective resolve of the nation's three principal political forces: the PRI, the PAN, and the PRD. This alliance, forged at the dawn of Enrique Peña Nieto's presidency, was dedicated to executing

---

[8] The only exception (the electoral reform of 2013) will be discussed in Section 5.3.4.

substantial and necessary reforms across a spectrum of policy areas, notably transforming the energy sector and advancing economic liberalization, each of which necessitated constitutional recalibration (del Tronco Paganelli and Hernández Estrada 2017, Mayer-Serra 2017).

Within the framework of the Pact for Mexico, a remarkable consensus was reached among the PRI, the PAN, and the PRD, leading to the ratification of a sweeping array of constitutional reforms ("Pacto por México" 2012). These included progressive changes in different topics such as anticorruption, transparency, telecommunications, and education, which demonstrated an unprecedented tripartite agreement aimed at modernizing the nation's infrastructural and institutional fabric. However, this unanimity did not extend to all reforms; notably, the electoral reform and the energy reform emerged as distinct outliers, with the latter becoming a particularly contentious issue within this tripartite alliance (del Tronco Paganelli and Hernández Estrada 2017).

The 2013 energy reform stands out as a contentious pivot within the Pact for Mexico, primarily due to the PRD's resistance to perceived encroachments upon national sovereignty. This led to a realignment of the PRI with the PAN, which held a pro-market perspective that was more amenable to the reform's objectives. The PAN's strategic position enabled it to negotiate the integration of its policy preferences into the energy reform and to extract a commitment from the PRI to support an impending political-electoral reform as part of the Pact's broader agenda (del Tronco Paganelli and Hernández Estrada 2017).

The political-electoral reform, eventually ratified in late 2013, instituted a raft of significant alterations to the political system. It saw the creation of the National Electoral Institute with expanded powers, an increase in the vote threshold for proportional representation, and provisions for the consecutive reelection of legislative and municipal officials. These changes, coupled with the energy reform (which sanctioned private sector participation in energy exploitation for the first time since the 1950s), signified a substantial shift in Mexico's energy model and a move towards strengthening the nation's democratic governance (Barrientos Del Monte and Añorve 2014).

The Pact for Mexico transcended mere policymaking; it epitomized a strategic political maneuver designed to forge wide-ranging coalitions capable of enacting constitutional reforms. The unanimity with which several reforms were approved underlines this approach. However, it is crucial to discern that the formation of such expansive alliances was not dictated by institutional mandates or exigencies. Instead, these coalitions were the product of deliberate political strategy, a testament to the power of negotiation and consensus-building across party lines. This climate of cooperation was not born out of institutional necessity[9] but rather from a concerted effort to achieve a shared vision for the nation's advancement. The political will to collaborate was the driving force behind this unified front, rendering the Pact for Mexico a pivotal catalyst in redefining Mexico's legislative achievements in the absence of any institutional compulsion.

5.3.5 Why Amend the Constitution and Not Produce Ordinary Legislation?

I demonstrated that trading across issues has been a very instrumental method to generate consensus among political parties in multiparty Mexico. A major enabler of this outcome is the centralization of Mexican parties. According to Velasco-Rivera (2021), negotiations are highly centralized; thus, agreements can be reached more easily. Political parties with congressional representation demonstrate a high degree of discipline owing to the regulation exerted by the national leadership (Nacif 2002). Given that the national leadership oversees the nomination procedures, legislators are incentivized to comply with directives from the leadership.

The consolidation of parliamentary discipline is reinforced by the institutional design inherent in the Mexican Congress. Various institutions bolster centralized decision-making. The most significant among these is the Political Coordination Board (JUCOPO), where the parliamentary leaders of political parties convene and forge consensuses. The JUCOPO is responsible for evaluating reform proposals once they have been examined by the committees and has the prerogative to schedule them for discussion on the floor once they have been previously agreed upon.

Once this consensus is achieved, enshrining it in the Constitution is a dominant strategy for two reasons: first, to tie their own hands, and second, to restrict the judicial branch from altering these agreements.

Tying the Political System's Hands

The process of incorporating political parties' agreements into the constitutional text serves as a mechanism to effectively lock these agreements in

---

[9] As Table 5.1 demonstrates, institutional necessity would require only two parties (the PRI and the PAN).

place, safeguarding them against potential reform and constitutional revision (Fix-Fierro and Valadés 2015). One significant aspect of this dynamic is the convergence of political parties in approving constitutional reforms with the intent to "protect" the understandings achieved between different political forces from potential changes in government and shifts in the majority within Congress. By enshrining these agreements within the Constitution, any future attempts to modify or overturn them would require a new consensus among political factions, thus creating a higher barrier for alteration. For example, a simple legislative majority would not be able to unilaterally alter these agreements through ordinary legislation (Salazar Ugarte 2013, Fix-Fierro 2017). This is due to the entrenched nature of constitutional provisions, which require a more extensive and rigorous process for amendment compared to ordinary legislation.

This is an important point that needs to be examined under the lens of the three-tiered system of rulemaking I discussed in the Introduction (Table I.2): changes that occur within the constitutional equilibrium (legislation and statutory interpretation by the courts); changes that occur outside the constitutional equilibrium (constitutional amendments); and changes of the constitution itself. The reason that we differentiate between Levels 1 and 2 (within the constitutional equilibrium and outside it) is that constitutional amendments are more difficult than ordinary legislation. However, what we see in Mexico is that the majorities necessary to pass legislation (the coalition between the PRI and the PAN) are also sufficient to pass constitutional amendments. As a result, when passing amendments becomes as easy as legislation, then the amendment strategy becomes dominant.

Restricting Checks by the Judiciary

Another advantage of constitutional amendments is the restriction of judicial interferences. Constitutional amendments cannot be superseded by the supreme court's decisions as ordinary legislation lies beyond the scope of the court's scrutiny, thereby shielding the incorporated agreements from legal challenges or potential invalidation by judicial interpretation. As a result, including the agreements in the constitution ensures that they remain immune to judicial interference and reinforces their binding nature.

However, as shown in this research, none of these arguments is indisputable or even as strong in Mexico compared to other countries. Constitutional amendments can be overruled by other constitutional amendments (and in Mexico this is done frequently), and the Supreme Court interprets the Constitution with unusually high frequency (see Section 5.1). Nevertheless, including agreements in the Constitution is a dominant strategy because it still provides them with a constitutional shield (no matter how ineffective, this is better than ordinary legislation or no legislation at all).

5.4 The Frequency of Threshold-Clearing Majorities and Oversized Coalitions

In Chapter 2, I described under what conditions a core will or will not exist. If it exists, modification of the constitution is impossible unless the status quo is outside the core; if it does not, it is feasible. In Section 5.1, I explained why Article 63 adds significant flexibility to the amendment rules of the Mexican Constitution (Article 135). In Section 5.3, I described how and why party coalitions emerged and included the amendment of the Constitution as one of their goals. I also explained why the states did not object to anything the parties wanted, including the decisions related to the centralization of power (which, in principle, should have been opposed). Now, I will synthesize all these arguments and see how often they describe the political situation in Mexico.

Figure 5.1 presents the profile of the sixty-eight constitutional amendments adopted in Mexico during the period under examination (from 2000 to 2013),[10] showing the institutional thresholds achieved, the composition of the coalitions, and the significance of amendments (as a function of the number of constitutional articles affected).

Coalitions

The shape of the points indicates the coalitions that promoted the amendments. We can see that the overwhelming majority of amendments – sixty-one out of sixty-eight, or 90 percent – were the result of an agreement between the three major parties. Only five out of sixty-eight were a PAN–PRI coalition, and two more were none of the above.

---

[10] This number is different from the 326 successful constitutional amendment initiatives presented in Section 5.3. This is because different initiatives for constitutional reform on the same subject are consolidated into a single document, which is prepared in the constitutional points committees of Congress (Fix-Fierro 2017).

5.4 CLEARING MAJORITIES AND OVERSIZED COALITIONS 143

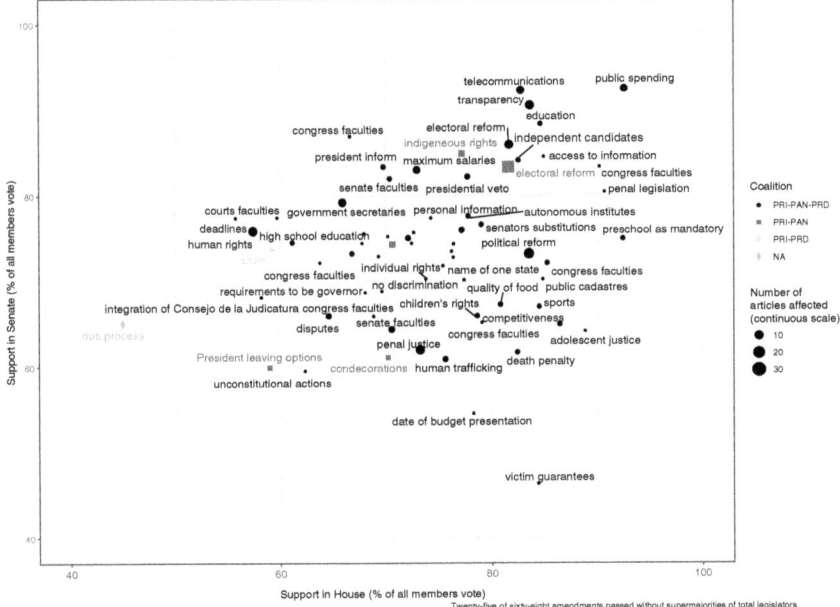

Figure 5.1 House and Senate support for constitutional amendments in Mexico from 2000 to 2013 by topic, coalition, and number of articles affected

Significance

The size of the points approximates the significance of the amendments: The more articles the reform affects, the greater the significance and, therefore, the greater the size of the circles will be.

A simple observation of Figure 5.1 indicates that the most significant amendments were achieved by the agreement of all three major parties with the exception of the electoral reform. The amendment on electoral reform, although included in the Pact of Mexico (and therefore signed by all three major parties), was approved in 2013 by the PRI and the PAN alone.[11] The PRD deviated from the convergence behavior, arguing that increasing the threshold for parties to maintain their registration, besides the introduction of immediate reelection, were modifications against minorities. In the record, PRD leaders claimed that the PRI and the PAN wanted to "perpetuate themselves in power, but the people will

---

[11] See discussion in Section 5.3.4.

know how to put an end to their lifelong ambitions" (Cámara de Diputados 2013).

I will mention only two important modifications included in this amendment that I touched on in this chapter. The first is the possibility of consecutive reelection of deputies (for up to four periods) and senators (for up to two) as well as the consecutive reelection of local legislators and members of the municipalities. The second is that the national voting threshold for a political party to maintain its registration increased from 2 percent to 3 percent. The ruling of this reform was discussed by the Senate on December 3, 2013, and was approved by 107 votes in favor and 16 against. For its part, the Chamber of Deputies voted on this matter on December 5, 2013, and approved it with 409 votes in favor and 69 against (Torres Alonso 2016, Zamitiz Gamboa 2017).

Institutional Constraints

The only articles that cleared a two-thirds qualified majority in both chambers of Congress are the ones in the first quadrangle of the picture. There are forty-four amendments that cleared both obstacles, four that did not clear the two-thirds restriction in either chamber, twelve that did not clear two-thirds in the Senate, and eight that did not clear two-thirds in the House.

Figure 5.2 presents the same configuration of amendments but focuses on the question generated by the participation levels of each chamber. As I argued in Section 5.1, if less than three-fourths of a chamber participate, then a simple majority of the chamber achieves the required two-thirds threshold (since one-half × three-fourths = two-thirds). However, as I have argued in Chapter 2, a simple majority requirement does not generate a core. Of course, it is possible to have a bicameral core in two dimensions under simple majority requirements in both chambers (as Figure 4.1b in Chapter 4 demonstrates), but Figure 5.2 gives an idea of how frequently low participation facilitates amendment adoption in Mexico: out of sixty-eight amendments, fourteen did not have a three-fourths participation in both chambers (indicated by a cross), thirteen did not have three-fourths participation in the House but did in the Senate (indicated by a square), nineteen did not have three-fourths in the Senate but did in the House (indicated by a triangle), and less than a third (twenty-two out of sixty-eight) had three-fourths participation in both chambers (indicated by a circle).

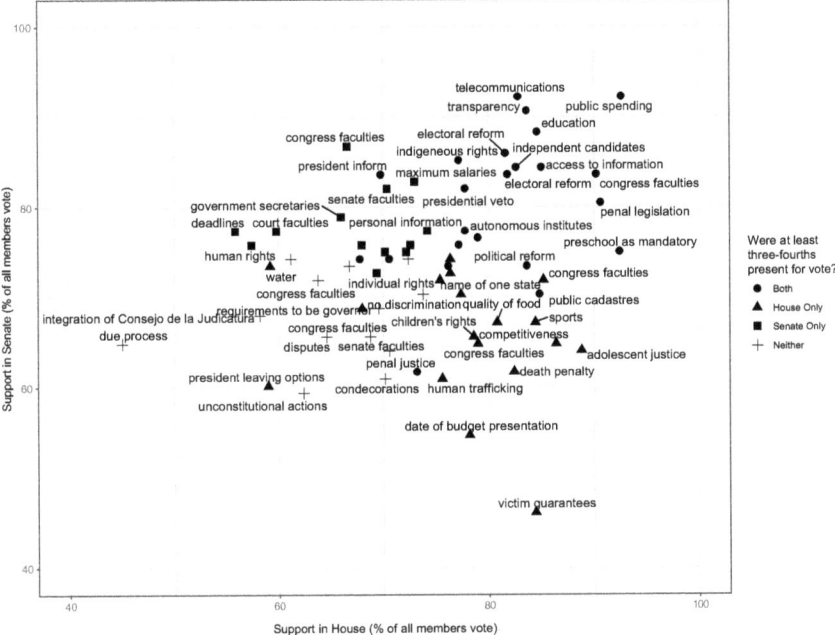

Figure 5.2 Congressional support for constitutional amendments in Mexico from 2000 to 2013

Conclusions

This chapter applies the analysis of Chapter 2 to Article 135 of the Mexican Constitution in order to calculate its core. I then argued that Article 65 significantly modifies this core (up to the point of elimination) because Article 135 can be applied only to half of the members of the House and/or the Senate, so this core may not even exist. I demonstrated that one-third of the constitutional amendments of Mexico in the period from 2000 to 2013 did not reach the two-thirds majority of the total members of the House or the Senate and that less than one-third of the deliberations had more than three-fourths of the members present in both chambers.

Next, I identified two additional reasons for why the Mexican Constitution is so frequently amended.

First is the fact that the Constitution is long and contradictory. While most of the analysts accept these two assessments, we have not seen them associated with the frequency of amendments in such a clear way. The argument here is that these two features create a high demand for amendments.

Second, I demonstrated that just as the institutions were not decisive in the period of the single-party dominance because the required thresholds were achieved automatically, the same thing happened during the multiparty period. Parties in Mexico are very disciplined (because of the electoral law), and, consequently, when they make an agreement, all their representatives (in the chambers or local governments) comply. In Section 5.4, we demonstrated that 90 percent of the amendments were by agreement of all three parties.

These agreements were made for political reasons. I argued that the birth of multipartyism in Mexico was due to such an agreement. With respect to the Constitution, a large part of these agreements involved the centralization of powers (Article 73). In addition, I identified political reasons such as NAFTA and the Pact for Mexico which explain party convergence to amend the Constitution. These are only some examples which reveal that once parties have incentives, they can reach agreements. Parties can also consider the Constitution as part of their domain. Once such agreements exist, it is a dominant strategy to enshrine and shield them in the Constitution.

Going back to ideas presented in Chapter 2, this chapter explained the reasons why parties may converge in such a way as to eliminate the core, just as a single party (the PRI) in the period of its dominance could bypass the institutions. This analysis explained in detail how and why the preferences converge and showed that in significant cases when they do not (like the electoral law) the votes represent the preferences, not the agreements. This is an alternative way of assessing the positions of the different actors as opposed to the cultural approaches discussed in Chapter 3. It requires specific analysis of the actors involved and their preferences (changing across issues and time) as opposed to responding to societal factors like political culture.

6

Constitutional Rigidity and Amendment Rate

> The amending clause ... describes and regulates ... amending power. *This is the most important part of the constitution.*
>
> John W. Burgess, *Political Science and Constitutional Law*
>
> Does the constitutional amendment rule matter at all?
>
> Ginsburg and Melton, "Does the Constitutional Amendment Rule Matter at All? Amendment Cultures and the Challenges of Measuring Amendment Difficulty"

In the Introduction, I provided an extensive set of references to the two competing assessments of constitutional amendment provisions included in every constitution. Here, I am using only two of them as excerpts to remind the reader that they are the subject of conflicting assessments. The point of view of Burgess seems self-evident and was the predominant approach until the empirical evidence that was collected (and included on the website www.constituteproject.org) enabled research to expand into empirical analysis. This then led to the dispute of constitutional rigidity on amendment rate, as the second excerpt suggests. Actually, above I used only the title of the article; the researchers themselves conclude after analyzing 790 current and previous constitutions that "the institutional variables are never statistically significant and, often, they do not even have the sign one would expect" (Ginsburg and Melton 2015: 711). I have addressed the theoretical part of these "no effect institutional variables" and the attribution of amendment frequencies to cultural variables in Chapter 3. There, I presented theoretical, empirical, and statistical objections to the argument that "it is not institutions; it is culture."

I remind the reader of these issues because the intuitive understanding that institutions matter has led to the expectation that constitutional rigidity should reduce the amendment rate, and one could argue that demonstrating this is a non-worthwhile enterprise.

However, I want to take issue with such an assessment. The reason for this is that we have significantly modified our understanding of the words "proof" and "evidence" since World War II. In fact, there have been two major revolutions in the social sciences since the end of World War II. The first was the rational choice revolution. If we place its date of birth with Arrow's Impossibility Theorem (in 1951),[1] we see an explosion of research following and demonstrating that intuition is not sufficient to establish sound beliefs. Regardless of whether people follow this research program or not, the word "proof" has a non-casual meaning. The second major revolution was the behavioral revolution. It is difficult to identify its date of birth, but it is associated with the University of Michigan, and it demonstrated that providing empirical examples is not enough, but one should analyze the whole population (or a random sample thereof) and use the appropriate statistical tools for it. Again, regardless of whether or not a researcher abides by the principles of the behavioral research program, we all understand that the word "evidence" has a much more precise meaning. Today these two revolutions have been incorporated into our beliefs, and we want theoretical justifications and empirical corroboration of propositions in order to consider them tenable. This is what I am doing in this book. In Chapter 2, I provided the theoretical argument that amendment rules translate into constitutional rigidity which affects the rate and significance of constitutional amendments.

In this chapter, I will apply the theoretical arguments of Chapter 2 on all democratic countries (numbering 103) and show that constitutional amendment rules have significant impact on the amendment rate. Using the veto players approach, I constructed an index of constitutional rigidity, which covers 103 democratic countries (those that had a POLITY2 score of five or above in 2013 [Marshall 2016]). Besides using the constitutional rigidity of the different countries, I also collect data on the significance of constitutional amendments. With these variables, I corroborate Burgess' claim. Most of the constitutional rigidity literature

---

[1] In "Social Choice and Individual Values," Arrow demonstrated that it is impossible to simultaneously satisfy five different but "obviously" highly desirable criteria in any social aggregation rule. The shock of this discovery was so great that in the beginning researchers started trying to prove that the proof was mistaken. Once the theorem was established, it dominated research for more than a decade, during which articles with the word "paradox" in their title were demonstrating that closer examination of intuitive beliefs was misleading. This is why I consider Arrow as the founder of the rational choice revolution despite the fact that he was preceded by other intellectuals (Black), sometimes by centuries (Condorcet, Lewis Carol).

only uses a subset of institutional rules and does not focus on democratic countries. As I said in the Introduction, restricting the analysis to democratic countries is like focusing as much as possible on "twins" and reducing the error term in our analysis.

In this chapter, I argue that there are three factors that cause empirical research to contradict Burgess' arguments: (1) the independent variable, (2) the dependent variable, and (3) the methodology used.

(1) The independent variable is a proxy for the size of the core. While most authors have used similar ideas, they have not been consistent; some analyses use only the institutional threshold, others use the number of veto players, others create a composite scalar measure depending on different criteria, and none of them use a combination of all these factors along with additional time or sequence constraints (as well as the impact of alternative procedures specified by the constitution). Previous work has analyzed a limited number of countries (around thirty). Ginsburg and Melton (2015) have used all countries, regardless of how democratic they are. I use only democratic countries in my sample and only for the period that they were democratic.[2]

(2) In the literature, the dependent variable is the rate of all constitutional amendments.[3] I will explain in this chapter why amendments should be weighted by significance, and I will divide amendments into three different categories: fundamental, significant, and insignificant. I will then perform three different tests: one on all amendments, one on the important ones (fundamental and significant), and one on just the fundamental ones.[4]

(3) The theory presented in Chapter 2 provides a necessary but insufficient condition for the size and rate of amendments. Therefore, it is inappropriate to use a linear model. Advancements in methodology indicate that the necessary but not sufficient conditions lead to two

---

[2] I use all 103 countries that were ranked at a five or above in the POLITY2 index in 2013 when I analyze the constitutions they have in place.
[3] It would be more appropriate to call the variable "amendment years" or, even better, "amendment events" since, if multiple amendments are introduced the same year, they are considered as being a single amendment. This is a reasonable choice since most of the time all of them are voted by using the same procedure. However, I will follow the literature on the matter and refer to "amendments" instead of "amendment events."
[4] These data are from the Comparative Constitutions Project dataset. I thank Tom Ginsburg for providing the data. See the discussion later in this chapter.

different predictions: one, on the size of the dependent variable, and two, on its variance (Goertz and Starr 2002, Goertz 2017). The appropriate method treats the predicted differences in variance (heteroskedasticity) as an asset instead of a liability in the estimation. I corroborate that constitutional rigidity leads to fewer and/or less significant amendments, and I show that constitutional flexibility may or may not lead to the adoption of more and/or significant amendments.

This chapter includes two appendixes. Appendix 6.A.1 presents the results of the heteroskedastic regressions (tables and figures) for different groups of amendments: first of the fundamental ones, then the combination of fundamental and significant ones, and finally of all amendments. Appendix 6.A.2 combines the results of the institutional analysis presented in this book with the cultural (or human capital) analyses presented in Chapter 3.

6.1 The Literature on Constitutional Rigidity

Constitutions systematically involve two types of items (in addition to Burgess' "most important" amending clauses): human rights and the rules of the political game. Both require stability – that is, they must be well known in advance, be respected by all participants, and remain constant (as long as they have not become obsolete). This is so all participants know their rights and obligations. For this reason, constitutions are designed to make modification difficult.

The multiplicity of these constitutional amendment provisions is extremely important for the way the political game is played in different countries. Stringent amendment rules can render political institutions almost "exogenous" as the outcome resulting from decisions made in the past is imposed on the current players. On the other hand, if these restrictions are weak, actors will include a constitutional revision in their agenda any time the actors disagree with the constitutional rules.

Studies on constitutional rigidity have been done at the normative and theoretical levels. The debate started between Thomas Jefferson, who advocated frequent changes to the US Constitution, and James Madison, who prevailed in establishing a long-standing one. Studies have also been done at the empirical level, including attempts to assess the level of constitutional rigidity in different countries. Given the variety of locking mechanisms in constitutions and the ability of founders to combine them either

6.1 THE LITERATURE ON CONSTITUTIONAL RIGIDITY

as supplements or as substitutes, the range of constitutional rigidity is extremely large with diverse empirical conclusions.

6.1.1 Measuring Constitutional Rigidity

In the literature, there are two major approaches to measuring constitutional rigidity. The first uses only institutional measures, while the second combines institutional measures with others such as the rate of amendments and other indicators that explain this rate. Focusing on the institutional factors alone, the level of constitutional rigidity may differ from one article of a constitution to the next.[5] The constitution may provide different provisions for the modification of different articles, such as using alternative political institutions. Similarly, it may be prohibited to amend certain articles like human rights or the regime type. Finally, there is a wide array of applicable revision procedures that range from multiple bodies to referendums, time delays that sometimes involve intermediate elections, and sometimes even the creation of special bodies, such as constitutional assemblies.

6.1.2 Institutional Criteria

Focusing on institutions, some authors only consider a subset of issues. For example, Lutz (1994) and Lijphart (2012) focus on the qualified majorities required in the amendment process, whereas Anckar and Karvonen (2015) focus mainly on the political actors involved (Lorenz 2005: 341–342, 344–345). Lutz (1994) studied eighty-two constitutions (the fifty US state constitutions and those of thirty countries), but Lorenz was not able to successfully apply Lutz's index to new countries (Lorenz 2005: 342). Lijphart (2012) created a fourfold typology, which divided countries based on the majority threshold required for approval. He finds that this classification correlates with the strength of judicial review (Lijphart 2012: 214–215). Schneier (2006) uses a similar method and classifies 101 constitutions into five categories and nineteen subcategories.

Other authors (e.g., Elster 2010, Lane 2011) use non-voting criteria such as time delays. Similarly, La Porta et al. (2004: 448) examine a group

---

[5] On the basis of this, Albert distinguishes constitutions as either "comprehensive" (if the whole constitution can be modified with the same rules), "restricted" (if different provisions are subject to different rules), or "exceptional" (where different rules are used exclusively for one provision or a set of related provisions) (Albert 2014).

of countries whose constitutions have remained unchanged since 1980. They measure constitutional rigidity on a scale from one to four, which is broken down in La Porta et al.'s Table 1:

> One point each is given if the approval of the majority of the legislature, the chief of the state, and a referendum is necessary in order to change the constitution. An additional point is given for each of the following: if a supermajority in the legislature (more than 66 percent of votes) is needed, if both houses of the legislature have to approve, if the legislature has to approve the amendment in two consecutive legislature terms, or if the approval of a majority of the state legislatures is required. (La Porta et al. 2004: 451)

Other authors, such as Rasch and Congleton (2006), use institutional information that they have on formal amendment rules. They then "create indexes of consensus and of the number of central government veto players or points of agreement required to secure a constitutional amendment" (Rasch and Congleton 2006: 546). Lorenz (2005) focuses on a mix of institutional and contextual variables and combines elements from Lutz, Lijphart, and Anckar and Karvonen to identify "the type of majority rule with the number of voting arenas or actors" (Lorenz 2005: 346).

6.1.3 Mixed Factors

Turning now to the combination of institutional and other factors, the most recent and sophisticated effort has been made by the Comparative Constitutions Project from Elkins et al. (2009). These authors start with the premise that constitutional rigidity should be calculated using a combination of the institutional procedures required for amendment and the actual rate, or lack thereof, of amendments. According to them, each component is not sufficient on its own. While they can assess the institutional component by looking at the constitution (though with difficulties that they enumerate and that this literature review corroborates), the rate of amendments depends on a host of social and historical factors: "Thus, we regress the amendment rate on a set of amendment procedure variables as well as a host of factors that should predict political reform more generally, including those factors included in our model of constitutional duration" (Ginsburg and Melton 2015: 695). Such factors include percentages of different ethnic groups, economic development, amendment rate, amendment rate squared, and so on (Elkins et al. 2009: 227–228). Tsebelis and Nardi (2016) use the same indicators in their analysis. Despite this, common statements in the literature, such as "constitutional rigidity [has] a negative effect on amendment frequency,"[6] cannot be accurately evaluated with the use of measures that include amendment rate as an ingredient of constitutional rigidity because they are affirming the consequent. This is the reason that I used purely institutional variables in my subsequent work and in this book. Ginsburg and Melton (2015) also do not include amendment rate as a component of constitutional rigidity.

6.1.4 Effect of Rigidity on Amendment Rate

Given the variety of variables included in the different indexes of constitutional rigidity, it is not surprising that there is low correlation among them (Ginsburg and Melton 2015: 698). Ginsburg and Melton find that "only three combinations yield a correlation greater than 0.5: Anckar and Karvonen with Lijphart, Lijphart with Lorenz, and Lorenz with Lutz. The other correlations are smaller than 0.5 and the correlation between the CCP and Lorenz measures is even negative" (Ginsburg and Melton 2015: 697). The reason for this negative correlation is probably because Ginsburg and Melton's analysis included social, economic, and other contextual indicators. In addition, as a series of authors point out, the correlation between the different measures of constitutional rigidity and amendment rate is low (Ferejohn 1997, Lorenz 2005, Rasch and Congleton 2006, Ginsburg and Melton 2015).

There is a potential explanation for this low correlation. The institutional indexes of rigidity are based mainly on one of two methods the founders of each country used to protect the constitution: either the number of veto players (institutions or actors required to agree to a constitutional amendment) or the required majorities in each one of them (Tsebelis 2017b). These methods are not independent – in fact, these methods are often used in a complementary way: bicameral legislatures require lower qualified majorities for approval than unicameral ones.[7] Depending on the weight of these two components,

---

[6] See Lutz (1994: 365–366), Rasch and Congleton (2006: 542), Dixon (2011: 106), and Lijphart (2012: 211).
[7] Eighty-nine percent of the countries that require just one body for constitutional changes also require a two-thirds majority or greater. Among countries that require two bodies, that percentage decreases to 63 percent, whereas only 52 percent of countries that require three bodies also require a two-thirds majority or greater. The most extreme countries (using only one of the two methods and generating the negative correlation) are Bulgaria and Mongolia on the one hand (requiring a three-fourths qualified majority from a single

Table 6.1 *Correlation of veto player constitutional rigidity index with other indexes*

Index	Correlation	p-value	Num. observations in common
Ginsburg and Melton (2015)	0.09	0.450	66
Anckar and Karvonen (2015)	0.16	0.263	52
La Porta et al. (2004)	0.44	0.004	41
Lijphart (2012)	0.23	0.252	26
Lorenz (2005)	0.59	0.000	34
Lutz (1994)	0.62	0.001	23
Rasch and Congleton (2006)	0.78	0.000	17

constitutional rigidity may take different values. As for the indexes involving components other than institutional ones, it goes without saying that the results will depend on the alternate variables included.

Table 6.1 presents the correlation between the veto player constitutional rigidity index calculated in Chapter 2 and the different other indexes of constitutional rigidity. It also presents the significance of the correlation (p-value) and the number of observations (number of countries in common) that generate it. The overall correlations are higher than the ones reported in Ginsburg and Melton (2015). In particular, the correlations are higher with the indexes of Lorenz (2005), Lutz (1994), and Rasch and Congleton (2006), who use different ways of combining institutional provisions (without covering them all) and their significance, although the number of countries covered is significantly lower.

I think, given the high p-value of my index with the last three indexes in Table 6.1, that the reason they do not get strong results in their analyses is the small number of countries covered.

6.2 Constitutional Amendment Theory and Tests

In Chapter 2 (around Figure 2.7), I presented the argument that high constitutional rigidity is a necessary but not sufficient condition for a low rate and small significance of amendments. This means that high rigidity

chamber) and Australia, Canada, Denmark, France, Iceland, Ireland, Italy, and Paraguay on the other, requiring a simple majority for approval in three different bodies, usually including a bicameral legislature. The interested reader can find details of constitutional amendment procedures in Appendix II.

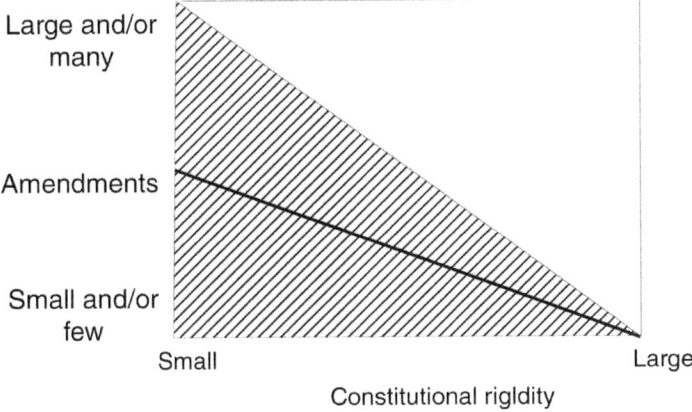

Figure 6.1 Constitutional rigidity and amendment size and/or rate

will necessarily lead to a low rate and significance of amendments, but low constitutional rigidity provides the opportunity for a high rate as well as a greater significance of constitutional amendments. However, whether these amendments will materialize depends on the preferences of the relevant actors.

Figure 6.1 presents a visual representation of this expectation. As a result, the relationship between constitutional rigidity and amendment rate will be heteroskedastic: At high levels of constitutional rigidity, amendments will be infrequent or even impossible, while at low levels of constitutional rigidity, amendments are possible but their rate will be high or low depending on other conditions (for example, political actors may not be willing to change the status quo despite the fact that it is easily amendable). The result of this argument is that the appropriate procedure to test the theoretical expectations is not a linear regression (as used in all of the previous empirical literature) but a heteroskedastic regression, where predictions are made not only about the average value of the amendment rate but also about its variance.

In Figure 6.2, I present a graph of all the democratic countries in a two-dimensional space: the independent variable is the veto player constitutional rigidity, and the dependent one is the amendment rate of the different countries (the number of amendment years divided by the number of democratic years).[8]

---

[8] I remind the reader that I am not considering countries that fall below five on the POLITY2 democracy scale.

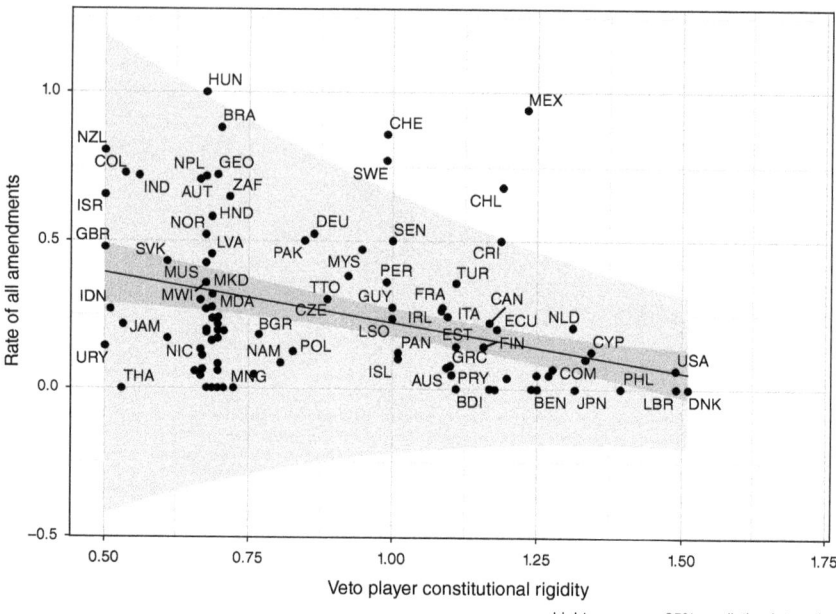

Figure 6.2 The effect of constitutional rigidity on the rate of all amendments (amendments of constitutions in effect in 2013 in all democratic countries)

There is one more variable that is expected to have a significant impact on the relationship: the significance of amendments. This heteroskedastic relationship will be stronger as the significance of the amendments increases because the actors will make more elaborate and accurate calculations and likely will not undertake them (if they think they may fail) or, even if they do, they will not succeed because of the difficulty of achieving the goal. This expectation regarding significant amendments is congruent with the findings on legislative output both in the US (at both the federal and state level) and from a comparative perspective. For example, Howell et al. (2000) divide federal legislation into three different categories: landmark, significant, and trivial. They find that while a divided government depresses the production of landmark legislation by about 30 percent, it has no substantive effect on the production of important, albeit not landmark, legislation and actually has a positive effect on the passage of trivial laws (Howell et al. 2000). In a study of policymaking in state legislatures, Crosson (2019) measures the size of the legislative core and finds substantively larger results when accounting for bill significance. Finally, Tsebelis (2002) divides legislation in European countries into two categories and finds that veto players and their distance are negatively correlated with the production of significant legislation but not with the production of nonsignificant pieces of legislation.

In conclusion, I expect to find a negative heteroskedastic relationship between constitutional rigidity and amendment rate, which will be more pronounced as the amendments' significance increases. To test this relationship, I measure the level of significance of the constitutional amendments in my sample.

I designed a survey that organized the constitutional data from Ginsburg and Melton by country – this way, country experts could evaluate the significance of all of the amendments in countries of their expertise (Ginsburg and Melton 2015). I posted the survey link on the constitutional law blog I-CONnect in addition to personally reaching out to a range of people from lists of country experts.

The questionnaire presented a three-class typology of amendment significance, consisting of "amendments of exceptional significance," "significant amendments," and "insignificant amendments." These categories break down as follows:

- Category 3 includes "amendments of exceptional significance" that, at the time of their passage, transformed the understanding of at least one area of the constitution of the country. In other words, amendments in this category transform how legislative bargaining or interbranch relations transpire, introduce an entirely new class of individual rights to a citizenry, or are subsequently deemed "unconstitutional" by the supreme court of a given country.
- Category 2 includes "significant amendments," which are changes that added or modified an important aspect of the constitution. These amendments alter (but do not transform) key institutional features of the legislative, executive, or judicial bodies of government (or their relation to each other), expand the electorate (but not fundamentally alter it) in some way, or add onto already existing individual rights.
- Category 1 is the residual category of "not significant or insignificant amendments." Given that the bar is very high for Categories 2 and 3, most amendments will belong to this residual category.

The survey elicited multiple sets of answers for numerous countries (from one to six).[9] In the case of discrepancies between sets of ratings,

---

[9] My team scored the countries for which I received no answer after several attempts.

I used the median rating.[10] If the median was not an integer but an interval (a possibility with two or four responders), I used the more conservative estimate (the lower of the two numbers).

6.3 Constitutional Rigidity and Significance of Amendments: Negative Heteroskedastic Relationships

With these data on the significance of constitutional amendments, I can test the relationship between constitutional rigidity and both amendment rate *and* significance. Chapter 2 expects this relationship to have three dimensions:

(1) On average, the rate of amendments will decline with constitutional rigidity.
(2) The variance of the relationship will decline with constitutional rigidity.
(3) The significance of the relationship will increase as a function of the significance of amendments.

In order to test these predictions, I use a heteroskedastic regression model. Heteroskedasticity is generally considered a liability in empirical estimations because it reduces the reliability of coefficients. My analysis *predicts* heteroskedasticity, so having a heteroskedastic relationship should not be seen as a liability. I expect not only a negative relationship between constitutional rigidity and the rate of amendments but also the variance of this rate. I also expect to find more significant results when the amendments are more significant. Appendix 6.A.1 presents the nine models, which I use to present the essence of my argument in Table 6.2.

This table examines three different categories of significance: first, all of the amendments (Categories 1, 2, and 3 in Appendix I); second, the more significant ones (Categories 2 and 3); and third, the fundamental ones (Category 3). For each category, three regressions are performed: the null model (assuming no relationship between constitutional rigidity and rate), the linear model (assuming a linear but not heteroskedastic relationship between constitutional rigidity and rate of amendment), and the heteroskedastic model (assuming a negative effect of rigidity on both the rate of constitutional amendments and the variance of this rate). In all three cases, I produce the added explanatory value of each model by

---

[10] This is true unless the answers indicated a violation of the instructions. For example, all amendments approved on the basis of constitutional rules but rejected by the constitutional court on the basis of substance (not procedure) were classified as 3 since (on the basis of the court's judgment) they were unconstitutional.

6.3 CONSTITUTIONAL RIGIDITY AND AMENDMENTS

Table 6.2 *Comparison of three models of effects of constitutional rigidity (null, mean only, and heteroskedastic) on amendment rate for POLITY2 ≥ 5 threshold 103 countries; likelihood ratio tests*

Significance	Models	Chi-square	$p(>$ Chi-square$)$
All amendments	Null vs. mean only	9.60	0.00194
	Mean only vs. heteroskedastic	2.63	0.10510
	Null vs. heteroskedastic	12.23	**0.00221**
Significant and fundamental	Null vs. mean only	7.02	0.00804
	Mean only vs. heteroskedastic	12.09	0.00050
	Null vs. heteroskedastic	19.11	**0.00007**
Fundamental amendments	Null vs. mean only	4.27	0.03883
	Mean only vs. heteroskedastic	76.37	1.00E+00
	Null vs. heteroskedastic	80.64	**1.00E+00**

reporting the *p*-values from a likelihood ratio test comparing the specified models.[11]

Table 6.2 underlines three main points. First, as predicted, the coefficients of constitutional rigidity are negative for both the mean rate and the variance of this rate. For each level of amendment significance, the explanatory power of the model increases from null to linear and then to heteroskedastic; the contribution of the mean or the variance varies for different levels of significance (for all amendments [1 + 2 + 3], the changes of rate provide the main part of the explanatory power of the model, while for more significant [2 + 3] or for fundamental [3] amendments most of the explanation is provided by the variance). Finally, and most importantly, the added value, denoted by the highlighted *p*-value of the difference between the null model and the heteroskedastic model, increases with the significance of amendments, moving from 0.001 for all

---

[11] The analyses in this chapter follow Tsebelis (2017b) with the only difference being that they cover countries above five in the POLITY2 scale instead of six as was covered in the article. As a result, I have 103 countries instead of 94, and although there is often more statistical significance in these current analyses, the substantive significance of results is exactly the same. In Appendix A.6.2, I expand the analysis to all the other cutoff points from the POLITY2 definition of democracy and show that the results remain qualitatively similar. The heteroskedastic regressions use the two-step GLS estimation procedure described on page 14 of Stata's hetregress manual. The likelihood ratio tests are based on maximum likelihood estimates because Stata does not compute the likelihood for the two-step GLS estimation.

amendments to 0.00005 for significant and fundamental amendments and to 1.00E+00 for fundamental amendments. In other words, the relationship between constitutional rigidity and the rate (number of amendment events over democratic years) of constitutional amendments is heteroskedastic as predicted, and the significance of this relationship increases with the significance of amendments under consideration. This new finding is consistent with the findings of the literature on legislation.

In Appendix 6.A.1, I provide the analytic results that produced Table 6.2 for the interested reader as well as the plots of constitutional rigidity with the different kinds of amendments. In Appendix 6.A.2, I replicate Table 6.2 for different cutoff points of democracy from the POLITY2 index and demonstrate the robustness of results. In Appendix 6.A.3, I use both the veto player rigidity index and the cultural variables from Chapter 3 in order to show that most of the cultural variables drop out when tested against the institutional ones.[12]

Conclusions

This chapter used the theoretical analysis of Chapter 2 to argue that constitutional rigidity affects amendment rate, but as a necessary condition only, and it will have higher results as a function of the significance of amendments. In order to produce the empirical results, I used the veto players constitutional rigidity index calculated in Chapter 2 in a heteroskedastic regression with three different levels of amendment significance. The results were always statistically significant. In addition, using an expert opinion survey, I constructed a variable for the importance of amendments. For the empirical analysis, I used the appropriate heteroskedastic regression and concluded that the more significant the amendments, the more my expectations were corroborated.

Constitutional rigidity affects the rate of significant amendments in the following ways: High rigidity makes amendments rare, but low rigidity simply enables amendments, which may or may not occur depending on political, social, or economic factors. As a result, low constitutional rigidity produces a higher average rate and higher variance of significant constitutional amendments. The higher the significance of amendments, the stronger the above relationship. This evidence corroborates Burgess' statement that I have referred to many times in this book and demonstrates why, if not analyzed correctly, the heteroskedastic data (who are

---

[12] The regressions in Appendix 6.A.3 are not heteroskedastic because the predicted heteroskedasticity goes in different directions.

necessarily noisy) lead to misleading and unwarranted conclusions that constitutional amendment rules have low significance or do not matter at all and should either be replaced by cultural explanations (Ginsburg and Melton 2015) or be completely ignored (Versteeg and Zackin 2016).

In this chapter, I demonstrated the direct use of constitutional rigidity: how and why it affects amendment rate, and how significance increases with the importance of amendments. However, there are also indirect effects of constitutional rigidity that we will study in the subsequent chapters.

Appendix 6.A.1

Here, I will present the results of the different models in more detail.

Table 6.A.1.1 presents the results of the heteroskedastic regression for fundamental amendments. Table 6.A.1.2 gives the results of the combination of fundamental and major amendments. Table 6.A.1.3 presents the results of all amendments.

Figure 6.A.1.1 gives the graphic representation of fundamental amendments. Figure 6.A.1.2 presents the fundamental and major amendments. (The graphic representation of all amendments is presented in the main text as Figure 6.2).

Table 6.A.1.1 *Results of the heteroskedastic regression for fundamental amendments (POLITY2 $\geq$ 5)*

	Null model	Mean-only model	Het. regression
n	103	103	103
Dependent variable: the fundamental amendment rate			
(Intercept)	0.043 ***	0.117 **	0.089 ***
	(0.011)	(0.037)	(0.026)
Veto players constitutional rigidity		−0.082 *	−0.057 *
		(0.039)	(0.024)
Dependent variable: the log-squared residuals of the OLS regression of the fundamental amendment rate on veto players constitutional rigidity			
(Intercept)		−4.408 ***	−0.189
		(0.139)	(0.468)
Veto players constitutional rigidity			−5.616 ***
			(0.502)

*** $p < 0.001$; ** $p < 0.01$; * $p < 0.05$.

Table 6.A.1.2 *Results of the heteroskedastic regression for the combination of fundamental and major amendments (POLITY2 ≥ 5)*

	Null model	Mean-only model	Het. regression
n	103	103	103
Dependent variable: the major and fundamental amendment rate			
(Intercept)	0.117 ***	0.249 ***	0.254 ***
	(0.015)	(0.051)	(0.050)
Veto players constitutional rigidity		−0.148 **	−0.152 **
		(0.055)	(0.046)
Dependent variable: the log-squared residuals of the OLS regression of the major and fundamental amendment rate on veto players constitutional rigidity			
(Intercept)		−3.720 ***	−2.110 ***
		(0.139)	(0.515)
Veto players constitutional rigidity			−2.016 ***
			(0.556)

*** $p < 0.001$; ** $p < 0.01$; * $p < 0.05$.

Table 6.A.1.3 *Results of the heteroskedastic regression on all amendments (POLITY2 ≥ 5)*

	Null model	Mean-only model	Het. regression
n	103	103	103
Dependent variable: the all amendment rate			
(Intercept)	0.253 ***	0.506 ***	0.519 ***
	(0.025)	(0.084)	(0.084)
Veto players constitutional rigidity		−0.284 **	−0.298 ***
		(0.090)	(0.084)
Dependent variable: the log-squared residuals of the OLS regression of all amendment rate on veto players constitutional rigidity			
(Intercept)		−2.714 ***	−2.022 ***
		(0.139)	(0.515)
Veto players constitutional rigidity			−0.910
			(0.557)

*** $p < 0.001$; ** $p < 0.01$; * $p < 0.05$.

CONCLUSIONS 163

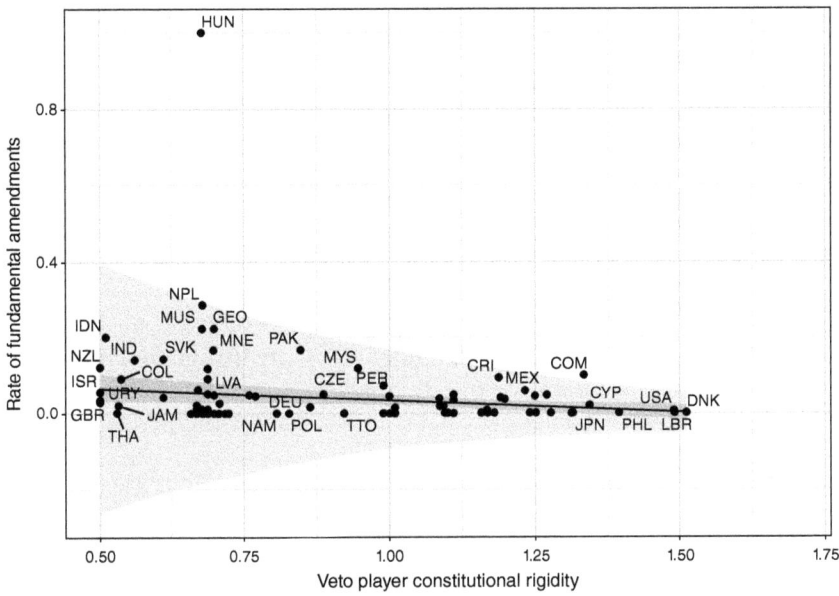

Figure 6.A.1.1 The effect of constitutional rigidity on the rate of fundamental amendments (amendments of constitutions in effect in 2013 in all democratic countries)

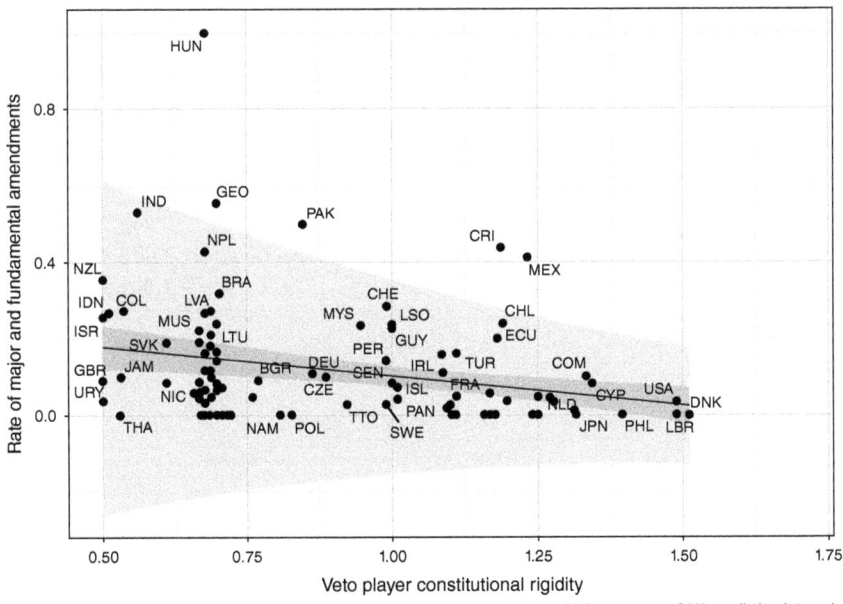

Figure 6.A.1.2 The effect of constitutional rigidity on the rate of significant and fundamental amendments (amendments of constitutions in effect in 2013 in all democratic countries)

Appendix 6.A.2

This appendix replicates Table 6.2 with different cutoff points from the POLITY2 index for democracy. The reader can verify that the results remain essentially highly significant despite the reduction in the number of cases. In addition, statistical significance increases with the substantive significance of amendments.

Table 6.A.2.1 *Comparison of three models of effects of constitutional rigidity (null, mean only, and heteroskedastic) on amendment rate for POLITY2 $\geq$ 6 threshold (ninety-five countries; likelihood ratio tests)*

Significance	Models	Chi-square	$p(>$ Chi-square$)$
All amendments	Null vs. mean only	10.00	0.00157
	Mean only vs. heteroskedastic	2.08	0.14880
	Null vs. heteroskedastic	12.08	**0.00238**
Significant and fundamental	Null vs. mean only	6.60	0.01022
	Mean only vs. heteroskedastic	12.26	0.00046
	Null vs. heteroskedastic	18.85	**0.00008**
Fundamental amendments	Null vs. mean only	4.19	0.04077
	Mean only vs. heteroskedastic	68.46	1.00E+00
	Null vs. heteroskedastic	72.65	**1.00E+00**

Table 6.A.2.2 *Comparison of three models of effects of constitutional rigidity (null, mean only, and heteroskedastic) on amendment rate for POLITY2 ≥ 7 threshold (eighty-three countries; likelihood ratio tests)*

Significance	Models	Chi-square	$p(>$ Chi-square$)$
All amendments	Null vs. mean only	5.23	0.02222
	Mean only vs. heteroskedastic	1.13	0.28679
	Null vs. heteroskedastic	6.36	**0.04151**
Significant and fundamental	Null vs. mean only	3.74	0.05317
	Mean only vs. heteroskedastic	10.30	0.00133
	Null vs. heteroskedastic	14.04	**0.00089**
Fundamental amendments	Null vs. mean only	1.93	0.16431
	Mean only vs. heteroskedastic	49.81	1.00E+00
	Null vs. heteroskedastic	51.74	**1.00E+00**

Table 6.A.2.3 *Comparison of three models of effects of constitutional rigidity (null, mean only, and heteroskedastic) on amendment rate for POLITY2 ≥ 8 threshold (seventy-two countries; likelihood ratio tests)*

Significance	Models	Chi-square	$p(>$ Chi-square$)$
All amendments	Null vs. mean only	4.34	0.03719
	Mean only vs. heteroskedastic	0.34	0.55854
	Null vs. heteroskedastic	4.68	**0.09613**
Significant and fundamental	Null vs. mean only	3.10	0.07825
	Mean only vs. heteroskedastic	7.16	0.00745
	Null vs. heteroskedastic	10.26	**0.00591**
Fundamental amendments	Null vs. mean only	1.55	0.21365
	Mean only vs. heteroskedastic	46.82	1.00E+00
	Null vs. heteroskedastic	48.37	**1.00E+00**

Table 6.A.2.4 *Comparison of three models of effects of constitutional rigidity (null, mean only, and heteroskedastic) on amendment rate for POLITY2 ≥ 9 threshold (fifty-four countries; likelihood ratio tests)*

Significance	Models	Chi-square	$p(>$ Chi-square$)$
All amendments	Null vs. mean only	7.26	0.00703
	Mean only vs. heteroskedastic	2.11	0.14666
	Null vs. heteroskedastic	9.37	**0.00923**
Significant and fundamental	Null vs. mean only	3.53	0.06028
	Mean only vs. heteroskedastic	12.32	0.00045
	Null vs. heteroskedastic	15.84	**0.00036**
Fundamental amendments	Null vs. mean only	1.47	0.22585
	Mean only vs. heteroskedastic	38.94	1.00E+00
	Null vs. heteroskedastic	40.40	**1.00E+00**

Table 6.A.2.5 *Comparison of three models of effects of constitutional rigidity (null, mean only, and heteroskedastic) on amendment rate for POLITY2 ≥ 10 threshold (thirty-five countries; likelihood ratio tests)*

Significance	Models	Chi-square	$p(>$ Chi-square$)$
All amendments	Null vs. mean only	5.00	0.02538
	Mean only vs. heteroskedastic	0.78	0.37602
	Null vs. heteroskedastic	5.78	**0.05554**
Significant and fundamental	Null vs. mean only	2.84	0.09168
	Mean only vs. heteroskedastic	8.39	0.00377
	Null vs. heteroskedastic	11.23	**0.00364**
Fundamental amendments	Null vs. mean only	1.88	0.17067
	Mean only vs. heteroskedastic	38.60	1.00E+00
	Null vs. heteroskedastic	40.48	**1.00E+00**

Appendix 6.A.3

This appendix presents two different tables, one of which runs the cultural variables all together and the other one at a time along with the constitutional rigidity (the 57 countries are the intersection of the 103 countries in this book with the countries in the Blake et al. [2023] article). This is the simplest appropriate empirical test, which confirms the conclusions of Chapter 3 for the more empirically minded reader. Actually, Chapter 3 argued that the cultural variables to be included required justification at the theoretical level, while here it becomes clear that even the empirical accuracy is questionable.

Table 6.A.3.1 *OLS regressions of different amendment rates (POLITY2 $\geq$ 5 cutoff) on constitutional rigidity and social capital (n = 57)*

	Fundamental amendments	Significant and fundamental	All amendments
n	57	57	57
(Intercept)	0.127 ***	0.288 ***	0.388 **
	(0.028)	(0.077)	(0.136)
Constitutional rigidity	−0.067 *	−0.158 *	−0.295 *
	(0.026)	(0.07)	(0.123)
Political trust	0.007	0.015	0.023
	(0.008)	(0.022)	(0.038)
Group membership	−0.01	−0.031	0.002
	(0.01)	(0.026)	(0.047)
Civic activism	−0.021	0.037	0.314 **
	(0.021)	(0.062)	(0.109)
R^2	0.171	0.111	0.211
Adj. R^2	0.107	0.043	0.15

*** $p < 0.001$; ** $p < 0.01$; * $p < 0.05$.

Table 6.A.3.2 *OLS regressions of different amendment rates (POLITY2 ≥ 5 cutoff) on constitutional rigidity and each indicator of social capital separately (n = 57)*

	Fundamental amendments	Fundamental and significant	All amendments	Fundamental amendments	Fundamental and significant	All amendments	Fundamental amendments	Fundamental and significant	All amendments
n	57	57	57	57	57	57	57	57	57
(Intercept)	0.103 ***	0.255 ***	0.510 ***	0.119 ***	0.288 ***	0.443 **	0.114 ***	0.248 ***	0.390 **
	(0.024)	(0.064)	(0.121)	(0.027)	(0.074)	(0.140)	(0.025)	(0.068)	(0.119)
Constitutional rigidity	−0.071 **	−0.152 *	−0.242	−0.071 **	−0.153 *	−0.244	−0.067 *	−0.156 *	−0.299 *
	(0.025)	(0.069)	(0.129)	(0.025)	(0.068)	(0.129)	(0.025)	(0.069)	(0.121)
Political trust	0.003	0.007	0.035						
	(0.008)	(0.020)	(0.038)						
Group membership				−0.010	−0.021	0.045			
				(0.009)	(0.024)	(0.045)			
Civic activism							−0.026	0.021	0.322 **
							(0.022)	(0.059)	(0.104)
R^2	0.128	0.086	0.076	0.146	0.097	0.079	0.149	0.086	0.204
Adj. R^2	0.096	0.052	0.042	0.115	0.063	0.045	0.118	0.052	0.174

*** $p < 0.001$; ** $p < 0.01$; * $p < 0.05$.

Data on the indicators of social capital are taken from Blake et al. (2023), which results in fifty-seven observations as in their cross-national analyses. While rigidity is significantly negatively associated with all kinds of amendments, among the social capital indicators only civic activism is significantly (and positively) associated only when looking at all amendments.

When considering each indicator of social capital separately, the result is the same as in Table 6.A.2.1: Only constitutional rigidity is significantly associated with amendment rates. Civic activism is the only social capital indicator that exhibits a significant relationship with one of the amendment-rate measures.

7

Time Inconsistency and Other Correlates of Constitutional Length

This chapter studies constitutional revision provisions at the theoretical level. Country constitutions systematically involve two categories of items: individual rights and the rules of the political game. The emphasis is on the word "systematically" because they may also include other elements.[1] Individual rights and the rules of the political game in a democracy must be well-known in advance and respected by all participants in the political game. In other words, they require stability over time, which I will call time consistency. For this reason, constitutions protect their text from change by making modification difficult. In Chapter 1 we saw such mechanisms, in Chapter 2 we studied how they work, and in Chapter 6 we corroborated our expectations: More veto players as well as higher required majorities for each one of them increase constitutional rigidity and make amendments overall more difficult and more rare.

As I discussed in Chapter 3, not all analyses share these arguments. A significant proportion argues that it is not institutions but culture that regulate the frequency of amendments. Others claim that instead of looking at the institutions researchers should base their analyses of constitutional rigidity on the frequency of amendments. For example, Marshfield (2018) writes, "A better measure of constitutional flexibility is a constitution's actual amendment rate because this presumably captures both the formal barriers to amendment contained in the amendment rules as well as cultural attitudes regarding formal amendment" (80). Versteeg and Zackin (2016) agree, saying, "The measure [of constitutional entrenchment] does not rely on formal amendment rules because these rules are mediated so dramatically by political norms" (661).

---

[1] These elements might include transitory provisions (as in Denmark and Portugal) or idiosyncratic elements (like the description of the flag in Spain and Turkey or the national anthem in Hungary and El Salvador).

Versteeg and Zackin confirm that the length of a constitution correlates with the frequency of amendments.

This institution-free analysis leads to a relativistic approach to constitutional length. Versteeg and Zackin (2016) argue that there is an alternative specific and flexible model of constitutions that had not been recognized by the theoretical literature: "We simply seek to demonstrate that the specific and flexible constitutions currently populating the globe are not simply failures to achieve brevity and entrenchment, but represent a plausible alternative solution to some of the agency problems associated with constitutional design."

This chapter, consistent with the institutional approach of the book, will be based on the constitutional rigidity approach and will develop a new concept called "time inconsistency," which combines constitutional rigidity and amendment frequency. The idea is the following: the founders of a constitution design the rules of amendment on the basis of how frequently (or, likely, how rarely) they think the constitution should be changed (as we showed in the previous chapter, the frequency of amendments should be lower if the required majority is three-fourths than if it is two-thirds). However, reality may impose different rules. The quality of the existing constitutional provisions and real-life conditions may lead to more or less frequent amendments than what was initially planned for. It is as if the country as a collective actor "changed its mind" with respect to the initially selected constitutional rigidity. I will call this difference "time inconsistency" and calculate it as the difference between actual amendment frequency and the frequency expected based on constitutional rigidity (as calculated in the previous chapter).

I find that time inconsistency correlates with the length of constitutions in all democratic countries. This is not a neutral feature of constitutional length. It is clearly a negative characteristic, and it brings us back to the traditional analyses of constitutions, according to which the "framework" constitutions (Dixon 2014) are the optimal choice. This discovery opens the door for further investigations of other negative associations of constitutional length – GDP per capita, corruption, inequality, and so on – which suggest that long constitutions are not a "plausible alternative solution" to constitutional design but are instead a suboptimal one.

This chapter is organized into three parts. In the first part, I present the interaction, in game form, between the founders of a constitution and the subsequent generations that may choose to revise it. In the second part, I define the time inconsistency concept and reexamine arguments presented by Tsebelis and Nardi (2016) as well as Tsebelis (2017b) who claim that time inconsistency is positively correlated with the length of a constitution. The difference is that these papers did not have the more advanced measures of constitutional rigidity generated in Chapter 2, so the results presented here are more empirically accurate. In addition, they cover more countries and (given that they lead to the same conclusions) provide a robustness check for these arguments. In the third part, I examine the implications of the time inconsistency argument and find that constitutional length is correlated not only with time inconsistency but also with a series of economic indicators (such as GDP per capita, inequalities, or corruption). The presentation is not only based on the 103 democratic countries but also uses the comparison of the fifty US states from the work of Brown (2022), who was able to perform more controlled comparisons and discover Granger causality between constitutional length and economic indicators.

7.1 The Intergenerational Constitutional Game

The founders of each constitution ultimately want to generate a document that will regulate the interactions of the political game for generations to come. Whether it is the rights of citizens or the interactions among the political actors, these rules have to be known and respected (and therefore known to be stable) by all political actors. Justice Scalia (1997) argues that "the whole purpose [of a constitution] is to prevent change – to embed certain rights in such a manner that future generations cannot readily take them away" (40), and Justice Brennan (1991) argues, "In my view, it is crucial to the durability and efficacy of a charter of personal liberties that it not be subject to easy alteration or suspension ... robust entrenchment forbidding compromise or requiring supermajoritarian approval for amendments seems to me best" (4).

On the other hand, if unforeseeable circumstances arise, these constitutional rules have to permit amendment. This is why there are constitutional provisions about the requirements for a constitutional revision.

The theoretical debate in constitutional design is between two major options with regard to the time horizon of constitutions: it can either be one anchored to and shaped by the citizens it represents or be one that stands the test of time. The former perspective represents that of Thomas Jefferson; the latter represents that of James Madison. The two addressed a fundamental question of the role played not only by a nation's governing document, the constitution, but also by the relation of the governors to the governed: Who decides the rules of the game? Are the living meant to be ruled, as Jefferson argued, by themselves in a revisited document, or should they be ruled by their forbearers through an enduring document?

Jefferson supported constitutional replacement in every generation to allow citizens to revisit institutions and rules, adapting them to changing circumstances. He supported replacing (or at least reevaluating in some form) constitutional bargains every generation, or about every nineteen years – which is, as Elkins et al. (2009: 129) note, the median survival time of constitutions in their sample. Madison, however, took issue with such a suggestion, arguing against instability and in favor of longevity. A government worthy of respect, in Madison's view, is one that is faithful to its citizens' wishes while also remaining steadfast in the face of short-lived fads and whimsical ideas. Additionally, long-standing constitutions, according to Madison, are more stable and less susceptible to the "ambition or corruption of one" and the "sagacious, the enterprising, and the moneyed few" (Madison 1788).

Figure 7.1 provides the game form of the considerations of founders and future generations. The founders have to decide on three different issues: (1) whether to include a subject matter in the constitution, (2) whether to include many provisions on the subject and make it restrictive, and (3) how much to lock it so it is protected against revisions. Each country gives different answers to these questions. This is why subjects

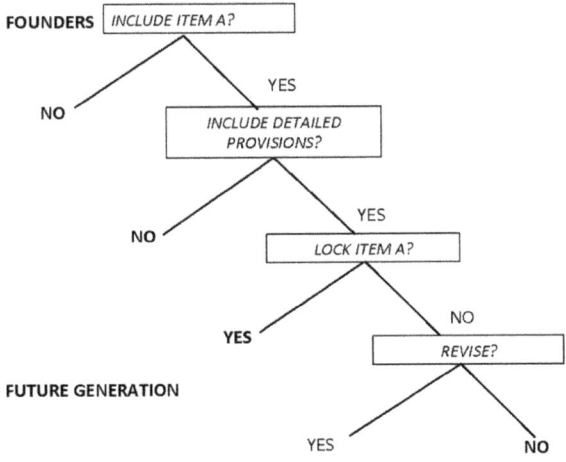

Figure 7.1 Writing and revising the constitution game

that exist in some constitutions are absent from others, and the locking mechanisms are different not only across countries but even within the same constitution (there may be some eternal clauses while the majority are amendable under specific rules).

For future generations, the question of a constitutional revision may arise, and the occurrence will be more frequent as the founders opt to incorporate more subjects and more detailed provisions. The success of such attempts at revisions will be higher the less locked the constitution is (as Chapter 6 demonstrated).

I have indicated with **bold** letters all the choices that lead to subgame perfect equilibria in this game form. One choice that does not lead to such an equilibrium, however, is the combination of constitutional detail (including a large number of provisions) and a failure to lock them sufficiently, along with the willingness of future generations to modify the constitutional provisions – that is, what Versteeg and Zackin (2016) call "specific and flexible constitutions … that represent a plausible alternative" (8).

The usual term in the economic literature for the description of such equilibria that are not subgame perfect is "time inconsistent." Economic theory has long underscored, since Kydland and Prescott's (1977) Nobel-winning article, "Rules Rather than Discretion," that time inconsistency ought to be avoided in economic policymaking. This is the standard reason that countries delegate monetary policy to central banks: to take it away from the hands of a government that will change preferences as a function of electoral cycles. This argument has been propagated in the creation of many other independent authorities as well, including environmental protection, mass media, medical regulations, and so on.

If institutions are created in order to avoid time inconsistency in **policies**, time inconsistency **a fortiori** should be avoided with respect to the **rules of the game** – that is, the constitution. In other words, constitutions that change often are subject to discretion rather than rules.[2]

---

[2] Typically, in the literature, the player with time-inconsistent preferences (who prefers to make one decision ex ante but changes their mind when the time comes) remains the same, but their preferences change. This is not, however, a necessary physical restriction. For example, the minister of finance may or may not change between the creation of an independent central bank and elections, but governments still anticipate time-inconsistent preferences between these two time periods. Thus, governments opt to create independent banks because preferences of the designated actor are likely to be time inconsistent. Similarly, in my analysis, the constitutional restrictions apply to all generations, including

On the basis of Figure 7.1, one can see that long constitutions (involving many detailed provisions) may lead to time-inconsistent outcomes. That is, despite their locking, they may lead future generations to overcome the obstacles and revise the constitution. The same thing is true about locking. If the rules become seriously obsolete, then locking may not be sufficient.

7.2 Implications and Data Analysis

The above analysis confirms two major points that have already been made in this book. First, constitutional amendments are out of (perfect) equilibrium behavior. Second, these amendments are a difficult enterprise that are actually undertaken only when solutions within the constitutional equilibrium (legislation or judicial interpretation) do not work.[3] Here I will introduce the concept of time inconsistency, measure it in a formal way, and then try to relate it to the length of a constitution. In the previous chapter, we related the constitutional rigidity of a country with its amendment frequency (or rate of amendments).

If we call fr the frequency of amendments, r the rigidity of the constitution, and k and a positive constants, we demonstrate that on average

$$fr = k - ar. \qquad (1)$$

Let us now call fr' the actual frequency of amendments in each country. On the basis of the discussion so far, we call the difference between the actual and the expected frequency of amendments time inconsistency (t):

$$t = fr' - fr. \qquad (2)$$

Combining (1) and (2), we conclude that

$$t = fr' - (k - ar). \qquad (3)$$

---

the one that made the constitution, who can also find themselves in front of an unfortunate provision that requires fast modification. The creation of collective inter-temporal actors like "government" or "nation" takes care of this same-player restriction.

[3] However, we have encountered in this book situations where constitutional amendments are *not* more difficult than ordinary legislation, like in Israel, India, the UK, or New Zealand where a simple majority is sufficient to amend the constitution, or like in Mexico (Chapter 5) where the political conjecture has generated conditions where the necessary majority for legislation also happens to be sufficient for constitutional amendments.

We will demonstrate that time inconsistency is proportional to length – that is, if we call l the (logarithm of) length of a constitution, then

$$t = b * l. \tag{4}$$

Before we move on to the empirical analysis, I want to demonstrate that besides the findings of Chapter 6 indicated by equation (1), there is now a significant new contribution to the literature. What was previously known in the literature is that the frequency of amendments is proportional to length. This finding was usually supported in an independent way by showing that longer constitutions will include more provisions and therefore will have a higher need for amendments (Lutz 1994: 357 and 359, Rasch and Congleton 2006: 542, Lijphart 2012: 207). However, more recently some researchers (Versteeg and Zackin 2016, Marshfield 2018) do not consider constitutional rigidity at all and replace it with amendment frequency. If one eliminates fr from equation (2), then (3) and (4) will lead to

$$fr' = b * l. \tag{5}$$

In other words, the actual frequency of amendments is proportional to the length of the constitution, which is what Versteeg and Zackin (2016) find in their analysis. But what escorts this noninstitutional approach is an association of length with the frequency of amendments instead of the association with time inconsistency that I demonstrate. The result is a relativistic approach to constitutional length (constitutions used to be short; now they are becoming longer, and there is nothing wrong with that). Here is the way they phrase it: "Specificity and flexibility are highly correlated with one another and appeared to have increased together in democratic constitutions... Their flexibility allows them to avoid the 'dead-hand' problem, since the living generation clearly acts as the principal in its frequent revision of the constitutional text" (Versteeg and Zackin 2016: 660). On the contrary, my analysis here makes the case that length is an undesirable characteristic associated with time inconsistency (as well as with other undesirable features that we will see). My expectation does not deviate from the assessment of most of the literature.

Let me start by replicating the findings of the literature with my data. Figure 7.2 shows the positive relationship between log length and amendment rate. Figure 7.3 presents the visual representation of my argument, which is that length is associated with time inconsistency. The slope of time inconsistency is less steep than the slope of amendment rate because time inconsistency is, by definition (see equation [3]), the actual rate minus the expected rate (on the basis of constitutional rigidity).

7.2 IMPLICATIONS AND DATA ANALYSIS

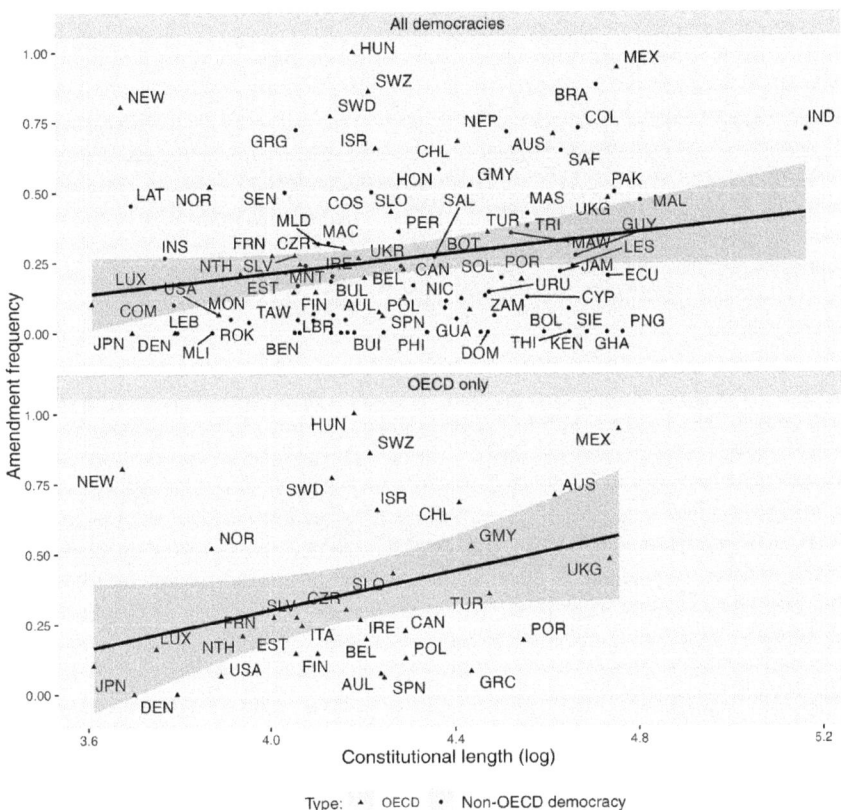

Figure 7.2 Amendment frequency and log length

As I said in the Introduction, I will start by replicating the analyses of Tsebelis and Nardi (2016) and Tsebelis (2017b), but I will use the constitutional rigidity measure introduced in this book instead of the more crude measures used in these articles. This way, we will have a more accurate assessment of the arguments. Tsebelis and Nardi (2016) only measure Organization for Economic Co-operation and Development (OECD) countries not only because the data were more easily available but also because they were expecting that the hypothesized relationships (in this case, time inconsistency and length) would be more discernible than in the wider set of democratic countries. Tsebelis (2017b) confirms this intuition but still uses alternative and rough indicators of rigidity.

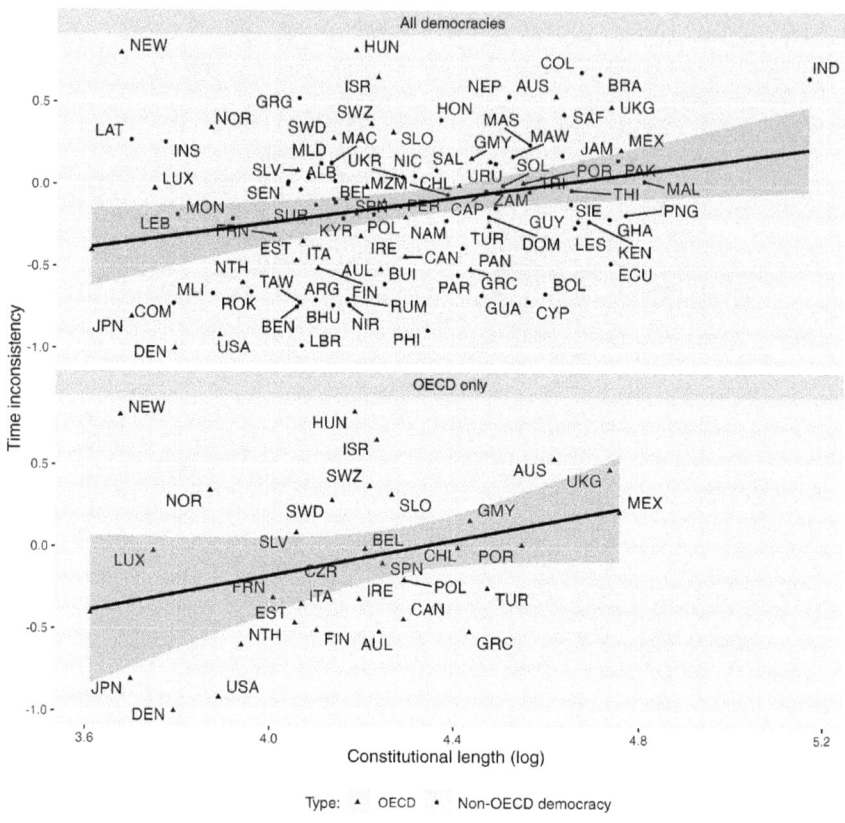

Figure 7.3 Time inconsistency and log length

Table 7.1 separates OECD countries from all democracies and uses the more theoretically founded and empirically accurate indicator of time inconsistency.

The first assessment is that the slope of OECD countries is steeper (0.45) than all democracies (0.34). However, the fact that there are three times more democratic countries than OECD countries makes the relationship significant for all the democratic countries but not for the OECD ones. This is true for the constants as well. The positive relationship in both cases indicates that longer constitutions have a higher time inconsistency (that is, the combination of rigidity and frequency of amendment). I will now consider this relationship more closely.

Table 7.1 *Time inconsistency as a function of constitution length*

	OECD	DEMOC
n	33	100
Log length	0.541	0.391 *
	(0.306)	(0.153)
Constant	−2.339	−1.795 *
	(1.318)	(0.667)
R^2	0.111	0.080

* $p < 0.05$.

7.3 Correlates of Length (Time Inconsistency, GDP per Capita, Corruption, Economic Inequality, Lack of Innovation, etc.)

In order to explain this time inconsistency, one needs to first understand the characteristics of long constitutions and then identify other factors that are associated with them.

7.3.1 What Is Length?

Constitutions can include three different kinds of provisions. First, constitutional provisions can regulate technical or innocuous matters that do not influence political behavior. Second, constitutions can contain aspirational goals, such as the right to work (included in many post–World War II constitutions), which do not impose any specific obligations on the government and are consequently not judicially enforceable (unsurprisingly, none of these countries have completely eradicated unemployment). Thirdly, constitutions contain restrictive or prescriptive statements, such as sections detailing government structure and citizens' rights. While these three categories might be straightforward at the theoretical level, empirically there is no reliable way of distinguishing between constitutions that contain many substantive restrictions and those that are simply "garrulous" (Voigt 2009). However, the frequency of amendments along with the difficulty of achieving such modifications indicates that long constitutions are restrictive because a country would not undertake the significant or formidable efforts required for amendments if these amendments were not deemed necessary. In other words, constitutional amendments are more likely to be made on restrictive provisions, not on innocuous ones.

Another question regarding length pertains to how words are distributed over topics in the constitution: Are there many topics with little discussion, a very detailed discussion of a few topics, or is it somewhere in between? The Comparative Constitutional Project dataset (Elkins et al. 2009) makes the distinction between the "scope" of a constitution (that is, the number of selected subjects included in it) and its "detail" (the number of words used to cover each subject on average). Obviously, the length of every constitution is the product of the two. Given this logical relationship, a regression predicting the length of a constitution (as a function of scope, detail, and their interaction) would provide a coefficient of 1 for the product term and an R^2 of 1. In other words, both variables cannot be used in the same equation. One could drop the distinction between these two variables and talk about their product (length). However, if we want to investigate along these lines, we can proceed as follows: It is known in the literature that more recent constitutions have a larger scope (i.e., they address more subjects); therefore, I can use the age of the constitution as a proxy for scope, provided the variable "age" is uncorrelated with "detail." As Figure 7.4 indicates, this is the case in all the countries of the world (regardless of whether they are democracies or not).

Now it is possible to identify the characteristics associated with length using the age of the constitution as a proxy for its scope. Table 7.2 examines the variables in the literature associated with the length of constitutions, focusing first on OECD member countries and then on all democracies. The variables I examine are age, detail, federalism, and legal origins. Again, the statistical significance is higher for all democracies than it is for OECD countries, but the coefficients are larger for OECD countries. The important finding is that "detail" has a positive coefficient and "age" (which is a proxy for "scope") has a small negative one. It is interesting that federalism has a negative but not significant effect, indicating that instead of expanding the constitution to include the interactions between federal and state governments the federal constitutions delegate many issues to the state governments. Also, the legal origins have no effect on the regressions. The conclusion is that across all democratic countries of the world, constitutional length is associated with more restrictions.

7.3.2 What Is Associated with Constitutional Length?

For long constitutions to be more time inconsistent – that is, to exhibit a higher number of amendments, despite locking – they must also lead to

7.3 CORRELATES OF LENGTH

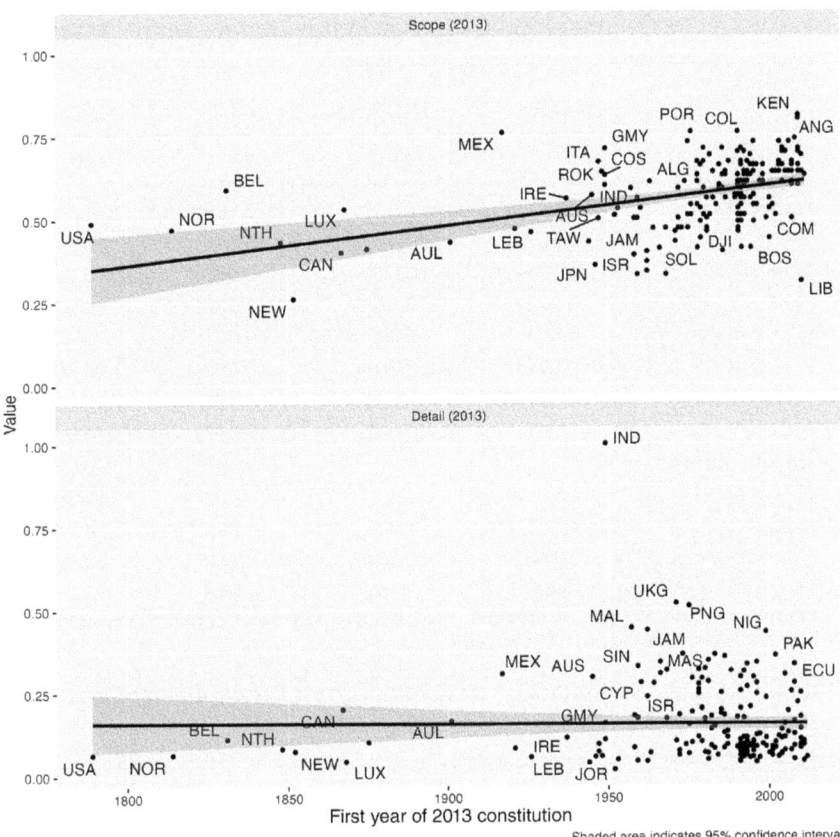

Figure 7.4 Scope and details in 187 countries

serious impediments to the political game in their corresponding countries. Tsebelis and Nardi (2016) identify two important correlates of constitutional length in OECD countries: GDP per capita and corruption.

Long constitutions are restrictive, and, as such, they prevent the adoption of policies that are desirable to the populations they regulate. This may be a reason for frequent constitutional amendments. One aggregate variable that would cause generalized dissatisfaction and would therefore cause constitutional revisions would be low GDP per capita. Table 7.3 corroborates the inverse relationship between constitutional length and GDP per capita (a relationship depicted graphically in Figure 7.5). In addition, with respect to corruption, Tsebelis and Nardi

Table 7.2 *Constitutional length as a function of country characteristics*

	OECD	DEMOC	OECD	DEMOC
n	33	99	33	99
Detail (calc)	2.401 **	1.839 ***	2.560 ***	1.869 ***
	(0.667)	(0.475)	(0.690)	(0.467)
Federalism	−0.108	−0.014	−0.088	−0.013
	(0.073)	(0.037)	(0.080)	(0.038)
Age of democracy	−0.003 *	−0.002 ***	−0.003	−0.002 *
	(0.001)	(0.001)	(0.002)	(0.001)
Legal origins	0.091	0.031	0.082	0.027
	(0.091)	(0.062)	(0.093)	(0.061)
Num amendments			−0.002	−0.001
			(0.002)	(0.002)
Constant	4.092 ***	4.045 ***	4.065 ***	4.041 ***
	(0.150)	(0.084)	(0.160)	(0.083)
R^2	0.807	0.758	0.815	0.759

*** $p < 0.001$; ** $p < 0.01$; * $p < 0.05$.

Table 7.3 *GDP per capita as a function of constitutional length and economic variables*

	OECD	DEMOC	OECD	DEMOC
n	32	97	30	70
Length (log)	−0.299 **	−0.442 **	−0.264 *	−0.225 *
	(0.108)	(0.149)	(0.103)	(0.101)
Education			0.001	0.006 ***
			(0.002)	(0.002)
Natural resources			0.002	−0.004
			(0.009)	(0.006)
Trade			0.001	0.000
			(0.001)	(0.001)
Investment			−0.015	−0.016 *
			(0.008)	(0.008)
Constant	5.767 ***	5.919 ***	5.819 ***	5.156 ***
	(0.449)	(0.650)	(0.485)	(0.539)
R^2	0.271	0.071	0.418	0.314

*** $p < 0.001$; ** $p < 0.01$; * $p < 0.05$.

Table 7.4 *GDP per capita as a function of length, economic variables, education, and corruption*

	OECD	DEMOC	OECD	DEMOC
n	30	70	30	70
Length (log)	−0.264 *	−0.225 *	−0.044	−0.025
	(0.103)	(0.101)	(0.103)	(0.079)
Education	0.001	0.006 ***	−0.000	0.003 *
	(0.002)	(0.002)	(0.001)	(0.001)
Natural resources	0.002	−0.004	−0.001	0.001
	(0.009)	(0.006)	(0.010)	(0.005)
Trade	0.001	0.000	0.001	0.001
	(0.001)	(0.001)	(0.001)	(0.001)
Investment	−0.015	−0.016 *	−0.007	−0.004
	(0.008)	(0.008)	(0.006)	(0.005)
Corruption (TPI)			−0.055 ***	−0.111 ***
			(0.011)	(0.011)
Constant	5.819 ***	5.156 ***	4.390 ***	3.652 ***
	(0.485)	(0.539)	(0.565)	(0.433)
R^2	0.418	0.314	0.696	0.744

*** $p < 0.001$; ** $p < 0.01$; * $p < 0.05$.

(2016) argue that causal links could be pointing in both directions: It could be that founders were captured by special interests who were asking for additional detailed provisions to be locked so that their privileges would be guaranteed. Alternatively, it may be that virtuous founders tried to include provisions in order to prevent or reduce the influence of organized interests.

Tsebelis and Nardi (2016) also anticipated that these relations would be clearer in OECD countries because these countries respect their constitutions, and, consequently, safer inferences can be made from the study of OECD countries. In Table 7.4, I include education and corruption as control variables (on top of the economic ones). This inclusion removes the statistical significance of length on GDP per capita, which occurs because corruption is strongly correlated with constitutional length as Figure 7.6 demonstrates.

However, more recent and controlled analyses give stronger results. Adam Brown (2022) examines the constitutions of the US states not in a cross-sectional analysis as I do but in a time-series comparison, finding

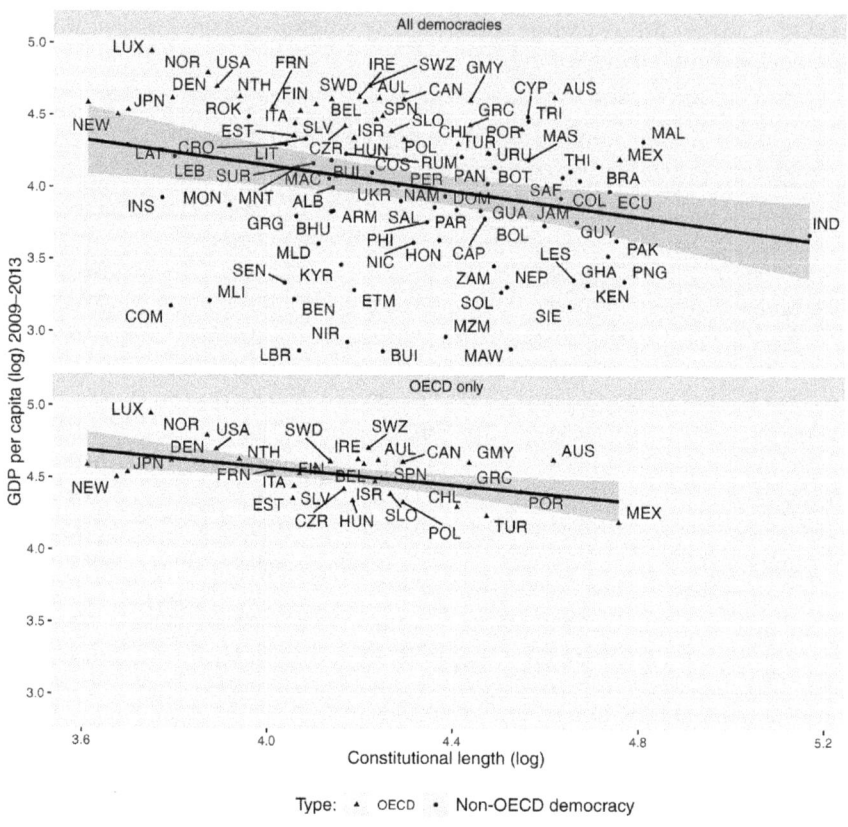

Figure 7.5 Log GDP and log length

that longer constitutions generate more amendments, more frequent judicial adjudications, and more negative economic indicators. I will here discuss his economic findings in more detail because they are indeed more convincing than the cross-country analysis of this book.

Brown does not find a relationship between length and constitutional rigidity and considers the assessment "long constitutions are restrictive" in Tsebelis (2017b) as a consequence of constitutional rigidity, while it is actually the result of more "detail" (see discussion around Figure 7.4 and Table 7.2 in this chapter).[4] Because of this, he proposes length itself as an independent variable. In the words of this book, he does not differentiate

---

[4] Chapter 6 does not present any relationship between length and constitutional rigidity.

7.3 CORRELATES OF LENGTH 185

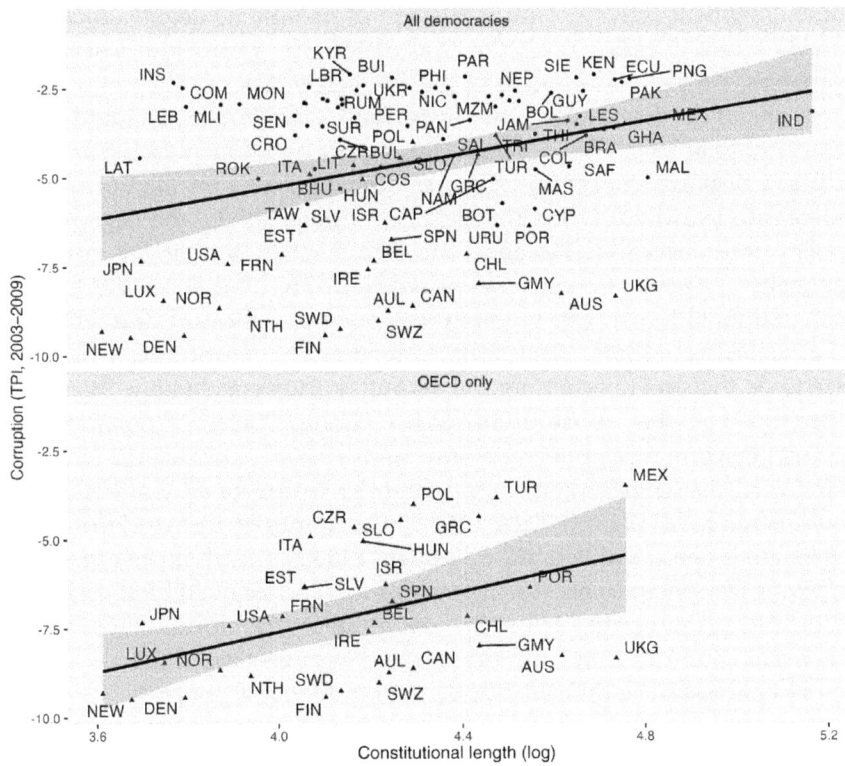

Figure 7.6 Corruption and log length

between "scope" (how many different topics are included in a constitution) and "detail" (how many words are used for each topic). His argument is that the inclusion of anything in the constitution (whether it be a different subject or more details in the text) is restrictive.

He also tests for a correlation between length and corruption and does not find any in his data. By contrast, he finds that more length was used in the constitutions adopted between 1870 and 1900 when political elites and authorities were mistrusted, not in relation to corruption.

Brown uses twenty years of constitutional history of the US states (except for Alabama) with biannual evaluation of constitutional length (which sometimes changes by 4,500 words!), as well as other control variables, and focuses on four dependent variables: GDP per capita, unemployment rate, the Gini coefficient of income inequality, and state policy innovativeness (Boehmke et al. 2018). He controls for a series of variables, such as the strength of parties, percentage of different minorities, age of the constitution, and number of amendments, and finds that constitutional length has a significant impact on all his dependent variables: a negative impact on GDP per capita, positive on the unemployment rate, positive on the Gini coefficient (inequalities), and negative on policy innovativeness. He goes one step further, testing for Granger causality – that is, he examines whether in his time series the lagged constitutional length can predict the economic indicators and whether the lagged economic indicators can predict constitutional length. He finds that the first but not the second is true, concluding, "We may therefore say that constitution length Granger-causes economic and policy performance, but economic and policy performance do not Granger-cause constitution length – and this is true for all four outcomes considered here" (Brown 2022: 136). This empirical evidence of the effect of length is consistent with my arguments but goes much further in terms of empirical evidence because it controls for a series of cultural variables (one can presume that US states are significantly more homogeneous than the countries I am considering) and because time series are much more conclusive causal evidence than cross-sectional analyses.

Conclusions

This chapter demonstrates that long constitutions are restrictive and generate a higher rate of amendments than what they were designed for (time inconsistency). Given the difficulty of performing constitutional revisions, such revisions are not likely to be undertaken without reason. They are likely to affect enforceable provisions that are hindering government majorities from acting the way they judge to be appropriate. In this sense, they are constraining majorities from making decisions according to their wishes, and they are confronting the democratic expression of the representatives of the people. Therefore, long constitutions are not just garrulous (Voigt 2009), but they are also restrictive, as Brown (2022) argues. Constitutional revisions may be due to design if a constitution is not rigid (that is, if amendment provisions are permissive). However, this chapter shows that the length of constitutions across all democratic countries of the world is correlated with time inconsistency – that is, the **combination** of locking and amendment frequency. This means that long constitutions do not just "represent a plausible alternative solution to some of the agency problems associated with constitutional design" (Versteeg and Zackin 2016) but represent a suboptimal solution as recognized for many years by the literature.

This chapter starts with an equilibrium analysis of the constitutional amendment provisions and shows that if constitutional amendments are to be successful in democracies then they require the support of majorities that exceed the limits specified by the amendment provisions of the constitution. More than that, this chapter demonstrates that the difference between the actual rate of amendments and the rate expected by the amendment provisions depends on the length of the constitution, and it shows that this length has an impact on the time inconsistency of the constitution (that is, the combination of locking and amendment frequency).

The usual means to eliminate time inconsistency in the literature is to delegate to an independent authority. This is not a possible solution in constitutional matters, though, because there is no higher authority than the people. If the people modify a constitution despite the obstacles included by the founders, it means that either there were radically new conditions or there was a design flaw due to potentially objectionable provisions being included and protected in the constitution. These provisions were later considered impediments either because the conditions changed or because large majorities changed their minds. Therefore, the best way to reduce time inconsistency is to avoid locking the constitution and/or avoid lengthy ones. Only rules that are widely accepted and are not likely to be overturned should be locked.

This is not the only argument in the literature. As I mentioned, Ginsburg and Melton (2015) argue that "the constitutions of India, Mexico, and Brazil, to take three prominent examples, are amended nearly every year. Such constitutions have the virtue of being frequently changed through internal mechanisms, avoiding the costly route of a total replacement. In such countries, we argue that the stakes of amendment are lower, and so cultural resistance to amend is less than in societies where it is infrequent" (689). Indeed, all three of these countries are highly time inconsistent, but the Indian case is due to the extremely lengthy constitution (the amendment rule is similar to legislation). In this respect, there is little formal difference between India and a country without a written constitution like the UK, where parliament can change any law it wants to by a simple majority. As for Brazil (with 68,000 words of constitutional text and a three-fifths majority required in both chambers on two different occasions for amendment), a detailed analysis is required. However, when analyzing the Brazilian Constitution, Couto and Arantes (2008) find that "The Brazilian constitution of 1988 presents a high rate of constitutional amending, with 62 amendments in twenty years (3.1 amendments per year); most of them sponsored by the Executive branch, aiming at implementing *public policies*" (Couto and Arrantes 2008: 1; emphasis mine). They argue that there is a high percentage of policymaking provisions inside the constitution, and they create a new measure of constitutional provisions, finding that 30 percent of them are policy related.[5] However, further research is required for these two cases. The Mexican case has already been discussed in Chapter 5 where I argued that the only visible "virtue" was political, being the attempt for wide-ranging coalitions. Further, these coalitions make constitutional amendments as easy as legislation and, consequently, a dominant solution for the parties.

The analysis presented in this chapter focuses on time inconsistency. The general approach in the time inconsistency literature is that, at the beginning of the game, institutional measures (rules) should be taken to prevent time inconsistency from manifesting itself (discretion).[6] With respect to constitutions, the analogy would be that "a constitution is Peter sober while the electorate is Peter drunk" (Holmes 1988: 195–196). Both Hayek (2006: 157) and Elster (2010) raise objections to such an approach. I argued that given the difficulty of constitutional change, adopted constitutional amendments were necessary, and I argued that the restrictions that were included in the original constitution are essentially undermining the essence of a document that sets the rules of the game. Therefore, it would be more reasonable to reduce the restrictive provisions (by reducing the length) instead of locking the constitutions more. Dixon (2014) has divided constitution writing into "codified-" and "framework-" styled approaches and provides legal arguments in favor of the latter style. I provide a similar empirically generated argument that long constitutions are restrictive. If my analysis is correct, the authors of the first constitution of a country should exercise constraint and not assume that they can lock anything they want in the constitution. Doing so leads to long, time-inconsistent constitutions. However, this is a "retroactive" suggestion with twenty-twenty hindsight. A prospective suggestion would be to have the people who engage in constitutional

---

[5] I thank Rogerio Arantes for familiarizing me with his work.
[6] Similarly, philosophy speaks about the "weakness of will," or "akrasia" as in Plato's (2008: 180–183) *Protagoras*.

revisions take the time to prune their constitutions. In other words, if a certain provision is restrictive, it would be more efficient to just drop it instead of replacing it with a different one.

What the correlation of length with time inconsistency indicates is that too many things are locked in constitutions, which results in the undermining of their effectiveness. Therefore, length and locking of constitutions is not a matter of culture but of arrogance and lack of restriction on the part of constitution writers. To use Jeremy Waldron's terms, "Any alternative conception that might be concocted by elected legislators next year or in ten years' time is so likely to be wrong-headed or ill motivated that his own formulation is to be elevated immediately beyond the reach of ordinary legislative revision" (Waldron 1999: 222). These arguments iterate on constitutional grounds the wisdom of the ages, such as the biblical verse Matthew 5:37 (English Standard Version): "Let what you say be simply 'Yes' or 'No'; anything more than this comes from evil," or even older sayings like "λακωνιζειν εστι φιλοσοφειν," or "brevity is the source of wit."[7] These assessments should be considered seriously when studying constitutions and should be abided by when writing constitutions.

---

[7] This is an accurate but very reduced English translation. (Ancient Spartans were very terse in their expression, and they had raised brevity of expression to a virtue equivalent to philosophy, which is what the proverb states.)

8

Constitutional Rigidity and Judicial Independence

Research on judicial independence (JI) has flourished since the pathbreaking article of Cooter and Ginsburg (1996) on judicial discretion. Cooter and Ginsburg (1996) argue that because judges have more discretion to shift policy when they are unafraid of being overruled, their discretion increases "*when the probability decreases of legislative repeal of their decisions*" (295), which they measure (among other factors) as the number of vetoes legislation has to clear.[1]

Today, a voluminous literature seeks to understand what exactly constitutes JI, identify how to measure it, and determine both its causes and its effects on other phenomena of interest. JI is thought to be essential to constraining state power and making agreements credible (North and Weingast 1989), and it leads to efficient investment, growth, and development (Barro 1997, Acemoglu et al. 2001, Feld and Voigt 2003), respect for human rights (Powell and Staton 2009), and democratic consolidation (North et al. 2000).

Starting with Feld and Voigt (2003), much of the literature distinguishes between de jure and de facto JI. De jure JI is generally defined as the independence guaranteed to judiciaries in formal legal documents (e.g., the constitution), whereas de facto JI is the amount of independence the judiciary enjoys in practice. The former is typically measured in terms of the presence or absence of a set of procedural factors (length of tenure, methods of appointment and removal, formal declaration of independence of the judiciary, etc.) (Keith 2002, Feld and Voigt 2003,

---

[1] They presented a brilliant (but limited) measure of judicial discretion, considering whether the courts alone (high discretion) or in cooperation with the legislature (medium discretion) had developed measures of strict liability for consumer product injuries. The default condition when the legislature develops the rules is classified as low discretion. Their empirical research corroborated their expectations.

La Porta et al. 2004), while the latter is measured by expert assessments (Howard and Carey 2004).[2]

Findings from this line of research indicate a weak relationship between the de facto and de jure JI: Researchers have shown that de facto JI, rather than de jure JI, is correlated with growth (Feld and Voigt 2003, Voigt et al. 2015), that de jure JI is weakly positively correlated with de facto JI (Hayo and Voigt 2007, 2019), that most components of de jure JI are uncorrelated with de facto JI (Melton and Ginsburg 2014), and that de jure JI is weakly negatively correlated with de facto JI (Ríos-Figueroa and Staton 2014, Metelska-Szaniawska and Lewkowicz 2021).

This set of findings implies that formal rules are ineffective at guaranteeing judicial independence. However, as Ríos-Figueroa and Staton (2014) argue, the theoretical motivation for why a specific rule should or should not contribute to judicial independence and the mechanisms by which it does so remains underdeveloped; therefore, researchers should be cautious in uncritically using indexes of rules as a measure for de jure JI. I concur with this assessment and take it one step further. To measure the relationship between formal institutional rules and the behaviors they condition, we need three things: a specific formal rule, a specific behavioral outcome, and a theorized mechanism by which the rule conditions the outcome.

To this end, instead of trying to establish a relationship between additive indexes of de jure provisions and de facto outcomes, I provide here a theoretical account of how a specific de jure feature of constitutions – the constitutional amendment rule – affects a specific de facto behavioral outcome: the capacity of a judiciary to strike down government legislation. I argue that as constitutions become more difficult to amend, high courts gain more *discretion* in their ability to strike down legislation without fearing a government override. By theoretically motivating the relationship between constitutional rigidity and judicial strikes, I can outline the conditions under which we will actually observe judicial strikes in terms of two theoretical quantities: the discretion afforded to judges by the constitution and the preferences of the judiciary over policy outcomes. When judges have a high level of discretion and their preferences over policy are not aligned with the government, they have considerable ability to strike down government legislation. In other words, they are independent of the government, with the amount of

---

[2] Evaluations and comparisons of the approaches can be found in Ríos-Figueroa and Staton (2014) and Linzer and Staton (2015).

independence increasing in both the level of discretion and the distance between judicial and government preferences. Conversely, when the judiciary has no discretion or is perfectly aligned with the government preference-wise, they will not be independent of the government, and, consequently, we will not observe independent behavior.

A parsimonious measure of JI directly follows from the definition of JI as being the frequency with which the judiciary alters or invalidates the policy of the *sitting* government, given the opportunity to do so. An example will clarify this definition: If the US Supreme Court decides to invalidate Obamacare while President Obama is in office, it will count as a demonstration of judicial independence, while if it makes this decision when President Trump is in office, it will not count as such.[3]

Using a measure of judicial discretion based on the constitutional rigidity index from Chapter 6, I estimate the effect of judicial discretion on JI. Because judicial preferences are unmeasurable except in rare cases, I deliberately exclude them from the analysis.[4] On the basis of the theorized relationship between preferences, discretion, and independence, I expect there to be a positive heteroskedastic relationship between judicial discretion and observable judicial independence such that at low levels of discretion, judicial independence is uniformly low, but at high levels of discretion, judicial independence varies between high or low depending on the judges' preferences. In addition, to control for the necessary condition for judicial independence that the decisions of the judiciary must be respected and enforced, I restrict my analysis to countries that are democratic (operationalized as countries that score over five on the POLITY2 index) on the basis that in democracies the decisions of the judiciary are likely to be respected.[5]

I test my theoretical expectation using data from the Comparative Law Project to calculate the rate of judicial strikes of government legislation

---

[3] It could not count as the opposite either; it could simply mean that the court agrees with the policy positions of President Trump.

[4] Judicial preferences are very difficult to measure. In fact, people have argued that they matter a lot (see Stone Sweet 2007 for France and Carrubba et al. 2012 for the US), but no systematic effort has been made to measure them in a comparative context. Actually, most of the time, unlike in the cases of the US and France where they are proposed by specific actors with (US) or without (France) other interference, usually the selection is the product of compromise, obscuring a preference assessment.

[5] It should be clear that the meaning as well as the measure of "judicial independence" will be different in a democratic and a nondemocratic country. Further, as some countries have "sham constitutions" (Law and Versteeg 2013), there will also be countries with a sham independent judiciary. Mixing these countries will just obfuscate the analysis.

and the constitutional rigidity index from Chapter 6 as a measure of judicial discretion over constitutional matters and show that the data support the hypothesized relationship between JI and discretion: As discretion increases, so too does the rate at which government legislation is struck down by the judiciary as well as its variance. I close with a discussion of directions for future research into JI. This chapter includes an appendix with the data used in the empirical analysis.

8.1 Literature Review

Judicial independence is often considered important for any well-functioning political system,[6] but the effect of JI on outcomes such as economic growth, democratic stability, and respect for human rights has been mixed. While an extensive literature from political economy has shown the positive relationship between institutional quality and economic growth (Acemoglu et al. 2002, 2005) and between property rights and economic growth (Acemoglu and Johnson 2005), there has been comparatively little research into the effect of JI on economic growth. Moreover, the research that does exist comes to contradictory conclusions: Glaeser et al. (2004) show that JI is uncorrelated with growth, whereas La Porta et al. (2004) show that JI is positively associated with economic and political rights. In a series of papers, Feld and Voigt claim that de facto JI, defined as the amount of independence that the judiciary enjoys in practice, is associated with economic growth but that de jure JI, defined as the amount of independence that is formally guaranteed to the judiciary in written legal texts, is uncorrelated with growth (Feld and Voigt 2003, Voigt et al. 2015). However, Dove (2015, 2016) shows that across the US states, JI is positively correlated with both entrepreneurship and economic freedom (using the procedure that judges are appointed by – a measure that would be considered to be de jure JI in the Feld and Voigt typology).

With respect to the relationship between JI and political rights, Howard and Carey (2004) show that "judicial independence is an important, if not absolutely necessary, condition for the development of political and civil liberties" (290). Keith et al. (2009) show that some indicators of JI (including the finality of court decisions and the absence of exceptional courts) are correlated with a reduction in state human rights abuse, but other indicators (such as guaranteed term lengths, fiscal autonomy for

---

[6] See North and Weingast (1989), North et al. (2000), and Randazzo et al. (2016).

judges, and judicial review) are not so correlated. Keith (2011) also shows that de facto JI is associated with respect for human rights.

The relationship between de jure and de facto JI is unclear: Hayo and Voigt (2007) show that de jure JI is the most important predictor of de facto JI, Ríos-Figueroa and Staton (2014) show that de jure JI is negatively correlated with de facto JI, Helmke and Rosenbluth (2009) show that de jure JI is uncorrelated with de facto JI, Keith (2011) shows that de jure JI is correlated with de facto JI, and Melton and Ginsburg (2014) show that only some combinations of de jure JI factors are predictive of de facto JI. More recently, Gutman and Voigt (2018, 2020) show that while de jure and de facto JI are completely uncorrelated at the world level, they are negatively correlated when restricting the sample to only democratic countries and positively correlated when restricting to only nondemocracies. Metelska-Szaniawska and Lewkowicz (2021) analyze JI in post-Soviet countries and find no relationship between de jure and de facto JI. The absence of a clear, observed relationship between de jure and de facto JI has led some scholars to investigate why such a gap exists in the first place. Voigt (2021) argues that the de jure–de facto gap is understudied and undertheorized and proposes a research program to investigate the determinants of the gap. Metelska-Szaniawska (2021) takes up Voigt's research program and shows that in post-Soviet constitutions, longer and more complicated constitutions are associated with larger de jure–de facto gaps.

There are reasons to be skeptical of these findings. First, there is no single agreed-upon definition of JI (Ríos-Figueroa and Staton 2014, Staton 2018). Second, since there is no way to observe JI directly, researchers must use proxies for which the relationship with JI is not always clear. As a result, there is inconsistency both within and across measures as to what constitutes an indicator of JI and whether a given indicator is associated with a higher or lower level of JI. The de jure–de facto split exacerbates this problem: It is frequently unclear whether measures are, in fact, proxying only de facto JI (as opposed to both de facto and de jure JI). I discuss each of these problems in the following sections.

8.1.1 Definition of JI

When analyzing JI, researchers must decide whether to define JI in terms of the *autonomy* that judges have from other branches of government and/or in terms of the ability of the judiciary to *influence* policy outcomes (that is, have their decisions implemented). Most scholars define JI strictly in terms of autonomy (e.g., Cox 1996, Kornhauser 2002,

Howard and Carey 2004, La Porta et al. 2004, Ríos-Figueroa 2007, Helmke and Rosenbluth 2009, Keith et al. 2009, Gibler and Randazzo 2011)[7] or as a combination of both autonomy and influence (Ferejohn and Kramer 2002, Feld and Voigt 2003). I will follow the general rule and focus on autonomy. Given that I restrict my empirical analysis to democratic countries, the implementation of judicial decisions can, in principle, be assumed.

8.1.2 Inconsistency within and across Measures of JI

A researcher's measure of JI can be problematic if it lacks internal consistency, which occurs when the chosen proxies do not match the definition of JI. Glaeser et al. (2004) and La Porta et al. (2004), for example, define JI as the ability of judges to enforce laws without interference (an autonomy-based measure) but measure JI in terms of whether judicial decisions are a source of law.

Internal consistency can also be a problem when researchers use measures of other related concepts as a proxy for judicial independence. For example, researchers such as Dove (2016) cite Barro (1997) as providing evidence that JI leads to economic growth, but Barro shows the effect of the *central bank* rather than *judicial* independence on growth. Similarly, Linzer and Staton (2015) include the Contract Intensive Money (CIM) score from Clague et al. (1999) in their composite measure of JI despite the CIM score reflecting the proportion of money in a given polity that is held in banking institutions.

This can also lead to inconsistency across measures since researchers are not all measuring the same concept. For example, Hayo and Voigt (2010) measure whether a constitution has an explicit statement of judicial independence, while Melton and Ginsburg (2014) are skeptical as to whether this will have an effect. Hayo and Voigt (2007) argue that judges who only serve one term are more independent, while Ríos-Figueroa and Staton (2014) argue that it is only important that the judge's term is longer than those who elected or appointed them. Melton and Ginsburg (2014) argue that judges with lifetime terms are more independent. Other concepts such as the number of judges,

---

[7] A typical autonomy-based definition of JI is "the extent to which a court may adjudicate free from institutional controls, incentives, and impediments imposed or intimidated by force, money, or extralegal, corrupt methods by individuals or institutions outside the judiciary, whether within or outside the government" (Howard and Carey 2004: 286).

selection procedure, removal procedure, salary insulation, changes to rules, and dependence on other branches are less debated but vary in terms of whether they are included in the measure altogether (Melton and Ginsburg 2014).

As a result, independent measures of JI may be uncorrelated even when trying to capture the same dimension of independence. For example, Haggard et al. (2008) show that the correlation between the La Porta et al. (2004) measure of JI and the measure used by the Word Economic Forum is only 0.15, even though both measures are attempting to capture the autonomy dimension of judicial independence.

8.1.3 Unclear Distinction between De Jure and De Facto JI

Both problems are also exacerbated by the strategies researchers use to distinguish between de jure and de facto JI. Tables 8.1 and 8.2 summarize

Table 8.1 *Measures of de facto judicial independence*

Source	Description
Howard and Carey (2004)	An ordinal measure of judicial autonomy with the levels fully independent, partially independent, or dependent based on US state department country reports
Henisz (2000)	A binary measure that uses the Political Executive Constraints measure and the Political Risk Service's Law and Order measure to get at the extent to which the judiciary is a constraint on the government
Cingranelli and Richards (2008)	An ordinal measure of judicial independence from none, partial, to full using state department country reports
Linzer and Staton (2015)	A continuous measure bounded by 0 and 1 measuring eight different components of de facto judicial independence using US state department human rights country reports as well as expert surveys
Feld and Voigt (2003)	A continuous measure bounded by 0 and 1 with eight different components of de facto judicial independence from expert surveys (note how much harder it is to get expert surveys on de facto as opposed to de jure judicial independence)
Hayo and Voigt (2007)	A continuous measure bounded between 0 and 1 with eight different components of de facto judicial independence collected with an expert survey

Table 8.2 *Measures of de jure judicial independence*

Source	Description
Hayo and Voigt (2007)	A continuous measure from 0 to 1 that includes twelve different variables collected from an expert survey
Hayo and Voigt (2010)	A selection of twenty-one variables from the Comparative Constitutions Project that they think are relevant in explaining judicial independence
Melton and Ginsburg (2014)	A measure of each aspect of judicial independence using data from the Comparative Constitutions Project (described in Table 8.4) on a 0 to 1 scale
Feld and Voigt (2003)	A continuous measure between 0 and 1 from twelve different indicators (twelve different variables described in Table 8.3) from expert surveys

existing measures of de facto and de jure JI in the literature, respectively, and Table 8.3 breaks down which indicators of de jure JI are used by each indicator. Starting with Feld and Voigt (2003), many researchers consider the two to be separate concepts, with de jure JI referring to the amount of JI guaranteed in legal texts and de facto JI to the amount of JI that exists in practice.

Despite the intent to distinguish between legally guaranteed and actually occurring independence, every measure of de facto JI mixes elements from both de jure and de facto JI. Measures based on expert surveys (e.g., Feld and Voigt 2003, Howard and Carey 2004, Cingranelli and Richards 2008) cannot ensure that the surveyed experts separate the influence of institutional guarantees in their assessment of the independence of a country's judiciary, and measures using procedural checklists include structural factors that should be associated more closely with the de jure concept.[8]

It is also not clear what the de jure concept is measuring. Most measures amount to aggregating a checklist of rules and procedures (e.g., Feld and Voigt 2003, Hayo and Voigt 2014). But, as Ríos-Figueroa and Staton (2014) argue, whether researchers recognize it or not, by using the de jure concept they are implicitly trying to capture the *incentives* that the written guarantees of independence provide the actors,

---

[8] For example, Feld and Voigt (2003) code a change to the formal legal rules as an indicator of low de facto JI.

Table 8.3 *Components of de jure judicial independence*

Description	Source(s)
Explicit statement of judicial independence	Hayo and Voigt (2010)
Measure of judicial tenure (one term)	Hayo and Voigt (2007)
Measure of judicial tenure (term longer than those that elected them)	Ríos-Figueroa (2011)
Measure of judicial tenure (lifetime term)	Melton and Ginsburg (2014), Feld and Voigt (2003)
Number of judges	Hayo and Voigt (2007)
Selection procedures	Melton and Ginsburg (2014), Feld and Voigt (2003), Hayo and Voigt (2010)
Removal procedures (cannot be removed or limited removal procedures)	Melton and Ginsburg (2014), Hayo and Voigt (2007, 2010)
Salary insulation (as well as access to other resources)	Melton and Ginsburg (2014), Hayo and Voigt (2007), Feld and Voigt (2003), Hayo and Voigt (2010)
Changes to rules (or lack thereof)	Hayo and Voigt (2007), Feld and Voigt (2003)
Dependence on other branches	Hayo and Voigt (2007)
Ability to initiate proceedings	Feld and Voigt (2003)
Publish decisions	Feld and Voigt (2003), Hayo and Voigt (2010)

rather than simply the semantic content of the written guarantees of JI. It is not clear a priori which rules should be included in a given measure of de jure JI, and, as a result, different measures of de jure JI (Feld and Voigt 2003, La Porta et al. 2004, Keith et al. 2009) are only weakly correlated with one another.

8.1.4 Composite Measures as a Corrective?

Recognizing the multiplicity of different measures of JI and the uneven coverage of these measures across both countries and time, some scholars have created composite measures of JI. Hayo and Voigt (2014, 2016) generate a time-series cross-sectional measure of de jure JI for 100 countries between 1950 and 2005 using factor analysis to extract the shared

8.1 LITERATURE REVIEW

information from a variety of structural indicators of JI; Linzer and Staton (2015) use a Bayesian Item-Response model to create a composite measure of de facto JI from 1948 to 2012 across over 200 countries by pooling information from a variety of existing de jure and de facto measures of JI (Feld and Voigt 2003, Howard and Carey 2004, Cingranelli and Richards 2008, Keith et al. 2009, economic and investment indexes from Clague et al. 1999, the Global Competitiveness Report, the International Country Risk Guide, the XCONST index from Polity IV).

It is unclear how to interpret Linzer and Staton's composite measure or what to do when other researchers use the Linzer and Staton measure of de facto JI to test the relationship between de jure and de facto JI given that the latent variable modeled by Linzer and Staton contains information from both de jure and de facto measures (Hayo and Voigt 2019).

8.1.5 Implications for Existing Findings

In sum, we should be skeptical of the validity of existing measures of JI and be cautious in accepting the lack of cohesive empirical findings from the literature at face value. Recall a central confusion from the literature: Feld and Voigt (2003) and Hayo and Voigt (2007, 2016, 2019) claim that de facto and not de jure JI is correlated with economic growth, but that there is a weak correlation between de facto and de jure JI, whereas Howard and Carey (2004) claim that de facto JI is correlated with political rights. La Porta et al. (2004) and Keith et al. (2009) claim that a de jure measure of JI is correlated with political and economic freedom and respect for human rights, respectively, and Melton and Ginsburg (2014) argue that certain combinations of indicators of de jure JI are correlated with de facto JI.

The inconsistency of these results is unsurprising, considering that the de jure measures from each of these projects are very weakly correlated (Ríos-Figueroa and Staton 2014). Regarding Howard and Carey's (2004) measure of de facto JI, based on US state department reports, their coding criteria mix de jure and de facto concepts. Feld and Voigt's (2003) de facto measure mixes in de jure concepts, and Melton and Ginsburg (2014) and Hayo and Voigt (2019) use the composite measure of de jure and de facto indicators from Linzer and Staton (2015).

Where do we go from here? In their review of measures of judicial independence, Ríos-Figueroa and Staton (2014) argue,

> It is not yet clear that we have identified well the rules (or sets of rules) that produce the incentives we hope to measure. The perennial question on whether and how institutions impact behavior, that is, the relationship between *de jure* and *de facto* judicial independence, requires thinking carefully about two sets of issues: the conditions under which tend to work effectively and the incentives set by specific institutions, such as the appointment, removal, or constitutional review powers of judges. *The length of judicial tenure as established in the constitution is a good measure if one wants to study the relationship between de jure and the actual length of tenure. But it is far less clear whether life tenure in the constitution produces "independent judicial behavior," even if the actual tenure is also long. The latter question requires a conceptual clarification of what amounts to independent judicial behavior; for instance, what we have identified as autonomy or influence and a theoretical model of how a long tenure incentivizes such behavior.* (Ríos-Figueroa and Staton 2014: 129; emphasis mine)

Similarly, Melton and Ginsburg (2014) argue that the relationship between individual components of de jure JI (such as selection procedure, judicial salary, judicial tenure, etc.) and de facto independence should be considered separately and theoretically justified.

I concur that theory is needed to map the relationship between specific rules and judicial independence and that our instinct with respect to the measurement of rules should be to disaggregate rather than aggregate. In addition, in order to properly measure the effects of specific rules (rather than aggregated indices), we first need to theorize about how the presence or absence of a rule affects specific judicial behaviors instead of aggregated indices of de facto JI based primarily on expert surveys.

To this end, in the next section, I return to the concept of judicial discretion and use it to motivate a theory of JI as the interaction between judicial discretion and the preferences of the judiciary.

8.2 Judicial Discretion, Preferences, and Independence

In this section, I follow Cooter and Ginsburg (1996) (see also Tsebelis 1995, 2002) who determine judicial discretion to be a function of the rigidity of legislative outcomes and argue that judicial control over constitutional outcomes is proportional to constitutional rigidity. Then, I offer a theory concerning the conditions under which we should observe independent behavior in terms of constitutional discretion and judicial preferences: when judicial preferences diverge from the government's and when discretion is high, the capacity for judges to behave independently will be high. However, since judicial preferences are nearly always unmeasurable, I predict that the relationship between behavioral indicators of judicial independence (such as the striking down of government legislation) and discretion will be heteroskedastic and positive due to the fact that judges may or may not rule against government policy when judicial discretion is high, and judges' preferences are unaligned with those of the government but will (almost) never rule against government policy when discretion is low. I also justify the measures I choose: for judicial independence, the proportion of a sitting government's legislation that the judiciary strikes down from the CompLaw dataset, and for discretion, the constitutional rigidity index from Tsebelis (2022).

8.2.1 Constitutional Discretion Is Proportional to Constitutional Rigidity

Cooter and Ginsburg (1996) argue that judicial discretion, defined as the extent to which the judiciary can use statutory interpretation,[9] increases as legislative override of judicial decisions becomes more difficult. Their logic is straightforward: when judges' preferences over policy diverge from those of the government, judges may wish to move policy closer to their ideal point by way of statutory interpretation. However, because the legislative veto players can, in most cases, come together to override the judiciary, the ability of the judiciary to interpret laws will be limited when the executive and legislative branches are aligned. Conversely, when the legislative veto players conflict, the judiciary may interpret laws to the extent that at least one of the legislative vetoes prefers the interpreted policy to the original.[10]

A generalization of the Cooter and Ginsburg argument is that as the number of veto players increases, so too does the discretion of the judiciary. Let us assume that a political system has three veto players (e.g., three parties in a coalition government or three political institutions in a presidential system).[11] Figure 8.1 presents the ideal points (preferences) in a two-dimensional space. Assume that the horizontal axis represents the left-right continuum and that the vertical axis represents

---

[9] That is, judicial decisions based on laws, not the constitution.
[10] The evidence for their proposition (discretion increases with the number of legislative veto players) is usually restricted to ordinary legislation. See Cooter and Ginsburg (1996) and Tsebelis (2002) for developed countries and Andrews and Montinola (2004) for developing countries.
[11] For a complete introduction to the theory of veto players, see Tsebelis (2002).

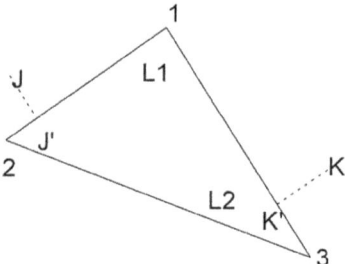

Figure 8.1 Legislative core: the court can make any statutory interpretation inside it

the environment. If each of these actors prefers points closer to their own preference over points further away, then they cannot change any policy located inside Triangle 123. Indeed, for any point inside this triangle, any movement of the status quo to the north will be objected to by Veto Player 3; any movement to the south will be objected to by Veto Player 1, and any movement to the east or west will be objected to by either 2 or 3. Therefore, a legislative change from point L1 to L2 is impossible because it will be objected to by Players 1 and 2, who will find the final outcome further away from their preferences. Similarly, a change from L2 to L1 will find Veto Player 3 objecting.[12]

This analysis can be used in order to explain judicial discretion since any decision inside the triangle cannot be overruled by the political system. If the judiciary in the corresponding country prefers L1 or L2, it can interpret the law accordingly without any fear of being overruled. In addition, the courts could modify their opinion (a delicate stare decisis case) from L1 to L2 without any interference from the political system. However, if it prefers points J or K, it will have to select points J' and K' in order to avoid a legislative decision overruling its interpretation. So, if the statutory interpretations are within the political core (Triangle 123), no reaction by the political system is possible. Therefore, the size of the legislative core is an appropriate proxy for the discretion of the judiciary with respect to regular legislation.

What would happen if the basis of the judicial decision is the constitution (constitutional interpretation) and not any particular law (statutory interpretation)? Then, instead of the legislative core of the political

---

[12] I remind the reader that decisions are made by unanimity since each veto player's agreement is required (by the definition of "veto player").

8.2 DISCRETION, PREFERENCES, AND INDEPENDENCE 203

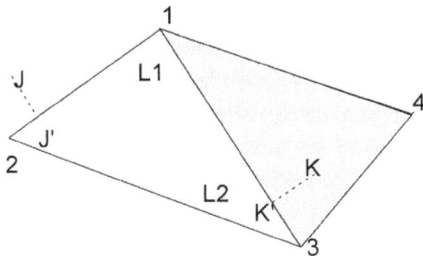

Figure 8.2 Constitutional core larger than legislative core: any constitutional interpretation within the constitutional core stands

system, we would have to base the analysis on the constitutional core. In most countries, it is more difficult to modify the constitution than the legislative status quo.[13]

Figure 8.2 gives a visual representation of this situation. I have added one more veto player than what was in Figure 8.1. The quadrilateral 1234 represents the constitutional core (the Veto Player 4 is also required for a constitutional revision). As a result, changes to the constitution inside Quadrilateral 1234 are impossible, and any constitutional interpretation inside this area becomes possible. The reader can verify from Figure 8.2 that while a judicial decision J would be overruled (no matter whether it was on statutory or constitutional grounds), a decision K would be overruled on statutory grounds but would be valid on constitutional grounds. So, in our hypothetical example, if the court had based its decision on the constitution, a legislative overrule would have been irrelevant, and a constitutional amendment would have been impossible. So, the larger the difference between the constitutional and the judicial core (the shaded area in Figure 8.2), the more empowered the judges are to make constitutional interpretations (as opposed to statutory ones).

Assuming the constitutional and supreme courts do not want to be overruled, they will exercise discretion proportionally to the size of the constitutional core. It follows that when considering discretion with respect to constitutional matters, it is appropriate to use the size of the constitutional core as a measure of constitutional discretion. For ordinary

---

[13] Exceptions to this rule are the UK, India, and New Zealand where a simple parliamentary majority is sufficient to modify any status quo. This situation sometimes entails confrontations between the legislature and the judiciary.

courts (or, more accurately, for statutory interpretations of any court), the determinant factor will be legislative overrule (i.e., the size of the legislative core of a country), while for constitutional decisions, the decisive factor will be the size of the constitutional core.

8.2.2 The Importance of Jurisdiction

The literature often focuses on higher courts, so there is relatively no work on lower courts (Burbank and Friedman 2002). This is because it is argued that the incentive structures of lower courts are different. Local courts may be independent of local governments, but they may also be highly reliant on senior judges (in particular for promotions) (Ramseyer and Rasmusen 2003). Lower court judges want to be promoted, whereas supreme court or constitutional court judges do not, which means that lower court judges will be more beholden to superior judges (Salzberger and Fenn 1999). In addition, it is thought that lower courts are more constrained than the supreme court (Burbank and Friedman 2002).

There are generally two different models for constitutional courts, generalized into the "American" and "European" Systems (Jacob et al. 1996). On the one hand, these models are different because they have different appointment mechanisms and different terms. For certain European courts, the appointment of judges is seen as nonpolitical – the process, usually through a constitutional tribunal, is often criticized for being too secret, unlike that of the appointment of Supreme Court justices in the US (Ferreres Comella 2009). We will test this expectation in Section 8.4. Unlike many ordinary judges, constitutional court judges often have term lengths and limits. This is because while the rulings of ordinary judges can be overruled by higher judges, constitutional judges are the final and only say in the matter (Ferreres Comella 2009). There are conflicting expectations about constitutional courts in the literature. Epstein et al. (2001) compare the characteristics of constitutional and supreme courts. They summarize the literature as follows:

> Some argue that [constitutional courts] are relatively unconstrained actors (e.g., Blankenburg 1996; Provine 1996; Stone 1994, 1995; Utter & Lundsgaard 1994), able to have "last licks" on matters that receive their attention. Others suggest that, even though these courts issue decisions that are final and formally binding, they are hardly untethered; they are instead constrained actors, those who must be attentive to preferences and likely actions of other relevant players in their systems of government, as well as to the institutional context in which they work, if they wish to issue efficacious

8.2 DISCRETION, PREFERENCES, AND INDEPENDENCE

decisions – decisions that the other players will respect and with which they will comply (e.g., Smithey 1999; Vanberg 1999). (Epstein et al. 2001: 123)

Table 8.4 presents a list of countries with constitutional courts (which will be included as a dummy variable in my empirical analysis).

The main difference between constitutional and ordinary courts is that constitutional courts provide the final say in constitutional matters (Finck 1997). At their most basic level, "constitutional courts have the power of judicial review and invalidation of unconstitutional statutes and statutory provisions" (Garlicki 2007: 67). In most cases, constitutional courts are added later on after the judicial system of a country is well established.

The distinction between constitutional and supreme courts started with Kelsen arguing the differences between the European and American models. Within systems that have a constitutional court, only

Table 8.4 *Countries with constitutional courts*

Albania	Luxembourg
Austria	Macedonia
Belgium	Moldova
Benin	Mongolia
Bolivia	Montenegro
Bulgaria	Niger
Burundi	Peru
Colombia	Poland
Croatia	Portugal
Czech Republic	Romania
Dominican Republic	Senegal
France	Serbia
Georgia	Slovakia
Germany	Slovenia
Guatemala	South Africa
Hungary	Spain
Indonesia	Taiwan
Italy	Thailand
Korea, Republic of	Turkey
Latvia	Ukraine
Lebanon	Zambia
Lithuania	

"a single court (usually called a 'constitutional court') can exercise judicial review; other courts are typically barred from so doing" (Epstein et al. 2001: 121). Because of this, constitutional courts are thought of as more centralized or concentrated and specialized (for example, in Germany), whereas supreme courts are seen as more decentralized or diffuse and general (Finck 1997, Horowitz 2006). This means that in systems with only an ordinary court, it can rule on whether an act is unconstitutional, but it can only do this "a posteriori," or after an act has occurred (Epstein et al. 2001). Here, centralized means a clear delineation in terms of how a case will reach a constitutional court. Ordinary courts deal with all legislation – if a country has a constitutional court and an ordinary court, the ordinary court will decide whether it is a constitutional matter. In practice, there is much more overlap between the constitutional court and the highest ordinary court (in some cases, a supreme court), which means that there can and will be tensions between the two (Garlicki 2007). For instance, in Germany, where the constitutional court has a vast amount of power, there are no clear and understood boundaries of the court's jurisdictions in practice (Garlicki 2007).

8.2.3 Judicial Preferences

To distinguish between cases where a court genuinely aligns with the government from those where the court aligns with the government under pressure, the positions of the executive, the legislature, the judiciary, and others must also be known (Cameron 2002). This approach can place a court into one of four categories. The first three, enumerated by Vanberg (2001), are (1) a friendly court where it shares the same preferences for the policy as the legislature, (2) a submissive court where it agrees that the policy is unconstitutional but will only do so when it knows that the legislature will abide by the court's decision, and (3) an assertive court where it will vote that a policy is unconstitutional regardless of the legislature's actions. Another possibility is (4) an authoritative court, which would force the executive to respect its preferences.

However, these distinctions require knowing the positions of the court in order to distinguish between a friendly, a submissive, an assertive, and an authoritative court. Therefore, in cases where the preferences of government actors are, in fact, measurable, it is possible to infer the positions of the judiciary from the rules governing judicial appointments and the positions of those who appoint. For instance, in countries where judges are appointed by legislators, the position of the legislatures can be a reliable proxy for the position of the judges. This is the case for a country like France where the "Conseil Constitutionnel members – being political appointees – are actually incapable of independent action and behave ... necessarily as partisans and not as judges" (Stone Sweet 2007: 73). Based on this, either the constitutional court legislates in the same manner as the parliament or it does not legislate at all, given that it is a product of appointees from the parliament (Stone Sweet 2007). This is similar to the case of the US, where, although not a constitutional court, the decisions of the Supreme Court can be predicted based on the position of the median justice in the majority coalition (Carrubba et al. 2012). This is because, in both cases, the nomination process of the judiciary is fairly transparent, making it known who appointed the judge, which makes the appointee a suitable proxy for the position of the judge. The nomination and appointment mechanisms can range from just a single actor, such as the head of state, to multiple actors, such as the head of state, one or multiple chambers of the legislature, and even approval from the judiciary. How many actors – as well as which actors – there are will determine how visible the process is as well as how applicable a proxy method of appointment may be.

8.2.4 JI as the Conjunction of Constitutional Rigidity and Judicial Preferences

When we can measure both the preferences of the government and the judiciary, we should expect the relationship between judicial preferences, discretion, and independence to be conditional: High discretion will be a necessary but not sufficient condition for JI. Indeed, if a court has no discretion, it will not be independent, but if it has high discretion, it still may not be independent. If the justices are appointed by a political actor, the appointees are likely to have identical preferences with their principal, and the court will not be considered independent.

However, since the preferences of members of the judiciary are unknown, we should expect that the relationship between the two variables will be heteroskedastic (just like the relationship between constitutional rigidity and amendment frequency; see Chapter 6).

Figure 8.3 makes this point visually. High constitutional rigidity generates high judicial discretion; however, this high discretion may or may not be used by the judiciary and, consequently, under these conditions judicial independence may be high or low. On the other hand, low constitutional rigidity leads necessarily to low judicial independence.

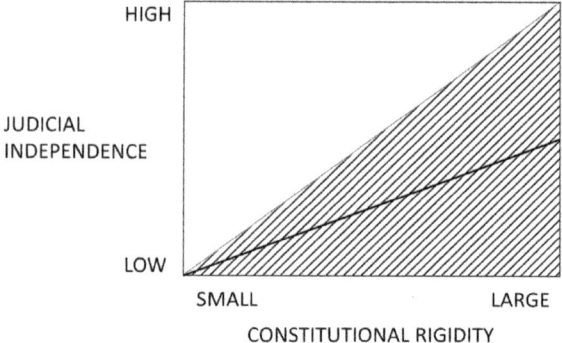

Figure 8.3 Low constitutional rigidity is a necessary condition for low judicial independence

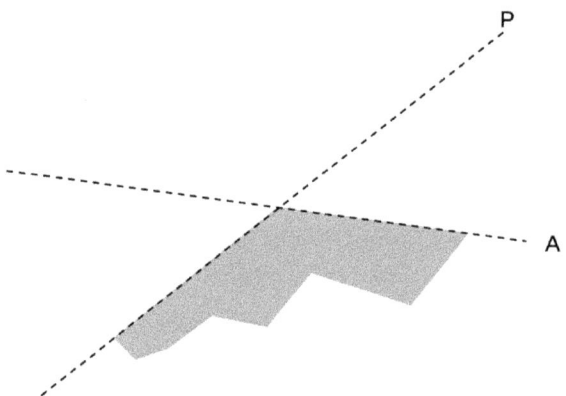

Figure 8.4 The win-set of the status quo subject to constraints on judicial decision-making

8.2.5 *Constitutional Strikes as a Measure of JI*

Figure 8.4 presents an abstraction of the set of outcomes that the majority of the constitutional court (from now on, the judiciary) prefers over the status quo (not presented in the figure). I call this set the win-set of the status quo, or W(SQ), which is the intersection of the majority of preferences and restrictions different judges impose on a piece of legislation to consider it compatible with the constitution. These preferences may include elements of political judgment (Gabel et al. 2024),[14] or they

---

[14] Such elements would generate circular indifference curves in two dimensions and spheres in multidimensional spaces.

may include absolute principles (like respect for human life), proportionality between such principles (human rights and freedom of expression),[15] or any other rule of textual interpretation one considers to be in play. The shaded area presents the intersection of the majority of such judicial preferences and constraints. In this simplified game, if the government makes a decision outside of W(SQ), it will be overruled by the judiciary on constitutional grounds. Therefore, under the conditions described above, the government will make a decision inside W(SQ). This model produces no judiciary strikes because they are anticipated by the government, and the proposed solutions are not objectionable by the judiciary. The only way that there would be judiciary overrule of government actions is if the government has a dominant strategy to provoke the judiciary and be overruled by it (or at least not care about it). Such a situation could happen if the government is involved in a Nested Game (Tsebelis 1991) where it cares about the payoffs provided in another arena (e.g., electoral) and not about the survival of its own legislation. An example of this would be a conservative government legislating against abortion rights in order to appeal to its supporters regardless of the fact that it will be overruled by the judiciary. Although such cases are possible, they cannot be the predominant explanation of disagreement between governments and the judiciary at a comparative level. In fact, they require the introduction of an additional actor (the public) and a special interaction between the government and this actor to determine (and explain) the actions of the government.

Figure 8.5 replicates the previous story with one difference that increases the realism of the model: What if the government does not have exact knowledge of W(SQ)? The lighter gray shaded area indicates the government's uncertainty over the judiciary's win-set of the status quo. Uncertainty stems from the fact that the government may not know the exact constitutional consequences of a particular policy decision and/or the preferences of the judiciary (just like researchers). As a result, these zones of uncertainty may be very wide indeed. In this scenario, the government may make a decision G in the zone of uncertainty that it intends to be approved by the judiciary but is instead struck down. What is the inference if we observe the judiciary striking down a government decision? First, we are in Figure 8.5 instead of Figure 8.4 (that is, the government is operating under incomplete information), and second, the

---

[15] Such elements would generate straight lines in two dimensions and hyperplanes in multidimensional spaces.

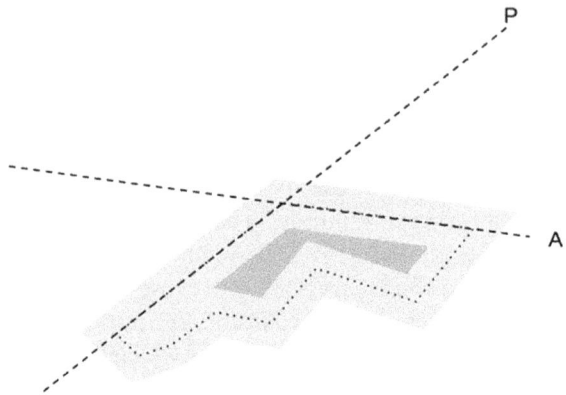

Figure 8.5 The win-set of the status quo subject to constraints on judicial decision-making, with uncertainty

judiciary has preferences different than the government and has affirmed these preferences. What is the inference if we observe no disagreement? There are several possibilities: first, it could be that the government was able to anticipate the preferences of the judiciary and made a proposal acceptable to it; second, it is possible that the judiciary does not have any significant differences from the government; and third, it may be that the judiciary is afraid to contradict the government. In other words, in the first case, the judiciary prevails; in the third, the government; and in the second, there is an identity of preferences. As a result, in the case of judicial approval, we can make no inference.

However, a lack of any disapproval of existing law should be counted as a disagreement between the government and the judiciary. We should identify the cases where the judiciary makes decisions conflicting with the decisions of the *current* government. Constitutionally overruling old laws is not an indication of JI, but it could be an indication that the laws have become obsolete or, even more perversely, that constitutional courts strike down old laws or provisions to suit the preferences of the current executive.[16] Therefore, I operationalize the JI variable as the percentage

---

[16] Examples of this include constitutional courts in Honduras, Costa Rica, Nicaragua, and Bolivia invalidating constitutional restrictions on presidential term limits to let the current president seek another election (Martínez-Barahona 2012, Landau et al. 2019a, Landau et al. 2019b). Similarly, the Ukrainian Constitutional Court struck down a constitutional revision that limited the power of the president six years after it was passed in order to empower the sitting president (Tyushka 2014).

8.2 DISCRETION, PREFERENCES, AND INDEPENDENCE

of cases that a constitutional court strikes down the decisions of the *current* government as unconstitutional over the total number of cases that the court votes them either up or down.

In sum, when the judiciary is not independent of the government, we will not see strikes against the sitting government's legislation; when the judiciary *is* independent of the government, we may or may not see strikes, depending on whether the preferences of the judiciary and the government align.

Some researchers have used the frequency of court overrule as a measure of judicial independence, although this is only the case for individual countries and is not always in terms of overruling against the sitting government. Their findings align with my expectation of a positive relationship between the size of the constitutional core and JI. For example, Santoni and Zucchini (2004) examine the Italian Constitutional Court from 1956 to 1992 and show that the frequency of disputes over the constitutionality of laws is increasing with the size of the constitutional core (defined as the number of parties needed to agree on a constitutional revision), though they do not restrict their analysis to only conflicts over legislation from a sitting government.[17] Similarly, Ríos-Figueroa (2007) analyzes all judicial decisions by the Mexican Supreme Court from 1994 to 2002 and shows that the judiciary is more likely to strike down legislation from the PRI when the fragmentation of the political system is high. Sánchez et al. (2011) include all Mexican Supreme Court rulings until 2007 and show that after the PRI lost the presidency in 2000 (and the political system became more fragmented), the Mexican Supreme Court became more likely to strike down laws of the sitting government via constitutional review.[18]

In order to replicate these analyses at the cross-national level, we need the indicator of constitutional rigidity developed in Chapter 6 along with decisions of constitutional courts in different countries rejecting laws from the government in power. The expectation is a heteroskedastic

---

[17] Actually, they do not include the constraint that the stricken legislation has to be produced by the incumbent government.

[18] It is also worth noting that Helmke and Rosenbluth (2009) argue that in some cases, judicial override of a weak sitting government can be taken as evidence that a judiciary is currying favor with a potential future government. While I do not dispute that it is possible that such strikes occur, I contend that these make up the minority of strikes compared to the vast majority that I believe to be a valid representation of judicial independence.

relationship between judicial discretion and the number of judicial decisions on the unconstitutionality of current government laws.

8.3 Looking Comparatively: The CompLaw Database

Creating a comparative dataset on courts is difficult for many reasons. First, comparability is very difficult. Each country conducts judicial reviews differently, making it difficult to compare one case to the next clearly. Second, it is difficult due to the large number of cases that pass through a judicial system each year, many of which are only accessible in a country's archives. Third, these two previous reasons are highly correlated with economic development and level of democracy, meaning that it is even harder to compare less-developed countries with more-developed countries. In addition to having information about cases, ideally there would also be information on the positions of the judges. While in some cases this is easier to measure, such as in the US or France, in most cases it is nearly impossible to measure the positions of judges. This is due to different appointment processes as well as the level of transparency of the courts.

The Comparative Law (CompLaw) Database (Carrubba et al. 2015, Gabel et al. 2024) addresses some of these problems by creating a comprehensive dataset that comparatively looks at constitutional cases around the world. It covers forty-five countries while coding at least 200 of the cases heard in each country in 2003. While this is by no means encompassing every case or every country, it is the first large-scale dataset of its kind providing comparative insights into multiple different systems of judicial review. Although it cannot evaluate the positions of the judges, it can provide data on how they decided on constitutional cases. CompLaw, like most existing data sources, only analyzes the highest court in a country with constitutional review, even when there are multiple high courts in a country. For data availability reasons, they also only include decisions that are published online. It does not include all cases – for example, if a country had fewer than 200 cases in 2003, then all 200 or fewer cases were coded, but if there were more than 200 cases in 2003, then they used a random sample to code at least 200 cases per country. Within each of the cases, the state, which can either be the state government or the federal government, has to be an active participant. Here, a case could be about a statute, an executive order, enforcement action, an administrative act, or a decree.

Within this dataset, there are many variables of interest. First, there is the admission date, which is when the case was admitted for review by the court. There is also the decision date, which is when the court decided the result. The policy date is when the policy was adopted by the government. Lastly in terms of dates, there is the date of the precipitating event, which is the date when the infraction occurred that gave rise to the case. In addition to these dates, there is the variable, which is extremely relevant to whether the court exercised constitutional review in its decision – this is coded as a dummy variable. Finally, they code how the court responded to the case – this is a categorical variable with four levels: 0, which is deemed constitutional; 1, which is deemed unconstitutional; 2, which is discussed but dismissed for procedural reasons; and 3, which is not discussed and dismissed for procedural reasons. For the purposes of this chapter, I am only interested in the first two levels: those that were deemed constitutional and those that were deemed unconstitutional.

I used the CompLaw Database to understand the relationship between the number of times a country's constitutional court rules a case as unconstitutional against the government and my measure of constitutional rigidity. While the existing data have each policy as the unit of analysis, I am interested in the country as the unit of analysis. I limited the countries to democratic ones (those that have a POLITY2 score of five or above). As described in the Introduction, I am only interested in cases where the court invalidates legislation of the current government.[19] To do this, I ensure that the government in office during the policy year is the same as the government in office during the decision date. For parliamentary governments, if there was an election it is considered a new government even if it has the same party composition. For presidential systems, I consider only the president as the government.

After cleaning the data, there is a sample of thirty countries with a POLITY2 score of five or above.[20] In order to aggregate the data to the country level, I calculate the percentage of strikes. The percentage of strikes is defined by the number of cases that the constitutional court rules as unconstitutional over the total number of cases that were deemed either constitutional (0) or unconstitutional (1). This is a better proxy of judicial independence because it only measures how often a court rules against its corresponding government, which is my definition of judicial

---

[19] This is like the example of Obamacare being invalidated during Obama's administration as opposed to during Trump's administration.
[20] The actual number of the intersection is thirty-one, but there was no case of either affirming or striking a current government decision in the Dominican Republic, which reduces the countries with data to thirty (see Appendix 8.A).

independence. This variable ranges from 0 with countries like Israel and India to 1 with countries like Italy, Canada, and Romania, where every case in 2003 was declared unconstitutional.

8.4 Method and Results

Using the CompLaw data, I test two hypotheses: (1) that the mean rate of judicial vetoes is increasing in constitutional rigidity and (2) that the variance of the rate of judicial vetoes is increasing in constitutional rigidity. To test both hypotheses, I fit a multiplicative heteroskedastic linear model of the form

$$y_i = x_i\beta_1 + z_i\beta_2 + \epsilon_i; \sigma_i^2 = e^{\{x_i\alpha\}},$$

where y_i is the rate of judicial strikes in country i, x_i is the level of constitutional rigidity, β_1 represents the correlation between constitutional rigidity and judicial strikes, z_i is a dummy variable indicating whether country i has a constitutional court, β_2 represents the correlation between a constitutional court and the rate of strikes, α represents the set of unknown parameters in the variance function, σ_i^2 is the variance in the rate of judicial strikes for country i, and ϵ_i is the error term for country i.[21] The idea is that this model tests two different predictions simultaneously: on the one hand, the average rate of judicial strikes, and on the other, its variance as functions of constitutional rigidity (as well as other unobserved factors).[22]

Figure 8.6 shows the relationship between the percentage of strikes and constitutional rigidity for countries with a POLITY2 score of five or above. It is a positive relationship, meaning that the higher the constitutional rigidity, the higher the expected strike percentage. In addition, Figure 8.6 shows that the 95 percent prediction interval, presented by the shaded area in the figure and dependent on the variance of the

---

[21] The model is fit using Harvey's two-step GLS estimator, where the residuals from an initial OLS regression are used to estimate the relationship between the independent variable and the variance of the dependent variable. For more information about multiplicative heteroskedastic regression, see www.stata.com/manuals/rhetregress.pdf. For a broader discussion about appropriate methods to use when testing the effects of necessary conditions, see Goertz and Starr (2002) and more recently Dul (2016) and Dul et al. (2020).

[22] The standard approach of correcting for the heteroskedasticity using, for example, heteroskedasticity-robust standard errors would be inappropriate because I would be correcting for one of the model's predictions!

8.4 METHOD AND RESULTS

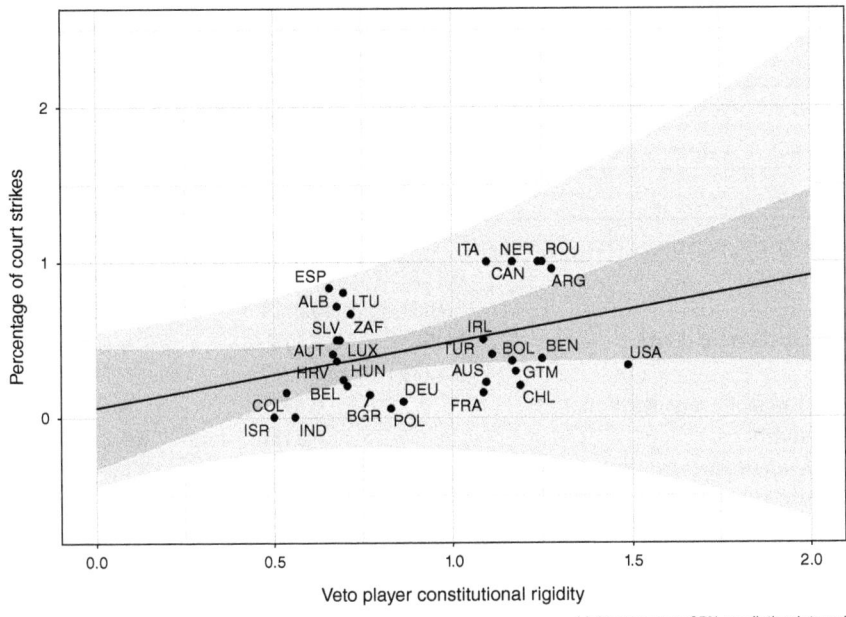

Figure 8.6 The effect of constitutional rigidity on court strikes

distribution, slightly expands when constitutional rigidity moves from 0.5 to 1.5. In other words, the relationship between constitutional rigidity and JI is positive and (slightly) heteroskedastic, as hypothesized.

Table 8.5 presents the numerical results of this calculation, including a dummy variable for the existence of a constitutional court (from Table 8.4). It shows that constitutional rigidity has a positive effect (both substantively and statistically significant) on the percentage of strikes (judicial independence).[23] On the other hand, the heteroskedasticity of the relationship, while positive as expected, is not statistically significant.[24] I attribute this lack of significance to the small number of countries and hope that, in the future, more data will become available (particularly

---

[23] The result is 0.462 with p-value 0.038.
[24] The result is 1.649 with p-value 0.268. If one eliminates the constitutional court dummy, the variance coefficient gets reduced to 1.526, and the p-value changes to 0.306. However, the results of the analysis do not change.

Table 8.5 *Effect of constitutional rigidity on percentage of strikes (sample: POLITY2 ≥ 5)*

	Base model	Mean-only model	Het. regression
n	30	30	30
Dependent variable: percentage of judicial strikes			
(Intercept)	0.412 ***	−0.027	−0.082
	(0.105)	(0.243)	(0.213)
Constitutional court	0.057	0.119	0.161
	(0.128)	(0.126)	(0.119)
Veto players constitutional rigidity		0.433	0.462 *
		(0.218)	(0.223)
Dependent variable: the log-squared residuals of the OLS regression of the percentage of judicial strikes on veto players constitutional rigidity and constitutional court			
(Intercept)	−3.072 ***		−3.319 *
	(0.299)		(1.43)
Veto players constitutional rigidity			1.649
			(1.491)

*** $p < 0.001$; ** $p < 0.01$; * $p < 0.05$.

Table 8.6 *Comparison of three models of effects of constitutional rigidity (base, mean only, and heteroskedastic) on judicial strikes for POLITY2 ≥ 5 threshold (likelihood ratio tests, n = 30)*

Models	Chi-square	p(> Chi-square)
Base vs. mean only	4.0822	0.04334
Mean only vs. heteroskedastic	1.0827	0.29809
Base vs. heteroskedastic	5.1649	**0.07559**

time series of court decisions). Table 8.6 is similar to Table 6.2 in Chapter 6, indicating the added value from the basic model (constant and existence of constitutional court) to the mean only model (where a constitutional rigidity variable is introduced) and to the heteroskedastic model (where the variance of constitutional rigidity is added). The final *p*-value is 0.076, which corroborates our analysis on the basis of Table 8.5.

In order to test the robustness of my results, I also applied Dul's method to test whether constitutional rigidity was a necessary condition for judicial strikes (Dul 2016, 2024). The test resulted in a p-value of 0.002 for the CE-FDH ceiling line (Dul et al. 2020), corroborating my hypothesis.

Conclusions

While JI has been frequently discussed in the literature, the underlying theory is not clear, and the empirical findings are not consistent. Starting from criticisms in the existing literature, I presented an alternative that is based on three different principles.

First, I gave a theoretical justification of my variables: I argued that the institutional basis of the analysis should be judicial discretion as determined by the constitutional rigidity of a country. Countries with high constitutional rigidity have high judicial discretion because the judges are not afraid that they will be overruled. In addition, I argued that assessing the independence of a branch famous for its opinions and decisions without explicitly modeling its preferences lacks a theoretical foundation. One can assess independence only when judges decide *according* to their preferences.[25] Consequently, knowing the preferences and beliefs of the judiciary is necessary to assess its independence. I therefore defined judicial independence as the interaction between judicial discretion and judicial preferences.

Second, instead of using an expert assessment of JI, I considered the percentage of times that the judiciary overrules the decisions of the other branches of government (over the number of cases that it either concurs or overrules). A decision to overrule cannot be considered anything but an indication of independence, while a decision to concur may have many motivations: it could be a sincere agreement of the judiciary, it could be deference because the appropriate decisionmaker is another branch, it could be fear of retaliation from the other branches, or it could be that the other branches anticipated the judicial decision and did not

---

[25] This is in addition to other matters of principle: for example, they may consider that particular decisions should be left to the legislative or the executive branch and use their decision to concur (even if they do not agree).

want to confront the judiciary. From the lack of manifest disagreement between the judiciary and other powers, no inference on judicial independence can be made. It is possible that expert assessments of JI include evaluations of agreements between the judiciary and other powers. For example, they can inflate the JI used in this chapter if they consider the lack of disagreement as an indication of deference, or they could deflate it if they consider it as an indication of timidity. However, there would be no way to make an intersubjectively testable assessment of these judgments.

Third, given the fact that one of my independent variables (judicial preferences) is unknown in the overwhelming majority of cases, I argued that the variance of my estimators would be affected. Consequently, I used the appropriate statistical technique: heteroskedastic regression, which explicitly models the heteroskedastic relationship between discretion and independence. This expectation was motivated by the theoretical analysis surrounding Figures 8.1 and 8.2 and was corroborated by the empirical tests in Figure 8.6 and Table 8.5. I want to point out that Brown (2022: ch. 4) evaluating the number of cases that state supreme courts strike government legislation in the US comes to similar conclusions while *including the distance of the court from the legislature*. Indeed, he finds a negative effect of the number of amendments (which in Chapter 6 I demonstrated is negatively correlated with constitutional rigidity) and a positive effect of ideological distance between the legislature and judiciary.

This chapter uses only one institutional variable (constitutional rigidity) as the basis for judicial independence. This choice does not mean that, in my opinion, other variables such as the identity of the person who appoints a judge cannot or should not be considered as a factor that affects JI, but it means that theoretical models of the effects of these variables should first be presented, and then we would and should be able to include them in the analysis.

I expect that the issue of data availability will be resolved and we will then be able to rely on time series of data in more countries than the thirty-one covered above. In addition, future research may use the indicator of JI calculated above to test the implications of JI on growth, human rights, and other variables, as discussed in the literature.

APPENDIX 8.A

Table 8.A.1 *Data used in the analysis (constitutional and unconstitutional judgments) from the Comparative Law Database*

Country	Unconst. judgments	Const. and unconst. judgments	Strikes	VP rigidity	Const. court
Albania	10	14	0.71428571	0.677	1
Argentina	22	23	0.95652174	1.277	0
Australia	2	9	0.22222222	1.093	0
Austria	35	86	0.40697674	0.667	1
Belgium	85	422	0.2014218	0.707	1
Benin	34	90	0.37777778	1.25	1
Bolivia	51	140	0.36428571	1.167	1
Bulgaria	10	69	0.14492754	0.77	1
Canada	1	1	1	1.167	0
Chile	42	206	0.2038835	1.19	0
Colombia	14	88	0.15909091	0.536	1
Croatia	6	25	0.24	0.697	1
Dominican Republic	0	0	Indeterminate	0.697	1
El Salvador	1	2	0.5	0.677	0
France	16	101	0.15841584	1.086	1
Germany	1	10	0.1	0.864	1
Guatemala	17	58	0.29310345	1.177	1
Hungary	59	162	0.36419753	0.677	1
India	0	8	0	0.56	0
Ireland	4	8	0.5	1.085	0
Israel	0	1	0	0.5	0
Italy	16	16	1	1.095	1
Lithuania	49	61	0.80327869	0.697	1
Luxembourg	2	4	0.5	0.687	1
Niger	3	3	1	1.24	1

Table 8.A.1 (*cont.*)

Country	Unconst. judgments	Const. and unconst. judgments	Strikes	VP rigidity	Const. court
Poland	1	18	0.05555556	0.828	1
Romania	14	14	1	1.249	1
South Africa	2	3	0.66666667	0.717	1
Spain	10	12	0.83333333	0.6576	1
Turkey	29	72	0.40277778	1.11	0
United States	1	3	0.33333333	1.489	0

9

Conclusions

This book presented an institutional analysis of amendment provisions. As such, in Lakatos' (1978) terms, it is part of a scientific research program based on the assumption that institutions matter, trying to identify how and why they do. This means that the significance of institutions is part of the *negative heuristic* of the program – that is, it is part of the assumptions that will not be abandoned within the research program. The reader may ask: What if empirical research found no evidence that institutions matter? This is exactly what we discussed in the Introduction as well as in Chapter 3. This book demonstrates in both Chapters 3 and 6 that the empirical analyses leading to the conclusion that institutions do not matter had some theoretical or methodological flaws that needed correction, following Lakatos' methodology. I also applied Lakatos' methodology in a positive way throughout the whole book and made a converse argument in Chapter 3. There, I explained what was wrong with previous cultural approaches to constitutional amendments without rejecting the research program of cultural analysis as a whole, instead arguing that we have to go back to the drawing board within this program. Therefore, the book is an application of the Lakatos hierarchy among heuristics in the area of constitutions and their amendments.

However, this conceptual hierarchy is not the only one that exists inside this book. I argued in the Introduction that there is a hierarchy (with three levels) of decisions: within the constitution (legislation by parliaments, statutory and constitutional interpretation by courts), outside the constitution (amendments), and constitutional replacement. These three levels require different rules and should not be confused with one another.[1] Confusion between constitution and legislation (making the constitution amendable as if it were legislation) degrades the constitution. It can happen at the empirical level by organizations,

---

[1] This is true unless specified by the constitution, as in the case of Israel, which generates different problems that I discussed in Chapter 1.

parties, or political actors who try to modify the constitution without following the amendment rules to promote their own interests (that is, to weaponize the constitution). They do this at the expense of democracy. It can also happen at the intellectual level (constitutional moments or unconstitutional constitutional amendments, as we discussed in the Introduction). While the proponents of these ideas do it out of respect for democracy, the result is that they disrespect the fact that the constitution is the rule about the rules.

This book justified the analysis of amendment rules, which is fundamental for understanding the institutions of a country. It is not a new idea, but the justification that the constitution comprises the rules about changing the rules and that they are respected in democracies provided the framework within which the book operates.

This book has chapters explaining the theoretical significance of amendment rules (Chapter 2) and the way the comparative index of constitutional rigidity was constructed. It also includes chapters explaining the variety of the institutions covered in it as well as some conflicts of particular actors about how these institutions should be used or changed (Chapter 1), indicating that the question of whether these rules matter is not shared by the actors on the ground. Finally, it also includes two chapters on cases where the amendment rules led to the failure of attempted amendments (Chapter 4) as well as the overuse of amendment provisions (Chapter 5).

Special attention was paid to referendums (Chapters 1, 2, and 4) because they are often used and because, in my mind, technological advances will lead to more frequent use of this particular institution. Therefore, understanding how they work and what their results are is likely to be particularly important.

Within this framework, I remain faithful to the principle of "follow the decisions" and study how, in different countries, the amendment rules have a fundamental impact on how easy it is to make amendments and how frequent and/or significant these amendments are likely to be. The amendment rules specify how many institutions are required to approve the change and what the conditions are (quorums, qualified majorities) in each one of them, looking at whether these rules operate in a conjunctive or disjunctive way. All these conditions have specific effects on the constitutional rigidity of a country, which in turn is expected to have effects in three different directions. These expectations are corroborated. First, the frequency and significance of amendments are inversely correlated with the constitutional rigidity of the country and its variance.

In addition, the more significant the amendments, the stronger this relationship is (Chapter 6). Second, the length of the constitution is correlated with a series of negative results like time inconsistency (itself a derivative of constitutional rigidity) as well as economic variables (GDP per capita, inequality, unemployment rate, and innovation; Chapter 7). Third, constitutional rigidity affects judicial independence of the supreme or constitutional court and its variance (Chapter 8).

The main contribution of this book is the combination of these ideas in a coherent framework: the theoretical approach, the way that the variable constitutional rigidity was created, the fact that it is a sufficient but not necessary condition for lack of amendments,[2] and, similarly, that it is a necessary but not sufficient condition for judicial independence. Both expectations require estimation of the results by heteroskedastic regression. They also enable the analysis to focus on one variable – that is, a necessary only *or* sufficient only condition.[3] So, to go back to Lakatos, there were no "inconsistencies," and the theory presented in the book was corroborated. The conclusions of this book can be the basis for further analyses where other researchers will evaluate the impact of their own variables (social, cultural, or any other sort) on constitutions, taking for granted the impact of amendment rules. In this sense, this book is the first step of a whole research agenda on constitutional amendments.

I mentioned in the beginning of the book that for a broad swathe of researchers the developments within nondemocratic countries are more interesting and more worthy of analysis than the ones within democratic countries. However, as I have argued in this book, these developments from an institutional perspective resemble random noise because they depend on other factors like authoritarian rulers; dictators; the military; civil wars; revolutions; social, ideological, or cultural groups; and so on. Such factors are not included in my analysis. This book demonstrated that institutions, in contrast, are *necessary* conditions, and data analysis is done under this assumption (through heteroskedastic regression). The implication is that if other variables are considered important, after the thorough explanation of the reasons for their relation to constitutional amendments they need to be applied through the same institutional framework. In other words, the results of this book must be considered the basis for further analyses.

---

[2] Alternatively, that lack of rigidity is a necessary but not sufficient condition for significant and frequent amendments.
[3] To be clear, not the *only* necessary or sufficient condition.

There has been an impressive development of constitutional analyses based on the actual text of the constitutions as presented and analyzed by the site Constitute (www.constituteproject.org). Their work has been cited extensively in this book. However, my results are significantly different. I explained the reasons for the differences: sometimes, it was the lack of the appropriate variables; at other times, it was the precision of these variables or the methodology. Here, I want to point out one other important dimension: *the significance of interdisciplinary research*. It seems like legal scholars are influenced by cultural arguments, as I argue in Chapter 3, yet these arguments either underestimate or misuse the institutional basis of comparative analysis, leading to the inability to use empirical evidence in a systematic way. Further, it may be the case that the hierarchy of rules I present in the Introduction that is based on equilibrium analysis is not as significant in legal analysis as it is on the impact of a change. Finally, from a legal point of view, there is no difference between long and short constitutions, as several legal scholars argue; however, the association with other (economic) variables may be negative, as demonstrated in this book.

The analysis undertaken here can be expanded. The obvious way would be to include more variables or to and expand it to nondemocratic countries. I discussed some of the arguments presented so far and explained why they have to be based on the analyses undertaken in this book as opposed to alternative explanations.

However, there are further institutional modifications that would increase the precision of the arguments presented in this book. For example, there could be more precise estimations of constitutional rigidity, such as estimating the difference between the two chambers of a bicameral legislature on a yearly basis as opposed to only once as I have done here. Even better would be the conceptual inclusion of coalitional politics, whether each chamber has its own coalitional structure or not, and the effect of this factor on constitutional rigidity. Another area would be the identification of the difference between two successive parliaments (in case they are required to agree for a constitutional amendment to be enacted) in exactly the same way as bicameralism. Such approaches would require different (time series) methodology for the analysis because instead of having one observation per country we would have several.

Another possible modification would be the further diversification of institutions. I have used an index of the summation of required institutional veto players and majorities within each one of them. I have used all the other institutional variations by adding or subtracting epsilons to which I assigned the value 0.01. What if a researcher wants to fine tune these epsilons even further or wants to argue that some particular ones should be evaluated very differently? The resulting different empirical analyses may have more accurate results.

Another interesting development is evaluating constitutional rigidity in different areas of constitutional decision-making. As I explained in Chapter 2, I calculate only the residual rule of constitutional amendments. However, this rule may not be operative in specific areas of decision-making. For example, if one wanted to analyze the evolution of human rights in different countries, a reevaluation of constitutional rigidity concerning these particular constitutional provisions would be necessary.

Finally, analyses of case studies covering specific countries (like in Chapters 4 and 5) or specific important constitutional amendments (Category 3 in my scale in Chapter 6) that change the political life in particular countries would improve our understanding of the role and significance of constitutions.

Appendix I

Country	Constitution year	Amendment year	Responses	Median value	VP rigid	POLITY2
Albania	1998	2007	2	1	0.677	9
Albania	1998	2008		2	0.677	9
Albania	1998	2012		1	0.677	9
Argentina	1983	1994	3	2	1.277	7
Argentina	1983	1997		1	1.277	7
Armenia	1995	2005	In house	3	0.677	5
Australia	1901	1907	1	1	1.093	10
Australia	1901	1910		1	1.093	10
Australia	1901	1929		1	1.093	10
Australia	1901	1942		3	1.093	10
Australia	1901	1946		3	1.093	10
Australia	1901	1967		1	1.093	10
Australia	1901	1977		1	1.093	10
Australia	1901	1985	2	1	1.093	10
Austria	1945	1946		1	0.667	10
Austria	1945	1948		1	0.667	10
Austria	1945	1954		No amendment	0.667	10
Austria	1945	1955		1	0.667	10
Austria	1945	1956		1	0.667	10
Austria	1945	1958		1	0.667	10
Austria	1945	1959		1	0.667	10
Austria	1945	1960		1	0.667	10
Austria	1945	1961		1	0.667	10
Austria	1945	1962		2	0.667	10
Austria	1945	1963		1	0.667	10

(cont.)

Country	Constitution year	Amendment year	Responses	Median value	VP rigid	POLITY2
Austria	1945	1964	1		0.667	10
Austria	1945	1968	2		0.667	10
Austria	1945	1969	1		0.667	10
Austria	1945	1972	1		0.667	10
Austria	1945	1973	1		0.667	10
Austria	1945	1974	2		0.667	10
Austria	1945	1975	2		0.667	10
Austria	1945	1977	1		0.667	10
Austria	1945	1979	2		0.667	10
Austria	1945	1981	1		0.667	10
Austria	1945	1982	1		0.667	10
Austria	1945	1983	2		0.667	10
Austria	1945	1984	2		0.667	10
Austria	1945	1986	1		0.667	10
Austria	1945	1987	1		0.667	10
Austria	1945	1988	2		0.667	10
Austria	1945	1990	1		0.667	10
Austria	1945	1991	1		0.667	10
Austria	1945	1992	2		0.667	10
Austria	1945	1993	2		0.667	10
Austria	1945	1994	3		0.667	10
Austria	1945	1996	2		0.667	10
Austria	1945	1997	1		0.667	10
Austria	1945	1998	1		0.667	10

Austria	1945	1999	1	0.667	10
Austria	1945	2000	1	0.667	10
Austria	1945	2001	1	0.667	10
Austria	1945	2002	1	0.667	10
Austria	1945	2003	1	0.667	10
Austria	1945	2004	1	0.667	10
Austria	1945	2005	2	0.667	10
Austria	1945	2007	2	0.667	10
Austria	1945	2008	1	0.667	10
Austria	1945	2009	1	0.667	10
Austria	1945	2010	1	0.667	10
Austria	1945	2011	1	0.667	10
Austria	1945	2012	2	0.667	10
Austria	1945	2013	1	0.667	10
Belgium	1831	1893	3	0.707	6
Belgium	1831	1920	2	0.707	9
Belgium	1831	1921	3	0.707	9
Belgium	1831	1968	1	0.707	10
Belgium	1831	1969	1	0.707	10
Belgium	1831	1970	3	0.707	10
Belgium	1831	1971	1	0.707	10
Belgium	1831	1980	2	0.707	10
Belgium	1831	1981	2	0.707	10
Belgium	1831	1983	2	0.707	10
Belgium	1831	1984	1	0.707	10
Belgium	1831	1985	1	0.707	10
Belgium	1831	1988	2	0.707	10

In house

(cont.)

Country	Constitution year	Amendment year	Responses	Median value	VP rigid	POLITY2
Belgium	1831	1989		1	0.707	10
Belgium	1831	1991		1	0.707	10
Belgium	1831	1993		3	0.707	10
Belgium	1831	1994		1	0.707	10
Belgium	1831	1996		1	0.707	10
Belgium	1831	1997		1	0.707	10
Belgium	1831	1998		1	0.707	10
Belgium	1831	1999		2	0.707	10
Belgium	1831	2000		1	0.707	10
Belgium	1831	2001		1	0.707	10
Belgium	1831	2002		1	0.707	10
Belgium	1831	2003		1	0.707	10
Belgium	1831	2004		1	0.707	10
Belgium	1831	2005		2	0.707	10
Belgium	1831	2007		1	0.707	8
Belgium	1831	2008		1	0.707	8
Belgium	1831	2012		1	0.707	8
Botswana	1966	1969	In house	2	0.667	6
Botswana	1966	1970		2	0.667	6
Botswana	1966	1972		1	0.667	6
Botswana	1966	1973		2	0.667	6
Botswana	1966	1978		1	0.667	6
Botswana	1966	1982		2	0.667	6
Botswana	1966	1983		1	0.667	6

Botswana	1966	1987		2	0.667	7
Botswana	1966	1992		1	0.667	7
Botswana	1966	1993		1	0.667	7
Botswana	1966	1997		3	0.667	8
Botswana	1966	1999		2	0.667	8
Botswana	1966	2002		2	0.667	8
Botswana	1966	2005		2	0.667	8
Brazil	1988	1992	1	2	0.702	8
Brazil	1988	1993		2	0.702	8
Brazil	1988	1994		2	0.702	8
Brazil	1988	1995		1	0.702	8
Brazil	1988	1996		1	0.702	8
Brazil	1988	1997		2	0.702	8
Brazil	1988	1998		1	0.702	8
Brazil	1988	1999		2	0.702	8
Brazil	1988	2000		1	0.702	8
Brazil	1988	2001		2	0.702	8
Brazil	1988	2002		1	0.702	8
Brazil	1988	2003		1	0.702	8
Brazil	1988	2004		2	0.702	8
Brazil	1988	2005		1	0.702	8
Brazil	1988	2006		1	0.702	8
Brazil	1988	2007		1	0.702	8
Brazil	1988	2008		1	0.702	8
Brazil	1988	2009		1	0.702	8
Brazil	1988	2010		1	0.702	8
Brazil	1988	2011		1	0.702	8

(*cont.*)

Country	Constitution year	Amendment year	Responses	Median value	VP rigid	POLITY2
Brazil	1988	2012		1	0.702	8
Brazil	1988	2013		2	0.702	8
Bulgaria	1991	2003	2	1	0.77	9
Bulgaria	1991	2005		1	0.77	9
Bulgaria	1991	2006		3	0.77	9
Bulgaria	1991	2007		2	0.77	9
Canada	1867	1893	1	1	1.167	9
Canada	1867	1907		1	1.167	9
Canada	1867	1915		2	1.167	9
Canada	1867	1916		1	1.167	9
Canada	1867	1927		1	1.167	10
Canada	1867	1930		1	1.167	10
Canada	1867	1940		2	1.167	10
Canada	1867	1943		1	1.167	10
Canada	1867	1946		1	1.167	10
Canada	1867	1949		2	1.167	10
Canada	1867	1951		2	1.167	10
Canada	1867	1952		1	1.167	10
Canada	1867	1960		1	1.167	10
Canada	1867	1964		2	1.167	10
Canada	1867	1965		1	1.167	10
Canada	1867	1974		1	1.167	10
Canada	1867	1975		1	1.167	10
Canada	1867	1982		3	1.167	10

Canada	1867	1983	1	1.167	10
Canada	1867	1986	1	1.167	10
Canada	1867	1987	1	1.167	10
Canada	1867	1992	1	1.167	10
Canada	1867	1993	1	1.167	10
Canada	1867	1997	1	1.167	10
Canada	1867	1998	1	1.167	10
Canada	1867	1999	2	1.167	10
Canada	1867	2001	1	1.167	10
Canada	1867	2011	1	1.167	10
Cape Verde	1992	1992	No amendment	0.667	8
Cape Verde	1992	1995	1	1	0.667	8
Cape Verde	1992	1999	2	0.667	8
Cape Verde	1992	2010	2	0.667	10
Chile	1980	1989	2	1.19	8
Chile	1980	1991	2	1	1.19	8
Chile	1980	1994	2	1.19	8
Chile	1980	1996	1	1.19	8
Chile	1980	1997	2	1.19	8
Chile	1980	1998	1	1.19	8
Chile	1980	1999	1	1.19	8
Chile	1980	2000	1	1.19	9
Chile	1980	2001	1	1.19	9
Chile	1980	2003	1	1.19	9
Chile	1980	2005	3	1.19	9
Chile	1980	2007	1	1.19	10
Chile	1980	2008	1	1.19	10

(cont.)

Country	Constitution year	Amendment year	Responses	Median value	VP rigid	POLITY2
Chile	1980	2009		2	1.19	10
Chile	1980	2011		1	1.19	10
Chile	1980	2012		1	1.19	10
Chile	1980	2013		1	1.19	10
Colombia	1991	1993	5	1	0.536	9
Colombia	1991	1995		1	0.536	7
Colombia	1991	1996		1	0.536	7
Colombia	1991	1997		1	0.536	7
Colombia	1991	1999		1	0.536	7
Colombia	1991	2000		1	0.536	7
Colombia	1991	2001		1	0.536	7
Colombia	1991	2002		2	0.536	7
Colombia	1991	2003		3	0.536	7
Colombia	1991	2004		2	0.536	7
Colombia	1991	2005		1	0.536	7
Colombia	1991	2007		1	0.536	7
Colombia	1991	2009		2	0.536	7
Colombia	1991	2011		3	0.536	7
Colombia	1991	2012		2	0.536	7
Colombia	1991	2013		1	0.536	7
Comoros	2001	2009	In house	3	1.333	9
Costa Rica	1949	1954	1	2	1.187	10
Costa Rica	1949	1956		2	1.187	10
Costa Rica	1949	1957		3	1.187	10

Costa Rica	1949	1958	1	1.187	10
Costa Rica	1949	1959	2	1.187	10
Costa Rica	1949	1961	2	1.187	10
Costa Rica	1949	1963	2	1.187	10
Costa Rica	1949	1965	2	1.187	10
Costa Rica	1949	1968	3	1.187	10
Costa Rica	1949	1969	3	1.187	10
Costa Rica	1949	1971	2	1.187	10
Costa Rica	1949	1972	2	1.187	10
Costa Rica	1949	1973	2	1.187	10
Costa Rica	1949	1975	3	1.187	10
Costa Rica	1949	1977	2	1.187	10
Costa Rica	1949	1981	2	1.187	10
Costa Rica	1949	1982	1	1.187	10
Costa Rica	1949	1984	1	1.187	10
Costa Rica	1949	1987	2	1.187	10
Costa Rica	1949	1989	3	1.187	10
Costa Rica	1949	1991	2	1.187	10
Costa Rica	1949	1993	2	1.187	10
Costa Rica	1949	1994	2	1.187	10
Costa Rica	1949	1995	2	1.187	10
Costa Rica	1949	1996	2	1.187	10
Costa Rica	1949	1997	2	1.187	10
Costa Rica	1949	1999	2	1.187	10
Costa Rica	1949	2000	2	1.187	10
Costa Rica	1949	2001	1	1.187	10
Costa Rica	1949	2002	3	1.187	10

(cont.)

Country	Constitution year	Amendment year	Responses	Median value	VP rigid	POLITY2
Costa Rica	1949	2003		2	1.187	10
Costa Rica	1949	2011		2	1.187	10
Croatia	1991	2000	In house	2	0.697	8
Croatia	1991	2001		2	0.697	8
Croatia	1991	2010		1	0.697	9
Cyprus	1960	1989		2	1.343	10
Cyprus	1960	1996	1	2	1.343	10
Cyprus	1960	2002		2	1.343	10
Cyprus	1960	2006		3	1.343	10
Cyprus	1960	2010		1	1.343	10
Cyprus	1960	2013		1	1.343	10
Czech Republic	1993	1998	In house	1	0.887	10
Czech Republic	1993	2000		1	0.887	10
Czech Republic	1993	2001		1	0.887	10
Czech Republic	1993	2002		3	0.887	10
Czech Republic	1993	2009		1	0.887	9
Czech Republic	1993	2012		2	0.887	9
Czech Republic	1993	2013		No amendment	0.887	9
Ecuador		2011	In house	2	1.18	5
El Salvador	1983	1991	1	1	0.677	7
El Salvador	1983	1992		1	0.677	7
El Salvador	1983	1993		1	0.677	7
El Salvador	1983	1994		1	0.677	7
El Salvador	1983	1996		1	0.677	7

El Salvador	1983	1999		1	0.677	7
El Salvador	1983	2000		2	0.677	7
El Salvador	1983	2003		No amendment	0.677	7
El Salvador	1983	2009		1	0.677	8
Estonia	1992	2003	In house	3	1.11	9
Estonia	1992	2007		1	1.11	9
Estonia	1992	2011		1	1.11	9
Finland	1999	2007	1	1	1.157	10
Finland	1999	2011		1	1.157	10
France	1958	1960	In house	2	1.086	5
France	1958	1962		3	1.086	5
France	1958	1963		1	1.086	5
France	1958	1974		2	1.086	8
France	1958	1976		1	1.086	8
France	1958	1992		2	1.086	9
France	1958	1993		1	1.086	9
France	1958	1995		1	1.086	9
France	1958	1996		1	1.086	9
France	1958	1998		1	1.086	9
France	1958	1999		2	1.086	9
France	1958	2000		1	1.086	9
France	1958	2003		1	1.086	9
France	1958	2005		1	1.086	9
France	1958	2008		2	1.086	9
Georgia	1995	2000	In house	2	0.697	5
Georgia	1995	2001		3	0.697	5
Georgia	1995	2002		1	0.697	5

(cont.)

Country	Constitution year	Amendment year	Responses	Median value	VP rigid	POLITY2
Georgia	1995	2003		2	0.697	5
Georgia	1995	2004	1	3	0.697	7
Georgia	1995	2005		2	0.697	7
Georgia	1995	2006		1	0.697	7
Georgia	1995	2008		2	0.697	6
Georgia	1995	2009		3	0.697	6
Georgia	1995	2010		3	0.697	6
Georgia	1995	2011		2	0.697	6
Georgia	1995	2012		1	0.697	6
Georgia	1995	2013		2	0.697	7
Germany	1949	1951	1	1	0.864	10
Germany	1949	1952		1	0.864	10
Germany	1949	1953		1	0.864	10
Germany	1949	1954		2	0.864	10
Germany	1949	1955		2	0.864	10
Germany	1949	1956		2	0.864	10
Germany	1949	1957		1	0.864	10
Germany	1949	1959		1	0.864	10
Germany	1949	1961		1	0.864	10
Germany	1949	1965		1	0.864	10
Germany	1949	1967		1	0.864	10
Germany	1949	1968		2	0.864	10
Germany	1949	1969		1	0.864	10
Germany	1949	1970		1	0.864	10

Germany	1949	1971		1	0.864	10
Germany	1949	1972		1	0.864	10
Germany	1949	1975		1	0.864	10
Germany	1949	1976		1	0.864	10
Germany	1949	1983		1	0.864	10
Germany	1949	1990		3	0.864	10
Germany	1949	1992		2	0.864	10
Germany	1949	1993		1	0.864	10
Germany	1949	1994		1	0.864	10
Germany	1949	1995		1	0.864	10
Germany	1949	1997		1	0.864	10
Germany	1949	1998		1	0.864	10
Germany	1949	2000		1	0.864	10
Germany	1949	2001		1	0.864	10
Germany	1949	2002		1	0.864	10
Germany	1949	2006		2	0.864	10
Germany	1949	2008		1	0.864	10
Germany	1949	2009		1	0.864	10
Germany	1949	2010		1	0.864	10
Germany	1949	2012		1	0.864	10
Greece	1975	1986	1	2	1.1	10
Greece	1975	2001		1	1.1	10
Greece	1975	2008		1	1.1	10
Guyana	1980	1992	In house	2	1	6
Guyana	1980	1995		2	1	6
Guyana	1980	2000		2	1	6
Guyana	1980	2001		2	1	6

(cont.)

Country	Constitution year	Amendment year	Responses	Median value	VP rigid	POLITY2
Guyana	1980	2003		3	1	6
Guyana	1980	2007		1	1	6
Honduras	1982	1984	In house	1	0.687	6
Honduras	1982	1986		2	0.687	5
Honduras	1982	1987		1	0.687	5
Honduras	1982	1988		1	0.687	5
Honduras	1982	1990		1	0.687	6
Honduras	1982	1991		1	0.687	6
Honduras	1982	1995		1	0.687	6
Honduras	1982	1996		1	0.687	6
Honduras	1982	1998		1	0.687	6
Honduras	1982	1999		1	0.687	7
Honduras	1982	2000		2	0.687	7
Honduras	1982	2001		1	0.687	7
Honduras	1982	2002		1	0.687	7
Honduras	1982	2003		2	0.687	7
Honduras	1982	2004		1	0.687	7
Honduras	1982	2005		1	0.687	7
Honduras	1982	2008		1	0.687	7
Honduras	1982	2011		1	0.687	7
Honduras	1982	2012		No amendment	0.687	7
Honduras	1982	2013		No amendment	0.687	7
Hungary	2011	2012	2	3	0.677	10
Hungary	2011	2013		3	0.677	10

Iceland	1944	1959	1	1	1.01	10
Iceland	1944	1968		2	1.01	10
Iceland	1944	1984		2	1.01	10
Iceland	1944	1991		2	1.01	10
Iceland	1944	1995		2	1.01	10
Iceland	1944	1999		1	1.01	10
Iceland	1944	2013		3	1.01	10
India	1949	1951	In house	3	0.56	9
India	1949	1952		1	0.56	9
India	1949	1954		1	0.56	9
India	1949	1955		2	0.56	9
India	1949	1956		3	0.56	9
India	1949	1959		2	0.56	9
India	1949	1960		1	0.56	9
India	1949	1961		2	0.56	9
India	1949	1962		2	0.56	9
India	1949	1963		2	0.56	9
India	1949	1964		2	0.56	9
India	1949	1966		1	0.56	9
India	1949	1967		1	0.56	9
India	1949	1969		3	0.56	9
India	1949	1971		2	0.56	9
India	1949	1972		3	0.56	9
India	1949	1973		2	0.56	9
India	1949	1974		1	0.56	9
India	1949	1975		3	0.56	7
India	1949	1976		3	0.56	7

(*cont.*)

Country	Constitution year	Amendment year	Responses	Median value	VP rigid	POLITY2
India	1949	1977		3	0.56	8
India	1949	1978		3	0.56	8
India	1949	1980		2	0.56	8
India	1949	1982		2	0.56	8
India	1949	1984		2	0.56	8
India	1949	1985		3	0.56	8
India	1949	1986		1	0.56	8
India	1949	1987		2	0.56	8
India	1949	1988		2	0.56	8
India	1949	1989		2	0.56	8
India	1949	1990		2	0.56	8
India	1949	1991		2	0.56	8
India	1949	1992		2	0.56	8
India	1949	1993		1	0.56	8
India	1949	1994		2	0.56	8
India	1949	1995		2	0.56	9
India	1949	1999		2	0.56	9
India	1949	2000		2	0.56	9
India	1949	2001		1	0.56	9
India	1949	2002		2	0.56	9
India	1949	2003		2	0.56	9
India	1949	2005		2	0.56	9
India	1949	2006		1	0.56	9
India	1949	2009		2	0.56	9

India	1949	2011		1	0.56	9
India	1949	2012		1	0.56	9
Indonesia	1959	1999	1	2	0.51	6
Indonesia	1959	2000		3	0.51	6
Indonesia	1959	2001		3	0.51	6
Indonesia	1959	2002		3	0.51	6
Ireland	1937	1939	2	1	1.085	8
Ireland	1937	1941		1	1.085	8
Ireland	1937	1972		3	1.085	10
Ireland	1937	1973		2	1.085	10
Ireland	1937	1979		1	1.085	10
Ireland	1937	1983		3	1.085	10
Ireland	1937	1984		1	1.085	10
Ireland	1937	1987		2	1.085	10
Ireland	1937	1992		2	1.085	10
Ireland	1937	1996		2	1.085	10
Ireland	1937	1997		1	1.085	10
Ireland	1937	1998		2	1.085	10
Ireland	1937	1999		3	1.085	10
Ireland	1937	2001		1	1.085	10
Ireland	1937	2002		2	1.085	10
Ireland	1937	2004		2	1.085	10
Ireland	1937	2009		2	1.085	10
Ireland	1937	2011		1	1.085	10
Ireland	1937	2012		2	1.085	10
Ireland	1937	2013		1	1.085	10
Israel	1958	1959	In house	1	0.5	10

(cont.)

Country	Constitution year	Amendment year	Responses	Median value	VP rigid	POLITY2
Israel	1958	1960		1	0.5	10
Israel	1958	1964		1	0.5	10
Israel	1958	1967		1	0.5	9
Israel	1958	1968		3	0.5	9
Israel	1958	1969		1	0.5	9
Israel	1958	1974		1	0.5	9
Israel	1958	1975		2	0.5	9
Israel	1958	1976		2	0.5	9
Israel	1958	1980		2	0.5	9
Israel	1958	1981		1	0.5	6
Israel	1958	1982		1	0.5	6
Israel	1958	1983		1	0.5	6
Israel	1958	1984		3	0.5	6
Israel	1958	1985		2	0.5	6
Israel	1958	1987		1	0.5	6
Israel	1958	1988		2	0.5	6
Israel	1958	1991		2	0.5	6
Israel	1958	1992		3	0.5	6
Israel	1958	1994		2	0.5	6
Israel	1958	1995		1	0.5	6
Israel	1958	1996		2	0.5	6
Israel	1958	1997		1	0.5	6
Israel	1958	1998		1	0.5	6
Israel	1958	2000		2	0.5	6

Israel	1958	2001		2	0.5	6
Israel	1958	2002		2	0.5	6
Israel	1958	2003		1	0.5	6
Israel	1958	2004		1	0.5	6
Israel	1958	2005		1	0.5	6
Israel	1958	2006		1	0.5	6
Israel	1958	2007		1	0.5	6
Israel	1958	2008		1	0.5	6
Israel	1958	2010		1	0.5	6
Israel	1958	2012		1	0.5	6
Israel	1958	2013		1	0.5	6
Italy	1947	1948	2	1	1.095	10
Italy	1947	1953		1	1.095	10
Italy	1947	1958		1	1.095	10
Italy	1947	1963		1	1.095	10
Italy	1947	1967		1	1.095	10
Italy	1947	1989		1	1.095	10
Italy	1947	1991		1	1.095	10
Italy	1947	1992		1	1.095	10
Italy	1947	1993		1	1.095	10
Italy	1947	1999		1	1.095	10
Italy	1947	2000		1	1.095	10
Italy	1947	2001		2	1.095	10
Italy	1947	2002		1	1.095	10
Italy	1947	2003		1	1.095	10
Italy	1947	2007		1	1.095	10
Italy	1947	2012		1	1.095	10

(cont.)

Country	Constitution year	Amendment year	Responses	Median value	VP rigid	POLITY2
Jamaica	1962	1971	In house	1	0.532	10
Jamaica	1962	1975		1	0.532	10
Jamaica	1962	1977		1	0.532	10
Jamaica	1962	1986		1	0.532	10
Jamaica	1962	1990		1	0.532	10
Jamaica	1962	1993		2	0.532	9
Jamaica	1962	1994		2	0.532	9
Jamaica	1962	1999		2	0.532	9
Jamaica	1962	2002		2	0.532	9
Jamaica	1962	2009		1	0.532	9
Jamaica	1962	2011		3	0.532	9
Latvia	1991	1994	In house	2	0.687	8
Latvia	1991	1996		2	0.687	8
Latvia	1991	1997		3	0.687	8
Latvia	1991	1998		2	0.687	8
Latvia	1991	2002		1	0.687	8
Latvia	1991	2003		3	0.687	8
Latvia	1991	2004		1	0.687	8
Latvia	1991	2005		1	0.687	8
Latvia	1991	2007		1	0.687	8
Latvia	1991	2009		2	0.687	8
Latvia	1991	2013	In house	No amendment	0.687	8
Lesotho	1993	1996		2	1	8
Lesotho	1993	1997		2	1	8

Lesotho	1993	2001		2	1	6
Lesotho	1993	2004		2	1	8
Lithuania	1992	1996	1	2	0.697	10
Lithuania	1992	2002		2	0.697	10
Lithuania	1992	2003		2	0.697	10
Lithuania	1992	2004		3	0.697	10
Lithuania	1992	2006		2	0.697	10
Luxembourg	1868	1919	In house	3	0.687	7
Luxembourg	1868	1948		2	0.687	10
Luxembourg	1868	1956		2	0.687	10
Luxembourg	1868	1972		2	0.687	10
Luxembourg	1868	1979		1	0.687	10
Luxembourg	1868	1983		1	0.687	10
Luxembourg	1868	1988	No amendment		0.687	10
Luxembourg	1868	1989		2	0.687	10
Luxembourg	1868	1994		1	0.687	10
Luxembourg	1868	1996		2	0.687	10
Luxembourg	1868	1998		1	0.687	10
Luxembourg	1868	1999		2	0.687	10
Luxembourg	1868	2000		2	0.687	10
Luxembourg	1868	2003		2	0.687	10
Luxembourg	1868	2004		2	0.687	10
Luxembourg	1868	2005		1	0.687	10
Luxembourg	1868	2006		2	0.687	10
Luxembourg	1868	2007		2	0.687	10
Luxembourg	1868	2008		1	0.687	10
Luxembourg	1868	2009		1	0.687	10

(*cont.*)

Country	Constitution year	Amendment year	Responses	Median value	VP rigid	POLITY2
Macedonia	1991	1992	1	1	0.687	6
Macedonia	1991	1998		1	0.687	6
Macedonia	1991	2001		2	0.687	6
Macedonia	1991	2003		1	0.687	9
Macedonia	1991	2005		1	0.687	9
Macedonia	1991	2009		1	0.687	9
Macedonia	1991	2011		1	0.687	9
Malawi	1994	1995		2	0.677	6
Malawi	1994	1997	1	1	0.677	6
Malawi	1994	1998		1	0.677	6
Malawi	1994	1999		1	0.677	6
Malawi	1994	2004		1	0.677	6
Malawi	1994	2010	1	2	0.677	6
Malaysia	1957	1958		1	0.947	10
Malaysia	1957	1959		No amendment?	0.947	10
Malaysia	1957	1960		2	0.947	10
Malaysia	1957	1961		No amendment?	0.947	10
Malaysia	1957	1962		3	0.947	10
Malaysia	1957	1963		3	0.947	10
Malaysia	1957	1964		1	0.947	10
Malaysia	1957	1965		2	0.947	10
Malaysia	1957	1966		1	0.947	10
Malaysia	1957	1968		1	0.947	10
Mauritius	1968	1969	In house	3	0.677	9

Mauritius	1968	1973	3		0.677	9
Mauritius	1968	1975	1		0.677	9
Mauritius	1968	1982	3		0.677	10
Mauritius	1968	1983	3		0.677	10
Mauritius	1968	1985	2		0.677	10
Mauritius	1968	1986	1		0.677	10
Mauritius	1968	1990	3		0.677	10
Mauritius	1968	1991	3		0.677	10
Mauritius	1968	1992	3		0.677	10
Mauritius	1968	1994	1		0.677	10
Mauritius	1968	1995	2		0.677	10
Mauritius	1968	1996	1		0.677	10
Mauritius	1968	1997	1		0.677	10
Mauritius	1968	2000	3		0.677	10
Mauritius	1968	2001	3		0.677	10
Mauritius	1968	2003	3		0.677	10
Mauritius	1968	2008	1		0.677	10
Mauritius	1968	2011	1		0.677	10
Mexico	1917	1997	1	2	1.232	6
Mexico	1917	1999	2		1.232	6
Mexico	1917	2000	1		1.232	8
Mexico	1917	2001	1		1.232	8
Mexico	1917	2002	1		1.232	8
Mexico	1917	2003	1		1.232	8
Mexico	1917	2004	1		1.232	8
Mexico	1917	2005	1		1.232	8
Mexico	1917	2006	2		1.232	8

(cont.)

Country	Constitution year	Amendment year	Responses	Median value	VP rigid	POLITY2
Mexico	1917	2007		2	1.232	8
Mexico	1917	2008		2	1.232	8
Mexico	1917	2009		1	1.232	8
Mexico	1917	2010		1	1.232	8
Mexico	1917	2011		2	1.232	8
Mexico	1917	2012		3	1.232	8
Mexico	1917	2013		2	1.232	8
Moldova	1994	1996	1	2	0.687	7
Moldova	1994	2000		3	0.687	7
Moldova	1994	2001		2	0.687	8
Moldova	1994	2002		2	0.687	8
Moldova	1994	2003		1	0.687	8
Moldova	1994	2006		1	0.687	9
Mongolia	1992	2001	In house	3	0.76	10
Mozambique	2004	2007	In house	1	0.67	5
Montenegro	2007	2013	In house	3	0.697	8
Namibia	1990	1998	In house	1	0.807	6
Namibia	1990	2010		1	0.807	6
Nepal	2007	2007	1	3	0.677	6
Nepal	2007	2008		3	0.677	6
Nepal	2007	2010		1	0.677	6
Nepal	2007	2011		1	0.677	6
Nepal	2007	2012		2	0.677	6
Netherlands	1848	1917	1	2	1.331	10

Netherlands	1848	1922	1	1.331	10
Netherlands	1848	1938	1	1.331	10
Netherlands	1848	1946	1	1.331	10
Netherlands	1848	1947	1	1.331	10
Netherlands	1848	1948	1	1.331	10
Netherlands	1848	1953	1	1.331	10
Netherlands	1848	1956	1	1.331	10
Netherlands	1848	1963	1	1.331	10
Netherlands	1848	1972	1	1.331	10
Netherlands	1848	1983	1	1.331	10
Netherlands	1848	1987	1	1.331	10
Netherlands	1848	1995	1	1.331	10
Netherlands	1848	1999	1	1.331	10
Netherlands	1848	2000	1	1.331	10
Netherlands	1848	2002	1	1.331	10
Netherlands	1848	2005	1	1.331	10
Netherlands	1848	2006	1	1.331	10
Netherlands	1848	2008	1	1.331	10
New Zealand	1852	1857	In house	1	0.5	10
New Zealand	1852	1863		2	0.5	10
New Zealand	1852	1881		2	0.5	9
New Zealand	1852	1891		2	0.5	9
New Zealand	1852	1892		3	0.5	9
New Zealand	1852	1893		3	0.5	10
New Zealand	1852	1894		3	0.5	10
New Zealand	1852	1902		3	0.5	10
New Zealand	1852	1907		3	0.5	10

(cont.)

Country	Constitution year	Amendment year	Responses	Median value	VP rigid	POLITY2
New Zealand	1852	1908		2	0.5	10
New Zealand	1852	1909		3	0.5	10
New Zealand	1852	1910		2	0.5	10
New Zealand	1852	1911		2	0.5	10
New Zealand	1852	1912		1	0.5	10
New Zealand	1852	1913		2	0.5	10
New Zealand	1852	1917		2	0.5	10
New Zealand	1852	1923		1	0.5	10
New Zealand	1852	1925		1	0.5	10
New Zealand	1852	1927		1	0.5	10
New Zealand	1852	1928		1	0.5	10
New Zealand	1852	1930		1	0.5	10
New Zealand	1852	1933		1	0.5	10
New Zealand	1852	1935		1	0.5	10
New Zealand	1852	1936		1	0.5	10
New Zealand	1852	1947		3	0.5	10
New Zealand	1852	1949		1	0.5	10
New Zealand	1852	1950		2	0.5	10
New Zealand	1852	1951		1	0.5	10
New Zealand	1852	1952		1	0.5	10
New Zealand	1852	1953		1	0.5	10
New Zealand	1852	1954		1	0.5	10
New Zealand	1852	1955		1	0.5	10
New Zealand	1852	1956		3	0.5	10

New Zealand	1852	1957	1	0.5	10
New Zealand	1852	1958	1	0.5	10
New Zealand	1852	1959	1	0.5	10
New Zealand	1852	1960	1	0.5	10
New Zealand	1852	1961	1	0.5	10
New Zealand	1852	1963	1	0.5	10
New Zealand	1852	1965	2	0.5	10
New Zealand	1852	1967	1	0.5	10
New Zealand	1852	1968	1	0.5	10
New Zealand	1852	1969	2	0.5	10
New Zealand	1852	1970	1	0.5	10
New Zealand	1852	1971	1	0.5	10
New Zealand	1852	1972	2	0.5	10
New Zealand	1852	1973	2	0.5	10
New Zealand	1852	1974	2	0.5	10
New Zealand	1852	1975	2	0.5	10
New Zealand	1852	1976	1	0.5	10
New Zealand	1852	1977	1	0.5	10
New Zealand	1852	1978	1	0.5	10
New Zealand	1852	1979	1	0.5	10
New Zealand	1852	1980	1	0.5	10
New Zealand	1852	1981	2	0.5	10
New Zealand	1852	1982	1	0.5	10
New Zealand	1852	1983	2	0.5	10
New Zealand	1852	1985	1	0.5	10
New Zealand	1852	1986	3	0.5	10
New Zealand	1852	1987	1	0.5	10

(cont.)

Country	Constitution year	Amendment year	Responses	Median value	VP rigid	POLITY2
New Zealand	1852	1988		1	0.5	10
New Zealand	1852	1989		1	0.5	10
New Zealand	1852	1990		3	0.5	10
New Zealand	1852	1991		1	0.5	10
New Zealand	1852	1992		1	0.5	10
New Zealand	1852	1993		3	0.5	10
New Zealand	1852	1994		1	0.5	10
New Zealand	1852	1995		2	0.5	10
New Zealand	1852	1996		1	0.5	10
New Zealand	1852	1997		1	0.5	10
New Zealand	1852	1998		2	0.5	10
New Zealand	1852	1999		1	0.5	10
New Zealand	1852	2000		2	0.5	10
New Zealand	1852	2001		3	0.5	10
New Zealand	1852	2002		1	0.5	10
New Zealand	1852	2003		3	0.5	10
New Zealand	1852	2004		1	0.5	10
New Zealand	1852	2005		2	0.5	10
New Zealand	1852	2006		1	0.5	10
New Zealand	1852	2007		2	0.5	10
New Zealand	1852	2008		2	0.5	10
New Zealand	1852	2009		2	0.5	10
New Zealand	1852	2010		2	0.5	10
New Zealand	1852	2011		1	0.5	10

New Zealand	1852	2012		1	0.5	10
New Zealand	1852	2013		1	0.5	10
Nicaragua	1987	1994		No amendment	0.61	6
Nicaragua	1987	1995	1	3	0.61	8
Nicaragua	1987	2000		2	0.61	8
Nicaragua	1987	2005		1	0.61	8
Nicaragua	1987	2007		1	0.61	9
Norway	1814	1898	2	2	0.677	10
Norway	1814	1899		1	0.677	10
Norway	1814	1901		1	0.677	10
Norway	1814	1902		1	0.677	10
Norway	1814	1903		1	0.677	10
Norway	1814	1905		3	0.677	10
Norway	1814	1907		1	0.677	10
Norway	1814	1908		1	0.677	10
Norway	1814	1910		1	0.677	10
Norway	1814	1911		1	0.677	10
Norway	1814	1913		2	0.677	10
Norway	1814	1914		1	0.677	10
Norway	1814	1916		1	0.677	10
Norway	1814	1917		1	0.677	10
Norway	1814	1919		1	0.677	10
Norway	1814	1920		1	0.677	10
Norway	1814	1922		1	0.677	10
Norway	1814	1923		1	0.677	10
Norway	1814	1925		1	0.677	10
Norway	1814	1926		1	0.677	10

(cont.)

Country	Constitution year	Amendment year	Responses	Median value	VP rigid	POLITY2
Norway	1814	1928	1	1	0.677	10
Norway	1814	1929	1	1	0.677	10
Norway	1814	1931	1	1	0.677	10
Norway	1814	1932	1	1	0.677	10
Norway	1814	1935	1	1	0.677	10
Norway	1814	1938	1	1	0.677	10
Norway	1814	1946	1	1	0.677	10
Norway	1814	1948	1	1	0.677	10
Norway	1814	1951	1	1	0.677	10
Norway	1814	1952	1	1	0.677	10
Norway	1814	1954	1	1	0.677	10
Norway	1814	1956	1	1	0.677	10
Norway	1814	1959	1	1	0.677	10
Norway	1814	1962	1	1	0.677	10
Norway	1814	1964	1	1	0.677	10
Norway	1814	1967	1	1	0.677	10
Norway	1814	1972	1	1	0.677	10
Norway	1814	1975	1	1	0.677	10
Norway	1814	1976	1	1	0.677	10
Norway	1814	1978	1	1	0.677	10
Norway	1814	1980	1	1	0.677	10
Norway	1814	1984	1	1	0.677	10
Norway	1814	1986	1	1	0.677	10
Norway	1814	1988	1	1	0.677	10

Norway	1814	1990		1	0.677	10
Norway	1814	1992		1	0.677	10
Norway	1814	1994		1	0.677	10
Norway	1814	1995		1	0.677	10
Norway	1814	2003		1	0.677	10
Norway	1814	2004		1	0.677	10
Norway	1814	2006		1	0.677	10
Norway	1814	2007		1	0.677	10
Norway	1814	2010		1	0.677	10
Norway	1814	2012		1	0.677	10
Pakistan	2002	2010	2	3	0.848	6
Pakistan	2002	2011		2	0.848	6
Pakistan	2002	2012		2	0.848	6
Panama	1972	1993	1	1	1.01	8
Panama	1972	1994		1	1.01	9
Panama	1972	2004		2	1.01	9
Paraguay	1992	2011	1	1	1.102	8
Peru	1993	2000	In house	3	0.99	5
Peru	1993	2002	1	2	0.99	9
Peru	1993	2004		1	0.99	9
Peru	1993	2005		1	0.99	9
Peru	1993	2009		1	0.99	9
Poland	1997	2006	6	1	0.828	10
Poland	1997	2009		1	0.828	10
Portugal	1976	1982	1	1	0.677	10
Portugal	1976	1989		2	0.677	10
Portugal	1976	1992		2	0.677	10

(cont.)

Country	Constitution year	Amendment year	Responses	Median value	VP rigid	POLITY2
Portugal	1976	1997		2	0.677	10
Portugal	1976	2001		2	0.677	10
Portugal	1976	2004		2	0.677	10
Portugal	1976	2005		2	0.677	10
Romania	1991	2003	In house	3	1.249	8
Senegal	2001	2003	In house	1	1	8
Senegal	2001	2006		1	1	8
Senegal	2001	2007		1	1	7
Senegal	2001	2008		2	1	7
Senegal	2001	2009		1	1	7
Senegal	2001	2012		1	1	7
Sierra Leone	1996	2008	In house	2	0.697	7
Slovak Republic	1992	1998	1	2	0.61	9
Slovak Republic	1992	1999		3	0.61	9
Slovak Republic	1992	2001		3	0.61	9
Slovak Republic	1992	2004		1	0.61	9
Slovak Republic	1992	2005		1	0.61	9
Slovak Republic	1992	2006		1	0.61	10
Slovak Republic	1992	2010		1	0.61	10
Slovak Republic	1992	2011		3	0.61	10
Slovak Republic	1992	2012		1	0.61	10
Slovenia	1991	1997	In house	2	0.687	10
Slovenia	1991	2000		3	0.687	10
Slovenia	1991	2003		3	0.687	10

Slovenia	1991	2004		1	0.687	10
Slovenia	1991	2006		2	0.687	10
Slovenia	1991	2013		1	0.687	10
Solomon Islands	1978	1982	In house	1	0.697	7
Solomon Islands	1978	1983		2	0.697	7
Solomon Islands	1978	1989		1	0.697	7
Solomon Islands	1978	1992		1	0.697	8
Solomon Islands	1978	2008		1	0.697	8
Solomon Islands	1978	2009		2	0.697	8
South Africa	1996	1997	3	1	0.717	9
South Africa	1996	1998		1	0.717	9
South Africa	1996	1999		1	0.717	9
South Africa	1996	2001		1	0.717	9
South Africa	1996	2002		1	0.717	9
South Africa	1996	2003		1	0.717	9
South Africa	1996	2005		1	0.717	9
South Africa	1996	2007		1	0.717	9
South Africa	1996	2008		1	0.717	9
South Africa	1996	2009		1	0.717	9
South Africa	1996	2012		1	0.717	9
South Korea	1948	1960	1	3	1.197	8
Spain	1978	1992	2	2	0.648	10
Spain	1978	2011		2	0.648	10
Surinam	1987	1992	In house	2	0.667	5
Sweden	1974	1975	2	1	0.99	10
Sweden	1974	1976		1	0.99	10
Sweden	1974	1977		1	0.99	10

(cont.)

Country	Constitution year	Amendment year	Responses	Median value	VP rigid	POLITY2
Sweden	1974	1978	1	1	0.99	10
Sweden	1974	1979	1	1	0.99	10
Sweden	1974	1981	1	1	0.99	10
Sweden	1974	1982	1	1	0.99	10
Sweden	1974	1983	1	1	0.99	10
Sweden	1974	1984	1	1	0.99	10
Sweden	1974	1985	1	1	0.99	10
Sweden	1974	1986	1	1	0.99	10
Sweden	1974	1987	1	1	0.99	10
Sweden	1974	1988	1	1	0.99	10
Sweden	1974	1989	1	1	0.99	10
Sweden	1974	1990	1	1	0.99	10
Sweden	1974	1991	1	1	0.99	10
Sweden	1974	1992	1	1	0.99	10
Sweden	1974	1993	1	1	0.99	10
Sweden	1974	1994	1	1	0.99	10
Sweden	1974	1995	1	1	0.99	10
Sweden	1974	1996	1	1	0.99	10
Sweden	1974	1997	1	1	0.99	10
Sweden	1974	1998	1	1	0.99	10
Sweden	1974	2000	1	1	0.99	10
Sweden	1974	2001	1	1	0.99	10
Sweden	1974	2002	1	1	0.99	10
Sweden	1974	2003	1	1	0.99	10

Sweden	1974		1	0.99	10
Sweden	1974		2	0.99	10
Sweden	1974		1	0.99	10
Switzerland	1999	2	1	0.99	10
Switzerland	1999		2	0.99	10
Switzerland	1999		1	0.99	10
Switzerland	1999		2	0.99	10
Switzerland	1999		2	0.99	10
Switzerland	1999		1	0.99	10
Switzerland	1999		1	0.99	10
Switzerland	1999		No amendment	0.99	10
Switzerland	1999		1	0.99	10
Switzerland	1999		1	0.99	10
Switzerland	1999		2	0.99	10
Switzerland	1999		No amendment	0.99	10
Switzerland	1999		1	0.99	10
Switzerland	1999		1	0.99	10
Taiwan	1947	1	3	0.75	9
Taiwan	1947		3	1.27	10
Trinidad and Tobago	1976	In house	1	0.923	8
Trinidad and Tobago	1976		1	0.923	8
Trinidad and Tobago	1976		1	0.923	8
Trinidad and Tobago	1976		1	0.923	8
Trinidad and Tobago	1976		1	0.923	8
Trinidad and Tobago	1976		1	0.923	9
Trinidad and Tobago	1976		1	0.923	9
Trinidad and Tobago	1976		1	0.923	9

(cont.)

Country	Constitution year	Amendment year	Responses	Median value	VP rigid	POLITY2
Trinidad and Tobago	1976	1995		1	0.923	9
Trinidad and Tobago	1976	1996		2	0.923	9
Trinidad and Tobago	1976	1999		1	0.923	10
Trinidad and Tobago	1976	2000		1	0.923	10
Trinidad and Tobago	1976	2006		1	0.923	10
Trinidad and Tobago	1976	2007		1	0.923	10
Turkey	1982	1987	4	2	1.187	7
Turkey	1982	1993		1	1.11	8
Turkey	1982	1995		2	1.11	8
Turkey	1982	1999		1	1.11	7
Turkey	1982	2001		2	1.11	7
Turkey	1982	2002		1	1.11	7
Turkey	1982	2004		2	1.11	7
Turkey	1982	2005		1	1.11	7
Turkey	1982	2006		1	1.11	7
Turkey	1982	2007		3	1.11	7
Turkey	1982	2010		2	1.11	7
Turkey	1982	2011		1	1.11	9
Ukraine	1996	2004	1	3	0.687	6
Ukraine	1996	2010		3	0.687	6
Ukraine	1996	2011		1	0.687	6
Ukraine	1996	2013		1	0.687	6
United Kingdom	1297	1911	In house	3	0.776	8
United Kingdom	1297	1914		1	0.5	8

262

United Kingdom	1297	1918	3	0.5	8
United Kingdom	1297	1925	1	0.5	10
United Kingdom	1297	1947	1	0.5	10
United Kingdom	1297	1948	1	0.5	10
United Kingdom	1297	1949	2	0.5	10
United Kingdom	1297	1950	1	0.5	10
United Kingdom	1297	1953	1	0.5	10
United Kingdom	1297	1955	1	0.5	10
United Kingdom	1297	1958	2	0.5	10
United Kingdom	1297	1962	1	0.5	10
United Kingdom	1297	1963	1	0.5	10
United Kingdom	1297	1967	1	0.5	10
United Kingdom	1297	1968	1	0.5	10
United Kingdom	1297	1969	1	0.5	10
United Kingdom	1297	1971	1	0.5	10
United Kingdom	1297	1972	3	0.5	10
United Kingdom	1297	1973	1	0.5	10
United Kingdom	1297	1975	1	0.5	10
United Kingdom	1297	1976	1	0.5	10
United Kingdom	1297	1977	1	0.5	10
United Kingdom	1297	1978	1	0.5	10
United Kingdom	1297	1979	1	0.5	10
United Kingdom	1297	1980	1	0.5	10
United Kingdom	1297	1981	1	0.5	10
United Kingdom	1297	1982	1	0.5	10
United Kingdom	1297	1983	1	0.5	10
United Kingdom	1297	1984	1	0.5	10

(cont.)

Country	Constitution year	Amendment year	Responses	Median value	VP rigid	POLITY2
United Kingdom	1297	1985		1	0.5	10
United Kingdom	1297	1986		1	0.5	10
United Kingdom	1297	1987		1	0.5	10
United Kingdom	1297	1988		1	0.5	10
United Kingdom	1297	1989		1	0.5	10
United Kingdom	1297	1990		1	0.5	10
United Kingdom	1297	1991		1	0.5	10
United Kingdom	1297	1992		1	0.5	10
United Kingdom	1297	1993		1	0.5	10
United Kingdom	1297	1994		1	0.5	10
United Kingdom	1297	1995		1	0.5	10
United Kingdom	1297	1996		1	0.5	10
United Kingdom	1297	1997		1	0.5	10
United Kingdom	1297	1998		2	0.5	10
United Kingdom	1297	1999		2	0.5	10
United Kingdom	1297	2000		1	0.5	10
United Kingdom	1297	2001		1	0.5	10
United Kingdom	1297	2002		1	0.5	10
United Kingdom	1297	2003		2	0.5	10
United Kingdom	1297	2004		1	0.5	10
United Kingdom	1297	2005		2	0.5	10
United Kingdom	1297	2006		2	0.5	10
United Kingdom	1297	2007		1	0.5	10
United Kingdom	1297	2008		1	0.5	10

United Kingdom	1297	2009	1	0.5	10
United Kingdom	1297	2010	1	0.5	10
United Kingdom	1297	2010	1	0.5	10
United Kingdom	1297	2011	2	0.5	10
United Kingdom	1297	2012	1	0.5	10
United Kingdom	1297	2013	1	0.5	10
United States	1789	1865	1	3	1.489	8
United States	1789	1868	2	1.489	8
United States	1789	1870	2	1.489	8
United States	1789	1913	2	1.489	10
United States	1789	1919	1	1.489	10
United States	1789	1920	2	1.489	10
United States	1789	1933	1	1.489	10
United States	1789	1951	2	1.489	10
United States	1789	1961	1	1.489	10
United States	1789	1964	2	1.489	10
United States	1789	1967	1	1.489	8
United States	1789	1971	1	1.489	8
United States	1789	1992	1	1.489	10
Uruguay	1985	1989	1	1	0.5	10
Uruguay	1985	1994	1	0.5	10
Uruguay	1985	1996	3	0.5	10
Uruguay	1985	2004	1	0.5	10
Zambia	1991	2009	In house	1	0.697	7

Appendix II

	OECD	VP rigidity formula	Euclidean distance for ‖lower-upper‖	VP rigidity with Euclidean distance for ‖lower-upper‖	Relevant articles
Albania	0	2/3 + e (all members)		0.677	177
Argentina	0	2/3 (lower) + 2/3 × ‖lower-upper‖ + 0.5 (convention)	0.165	1.277	30
Armenia	0	2/3 parl.		0.67	202–208
Australia	1	0.5 (lower) + 0.5 × ‖lower-upper‖ + 0.5 (ref.) + e (maj. of states' voters)	0.165	1.093	128
Austria	1	2/3	0.251	0.667	44 but also 42–45
Belgium	1	2/3 (lower) + 2/3 ‖lower-upper‖ + e (2/3 present)	0.045	0.707	46, 77, 195–77, 198
Benin	0	3/4 + 0.5 (ref.) − e (other route) + e (all members)		1.25	154–156
Bhutan	0	3/4 of parl. + 0.5 − e (king or ref.)		1.24	2, 33–35
Bolivia	0	2/3 + 0.5 (ref.)	0.054	1.167	411
Botswana	0	2/3		0.667	88–89
Brazil	0	3/5 (lower) + 3/5 ‖lower-upper‖ + e (two rounds)	0.153	0.702	60
Bulgaria	0	3/4 + e (3 ballots) − e (alt route: 2/3 2x) + e (all members for maj.) + e (at least 2 months before discussion)		0.77	153–163
Burundi	0	4/5 (lower) + 4/5 ‖lower-upper‖ − e (alt route: pres. can send to ref.) + e (abs. maj. to initiate amendment) + e (all members for maj.)	0.375	1.11	297–300

(cont.)

	OECD	VP rigidity formula	Euclidean distance for ‖lower-upper‖	VP rigidity with Euclidean distance for ‖lower-upper‖	Relevant articles
Canada	1	0.5 + 2/3 + e (50% pop. representation) – e (alt: instead of senate, pass 2x in house > 180 days apart)	0.401	1.167	35, 38–49, 52
Cape Verde	0	2/3 members – e (pres. cannot refuse to prom.) + e (all members for maj.)		0.667	173, 179, 309–315
Chile	1	3/5 (lower) + 3/5 ‖lower-upper‖ + 0.5 (pres.) – e (can override pres.) + e (all members for maj.)	0.15	1.19	127–129
Colombia	0	0.5 (lower) + 0.5 ‖lower-upper‖ + e (two discussions) – e (alt: can do constituent assembly) – e (alt: ref.)	0.092	0.536	155, 374–379
Comoros	0	2/3 + 2/3 (councils) – e (alt: councils or ref.) + e (all members for maj.)		1.333	42
Costa Rica	0	2/3 + e (multiple debates and delays) + 0.5 (pres.) + e (all members for maj.)		1.187	195–196
Croatia	0	2/3 + e (maj. vote to decide yes/no on amendment) + e (maj. draft approval) + e (all members for maj.)		0.697	87, 147–150
Cyprus	0	2/3 (turkish community) + 2/3 (greek community) + e (all members for maj.)		1.343	182

Czech Republic	1	3/5 (lower) + 3/5 ‖lower-upper‖ + e (all members for maj.)	0.461	0.887	9, 39, 41, 62, Appendix B #8
Denmark	1	0.5 + 0.5 (post-election) + 0.5 (ref.) + e (40% voters say yes)		1.51	88
Dominican Republic	0	2/3 + e (maj. in both houses) + e (two chambers) + e (maj. present in both houses for joint session)	0.551	0.697	93, 99, 120, 267–272
East Timor	0	2/3 + e (120 days advance notice for proposals)		0.677	154–157
Ecuador	0	2/3 (of NA) + (0.5 ref.) + e (time)		1.18	84, 103, 106, 120, 441–444
El Salvador	0	2/3 + e (agreement by 0.5 + 1 members for proposal)		0.677	246, 248
Estonia	1	3/5 (parl.) + 0.5 (ref.) + e (time between 3 readings) + e (3 readings) + e (all members for maj.) – e (alt) – e (alt)		1.11	78, 161–168
Finland	1	0.5 (first vote) + 2/3 (second vote, post elections) – e (alt)		1.157	73, 94, 95
France	1	0.5 (lower) + 0.5 ‖lower-upper‖ + 0.5 (ref) + e (time for bill consideration: tabling delays) – e (alt path)	0.171	1.086	42, 89
Georgia	0	2/3 + e (amendment suggestion needs 50% of members) + e (delay for discussion after draft pub.) + e (all members for maj.)		0.697	68.4, 102, 103
German Federal Republic	1	2/3 (lower) + 2/3 ‖lower-upper‖ + e (all members for maj.)	0.281	0.864	79
Ghana	0	2/3 + e (pub. 2x in gazette, 3 months apart) + e (3 readings) + e (2/3 at second AND third reading) + e (all members for maj.)		0.707	289–292

(cont.)

	OECD	VP rigidity formula	Euclidean distance for ‖lower-upper‖	VP rigidity with Euclidean distance for ‖lower-upper‖	Relevant articles
Greece	1	0.5 (first vote) + 3/5 (second vote after elections) – e (alt path for revisions: 3/5 + 0.51) + e (two rounds of votes in first round [mult. Readings])		1.1	110
Guatemala	0	2/3 + 0.5 + e (all members for maj.)		1.177	173, 277–281
Guyana	0	Maj. + ref. + e (2–6 months to submit to ref.) – e (alt route: 2/3)		1	66, 164
Honduras	0	2/3 + e (all members for maj.) + e (ratify in subsequent session)		0.687	5, 218, 373, 374
Hungary	1	2/3 + e (all members for maj.)		0.677	s, 1.2, 8.3
Iceland	1	0.5 (first vote) + 0.5 (second vote, post elections) + e (pres. confirms)		1.01	79
India	0	0.5 (lower) + 0.5 ‖lower-upper‖ + e (2/3 members present)	0.099	0.56	368
Indonesia	0	0.5 (lower) + 0.5 ‖lower-upper‖ + e (2/3 members present)	0	0.51	37
Ireland	1	0.5 (lower) + 0.5 ‖lower-upper‖ + 0.5 (ref.)	0.17	1.085	46–47
Italy/Sardinia	1	0.5 (lower) + 0.5 ‖lower-upper‖ + e (two debates) + e (time: 3 months between debates) + 0.5 (ref.) – e (alt route: 2/3, no ref.)	0.17	1.095	138 (referendum Art. 75)

Country		Procedure			
Israel	1	0.5 (lower house)		0.5	
Jamaica	0	0.5 (lower) + 0.50 ‖lower-upper‖ + e (all members for maj.) + e (wait 3 months for debate)	0.024	0.532	49
Japan	1	2/3 (lower) + 2/3 ‖lower-upper‖ + 0.5 (ref.) + e (all members for maj.)	0.208	1.315	96
Kenya	0	2/3 (lower) + 2/3 ‖lower-upper‖ + e (3 readings) + e (certificate) + e (all members for maj.)	0.04	0.723	94.3, 255, 256, 257
Korea, Republic of	1	2/3 + 0.5 (ref.) + e (maj. to introduce amendment) + e (delay of 20 days to consider amendments) + e (all members for maj.)		1.197	128–130
Kyrgyz Republic	0	2/3 + e (time: 6 months or less to adopt amendments after proposal) + e (3 readings) + e (2 months between readings) + e (all members for maj.)		0.707	74.2, 97.6, 114
Latvia	1	2/3 + e (2/3 present) + e (3 readings)		0.687	76–79
Lebanon	0	2/3 + e (time: 4 months) + e (all members for maj.)		0.687	65, 76–79
Lesotho	0	0.5 (lower) + 0.5 ‖lower-upper‖ + 0.5 (ref.) + e (time: limit for holding ref.) − e (alt: 2/3)	0	1	85
Liberia	0	2/3 (lower) + 2/3 ‖lower-upper‖ + 2/3 (ref.) + e (2/3 approval for ref.) + e (time: 1 year wait for ref.) + e (all members for maj.)	0.19	1.49	87, 91–93
Lithuania	1	2/3 + e (time: 1-month delay) + e (signs and promulgates) + e (all members for maj.)		0.697	67, 147, 148, 149

(cont.)

	OECD	VP rigidity formula	Euclidean distance for ‖lower-upper‖	VP rigidity with Euclidean distance for ‖lower-upper‖	Relevant articles
Luxembourg	1	2/3 + e (two rounds of votes) + e (3 months between votes) − e (can substitute ref. for second round of voting) + e (all members for maj.)		0.687	114
Macedonia (Former Yugoslav Republic of)	0	2/3 + e (second round of voting; need maj.) + e (all members for maj.)		0.687	129–131, amend. 18
Malawi	0	2/3 + e (all members for maj.)		0.677	195–197, schedule
Malaysia	0	2/3 (lower) + 2/3 ‖lower-upper‖ + e (3 readings) + e (all members for maj.)	0.39	0.947	159, 161e
Mali	0	2/3 (NA) + 0.5 (ref.)		1.17	118
Mauritius	0	2/3 + e (all members for maj.)		0.677	46–47
Mexico	1	2/3 (lower) + 2/3 ‖lower-upper‖ + 0.5 (states) − e (half members for maj.)	0.083	1.212	135
Moldova	0	2/3 + e (6 months between initiative and passage) + e (all members for maj.)		0.687	63, 141–143
Mongolia	0	3/4 + e (all members for maj.)		0.76	26, 68–70
Montenegro	0	2/3 + e (public hearing [1 month+]) + e (two votes of 2/3) + e (all members for maj.)		0.697	155–157

Mozambique	0	2/3 NA		0.67	291, 292, 295
Namibia	0	2/3 (lower) + 2/3 ‖lower-upper‖ – e (alt route: ref. if second chamber does not approve) + e (all members for maj.)	0.21	0.807	131, 132
Nepal	0	2/3 + e (all members for maj.)		0.677	148
Netherlands	1	1/2 (lower) + 1/2 ‖lower-upper‖ + 2/3 (lower) + 2/3 ‖lower-upper‖	0.124	1.312	137–142
New Zealand	1	Maj.		0.5	See text at right
Nicaragua	0	3/5 + e (commission)		0.61	141, 191–195
Niger	0	3/4 + 0.5 (ref.) – e (alt: 4/5)		1.24	173–175
Norway	1	2/3 + e (previous proposal)		0.677	112
Pakistan	0	2/3 + 1/3 ‖lower-upper‖ + e (all members for maj.)	0.513	0.848	238, 239
Panama	0	Maj. (abs.) + maj. (abs., second) + e (gazette) + e (3 readings) – e (alt)		1.01	313–314
Papua New Guinea	0	2/3 parl. + e (time)		0.68	13, 14
Paraguay	0	0.5 (lower) + 0.5 ‖lower-upper‖ + 0.5 (ref.) + e (180 days to call ref.)	0.184	1.102	289–290
Peru	0	Abs. maj. + 0.5 ref. – e (alt: 2/3)		0.99	32, 101.4, 206
Philippines	0	3/4 (lower) + 3/8 ‖lower-upper‖ + 0.5 (pleb.) + e (60–90 days to hold pleb.) – e (alt: constitutional convention) – e (initiative)	0.411	1.394	17
Poland	1	2/3 (lower) + 2/3 ‖lower-upper‖ + e (adopt twice) + e (60 days to adopt second time)	0.212	0.828	235
Portugal	1	2/3 + e (all members for maj.)		0.677	284–289

(cont.)

	OECD	VP rigidity formula	Euclidean distance for ‖lower-upper‖	VP rigidity with Euclidean distance for ‖lower-upper‖	Relevant articles
Romania	0	2/3 (lower) + 2/3 ‖lower-upper‖ + 0.5 (ref.) − e (alt: 3/4 joint session) + e (all members for maj.)	0.124	1.249	150–152
Senegal	0	0.5 (lower) + 0.5 (ref.) − e (alt: 3/5) + e (second chamber)		1	71, 103
Sierra Leone	0	2/3 + e (publish in ≥ 2 issues of gazette, at least 9 days apart) + e (3 readings) + e (all members for maj.)		0.697	108
Slovakia	1	3/5 + e (all members for maj.)		0.61	84.4, 152.1
Slovenia	1	2/3 + e (2/3 approval of proposal) + e (all members for maj.)		0.687	168–171
Solomon Islands	0	2/3 + e (two readings) + e (give bill to speaker 4 weeks in advance) + e (all members for maj.)		0.697	61
Somalia	0	2/3 of both chambers + e (committee) + 0.5 ref.		1.17	57, 63, 71
South Africa	0	2/3 + e (30 days before bill publish in gazette) + e (submit to provincial legislatures) + e (submit comments to speaker) + e (wait 30 days for introducing or tabling) + e (all members for maj.)	0.048	0.717	74

Spain	1	3/5 (lower) + 3/5 ‖lower-upper‖ − e (alt: joint session) − e (alt: can pass 2/3 in the lower house and maj. in upper) + e (all members for maj.)	0.096	0.6576	75, 87, 166–169
Surinam	0	2/3 NA		0.667	72, 83, 181(2)
Sweden	1	0.5 (first vote) + 0.5 (second vote) + e (9-month delay between two votes) − e (alt: abs. maj. + ref.) − e (alt: 3/4 with maj. present)		0.99	8.5.14–17, 8.8.21
Switzerland	1	0.5 (people) + 0.5 (cantons) − e (alt: parl. route)	0.239	0.99	4.2.138, 4.2.139, 4.2.140, 4.2.142, 6.1.192–195
Taiwan before 2000	0	3/4 + e (3/4 present) − e (alt procedure)		0.75	Additional articles to the Constitution of the Republic of China (Fourth Revision); Art. 27 and 174 of the Constitution
Taiwan after 2000	0	3/4 + 0.5 + e (ref. turnout) + e (3/4 present)		1.27	Additional Article 12 (replaces 174) (previously discussed in Art. 27, 30, 174, additional Art. 1)
Thailand	0	0.5 (lower) + 0.5 ‖lower-upper‖ + e (maj. of all members) + e (3 readings) + e (15-day delay between second and third readings)	0	0.53	291

275

(cont.)

	OECD	VP rigidity formula	Euclidean distance for ‖lower-upper‖	VP rigidity with Euclidean distance for ‖lower-upper‖	Relevant articles
Trinidad And Tobago	0	2/3 (lower) + 2/3 ‖lower-upper‖ + e (all members for maj.)	0.37	0.923	18.4, 54
Tunisia	0	1/2 pres. + 2/3 (assembly) + e (initial approval by maj.) − e (alt route)		1.167	76–78
Turkey before 1987	1	2/3 + 0.5 (pres.) + e (two rounds of debate) + e (all members for maj.)		1.19	
Turkey after 1987	1	3/5 + 0.5 (pres.) + e (two rounds of debate) + e (all members for maj.) − e (alt: 2/3)		1.11	
Ukraine	0	2/3 + e (maj. approval in previous round) + e (all members for maj.)		0.687	154–159
United Kingdom before 1911	0	0.5 (lower) + 0.5 ‖lower-upper‖	0.551	0.776	
United Kingdom after 1911	1	0.5 (maj. in LH)		0.5	
Uruguay	0	0.5 (ref.)	0.035	0.5	331
USA	1	2/3 (lower) + 2/3 ‖lower-upper‖ + 3/4 − e (alt) − e (alt) + e (all members for maj.)	0.123	1.489	5
Yugoslavia (Serbia)	0	2/3 + e (all members for maj.)		0.677	203–205 + AD97
Zambia	0	2/3 + e (public in gazette) + e (3 readings) + e (all members for maj.)		0.697	79

BIBLIOGRAPHY

Acemoglu, D. & Johnson, S. (2005). Unbundling institutions. *Journal of Political Economy*, 113(5), 949–995. https://doi.org/10.1086/432166

Acemoglu, D., Johnson, S., & Robinson, J. A. (2001). The colonial origins of comparative development: An empirical investigation. *American Economic Review*, 91(5), 1369–1401. https://doi.org/10.1257/aer.91.5.1369

(2002). Reversal of fortune: Geography and institutions in the making of the modern world income distribution. *The Quarterly Journal of Economics*, 117(4), 1231–1294. https://doi.org/10.1162/003355302320935025

(2005). Institutions as a fundamental cause of long-run growth. *Handbook of Economic Growth*, 1, 385–472. https://doi.org/10.1016/s1574-0684(05)01006-3

Achen, C. H. (2000, July). Why lagged dependent variables can suppress the explanatory power of other independent variables. *Annual Meeting of the Political Methodology Section of the American Political Science Association, University of California, Los Angeles*, 20(22), 7–20.

Ackerman, B. A. (1991). *We The People*, vol. 1. Cambridge, MA: Harvard University Press.

Adamičková, N. & Königová M. (2016). Lidé mají dostat právo sáhnout při ohrožení státu po zbrani. Online article. www.novinky.cz/domaci/clanek/lide-maji-dostat-pravo-sahnout-pri-ohrozeni-statu-po-zbrani-40018504

Adjolohoun, S. H. (2017, May 16). Benin's fourth failed constitutional reform effort: The decisive legacy of participatory processes. Online article. https://constitutionnet.org/news/benins-fourth-failed-constitutional-reform-effort-decisive-legacy-participatory-processes

Albert, R. (2009). Nonconstitutional amendments. *The Canadian Journal of Law and Jurisprudence*, 22(1), 5–47.

(2010). Constitutional handcuffs. *Arizona State Law Journal*, 42(3), 663–716.

(2014). The structure of constitutional amendment rules. *Wake Forest Law Review*, 49, 913.

(2015a). Amending constitutional amendment rules. *International Journal of Constitutional Law*, 13(3), 655–685. https://doi.org/10.1093/icon/mov040

(2015b). Constitutional amendment by stealth. *McGill Law Journal*, 60(4), 673–736. https://doi.org/10.7202/1034051ar

(2015c). How unwritten constitutional norms change written constitutions. *Dublin University Law Journal*, 38(2), 387–418.

(2015d). The unamendable core of the United States constitution. In A. Koltay (ed.), *Comparative Perspectives on the Fundamental Freedom of Expression*. Budapest: Wolters Kluwer. 13–40.

(2018). Constitutional amendment and dismemberment. *Yale Journal of International Law*, 43, 1–85.

(2019). *Constitutional Amendments: Making, Breaking, and Changing Constitutions*. Oxford: Oxford University Press.

Albert, R., Nakashidze, M., & Olcay, T. (2018). The formalist resistance to unconstitutional constitutional amendments. *Hastings Law Journal*, 70, 639–670.

Alessandri Palma, A. (1967). *Recuerdos de Gobierno*, vols. 1 & 2. Santiago: Editorial Nascimento.

Amar, A. R. (1994). The consent of the governed: Constitutional amendment outside Article V. *Columbia Law Review*, 94(2), 457–508.

American Civil Liberties Union. (n.d.). Background on the flag desecration amendment. Online article. www.aclu.org/other/background-flag-desecration-amendment

Anckar, D. & Karvonen, L. (2015). Constitutional amendment methods in the democracies of the world. In P. Mikuli, A. Kulig, J. Karp, & G. Kuca (eds.), *Ustroje tradycje i porownania*. Warsaw: Wydawnictwo Sejmowe. 205–218.

Andrade Geywitz, C. (1991). *Reforma de la Constitución Política de la República de Chile de 1980*. Santiago: Editorial Jurídica de Chile.

Andrews, J. T. & Montinola, G. R. (2004). Veto players and the rule of law in emerging democracies. *Comparative Political Studies*, 37(1), 55–87. https://doi.org/10.1177/0010414003260125

Ansa. (2016, January 20). Renzi, se perdo referendum vado a casa. Online article. www.ansa.it/sito/notizie/topnews/2016/01/20/renzi-se-perdo-referendum-vado-a-casa_38468242-2355-4f1f-9312-9f22046f7548.html

Arellanes Jiménez, P. E. (2014). El Tratado de Libre Comercio de América del Norte: Antes, durante y después, afectaciones jurídicas en México. *IUS Revista del Instituto de Ciencias Jurídicas de Puebla*, 8(3), 257–274.

Associated Press. (2023a, January 21). Slovakia holds referendum to enable snap election. Online article. https://apnews.com/article/politics-slovakia-government-zuzana-caputova-bdee67a3c96d635187d8e94d2683ce0b?utm_source=copy&utm_medium=share

(2023b, January 25). Slovakia parliament changes constitution to enable snap vote. Online article. https://apnews.com/article/politics-slovakia-government-zuzana-caputova-bdee67a3c96d635187d8e94d2683ce0b

Aus, J. P. (2008). The mechanisms of consensus: Coming to agreement on community asylum policy. In D. Naurin & H. Wallace (eds.), *Unveiling the Council of the European Union: Games Governments Play in Brussels*. New York: Palgrave Macmillan. 99–118.

Australian Electoral Commission. (2024, March 10). Referendums FAQs. Website. https://web.archive.org/web/20240310091603/https://www.aec.gov.au/referendums/aec/faqs.html

Ballotpedia. (n.d.). Single-subject rule for ballot initiatives. Online article. https://ballotpedia.org/Single-subject_rule_for_ballot_initiatives

Bank, M. (2016). Parliament gears up to debate new EU firearms legislation. Online article. www.theparliamentmagazine.eu/news/article/parliament-gears-up-to-debate-new-eu-firearms-legislation

Bánkuti, M., Halmai, G., & Scheppele, K. L. (2015). Hungary's illiberal turn: Disabling the constitution. In *The Hungarian Patient: Social Opposition to an Illiberal Democracy*. Budapest: Central European University Press. 37–46.

Bárcena Juárez, S. A. (2017). Involucramiento legislativo sin reelección: La productividad de los diputados federales en México, 1985–2015. *Política y Gobierno*, 24(1), 45–79.

Barrientos Del Monte, F. & Añorve, D. (2014). México 2013: Acuerdos, reformas y descontento. *Revista de Ciencia Política (Santiago)*, 34(1), 221–247. https://doi.org/10.4067/S0718-090X2014000100011

Barro, R. J. (1997). *Determinants of Economic Growth: A Cross-Country Empirical Study*. Cambridge, MA: MIT Press.

Becerra, R., Salazar, P., & Woldenberg, J. (2011). *La Mecánica del Cambio Político en México: Elecciones, Partidos y Reformas*. Mexico City: Cal y Arena.

Benoit, K. (2001). Evaluating Hungary's mixed-member electoral system. In *Mixed-Member Electoral Systems: The Best of Both Worlds?* Oxford: Oxford University Press. 477–493.

Bergman, M. E. (2019). Rejecting constitutional reform in the 2016 Italian referendum: Analyzing the effects of perceived discontent, incumbent performance and referendum-specific factors. *Contemporary Italian Politics*, 11(2), 177–191.

Bernaschina, M. (1956). Génesis de la Constitución de 1925. *Anales de la Facultad de Ciencias Jurídicas y Sociales*, 3(5), 46–65.

Blake, W., Cozza, J., Armstrong, D., & Friesen, A. (2023). Social capital, institutional rules, and constitutional amendment rates. *American Political Science Review*, 118(2), 1075–1083. https://doi.org/10.1017/S0003055423000606

Boehmke, F. J., Brockway, M., Desmarais, B., Harden, J. J., LaCombe, S., Linder, F., et al. (2018). State innovativeness: Dynamic rate scores from SPID v.1.0. *Harvard Dataverse*. https://doi.org/10.7910/DVN/GMVOI5

Boros, T. (2013). Constitutional amendments in Hungary: The government's struggle against the constitutional court. Online article. www.policysolutions.hu/userfiles/elemzes/21/nachrichten_aus_ungarn_februar_2013.pdf

Bowman, G. (2006). The art of legislative drafting. *Amicus Curiae*, 2006(64), 2–9.

Brennan, W. J., Jr. (1991). Why have a bill of rights? *Valparaiso University Law Review*, 26(1), 1–19.

Breuer, A. (2008). Policymaking by referendum in presidential systems: Evidence from the Bolivian and Colombian cases. *Latin American Politics and Society*, 50(4), 59–89.

Brown, A. J. (2008). In pursuit of the "genuine partnership": Local government and federal constitutional reform in Australia. *University of New South Wales Law Journal*, 31(2), 435–466.

Brown, A. R. (2022). *The Dead Hand's Grip: How Long Constitutions Bind States*. Oxford: Oxford University Press.

Brunner, M. (2013). *Parliaments and Legislative Activity: Motivations for Bill Introduction*. Wiesbaden: Springer Fachmedien Wiesbaden.

Buchanan, J. M. & Tullock, G. (1965). *The Calculus of Consent: Logical Foundations of Constitutional Democracy*, vol. 100. Ann Arbor, MI: University of Michigan Press.

Bucur, C. & Rasch, B. E. (2019). Institutions for amending constitutions. In R. D. Congleton., B. Grofman, & S. Voigt (eds.), *The Oxford Handbook of Public Choice*, vol. 2. Oxford: Oxford University Press. 156–176.

Bulkan, A. (2004). Democracy in disguise: Assessing the reforms to the fundamental rights provisions in Guyana. *Georgia Journal of International & Comparative Law*, 32, 613.

Bunikowski, D. (2018). The constitutional crisis in Poland, Schmittian questions and Kaczyński's political and legal philosophy. *Journal of Contemporary European Studies*, 26(3), 285–307.

Burbank, S. B. & Friedman, B. (2002). Reconsidering judicial independence. In S. B. Burbank & B. Friedman (eds.), *Judicial Independence at the Crossroads: An Interdisciplinary Approach*. Thousand Oaks, CA: SAGE Publications. 9–42. https://doi.org/10.4135/9781452229577.n2

Burgess, J. W. (1890). *Political Science and Constitutional Law*, vols. 1 & 2. Boston: Ginn & Company.

Cadem. (2022). Encuesta Plaza Pública Segunda Semana De Septiembre: Estudio 452. Pamphlet. https://cadem.cl/wp-content/uploads/2022/09/PP-452-67-esta-de-acuerdo-con-que-Chile-tenga-una-nueva-Constitucion.pdf

Cámara de Diputados. (2013). Aprueban diputados reformas constitucionales en materia político-electoral. Online article. www3.diputados.gob.mx/camara/005_comunicacion/a_boletines/2013_2013/diciembre_diciembre/05_05/2701_aprueban_diputados_reformas_constitucionales_en_materia_politico_electoral

(2023). Reformas Constitucionales por Decreto en orden cronológico. Website. www.diputados.gob.mx/LeyesBiblio/ref/cpeum_crono.htm

Cameron, C. M. (2002). Judicial independence: How can you tell it when you see it? And, who cares? In S. B. Burbank & B. Friedman (eds.), *Judicial Independence at the Crossroads: An Interdisciplinary Approach*. Thousand Oaks, CA: SAGE Publications. 134–147. https://doi.org/10.4135/9781452229577.n6

Cantú, F. (2019, June 24). The fingerprints of fraud: Evidence from Mexico's 1988 presidential election. *American Political Science Review*, 113(3), 710–726. https://doi.org/10.1017/S0003055419000285

Cárdenas Gracia, J. (1994). *Transición política y reforma constitucional en México*. Mexico City: Universidad Nacional Autónoma de México.

(1998). Hacia una constitución normativa. In *El significado actual de la Constitución: Memoria del simposio internacional*. Mexico City: Universidad Nacional Autónoma de México. 93–118.

Carrubba, C. J., Friedman, B., Martin, A. D., & Vanberg, G. (2012). Who controls the content of Supreme Court opinions? *American Journal of Political Science*, 56(2), 400–412. https://doi.org/10.1111/j.1540-5907.2011.00557.x

Carrubba, C. J., Gabel, M., Helmke, G., Martin, A. D., & Staton, J. K. (2015). When parchment barriers matter: De jure judicial independence and the concentration of power. Unpublished manuscript.

Cassel, D. (2009). Honduras: Coup d'état in constitutional clothing? *American Society of International Law Insights*, 13(9).

Ceccarini, L. & Bordignon, F. (2017). Referendum on Renzi: The 2016 vote on the Italian constitutional revision. *South European Society and Politics*, 22(3), 281–302.

Centre for Population. (2024, July 16). National, state and territory population: September 2023. Website. https://web.archive.org/web/20240716120843/https://population.gov.au/data-and-forecasts/key-data-releases/national-state-and-territory-population-september-2023

Cheibub, J., Elkins, Z., & Ginsburg, T. (2014). Beyond presidentialism and parliamentarism. *British Journal of Political Science*, 44(3), 515–544. https://doi.org/10.1017/S000712341300032X

Chetty, R., Jackson, M. O., Kuchler, T., Stroebel, J., Hendren, N., Fluegge, R. B., et al. (2022). Social capital I: Measurement and associations with economic mobility. *Nature*, 608(7921), 108–121.

Cincurova, S., Inotai, E., Gosling, T., & Ciobanu, C. (2023, January 20). Democracy digest: Slovakia set for referendum and early election. Online article. https://balkaninsight.com/2023/01/20/democracy-digest-slovakia-set-for-referendum-and-early-election/

Cingranelli, D. L. & Richards, D. L. (2008). The Cingranelli-Richards (CIRI) Human Rights Data Project. Website. www.humanrightsdata.com

Clague, C., Keefer, P., Knack, S., & Olson, M. (1999). Contract-intensive money: Contract enforcement, property rights, and economic performance. *Journal of Economic Growth*, 4(2), 185–211. https://doi.org/10.1023/a:1009854405184

Constitute Project. (2015). Mexico's constitution of 1917 with amendments through 2015. Website. www.constituteproject.org/countries/Americas/Mexico?lang=en

Contiades, X. & Fotiadou, A. (2016). The determinants of constitutional amendability: Amendment models or amendment culture? *European Constitutional Law Review*, 12(1), 192–211. https://doi.org/10.1017/S157401961600002X

Cooter, R. D., & Ginsburg, T. (1996). Comparative judicial discretion: An empirical test of economic models. *International Review of Law and Economics*, 16(3), 295–313. https://doi.org/10.1016/0144-8188(96)00018-X

Couto, C. G. & Arantes, R. B. (2008). Constitution, government and democracy in Brazil. *World Political Science*, 4(2), 1–33.

Cox, A. (1996). The independence of the judiciary: History and purposes. *University of Dayton Law Review*, 21(3), 565–584.

Cramton, R. C. (1964). The powers of the Michigan Civil Rights Commission. *Michigan Law Review*, 63(1), 5–58.

CRC special report: Michigan constitutional issues – A brief Michigan constitutional history. (2010a, February). *Citizens Research Council of Michigan*, (360-02).

CRC special report: Michigan constitutional issues – Amending the Michigan constitution: Trends and issues. (2010b, March). *Citizens Research Council*, (360-03).

Crosson, J. M. (2019). Stalemate in the states: Agenda control rules and policy output in American legislatures. *Legislative Studies Quarterly*, 44(1), 3–33.

Cuesta-López, V. (2012). The Spanish agenda initiative and the reform of its legal regime: A new chance for participatory democracy? In *Citizens' Initiatives in Europe*. London: Palgrave Macmillan. 193–211.

Čuroš, P. (2022, September 28). Mária Kolíková is leaving. Online article. https://verfassungsblog.de/maria-kolikova-is-leaving/

(2023). Attack or reform: Systemic interventions in the judiciary in Hungary, Poland, and Slovakia. *Oñati Socio-legal Series*, 13(2), 626–658.

Davala, M. & Chudo, R. (2021, January 27). Amendment to the Constitution of the Slovak Republic focuses on reform of the judiciary. Online article. www.hkv.sk/en/amendment-to-the-constitution-of-the-slovak-republic-focuses-on-reform-of-the-judiciary/

De Londras, F. & Morgan, D. G. (2013). Constitutional amendment in Ireland. In X. Contiades (ed.), *Engineering Constitutional Change*. London: Routledge. 179–202.

Debre, I. & Federman, J. (2023, January 4). Israel's new government unveils plan to weaken Supreme Court. Online article. https://apnews.com/article/politics-israel-government-benjamin-netanyahu-5b240d4bc5d2fb8f533694fc6b7b7809

del Tronco Paganelli, J. & Hernández Estrada, M. I. (2017). Los cambios de política de tercer orden: Recursos, ideas y actores de veto en las reformas energética y educativa (México 2013–2014). *Revista Mexicana de Análisis Político y Administración Pública*, 6(2), 67–92.

Di Mauro, D. & Memoli, V. (2018). Targeting the government in the referendum: The aborted 2016 Italian constitutional reform. *Italian Political Science Review/Rivista Italiana di Scienza Politica*, 48(2), 133–154.

Dishon, N. (2018). Temporary constitutional amendments as a means to undermine the democratic order: Insights from the Israeli experience. *Israel Law Review*, 51(3), 389–425.

Dixon, R. (2011). Constitutional amendment rules: A comparative perspective. In R. Dixon & T. Ginsburg (eds.), *The Research Handbook in Comparative Constitutional Law*. Northampton, MA: Elgar Publishing. 96–111.

(2014, August 18). Partial constitutional codes. *UNSW Law Research Paper*, (2014–37). http://dx.doi.org/10.2139/ssrn.2482377

(2019, October 26). Constitutional design deferred. *UNSW Law Research Paper*, (18–63). https://dx.doi.org/10.2139/ssrn.3251095

Dixon, R. & Baldwin, G. (2019, March). Globalizing constitutional moments? A reflection on the Japanese Article 9 debate. *The American Journal of Comparative Law*, 67(1), 145–176. https://doi.org/10.1093/ajcl/avz002

Dixon, R. & Holden, R. (2012). Constitutional amendment rules: The denominator problem. In T. Ginsburg (ed.), *Comparative Constitutional Design, Comparative Constitutional Law and Policy*. Cambridge: Cambridge University Press. 195–218.

Dixon, R. & Landau, D. (2015). Transnational constitutionalism and a limited doctrine of unconstitutional constitutional amendment. *International Journal of Constitutional Law*, 13(3), 606–638.

(2018). Tiered constitutional design. *The George Washington Law Review*, 86 (438), 438–512.

Dixon, R. & Uhlmann, F. (2018). The Swiss Constitution and a weak-form unconstitutional amendment doctrine? *International Journal of Constitutional Law*, 16(1), 54–74.

Domin, M. (2019, February 8). A part of the constitution is unconstitutional, the Slovak Constitutional Court has ruled. Online article. https://verfassungsblog.de/a-part-of-the-constitution-is-unconstitutional-the-slovak-constitutional-court-has-ruled/

Dove, J. A. (2015). The effect of judicial independence on entrepreneurship in the US states. *Economic Systems*, 39(1), 72–96. https://doi.org/10.1016/j.ecosys.2014.06.006

(2016). Judicial independence and economic freedom in the US states. *Applied Economics Letters*, 23(1), 78–83. https://doi.org/10.1080/13504851.2015.1051649

Doyle, O. & Walsh, R. (2020). Deliberation in constitutional amendment: Reappraising Ireland's deliberative mini-publics. *European Constitutional Law Review*, 16(3), 440–465.

Drugda, Š. (2021, September 14). The People v their representatives. Online article. https://verfassungsblog.de/the-people-v-their-representatives/

Dul, J. (2016). Necessary condition analysis (NCA) logic and methodology of "necessary but not sufficient" causality. *Organizational Research Methods*, 19(1), 10–52. https://doi.org/10.1177/1094428115584005

(2024). A different causal perspective with necessary condition analysis. *Journal of Business Research*, 177, 114618. https://doi.org/10.1016/j.jbusres.2024.114618

Dul, J., Van der Laan, E., & Kuik, R. (2020). A statistical significance test for necessary condition analysis. *Organizational Research Methods*, 23(2), 385–395. https://doi.org/10.1177/1094428118795272

Dunn, J. A., Jr. (1974). The revision of the constitution in Belgium: A study in the institutionalization of ethnic conflict. *Western Political Quarterly*, 27(1), 143–163.

Dura, J. (2023). Proposed restrictions on amending North Dakota constitution to go to voters. Online article. https://bismarcktribune.com/news/state-and-regional/govt-and-politics/proposed-restrictions-on-amending-north-dakota-constitution-to-go-to-voters/article_360cea56-d32d-11ed-bc2a-8f3475341a5e.html

Economist. (2015, October 17). Not just hand-waving. Online article. www.economist.com/news/europe/21674774-italian-government-was-byword-instability-and-indecision-no-more-not-just-hand-waving

Elazar, D. J. (1984). *American Federalism: A View from the States*, 3rd ed. New York: HarperCollins.

Eldes, A., Fong, C., & Lowande, K. (2024). Information and confrontation in legislative oversight. *Legislative Studies Quarterly*, 49(2), 227–256. https://doi.org/10.1111/lsq.12440

Elkins, Z., Ginsburg, T., & Melton, J. (2009). *The Endurance of National Constitutions*. Cambridge: Cambridge University Press.

Elklit, J. (2010). Denmark. In D. Nohlen & P. Stöver (eds.), *Elections in Europe: A Data Handbook*. Baden-Baden, DE: Nomos Publishing House. 501–564.

Elster, J. (2010). *Ulysses Unbound: Studies in Rationality, Precommitment, and Constraints*. New York: Cambridge University Press.

Ely, J. H. (1973). The wages of crying wolf: A comment on Roe v. Wade. *Yale Law Journal*, 82(5), 920–949.

Epstein, L., Knight, J., & Shvetsova, O. (2001). The role of constitutional courts in the establishment and maintenance of democratic systems of government. *Law and Society Review*, 35(1), 117–164. https://doi.org/10.2307/3185388

Escalante Gonzalbo, F. E. (2015). *Historia mínima del neoliberalismo*. Mexico City: El Colegio de Mexico AC.

European Commission for Democracy through Law (Venice Commission). (2010, January 19). Report on constitutional amendment adopted by the Venice Commission at its 81st Plenary Session (Venice, 11–12 December 2009). CDL-AD(2010)001.

Farrell, D., Harris, C., & Suiter, J. (2016). Bringing people into the heart of constitutional design: The Irish Constitutional Convention of 2012–14. In X. Contiades & A. Fotiadou (eds.), *Participatory Constitutional Change: The People as Amenders of the Constitution*. London: Routledge. 120–131.

Feld, L. P. & Voigt, S. (2003). Economic growth and judicial independence: Cross-country evidence using a new set of indicators. *European Journal of Political Economy*, 19(3), 497–527. https://doi.org/10.1016/s0176-2680(03)00017-x

Ferejohn, J. A. (1997). The politics of imperfection: The amendment of constitutions. *Law & Social Inquiry*, 22(2), 501–530. www.jstor.org/stable/828796

Ferejohn, J. A. & Kramer, L. D. (2002). Independent judges, dependent judiciary: Institutionalizing judicial restraint. *New York University Law Review*, 77(4), 962–1039.

Ferejohn, J. A., McKelvey, R. D., & Packell, E. W. (1984). Limiting distributions for continuous state Markov voting models. *Social Choice and Welfare*, 1, 45–67.

Ferreres Comella, V. (2009). *Constitutional Courts and Democratic Values: A European Perspective*. New Haven, CT: Yale University Press.

Finck, D. E. (1997). Judicial review: The United States Supreme Court versus the German Constitutional Court. *Boston College International and Comparative Law Review*, 20(1), 123.

Finer, H. (1949). *The Theory and Practice of Modern Government*. New York: Henry Holt and Company.

Finke, D., König, T., Proksch, S. O., & Tsebelis, G. (2013). *Reforming the European Union: Realizing the Impossible*. Princeton, NJ: Princeton University Press.

Fix-Fierro, H. (2017). ¿Por qué se reforma tanto la Constitución mexicana de 1917? Hacia la renovación del texto y la cultura de la Constitución. In G. Esquivel, F. Ibarra Palafox, & P. Salazar Ugarte (eds.), *Cien ensayos para el centenario: Constitución Política de los Estados Unidos Mexicanos*. Mexico City: Instituto de Investigaciones Jurídicas UNAM (Estudios Políticos). 143–162.

Fix-Fierro, H. & Valadés, D. (2015). Toward the reorganization and consolidation of the text of the Constitution of the United Mexican States of 1917: Introductory essay. Online article. https://archivos.juridicas.unam.mx/www/bjv/libros/9/4050/2a.pdf

(2016). *Constitución Política de los Estados Unidos Mexicanos: Texto reordenado y consolidado*. Mexico City: Instituto de Investigaciones Jurídicas de la Universidad Nacional Autónoma de México.

Follain, J. (2015, October 13). Renzi wins vote to overhaul Roman Senate in blow to elite. Online article. www.bloomberg.com/news/articles/2015-10-13/renzi-wins-vote-to-overhaul-roman-senate-in-blow-to-elite

Fruhstorfer, A. (2016). Moldova. In *Constitutional Politics in Central and Eastern Europe*. Wiesbaden: Springer VS. 359–387.

Fuentes, C. (2006). *Looking Backward, Defining the Future: Constitutional Design in Chile 1980–2005*. Philadelphia: Annual Meeting of the American Political Science Association.

(2015). Shifting the status quo: Constitutional reforms in Chile. *Latin American Politics and Society*, 57(1), 99–122.

(2018). Debate constitucional en Chile¿ Reemplazo vía enmienda? *Política y Gobierno*, 25(2), 469–483.

Fukuyama, F. (1995). Social capital and the global economy. *Foreign Affairs*, 74, 89.

Gabel, M., Carrubba, C. J., Helmke, G., Martin, A. D., Staton, J. K. Ward, D., et al. (2024). CompLaw: A coding protocol and database for the comparative study of judicial review. *Journal of Law and Courts*, 1–27. https://doi.org/10.1017/jlc.2024.4

Garcia, J. F. (2023). A failed but useful constitution-making process: How Bachelet's process contributed to constitution-making in Chile. *Global Constitutionalism*, 13(1), 1–11.

Garlicki, L. (2007). Constitutional courts versus supreme courts. *International Journal of Constitutional Law*, 5(1), 44–68. https://doi.org/10.1093/icon/mol044

Gardbaum, S. (2018). What makes for more or less powerful constitutional courts? *Duke Journal of Comparative & International Law*, 29, 1.

Gerkrath, J. (2013). Some remarks on the pending constitutional change in the Grand Duchy of Luxembourg. *European Public Law*, 19, 449.

Gerlach, P. & Eriksson, K. (2021). Measuring cultural dimensions: External validity and internal consistency of Hofstede's VSM 2013 Scales. *Frontiers in Psychology*, 12, 662604.

Gibler, D. M. & Randazzo, K. A. (2011). Testing the effects of independent judiciaries on the likelihood of democratic backsliding. *American Journal of Political Science*, 55(3), 696–709. https://doi.org/10.1111/j.1540-5907.2010.00504.x

Giles Navarro, C. A. (2018). Las reformas a la Constitución Política de los Estados Unidos Mexicanos. *Instituto Belisario Domínguez*, 33, 1–11.

Ginsburg, T. & Huq, A. (2018). Democracy's near misses. *Journal of Democracy*, 29(4), 16–30.

Ginsburg, T. & Melton, J. (2015). Does the constitutional amendment rule matter at all? Amendment cultures and the challenges of measuring amendment difficulty. *International Journal of Constitutional Law*, 13(3), 686–713.

Glaeser, E. L., La Porta, R., Lopez-de-Silanes, F., & Shleifer, A. (2004). Do institutions cause growth? *Journal of Economic Growth*, 9(3), 271–303. https://doi.org/10.1023/b:joeg.0000038933.16398.ed

Goldenberg, T. (2023, February 2). Israeli AG: Netanyahu cannot be involved in legal overhaul. Online article. https://apnews.com/article/politics-israel-government-benjamin-netanyahu-fraud-d93f12b9ba68e89f8dceb5743833ff03

Goertz, G. (2017). *Multimethod Research, Causal Mechanisms, and Case Studies: An Integrated Approach*. Princeton, NJ: Princeton University Press.

Goertz, G. & Starr, H. (2002). *Necessary Conditions: Theory, Methodology, and Applications*. Lanham, MD: Rowman & Littlefield.

Goguel, F. (1963). Le référendum du 28 Octobre et les élections des 18-25 Novembre 1962. *Revue française de science politique*, 13(2), 289-314.

Goldey, D. B. (1963). The French referendum and election of 1962: The national campaigns. *Political Studies*, 11(3), 287-307.

Goldman, B. T. (2012). The switch in time that saved nine: A study of Justice Owen Roberts's vote in West Coast Hotel Co. v. Parrish. Online article. https://repository.upenn.edu/handle/20.500.14332/8554

Goossens, J. & Cannoot, P. (2015). Belgian federalism after the sixth state reform. *Perspectives on Federalism*, 7(2), 29-55.

Goossens, J. & Hendriks, F. (2021). Belgium. In J. Martí-Henneberg (ed.), *European Regions, 1870-2020*. New York: Springer. 21-29.

González Oropeza, M. (1998). Una nueva constitución para México. In *El significado actual de la Constitución: Memoria del simposio internacional*. Mexico City: Universidad Nacional Autónoma de México. 309-317.

González-Ocantos, E. & Meléndez, C. (2024). Rethinking the role of issue-voting in referenda: Conjoint and vote choice analyses of preferences for constitutional change in Chile. *Comparative Politics*, 56(2), 219-242.

Gutmann, J. & Voigt, S. (2018). The rule of law: Measurement and deep roots. *European Journal of Political Economy*, 54, 68-82. https://doi.org/10.1016/j.ejpoleco.2018.04.001

(2020). Judicial independence in the EU: A puzzle. *European Journal of Law and Economics*, 49(1), 83-100. https://doi.org/10.1007/s10657-018-9577-8

Haggard, S., MacIntyre, A., & Tiede, L. (2008). The rule of law and economic development. *Annual Review of Political Science*, 11, 205-234. https://doi.org/10.1146/annurev.polisci.10.081205.100244

Halbfinger, D. & Rasgon, A. (2020, June 9). Israel court rejects law legalizing thousands of settlement homes. Online article. www.nytimes.com/2020/06/09/world/middleeast/israel-supreme-court-west-bank-settlements.html

Hamon, L. (1963). Voting patterns in Gaullist France: An analysis of the last referendum and elections. *The World Today*, 19(4), 146-155.

Harrison, C. (2022, May 20). A look at what is – and isn't – in Chile's constitutional draft. Online article. www.as-coa.org/articles/look-what-and-isnt-chiles-constitutional-draft

Hayek, F. (2006). *The Constitution of Liberty*. New York: Routledge.

Hayo, B. & Voigt, S. (2007). Explaining de facto judicial independence. *International Review of Law and Economics*, 27(3), 269-290. https://doi.org/10.1016/j.irle.2007.07.004

(2010). Determinants of constitutional change: Why do countries change their form of government? *Journal of Comparative Economics*, 38(3), 283–305. https://doi.org/10.1016/j.jce.2010.07.007

(2014). Mapping constitutionally safeguarded judicial independence: A global survey. *Journal of Empirical Legal Studies*, 11(1), 159–195. https://doi.org/10.1111/jels.12038

(2016). Explaining constitutional change: The case of judicial independence. *International Review of Law and Economics*, 48, 1–13. https://doi.org/10.1016/j.irle.2016.06.003

(2019). The long-term relationship between de jure and de facto judicial independence. *Economics Letters*, 183, 108603. https://doi.org/10.1016/j.econlet.2019.108603

Heiss, C. & Navia, P. (2007). You win some, you lose some: Constitutional reforms in Chile's transition to democracy. *Latin American Politics and Society*, 49(3), 163–190.

Helmke, G. & Rosenbluth, F. (2009). Regimes and the rule of law: Judicial independence in comparative perspective. *Annual Review of Political Science*, 12, 345–366. https://doi.org/10.1146/annurev.polisci.12.040907.121521

Hendrix, S. (2023, October 11). As Israel reels, Netanyahu agrees to share power with opposition party. Online article. www.washingtonpost.com/world/2023/10/11/israel-unity-government-netanyahu-gantz/

Henisz, W. J. (2000). The institutional environment for economic growth. *Economics & Politics*, 12(1), 1–31. https://doi.org/10.1111/1468-0343.00066

High Court. (2006, December 14). Zappone & Anor -v- Revenue Commissioners & Ors. Website. https://web.archive.org/web/20150923230051/http://www.bailii.org/ie/cases/IEHC/2006/H404.html

Hill, D. B. (1981). Political culture and female political representation. *The Journal of Politics*, 43(1), 159–168.

Hofstede, G. (2001). *Culture's Consequences: Comparing Values, Behaviors, Institutions and Organizations Across Nations*. Thousand Oaks, CA: Sage.

Hofstede, G., Hofstede, G. J., & Minkov, M. (2010). *Cultures and Organizations: Software of the Mind*, 3rd ed. New York: McGraw-Hill.

Holmes, S. (1988). Precommitment and the paradox of democracy. In J. Elster & R. Slagstad (eds.), *Constitutionalism and Democracy*. Cambridge: Cambridge University Press. 195–240.

Horowitz, D. L. (2006). Constitutional courts: A primer for decision makers. *Journal of Democracy*, 17(4), 125–137. https://doi.org/10.1353/jod.2006.0063

Howard, R. M. & Carey, H. F. (2004). Is an independent judiciary necessary for democracy? *Judicature*, 87, 284–291.

Howell, W., Adler, S., Cameron, C. & Riemann, C. (2000). Divided government and the legislative productivity of Congress. *Legislative Studies Quarterly*, 25(2), 285–312.

Ibarra Palafox, F. (2016). Identidad y constitucionalismo. Reflexiones sobre la reforma constitucional y su vigencia. In L. R. Guerrero Galván & C. M. Pelayo Moller (eds.), *100 años de la Constitución Mexicana: de las garantías individuales a los derechos humanos*. Mexico City: Instituto de Investigaciones Jurídicas UNAM. 59-74.

Ingles, J. & Kasler, K. (2023, August 8). Ohio voters reject measure that would have made it harder to change constitution. Online article. www.npr.org/2023/08/08/1191679261/ohio-election-results-issue1-abortion-state-constitution-amendment-ballot-voters

Jacob, H., Blankenburg, E., Kritzer, H. M., Provine, D. M., & Sanders, J. (1996). *Courts, Law, and Politics in Comparative Perspective*. New Haven, CT: Yale University Press.

Kalyvas, A. (2012). Constituent power. In A. Ophir & A. L. Stoler (eds.), *Political Concepts: A Critical Lexicon*. New York: Fordham University Press. 87-117.

Keith, L. C. (2002). Constitutional provisions for individual human rights (1977-1996): Are they more than mere "window dressing"? *Political Research Quarterly*, 55(1), 111-143. https://doi.org/10.1177/106591290205500105

(2011). *Political Repression: Courts and the Law*. Philadelphia: University of Pennsylvania Press.

Keith, L. C., Tate, C. N., & Poe, S. C. (2009). Is the law a mere parchment barrier to human rights abuse? *The Journal of Politics*, 71(2), 644-660. https://doi.org/10.1017/S0022381609090513

Kim, J. (2021). Some reflections on constitutional amendment movement in the first half of Moon Jae-In government: With special reference to the role of the judicial bodies. *Korea Observer*, 52(4), 575-601.

Kingsley, P. (2023a, September 12). Israel's Supreme Court weighs law that limits its own power. Online article. www.nytimes.com/2023/09/12/world/middleeast/israel-supreme-court-power-limit.html

(2023b, January 12). Netanyahu surges ahead with judicial overhaul, prompting fury in Israel. Online article. www.nytimes.com/2023/01/12/world/middleeast/netanyahu-israel-judicial-reform.html

Klug, H. (2015). The Constitution in comparative perspective. In M. Tushnet, M. A. Graber, & S. Levinson (eds.), *The Oxford Handbook of the U.S. Constitution*. New York: Oxford University Press. 943-966.

Kornhauser, L. A. (2002). Is judicial independence a useful concept? In S. B. Burbank & B. Friedman (eds.), *Judicial Independence at the Crossroads: An Interdisciplinary Approach*. New York: SAGE Publications. 45-55.

Krehbiel, K. (1998). *Pivotal Politics: A Theory of U.S. Lawmaking*. Chicago: University Of Chicago Press.

Kydland, F. E. & Prescott, E. C.. (1977, June). Rules rather than discretion: The inconsistency of optimal plans. *The Journal of Political Economy*, 85(3), 473-491.

La Porta, R., Lopez-de-Silanes, F., Pop-Eleches, C., & Shleifer, A. (2004). Judicial checks and balances. *Journal of Political Economy*, 112(2), 445–470. https://doi.org/10.1086/381480

Lakatos, I. (1978). *The Methodology of Scientific Research Programmes.* Cambridge: Cambridge University Press.

Ľalík, T. (2020a). The Slovak Constitutional Court on unconstitutional constitutional amendment (PL. ÚS 21/2014). *European Constitutional Law Review*, 16(2), 328–343. https://doi.org/10.1017/S1574019620000140

(2020b, December 18). Slovakia on its way to illiberal democracy: Nullifying the power of the constitutional court to review constitutional amendments. Online article. www.iconnectblog.com/slovakia-on-its-way-to-illiberal-democracy-nullifying-the-power-of-the-constitutional-court-to-review-constitutional-amendments/

Landau, D. E. & Dixon, R. (2023). Utopian constitutionalism in Chile. *Global Constitutionalism*, 13(1), 1–11. https://doi.org/10.1017/S2045381723000266

Landau, D. E., Dixon, R., & Roznai, Y. (2019a). From an unconstitutional constitutional amendment to an unconstitutional constitution? Lessons from Honduras. *Global Constitutionalism*, 8(1), 40–70. https://doi.org/10.1017/s2045381718000151

Landau, D. E., Roznai, Y., & Dixon, R. (2019b). Term limits and the unconstitutional constitutional amendment doctrine: Lessons from Latin America. In A. Baturo & R. Elgie (eds.), *The Politics of Presidential Term Limits.* Oxford: Oxford University Press. 53–74.

Lane, J. (2011). *Constitutions and Political Theory.* Manchester: Manchester University Press.

Law, D. S. & Versteeg, M. (2013). Sham constitutions. *California Law Review*, 101(4), 863–952.

Lehoucq, F. (2002). The 1999 elections in Guatemala. *Electoral Studies*, 21(1), 107–114.

Lieber, D. & Amon, M. (2023, June 29). Israel's Netanyahu revives judicial overhaul stripped of most controversial piece. Online article. www.wsj.com/articles/netanyahu-revives-judicial-overhaul-stripped-of-most-controversial-piece-33160de

Lieber, D. & Boxerman, A. (2022, November 15). Israel's right-wing lawmakers aim to remake supreme court. Online article. www.wsj.com/articles/israels-right-wing-lawmakers-aim-to-remake-supreme-court-11668506325

Lijphart, A. (2012). *Patterns of Democracy: Government Forms and Performance in Thirty-Six Democracies*, 2nd ed. New Haven, CT: Yale University Press.

Linzer, D. A. & Staton, J. K. (2015). A global measure of judicial independence, 1948–2012. *Journal of Law and Courts*, 3(2), 223–256. https://doi.org/10.1086/682150

Lorenz, A. (2005). How to measure constitutional rigidity: Four concepts and two alternatives. *Journal of Theoretical Politics*, 17(3), 339–361.

(2016). How differently actors cope with demanding constitutional amendment rules: Two types of constitutional politics in federal democracies. *Regional & Federal Studies*, 26(5), 729–748.

Lupia, A. (1994). Shortcuts versus encyclopedias: Information and voting behavior in California insurance reform elections. *American Political Science Review*, 88, 63–76.

(2006). How elitism undermines the study of voter competence. *Critical Review*, 18, 217–232.

Lutz, D. S. (1994). Toward a theory of constitutional amendment. *American Political Science Review*, 88(2), 355–370.

(2006). *Principles of Constitutional Design*. Cambridge: Cambridge University Press.

Madison, J. (1788). The Federalist No. 62. Website. https://founders.archives.gov/documents/Hamilton/01-04-02-0212

Magaloni, B. (2006). *Voting for Autocracy: Hegemonic Party Survival and its Demise in Mexico*. Cambridge: Cambridge University Press.

Mansoor, S. (2023, March 27). Netanyahu is beholden to the Israeli far-right on the judicial overhaul plan. Online article. https://time.com/6266434/israel-protests-netanyahu-far-right/

Marshall, M. G. (2016). Polity IV Project: Political regime characteristics and transitions, 1800–2013. Website. www.systemicpeace.org/polity/polity4.htm

Marshfield, J. L. (2017). Court and informal constitutional change in the states. *New England Law Review*, 51(453), 453–518.

(2018). The amendment effect. *Boston University Law Review*, 98(1), 55–126.

Martínez-Barahona, E. (2012). Constitutional courts and constitutional change: Analyzing the cases of presidential re-election in Latin America. In D. Nolte & A. Schilling-Vacaflor (eds.), *New Constitutionalism in Latin America*. Farnham, UK: Ashgate. 289–312.

Mayer-Serra, C. E. (2017). Reforma de la Constitución: la economía política del Pacto por México. *Revista Mexicana de Ciencias Políticas y Sociales*, 62(230), 21–49. https://doi.org/10.1016/S0185-1918(17)30016-8

McKernan, B. (2023, September 12). What is Israel's judicial overhaul about and what happens next? Online article. www.theguardian.com/world/2023/jul/24/what-is-israel-judicial-overhaul-vote-about-what-happens-next

Melton, J. & Ginsburg, T. (2014). Does de jure judicial independence really matter? A reevaluation of explanations for judicial independence. *Journal of Law and Courts*, 2(2), 187–217. https://doi.org/10.1086/676999

Metelska-Szaniawska, K. (2021). Post-socialist constitutions: The de jure–de facto gap, its effects and determinants. *Economics of Transition and Institutional Change*, 29(2), 175–196. https://doi.org/10.1111/ecot.12261

Metelska-Szaniawska, K. & Lewkowicz, J. (2021). Post-socialist illiberal democracies: Do de jure constitutional rights matter? *Constitutional Political Economy*, 32(2), 233–265. https://doi.org/10.1007/s10602-020-09316-4

Ministerio del Interior. (1925). *Actas Oficiales de las Sesiones celebradas por la Comisión y Sub-comisiones encargadas del estudio del Proyecto de Nueva Constitución Política de la República*. Santiago: Imprenta Universitaria.

Mitchell, J. (2023, April 23). North Dakota voters to decide on constitutional initiative procedures in 2024. Online article. https://news.ballotpedia.org/2023/04/18/north-dakota-voters-to-decide-on-constitutional-initiative-procedures-in-2024/

Mondak, J. J. & Canache, D. (2014). Personality and political culture in the American states. *Political Research Quarterly*, 67(1), 26–41.

Morisey, M. (2007). Flag desecration, religion and patriotism. *Rutgers Journal of Law & Religion*, 9, 1.

Nacif, B. (2002). Understanding party discipline in the Mexican Chamber of Deputies: The centralized party model. In B. Nacif & S. Morgenstern (eds.), *Legislative Politics in Latin America*. Cambridge: Cambridge University Press. 254–284.

Nanda, V. P. (1974). The constitutional framework and the current political crisis in India. *Hastings Constitutional Law Quarterly*, 2, 859.

Nash, J. (1951). Non-cooperative games. *Annals of Mathematics*, 54, 286–295.

Navia, P. (2018). If you can fix it, why replace it? Democratizing the Pinochet Constitution in Chile. *Política y Gobierno*, 25(2), 485–499.

Negretto, G. L. (2012). Replacing and amending constitutions: The logic of constitutional change in Latin America. *Law & Society Review*, 46(4), 749–779.

Negri, F. & Rebessi, E. (2018). Was Mattarella worth the trouble? Explaining the failure of the 2016 Italian constitutional referendum. *Italian Political Science Review/Rivista Italiana di Scienza Politica*, 48(2), 177–196.

Neuborne, B. (2003). The supreme court of India. *International Journal of Constitutional Law*, 1(3), 476–510.

Nev. Const. art. 16, § 1.

Nev. Const. art. 19, § 2.

Nevada Secretary of State. (n.d.). Petition district maps. Website. www.nvsos.gov/sos/elections/initiatives-referenda/petition-district-maps

New York Times. (2005, June 10). Israeli Supreme Court backs Gaza pullout plan. Online article. www.nytimes.com/2005/06/10/world/africa/israeli-supreme-court-backs-gaza-pullout-plan.html

Nicas, J. (2023, December 17). Chile's Left forced a new constitution: Then the Right took control. Online article. www.nytimes.com/2023/12/17/world/americas/chile-constitution-referendum-vote.html

North, D. C. & Weingast, B. R. (1989). Constitutions and commitment: The evolution of institutions governing public choice in seventeenth-century England. *The Journal of Economic History*, 49(4), 803–832. https://doi.org/10.1017/s0022050700009451

North, D. C., Summerhill, W., & Weingast, B. (2000). Order, disorder and economic change: Latin America vs. North America. In B. Bueno de Mesquita

& H. L. Root (eds.), *Governing for Prosperity*. New Haven, CT: Yale University Press. 17–58.

Oliver, J. E. & Wood, T. J. (2014). Conspiracy theories and the paranoid style(s) of mass opinion. *American Journal of Political Science*, 58(4), 952–966.

Orange Files. (2013, October 21). Amendments to the fundamental law. Online article. https://theorangefiles.hu/amendments-to-the-fundamental-law/

Orozco Pulido, J. M. (2020). Drafting a constitution is not drafting a statute: An analysis of the Mexican Constitution and hyper-amending pathologies from the legislative drafting perspective. *Mexican Law Review*, 13(1), 203–217. https://doi.org/10.22201/iij.24485306e.2020.1.14814

Ortiz Gallegos, J. E. (2007). Los círculos feudales de la política en México. *Este país*, 1–10.

Pacto por México. (2012). Online article. www.foroconsultivo.org.mx/FCCyT/sites/default/files/pacto_por_mexico.pdf

PLAC. (2014). A step-by-step process of amending the Nigerian Constitution. Online article. https://placng.org/i/wp-content/uploads/2021/05/Step-by-Step-Guide-to-the-Process-of-Amending-the-Nigerian-Constitution.pdf

Plato. (2008). N. Denyer (ed.), *Protagoras*. Cambridge: Cambridge University Press.

Plevák, O. (2021, July 23). Firearm ownership rights embedded into Czech constitution. Online article. www.euractiv.com/section/politics/short_news/firearm-ownership-rights-embedded-into-czech-constitution/

Pou Giménez, F. (2018). Constitutionalism old, new and unbound: The case of Mexico. In C. Crawford & D. Bonilla Maldonado (eds.), *Constitutionalism in the Americas*. Cheltenham, UK: Edward Elgar Publishing Limited. 155–187.

Powell, E. J. & Staton, J. K. (2009). Domestic judicial institutions and human rights treaty violation. *International Studies Quarterly*, 53(1), 149–174. https://doi.org/10.1111/j.1468-2478.2008.01527.x

Pozas-Loyo, A. & Saavedra-Herrera, C. (2021). Mexico. *The International Review of Constitutional Reform: 2020*. Austin: University of Texas. 208–211.

Pozas-Loyo, A., Saavedra-Herrera, C., & Pou-Giménez, F. (2022, September 2). When more leads to more: Constitutional amendments and interpretation in Mexico 1917–2020. *Law & Social Inquiry*, 1–32. https://doi.org/10.1017/lsi.2022.35

Putnam, R. D. (2001). *Bowling Alone: The Collapse and Revival of American Community – Revised and Updated*. New York: Simon and Schuster.

Putnam, R. D., Leonardi, R., & Nonetti, R. Y. (1993). *Making Democracy Work: Civic Traditions in Modern Italy*. Princeton, NJ: Princeton University Press.

Raifeartaigh, U. N. (1997). Reconciling bail law with the presumption of innocence. *Oxford Journal of Legal Studies*, 17, 1.

Ramseyer, J. M. & Rasmusen, E. (2003). *Measuring Judicial Independence: The Political Economy of Judging in Japan*. Chicago: University of Chicago Press.

Randazzo, K. A., Gibler, D. M., & Reid, R. (2016). Examining the development of judicial independence. *Political Research Quarterly*, 69(3), 583–593. https://doi.org/10.1177/1065912916656277

Rasch, B. E. (2000). Parliamentary floor voting procedures and agenda setting in Europe. *Legislative Studies Quarterly*, 25(1), 3–23.

Rasch, B. E. & Congleton, R. D. (2006). Amendment procedures and constitutional stability. In R. D. Congleton & B. Swedenborg (eds.), *Democratic Constitutional Design and Public Policy: Analysis and Evidence*. Cambridge, MA: MIT Press. 536–561.

Reuters. (2020a, July 6). Ahead of run-off vote, Polish president proposes constitutional ban on gay adoption. Online article. www.reuters.com/article/us-poland-election/ahead-of-run-off-vote-polish-president-proposes-constitutional-ban-on-lgbt-adoption-idUSKBN2471FT/

Reuters. (2020b, April 15). Poland's PiS seeks constitutional change to extend president's term. Online article. www.reuters.com/article/us-health-coronavirus-poland-constitutio/polands-pis-seeks-constitutional-change-to-extend-presidents-term-idUSKCN21X3CJ/

Rice, T. M. & Sumberg, A. F. (1997). Civic culture and government performance in the American states. *Publius: The Journal of Federalism*, 27(1), 99–114.

Ríos-Figueroa, J. (2007). Fragmentation of power and the emergence of an effective judiciary in Mexico, 1994–2002. *Latin American Politics and Society*, 49(1), 31–57. https://doi.org/10.1111/j.1548-2456.2007.tb00373.x

(2011). Institutions for constitutional justice in Latin America. In G. Helmke & J. Ríos-Figueroa (eds.), *Courts in Latin America*. Cambridge: Cambridge University Press. 27–54.

Ríos-Figueroa, J. & Staton, J. K. (2014). An evaluation of cross-national measures of judicial independence. *The Journal of Law, Economics, & Organization*, 30(1), 104–137. https://doi.org/10.1093/jleo/ews029

Rivera León, M. A. (2017). Understanding constitutional amendments in Mexico: Perpetuum mobile constitution. *Mexican Law Review*, 9, 3–27.

Rogoff, M. A. (2008). Fifty years of constitutional evolution in France: The 2008 amendments and beyond. *The Financial Crisis of 2008: French and American Responses – Proceedings of the 2010 Franco-American Legal Seminar*. https://dx.doi.org/10.2139/ssrn.1793210

Roy, T. & Swamy, A.V. (2022). Land rights. In *Law and the Economy in a Young Democracy*. Chicago: University of Chicago Press. 15–44.

Roznai, Y. (2017). Unconstitutional constitutional change. *New England Law Review*, 51(3), 555–577.

(2022). Constitutional transformation: Hungary. In D. S. Law (ed.), *Constitutionalism in Context*. Cambridge: Cambridge University Press. 136–156.

Sadurski, W. (2020a). Constitutional democracy in the time of elected authoritarians. *International Journal of Constitutional Law*, 18(2), 324–333.

(2020b). Constitutional design: Lessons from Poland's democratic backsliding. *Constitutional Studies*, 6(1), 59–79.

Salazar Ugarte, P. (2013). *Política Y Derecho: Derecho y garantías – Cinco ensayos latinoamericanos*. Mexico City: Fontamara.

Salzberger, E. & Fenn, P. (1999). Judicial independence: Some evidence from the English Court of Appeal. *The Journal of Law and Economics*, 42(2), 831–847. https://doi.org/10.1086/467444

Sánchez, A., Magaloni, B., & Magar, E. (2011). Legalist versus interpretativist: The Supreme Court and the democratic transition in Mexico. In G. Helmke & J. Ríos-Figueroa (eds.), *Courts in Latin America*. Cambridge: Cambridge University Press. 187–218.

Santoni, M. & Zucchini, F. (2004). Does policy stability increase the constitutional court's independence? The case of Italy during the first republic (1956–1992). *Public Choice*, 120(3), 439–401. https://doi.org/10.1023/b:puch.0000044291.11088.75

Sartori, G. (1970). Concept misformation in comparative politics. *American Political Science Review*, 64(4), 1033–1053.

Sauer, C. (2021, October 28). Luxembourg's constitutional crescendo: Will incremental reforms succeed where overhaul failed? Online article. https://constitutionnet.org/news/luxembourgs-constitutional-crescendo-will-incremental-reforms-succeed-where-overhaul-failed

Scalia, A. & Gutmann, A. (1997). *A Matter of Interpretation: Federal Courts and the Law: An Essay*. Princeton, NJ: Princeton University Press.

Schneier, E. V. (2006). *Crafting Constitutional Democracies: The Politics of Institutional Design*. Oxford: Rowman & Littlefield.

Schwartz, S. (1992). Universals in the content and structure of values: Theoretical advances and empirical tests in 20 countries. *Advances in Experimental Social Psychology*, 25, 1–65.

Serna de la Garza, J. M. (2016). *El sistema federal mexicano: trayectoria y caracterísiticas*. Mexico City: Instituto de Investigaciones Jurídicas.

Sharkansky, I. (1969). The utility of Elazar's political culture: A research note. *Polity*, 2(1), 66–83.

Shepsle, K. A. & Weingast, B. R. (1987). The institutional foundations of committee power. *American Political Science Review*, 81(1), 85–104. https://doi.org/10.2307/1960780

Smyth, J. C. (2023a, May 15). GOP state lawmakers try to restrict ballot initiatives, partly to thwart abortion protections. Online article. https://apnews.com/article/democracy-ballot-initiatives-abortion-republicans-ohio-missouri-c48033311370f071ccece0da975818cb

(2023b, November 24). Ohio voters just passed abortion protections: When and how they take effect is before the courts. Online article. https://apnews.com/article/abortion-ohio-constitutional-amendment-republicans-courts-fb1762537585350caeee589d68fe5a0d

Soederberg, S. (2005). The rise of neoliberalism in Mexico: From a developmental to a competition state. In S. Soederberg, G. Menz, & P. G. Cerny (eds.), *Internalizing Globalization: The Rise of Neoliberalism and the Decline of National Varieties of Capitalism*. London: Palgrave Macmillan UK. 167–182.

Sosa, E. (2015). The movement against the coup in Honduras. In *Handbook of Social Movements Across Latin America*. Dordrecht: Springer. 313–326.

Stanton, K. A. (1997a). The transformation of a political regime: Chile's 1925 constitution. Conference paper. Guadalajara: 1997 Meeting of the Latin American Studies Association.

(1997b). Transforming a political regime: The Chilean Constitution of 1925. Doctoral dissertation. Chicago: University of Chicago, Dept. of Political Science.

Staton, J. K. (2018). Judicial independence research beyond the crossroads. In R. M. Howard & K. A. Randazzo (eds.), *Routledge Handbook of Judicial Behavior*. London: Routledge. 355–369.

Steuer, M. & Láštic, E. (2024). The Slovak constitutional court: The promise of Dworkinian adjudication? In K. Pócza (ed.), *Constitutional Review in Central and Eastern Europe*. London: Routledge. 244–273.

Stohler, S., Bateman, D., & Woodward Burns, R. (2022). Judicial power and the shifting purpose of Article V. *Studies in American Political Development*, 36(2), 84–103.

Stone Sweet, A. (2007). The politics of constitutional review in France and Europe. *International Journal of Constitutional Law*, 5(1), 69–92. https://doi.org/10.1093/icon/mol041

Strøm, K., Müller, W. C., & Bergman, T. (eds.). (2003). *Delegation and Accountability in Parliamentary Democracies, Comparative Politics*. Oxford: Oxford University Press.

Student. (1931). The Lanarkshire milk experiment. Biometrika, 23(3/4), 398–406. https://doi.org/10.2307/2332424

Sturm, A. L. (1963). *Constitution-Making in Michigan, 1961–1962: Michigan Governmental Studies No. 43*. Ann Arbor, MI: Institute of Public Administration, University of Michigan.

Tarabar, D. & Young, A. T. (2021). What constitutes a constitutional amendment culture? *European Journal of Political Economy*, 66, 101953.

Thomson, R., Stokman, F. N., Achen, C. H., & König, T. (eds.). (2006). *The European Union Decides*. Cambridge: Cambridge University Press.

Tiernan, S. (2020). *The History of Marriage Equality in Ireland: A Social Revolution Begins*. Manchester: Manchester University Press.

Torres Alonso, E. (2016). Pacto por México: Una nueva vuelta de tuerca al reformismo mexicano. *RAIGAL. Revista Interdisciplinaria de Ciencias Sociales*, 2, 8–22.

Torres-Artunduaga, C. & García-Jaramillo, S. (2020). Democratizing the doctrine of unconstitutional constitutional amendments: The puzzle of amending the judiciary branch. *ICL Journal*, 14(1), 1–42.

Tribe, L. H. (1995). Taking text and structure seriously: Reflections on free-form method in constitutional interpretation. *Harvard Law Review*, 108(6), 1221–1303.

Tsebelis, G. (1991). *Nested Games*. Berkeley: University of California Press.

(1995). Decision making in political systems: Veto players in presidentialism, parliamentarism, multicameralism and multipartyism. *British Journal of Political Science*, 25(3), 289–325. https://doi.org/10.1017/s0007123400007225

(2002). *Veto Players: How Political Institutions Work*. Princeton, NJ: Princeton University Press.

(2012). The rules of decisionmaking in EU institutions. In T. Eger & H. B. Schäfer (eds.), *Research Handbook on the Economics of European Union Law*. Northampton, MA: Edward Elgar. 29–54.

(2017a). Compromesso astorico: The role of the senate after the Italian constitutional reform. *Italian Political Science Review/Rivista Italiana di Scienza Politica*, 47(1), 87–104.

(2017b). The time inconsistency of long constitutions: Evidence from the world. *European Journal of Political Research*, 56(4), 820–845.

(2018a). Back to the Pinochet Constitution: A response. *Política y Gobierno*, 25(2), 501–510.

(2018b). How can we keep direct democracy and avoid "Kolotoumba." *Homo Oeconomicus*, 35(1), 81–90.

(2018c). Veto players and constitutional change: Can Pinochet's constitution be unlocked? *Política y Gobierno*, 25(1), 3–30.

(2022). Constitutional rigidity matters: A veto players approach. *British Journal of Political Science*, 52(1), 280–299. https://doi.org/10.1017/S0007123420000411

Tsebelis, G. & Alemán, E. (2005). Presidential conditional agenda setting in Latin America. *World Politics*, 57(3), 396–420.

Tsebelis, G. & Atilano-Robles, E. (2024). Why are constitutional amendments in Mexico so frequent? *Journal of Politics in Latin America*, 0(0). https://doi.org/10.1177/1866802X241254400

Tsebelis, G. & Hahm, H. (2014). Suspending vetoes: How the euro countries achieved unanimity in the fiscal compact. *Journal of European Public Policy*, 21(10), 1388–1411. https://doi.org/10.1080/13501763.2014.929167

Tsebelis, G. & Nardi, D. J. (2016). A long constitution is a (positively) bad constitution: Evidence from OECD countries. *British Journal of Political Science*, 46(02), 457–478.

Tyushka, A. (2014). A liberationist constitution? Maidan's revolutionary agenda and challenges for constitutional reform in Ukraine. *European View*, 13(1), 21–28. https://doi.org/10.1007/s12290-014-0291-9

Uitz, R. (2015). Can you tell when an illiberal democracy is in the making? An appeal to comparative constitutional scholarship from Hungary. *International Journal of Constitutional Law*, 13(1), 279–300.

Uleri, P. V. (2012). Institutions of citizens' political participation in Italy: Crooked forms, hindered institutionalization. In *Citizens' Initiatives in Europe*. London: Palgrave Macmillan. 71–88.

Valenzuela, A. (1977). *Political Brokers in Chile: Local Government in a Centralized Polity*. Durham, NC: Duke University Press.

Vanberg, G. (2001). Legislative-judicial relations: A game-theoretic approach to constitutional review. *American Journal of Political Science*, 45, 346–361.

Vandenbosch, S. (1991). Political culture and corporal punishment in public schools. *Publius: The Journal of Federalism*, 21(2), 117–121.

VanderMay, M. C. (1996). The role of the judiciary in India's constitutional democracy. *Hastings International and Comparative Law Review*, 20, 103.

Velasco-Rivera, M. (2019). The political sources of onstitutional amendment (non) difficulty in Mexico. In R. Albert, C. Bernal, & J. Z. Benvindo (eds.), *Constitutional Change and Transformation in Latin America*. London: Bloomsbury Publishing. 243–268.

 (2021). Constitutional rigidity: The Mexican experiment. *International Journal of Constitutional Law*, 19(3), 1042–1061. https://doi.org/10.1093/icon/moab087

Venice Commission. (2012, June 20). Opinion on the revision of the Constitution of Belgium (Opinion No. 679 / 2012). Online article. www.venice.coe.int/webforms/documents/default.aspx?pdffile=CDL-AD%282012%29010-e

Versteeg, M. & Zackin, E. (2016). Constitutions unentrenched: Toward an alternative theory of constitutional design. *American Political Science Review*, 110(4), 657–674.

Vial, G. (1987). "La Constitución de 1925", *Historia de Chile, 1891–1973*, vol. 3. Santiago: Editorial Santillana del Pacífico.

Voigt, S. (2009, December). Explaining constitutional garrulity. *International Review of Law and Economics*, 29(4), 290–303.

 (2021). Mind the gap: Analyzing the divergence between constitutional text and constitutional reality. *International Journal of Constitutional Law*, 19(5), 1778–1809. https://doi.org/10.1093/icon/moab060

Voigt, S., Gutmann, J., & Feld, L. P. (2015). Economic growth and judicial independence, a dozen years on: Cross-country evidence using an updated set of indicators. *European Journal of Political Economy*, 38, 197–211. https://doi.org/10.1016/j.ejpoleco.2015.01.004

Von Neumann, J. & Morgenstern, O. (1944). *Theory of Games and Economic Behavior*. Princeton, NJ: Princeton University Press.

Vrbin, T. (2023, March 6). Heightened requirements to put measures on the Arkansas ballot awaits Sanders' signature. Online article. https://arkansasadvocate.com/2023/03/06/heightened-requirements-to-put-measures-on-the-arkansas-ballot-awaits-sanders-signature/

Waldron, J. (1999). *Law and Disagreement*. Oxford: Oxford University Press.

White House. (2023, April 29). Remarks by President Biden at the White House Correspondents' Dinner. Website. www.whitehouse.gov/briefing-room/speeches-remarks/2023/04/30/remarks-by-president-biden-at-the-white-house-correspondents-dinner/

Williams, K. (2018). Keeping and bearing arms in Czech. In *Taming the Corpus*. Cham: Springer. 147–166.

Wilson, K. G., Sandoz, E. K., Kitchens, J., & Roberts, M. (2010). The Valued Living Questionnaire: Defining and measuring valued action within a behavioral framework. *The Psychological Record*, 60, 249–272.

Woldenberg, J. (2012). *Historia mínima de la transición democrática en México*. Mexico City: El Colegio de Mexico AC.

Wolff, J. (2020). The turbulent end of an era in Bolivia: Contested elections, the ouster of Evo Morales, and the beginning of a transition towards an uncertain future. *Revista de Ciencia Política*, 40(2), 163–186.

Yap, P. J. (2015). The conundrum of unconstitutional constitutional amendments. *Global Constitutionalism*, 4(1), 114–136.

Zamitiz Gamboa, H. (2017). La reforma político-electoral 2014–2015: ¿híbrido institucional o avance gradual del sistema democrático en México? *Estudios Políticos*, 40, 11–46.

Zamora, S. (1992). The Americanization of Mexican law: Non-trade issues in the North American Free Trade Agreement. *Law and Policy in International Business*, 24, 391.

Zernike, K. & Wines, M. (2023, April 23). Losing ballot issues on abortion, G.O.P. now tries to keep them off the ballot. Online article. www.nytimes.com/2023/04/23/us/republicans-abortion-voting

INDEX

Achen, Christopher, 54, 86, 88
Ackerman, Bruce, 11–13
acquis communautaire, 83
Albert, Richard, xv, 1, 7, 11, 14, 16, 55, 78–81, 151
amendment culture, 2, 78, 82, 85, 89, 130
amendment difficulty, 2, 78–79, 82
amendment provisions, xiii, 19–20, 25, 69, 80, 115, 123, 126–127, 147, 150, 186, 221–222
amendment rate, 2, 82–83, 90, 126, 147–148, 152–153, 155, 157–158, 160–161, 169–170, 176
Anckar, Dag, 1, 126, 151–154
Argentina, 98, 219
Armstrong II, David, 91–92, 94–97, 167, 169
Arrow, Kenneth, 148
Atilano-Robles, Edwin, 127
Australia, 36, 98, 154, 219
Austria, 64, 71, 73, 205, 219

Belgium, 29, 205, 219
Benin, 27, 205, 219
bicameral core, 61, 100, 103, 144
bicameral legislature, 60–61, 64, 71–72, 153–154, 224
Blake, William, 91–96, 97, 167, 169
Botswana, 36
Brown, Adam, 9, 172, 183, 185–186, 218
Burgess, John, 1, 58, 147–148, 150, 160

Carrubba, Clifford, 192, 207, 212
centralization of power, 142
Chile, xiv, 6–9, 21, 65, 70, 98–99, 102–103, 108–110, 113–117, 123–124, 219

citizen initiatives, 35
civic activism, 93–94, 96–97, 169
civil society participation, 96
Colombia, 14, 33, 38, 98, 205, 219
CompLaw Database, 201, 212, 214
concertacesiones, 133, 135
Congleton, Roger, 1, 152–154, 176
constituent assembly, 109–110, 115, 124, 268
constituent power, 13, 47
constitutional amendment, 2, 7, 11–14, 19–20, 23–28, 31, 33–36, 40, 46–48, 50, 52, 54, 65–66, 69–70, 73, 76, 78–79, 82, 90–93, 95, 97, 102, 108, 112, 114–115, 124, 127, 129, 131, 136, 142, 147–148, 150, 152–154, 161, 187, 191, 203, 224
constitutional change, 7, 14, 18, 36, 40, 46, 52, 54, 57, 68, 83, 85, 114, 188
constitutional convention, 9, 18, 49–50, 273
constitutional core, 54, 56–58, 60, 63–65, 100, 103, 106–107, 111, 127–128, 203, 211
constitutional court, 46, 92, 125, 204–205, 207, 211, 213–215, 223
constitutional entrenchment, 2, 83, 130, 170
constitutional equilibrium, 6–9, 12, 14, 16, 19, 54, 93, 141, 175
constitutional flexibility, 2, 28, 83, 150, 170
constitutional interpretation, 8–10, 12, 19, 47–48, 202–203, 221
constitutional length, 171, 176, 180–183, 185
constitutional moments, 11, 13, 222

constitutional reform, 25, 102, 107, 109–110, 113–114, 118, 129, 142
constitutional replacement, 54, 65, 85, 116, 173, 221
constitutional revision, xiv, 27, 30, 32, 50, 59, 64, 70, 72, 79, 100, 102–103, 107, 111, 114, 141, 150, 170, 172, 174, 203, 210–211
constitutional rigidity, xiii–xiv, 1–3, 5, 17, 19–22, 24, 55, 65–66, 69–70, 72–73, 80, 82–83, 85–86, 91, 93, 96, 129, 132, 147–148, 150–155, 157–161, 167, 169–172, 175–176, 184, 191–193, 200, 207, 211, 213–215, 217–218, 222, 224
Cooter, Robert, 190, 201
core, xv, 20, 40, 45, 54–55, 57–66, 68–69, 74, 97, 99–101, 103, 106–107, 116, 123, 127–128, 142, 144–146, 149, 156, 202–203, 211
corruption, 34, 41, 45, 171, 173, 179, 181, 183, 185
Costa Rica, 18, 33, 210
Cozza, Joseph, 91–92, 94–97, 167, 169
cultural theories, 21
Czech Republic, 25, 73, 98, 205

de facto judicial independence, 196, 200
de jure judicial independence, 196
decision-making rules, 52
democracy, 2, 8, 12, 14–15, 17, 42, 45, 77, 85, 97, 155, 159–160, 170, 212, 222
democratic consolidation, 190
Denmark, 36, 154, 170
Dixon, Rosalind, 1, 11–12, 14–15, 35, 77, 115, 153, 171, 188, 210

economic development, 88, 134, 152, 212
Elkins, 130, 152, 173
entrenchment, 24, 171–172
eternal provisions, 32
eternity clauses, 14

federalism, 31, 180
Feld, Lars, 190–191, 193, 195–199

Ferejohn, John, 67, 153, 195
Finke, Daniel, 205–206
Fix-Fierro, Héctor, 131, 141–142
France, 7, 16, 34, 65, 98, 120–122, 154, 192, 205, 207, 212, 219
Friedman, Barry, 192, 204, 207
Friesen, Amanda, 91–92, 94–97, 167, 169
Fuentes, Claudio, xv, 113–114

game theory, 55
Germany, 14, 32, 72–73, 98, 205–206, 219
Ginsburg, Tom, xv, 2, 15, 73, 76, 82–85, 87, 89–90, 126, 129–130, 147, 149, 152–154, 157, 161, 173, 187, 190–191, 194–195, 197–201
Greece, 8, 27, 35, 70, 73, 98
Guatemala, 7, 73, 98, 205, 219
Guyana, 33–34

Hayo, Bernd, 83, 191, 194–199
Helmke, Gretchen, 194–195, 211–212
heteroskedasticity, 150, 158, 160
Howard, Robert, 191, 193, 195, 197, 199
human rights, 15, 41, 49, 71, 150–151, 190, 193, 199, 209, 218, 225
Hungary, 42–43, 98, 170, 205, 219

India, 14, 38, 47, 98, 130, 175, 187, 203, 214, 219
institutional approach, 3, 21, 94, 171, 176
institutional constraints, 83, 127
Ireland, 38, 43, 47–48, 65, 121, 154, 219
Israel, 24, 40, 42, 47, 70, 96, 175, 214, 219, 221
Italy, xiv, 6, 21, 35, 65, 70, 77, 98–99, 101, 103, 111–112, 115–117, 123–125, 154, 205, 214, 219

judicial discretion, 190, 192–193, 200, 202, 207, 212, 217
judicial independence, 3, 83, 132, 190–193, 195–197, 199–201, 207, 211, 213, 215, 217–218, 223
judicial review, 39–40, 43–44, 82, 87, 151, 194, 205, 212

Karvonen, Lauri, 1, 126, 151–154
Keith, Linda, 190, 193, 195, 198–199
Knight, Jack, xv, 204
König, Thomas, 54, 121
Kydland, Finn, 174

La Porta, Rafael, 152, 154, 190, 193, 195–196, 198–199
Lakatos, Imre, 84, 91, 221, 223
Landau, David, 7, 11, 14–15, 77, 115, 210
legal origins, 180
Lijphart, Arend, 1, 71, 111, 126, 151–154, 176
Linzer, Drew, 191, 195–196, 199
Lopez-de-Silanes, Florencio, 151, 191, 193, 195–196, 198–199
Lorenz, Astrid, 1, 126, 151, 153–154
Lutz, Donald, 1, 126, 132, 151–154, 176
Luxembourg, 31, 73, 205, 219

Marshfield, Jonathan, 2, 83, 170, 176
Martin, Andrew, 192, 207, 212
Melton, James, 2, 73, 76, 82–85, 88–90, 126, 129, 147, 149, 152–154, 157, 161, 173, 187, 191, 194–195, 197–200
Mexico, xiv, 6, 9, 21, 55, 60, 62, 74, 98, 126–130, 133–139, 141–146, 175, 187
Michigan, xv, 49–51, 148
Moldova, 36, 98, 205

necessary conditions, 22, 97, 214, 223
Negretto, xv, 71, 74, 126
Nevada, 37–38
Nigeria, 33
North Dakota, 51

Ohio, 50–51

PAN, 134–142
Poe, Steven, 193, 195, 198–199
Poland, 26, 98, 205, 220
policy space, 56, 66
political culture, 77, 94, 146
political parties, 42, 55, 94, 97, 109, 113, 118, 122, 130, 133–134, 137–138, 140

Polity, 19, 70, 73, 148–149, 160, 192, 199, 213–214
Pop-Eleches, Cristian, 151, 190, 193, 195–196, 198–199
popular initiatives, 68
PRD, 134, 136–139, 143
Prescott, Edward, 174
PRI, 55, 127, 133–142, 146, 211
Prokch, Sven-Oliver, 121
Putnam, Robert, 76–77, 92

qualified majorities, 10, 20, 23, 69, 73, 127, 151, 153, 222
quorum requirements, 20, 118

Rasch, Bjørn, xv, 1, 83, 116, 152–154, 176
referendums, 20, 23, 28, 36–38, 48–49, 52, 65, 70, 99, 116, 118, 120–121, 124–125, 151, 222
rigidity index, 21, 73–74, 154, 160, 192–193, 201
Ríos-Figueroa, Julio, xv, 191, 194–195, 197–199, 211
Rosenbluth, Frances, 194–195, 211
Roznai, Yaniv, 11, 43–44, 210

separation of powers, 44, 69
Shleifer, Andrei, 151, 190, 193, 195–196, 198–199
single-subject rule, 52
Slovakia, 44, 46, 205
social capital, 91–94, 97, 169
South Korea, 26, 98
Spain, 7, 35, 98, 170, 205, 220
Stanton, Kimberly, 108–110
Staton, Jeffrey, 190–191, 194–197, 199, 212
statutory interpretation, 8, 10, 141, 201–202
sufficient conditions, 64, 149
supreme courts, xiv, 205
Switzerland, 35, 73, 98

Tarabar, Danko, 89, 91
term limits, 7, 15, 34, 38, 51, 210
time inconsistency, 2, 19, 21, 171, 174–176, 178, 186–189, 223

Tsebelis, George, 28, 67, 72, 74, 98, 108, 114, 121, 132–133, 152–153, 156, 159, 172, 177, 181, 184, 200–201, 209

Ukraine, 46, 98, 205
unconstitutional constitutional amendments, 14, 222
United States, 25, 98, 122, 129, 137, 172, 204, 207, 212, 220
Uribe, Alvaro, 14, 34, 36

Vanberg, Georg, 192, 205–207
Velasco-Rivera, Mariana, 126–127, 140
Versteeg, Mila, 2, 83, 130, 161, 170–171, 174, 176, 187, 192
veto players, xiii, 54, 69, 71–73, 148, 152–153, 157, 160, 170, 201, 224
Voigt, Stefan, 83, 179, 186, 190–191, 193–199

Weingast, Barry, 54, 190, 193
win-set, 20, 60, 64, 66, 69, 74, 111, 116, 208–209
World Values Survey, 95, 97

Zackin, Emily, 2, 83, 130, 161, 170–171, 174, 176, 187

For EU product safety concerns, contact us at Calle de José Abascal, 56–1°,
28003 Madrid, Spain or eugpsr@cambridge.org.

www.ingramcontent.com/pod-product-compliance
Ingram Content Group UK Ltd.
Pitfield, Milton Keynes, MK11 3LW, UK
UKHW021939010525
458033UK00020B/504